THE UNNAMING OF KROEBER HALL

THE UNNAMING OF KROEBER HALL

LANGUAGE, MEMORY, AND INDIGENOUS CALIFORNIA

ANDREW GARRETT

The MIT Press
Cambridge, Massachusetts
London, England

The MIT Press would like to thank the anonymous peer reviewers who provided comments on drafts of this book. The generous work of academic experts is essential for establishing the authority and quality of our publications. We acknowledge with gratitude the contributions of these otherwise uncredited readers.

This book was set in Bembo by Westchester Publishing Services. Printed and bound in the United States of America.

Library of Congress Cataloging-in-Publication Data

Names: Garrett, Andrew, 1961– author.
Title: The unnaming of Kroeber Hall : language, memory, and Indigenous California / Andrew Garrett.
Description: Cambridge, Massachusetts : The MIT Press, 2023. | Includes bibliographical references and index.
Identifiers: LCCN 2023007497 (print) | LCCN 2023007498 (ebook) | ISBN 9780262547093 (paperback) | ISBN 9780262377270 (epub) | ISBN 9780262377263 (pdf)
Subjects: LCSH: Kroeber Hall (Berkeley, California) | Kroeber, A. L. (Alfred Louis), 1876–1960. | Anthropological ethics. | Indians of North America—California—Languages. | University of California, Berkeley—History.
Classification: LCC LD765.K76 G37 2023 (print) | LCC LD765.K76 (ebook) | DDC 378.794/67—dc23/eng/20230517
LC record available at https://lccn.loc.gov/2023007497
LC ebook record available at https://lccn.loc.gov/2023007498

10 9 8 7 6 5 4 3 2 1

For Leslie

Every story should have a foundation; explain where something began and came from, and if you do not know the foundation, do not try to teach.
—Robert Spott, 1941

What is that thought so great and so sacred that cannot be expressed in our own language, that we should seek to use the white man's words?
—Juan Dolores, 1901

CONTENTS

FIGURES AND TABLES

FIGURES

TABLES

ABBREVIATIONS

ALK	A. L. Kroeber Papers, 1869–1972. BANC MSS C-B 925, Bancroft Library, UCB
ALKFP	A. L. Kroeber Family Photographs, ca. 1870–1969. BANC PIC 1978.128, Bancroft Library, UCB
ASTP	Army Specialized Training Program
BIA	Bureau (formerly Office) of Indian Affairs
BNRC	Building Name Review Committee, UCB
CLA	California Language Archive, Department of Linguistics, UCB
DAR	Daughters of the American Revolution
DKH	Documents relating to the unnaming of Kroeber Hall (Garrett 2021)
ED	Ethnological Documents of the Department and Museum of Anthropology, 1875–1958. BANC FILM 2216, Bancroft Library, UCB (cited by reel and folder number)
FBP	Franz Boas Papers. Mss.B.B61, American Philosophical Society
GPAHP	George and Phoebe Apperson Hearst Papers, 1849–1926. BANC MSS 72/204c, Bancroft Library, UCB
KFP	Kroeber Family Papers, ca. 1802–1972. BANC MSS 82/132 c, Bancroft Library, UCB
LSA	Linguistic Society of America
NAA	National Anthropological Archives, Smithsonian Institution
NAGPRA	Native American Graves Protection and Repatriation Act
NCIA	Northern California Indian Association
PAHMA	Phoebe A. Hearst Museum of Anthropology, UCB
RDA	Records of the Department of Anthropology, 1901–. CU-23, University Archives, Bancroft Library, UCB

TKP	Theodora Kroeber Papers, 1881–1983. BANC MSS 69/145c, Bancroft Library, UCB
TKQP	Theodora Kroeber Quinn Papers, AA-15, Arizona State Museum Library, University of Arizona
UC(B)	University of California (Berkeley)
UCOPAF	UC Office of the President, Alphabetical Files, 1885–1913. CU-5, Series 1, University Archives, Bancroft Library, UCB
UKLG	Ursula K. Le Guin Papers, ca. 1930s–2018. Coll. 270, Special Collections & University Archives, University of Oregon
YWCA	Young Women's Christian Association

ACKNOWLEDGMENTS

I wrote this book in response to events at the University of California, Berkeley, where I work in the linguistics department. The discourse surrounding those events often expressed a sense of history that did not match my own understanding of my predecessors' work. Even within a single university community, people imagine their pasts very differently. This book is my way of grappling with dissonant memories of early-twentieth-century California anthropology and linguistics.

Though I write about many subjects here, I have a linguist's perspective, interests, and disciplinary formation. I am not trained in anthropology, history, Native American studies, cultural criticism, or archives scholarship. I know my background shows, but I have tried to be aware of multiple points of view, kinds of learning, and personal experiences, and to find empathy for others.

My thinking about Indigenous language work owes an incalculable debt to Yurok and Karuk friends and teachers. Those who shared their language with me include elders who have passed on: *'aawokw* Aileen Figueroa, Ollie Foseide, Jimmie James, Glenn Moore Sr., Archie Thompson, and Georgiana Trull (Yurok); and *kêemachkoo* Lucille Albers, Sonny Davis, and Vina Smith (Karuk). They were generous hosts and teachers whose foresightful commitment to their families and communities will matter for generations to come. And among dozens of Karuk and Yurok people I have learned with, I am especially grateful to Leo Canez, Victoria Carlson, Susan Gehr, James Gensaw, Annelia Hillman, Julian Lang, Carole Lewis, Barbara McQuillen, Seafha Ramos, Crystal Richardson, *'aawokw* Kathleen Vigil, and Brittany Vigil-Burbank. They have helped teach me what linguistics is for.

At Berkeley, I am lucky to be part of an eclectic, vibrant community of linguists. I am particularly grateful to the colleagues and students with whom I have often discussed matters that I write about here. They include

Patricia Baquedano-López, Chris Beier, Leanne Hinton, Larry Hyman, Peter Jenks, Keith Johnson, Lev Michael, Line Mikkelsen, Beth Piatote, Hannah Sande, and students in seminars on language revitalization and on the languages of California. I would not have been able to undertake this project without all I have learned from them.

For their kindness, I also thank the many other colleagues and friends at Berkeley and elsewhere who have offered criticisms, discussion, information, and suggestions. They include Sabrina Agarwal, Uldis Balodis, Heidi Barlese, Kayla Begay, Adam Benkato, Joan Berman, Fallon Burner, Gabriela Caballero, Lisa Conathan, Meg Conkey, Nicholas Cortez, Theo Downes-Le Guin, Paul Fine, Alice Gaby, Todd Hickey, Edwin Ko, Gavin Kroeber, Julian Lang, Caroline Le Guin, Elisabeth Le Guin, Kent Lightfoot, Erik Hans Maier, Julia Nee, Julie Phillips, Tony Platt, Ruth Rouvier, Clare Sandy, Nancy Scheper-Hughes, Amalia Skilton, Bob Skotheim, Carolyn Smith, Justin Spence, Orin Starn, Michael Swanton, and Tony Woodbury. All have broadened my thinking. Where we disagree, I hope I have learned from our disagreements.

The late Victor Golla and Ira Jacknis taught me much over the years, in person and through their writing, about California linguistics and anthropology, respectively. In 2021, they both passed away in their intellectual prime. Some of what follows was written as imagined conversations with Ira or Victor. I wish these could have come to pass.

For detailed, generous, insightful comments on a complete draft of this book, I thank Claire Bowern, Jim Clifford, Les Field, Leslie Kurke, Yoram Meroz, Zach O'Hagan, Katie Sardinha, and two anonymous reviewers for the MIT Press. They have made this much better than it could otherwise have been.

Archives and museums have contributed crucial material to this book. At Berkeley, I am indebted to Mary Elings, Lorna Kirwan, Susan McElrath, Theresa Salazar, Lee Ann Titangos, and their colleagues at the Bancroft Library; Michael Black, Caroline Fernald, Lauren Kroiz, Paolo Pellegatti, Linda Waterfield, and others at the Phoebe A. Hearst Museum of Anthropology; and Ronald Sprouse at the California Language Archive. Valuable assistance was also provided by Brian Carpenter and Paul Sutherland at the American Philosophical Society; Teresa Mora at the UC Santa Cruz Special Collections & Archives; John Seamans at the National Archives at San Francisco; Ken MacLennan at Pleasanton's Museum on Main; Caroline Kinsley and Jannelle Weakly at the Arizona State Museum; Nicolette Bromberg at the University of Washington Libraries Special Collections; Laura E. Rocke at the Special Collections and University Archives Department, University of Nevada, Reno; and Special Collections & University Archives staff at the University of Oregon. The HathiTrust Emergency Temporary Access Service was a critical resource in 2020–2021, opening the entire HathiTrust Digital Library while Berkeley libraries were closed.

At the MIT Press, I am grateful to Phil Laughlin, Haley Biermann, and Jim Mitchell, who have made the process of turning this into a real book as painless as I could imagine. Madhulika Jain at Westchester Publishing was very helpful throughout the production process. For meticulous copyediting and indexing, I am grateful to Susan Campbell and Erika Millen, respectively. For permission to reproduce manuscript images and photographs from several Kroeber collections in the Bancroft Library, thanks to Arthur Kroeber on behalf of the Kroeber family. Thanks also to Scott Braley and Irene Yi for sharing their marvelous photographs.

This book is partly about recent events. I began writing it in the summer of 2020 and finished in 2022. A few additions and corrections were possible in March 2023 before the final text went to the compositor. All websites and links cited in the notes and references were checked in September 2022 and were then correct and accurately quoted.

I live and work on the traditional, ancestral, and unceded land of the Ohlone people, whose historical relationships with the land continue today. The language of this land is Chochenyo.

Ohlone creativity and resilience inspire Indigenous people worldwide. I hope that I and others at the colonial university that occupies their land, and in the many archives, museums, and scholarly disciplines that possess and use the cultural and linguistic heritage of Indigenous people, are also inspired to better serve those people's needs by listening, by hearing them, and by welcoming them as colleagues, students, teachers, and the owners of that heritage.

THE UNNAMING OF KROEBER HALL

1

KROEBER HALL

> "Finding what other makers made, speaking it, printing it, recovering it from neglect or oblivion, relighting the light of the word—this is the chief work of my life."
>
> —Orrec Caspro, in Ursula K. Le Guin, *Voices*, 2006

In 1901, the University of California initiated a systematic program to document the cultures and languages of California's Indigenous people and to collect their artifacts and even their ancestral remains. Today, as a result, more than any other American university, UC Berkeley has museums and archives filled with its own state's Native cultural heritage. The ownership and uses of this heritage have been contested for over a century.

I have taught at Berkeley since 1995. In 2019, an Indigenous California language activist and cultural leader visiting a seminar in my department said she felt physically sick on the Berkeley campus. Being present in places where I find joy in working reminded her of thousands of Native American ancestral remains stored in boxes on campus, and of objects of cultural value that are no longer with their makers. It recalled three centuries of colonization that have decimated and transformed Indigenous communities, and decades of extraction of tangible and intangible cultural heritages.

The materials and documentation of cultural heritage now stored at universities like Berkeley were taken or recorded by scholars and scientists who believed that Indigenous cultures would vanish as modernity effaced local ways everywhere. They assumed that what they ignored would be lost forever and that humanity would benefit from the knowledge and cultural expressions they collected. They also had privileged positions and the freedom to make choices in a destructive colonial regime. How we remember their choices, how we name their work, and what we forget or leave unnamed are the central questions of this book.

Over many years and from multiple perspectives, at least since Vine Deloria's *Custer Died for Your Sins* (1969), numerous writers have critiqued the early-twentieth-century interactions of academic and Indigenous communities in the United States. Within this broad landscape, the California situation is distinctive. Only there did a public university, in the immediate aftermath of genocide, take up what it described as the mission of documenting its state's Indigenous cultures and languages. UC peers early in the twentieth century were private universities in the eastern United States, like Columbia and Harvard, which showed no interest in the Native people of their regions.[1]

No small part in this history is played by my academic field, linguistics. American linguistics coalesced from two disciplines, one in anthropology (linguistic anthropology) and the other (historical linguistics) traditionally concerned with European and Asian languages with long written traditions. The Berkeley campus has two buildings that were named for foundational figures in linguistics: two of the twenty-nine signatories of the 1924 call for a Linguistic Society of America (LSA). That event marked the beginning of the professionalization of American linguistics and the end of an era when linguistics, anthropology, and folklore had far more porous disciplinary boundaries than they do today.[2]

The two academic disciplines that gave rise to linguistics in the United States are represented by the UC signatories of the LSA call: Benjamin Ide Wheeler, a historical linguist who was UC president from 1899 to 1919; and the anthropologist and linguist Alfred Kroeber, LSA president in 1940. Kroeber was one of only four LSA presidents who also led the American Folklore Society (in 1906) and the American Anthropological Association (in 1917–1918), signifying a combination of commitments that is rare today.[3] As if to recognize the two disciplines, Wheeler Hall was dedicated in 1917, and Kroeber Hall in 1960, a few months before Kroeber's death (see figures 1.1–1.2).

Berkeley's anthropology museum and departments of anthropology and art practice occupied Kroeber Hall for sixty years. In January 2021, after a decision promoted by campus activists; supported by hundreds of campus community members and multiple student groups; endorsed by a high-level committee of faculty, students, and staff; and made by

Figure 1.1
Dedication of Kroeber Hall, March 1960 (*Oakland Tribune*, 7 March 1960, p. 12). Left to right: UC Berkeley Chancellor Glenn Seaborg, Alfred Kroeber, UC Regent Catherine Hearst, and UC President Clark Kerr.

the university administration, Kroeber's name was removed from the building.

This book is about Alfred Kroeber's legacy and the unnaming of Kroeber Hall. Kroeber spent many years documenting California's Indigenous languages and cultures, and trained or inspired students and younger colleagues to do the same. The result was a unique corpus of written materials and sound recordings, accessible and valued today. In both academic and popular work, Kroeber argued forcefully against contemporary racism and eugenics; he collaborated with Indigenous scholars and uplifted their work, and advocated for Native cultural and land rights. How did he come to be excoriated as "racist" and "astonishingly detached from ethical standards" at his own institution? Why did its

Figure 1.2
Alfred Kroeber at Kroeber Hall, 1960 (ALKFP Box 1). The lettering on the building was later replaced and raised (as seen in figure 10.1).

leaders conclude that Kroeber's "views and writings stand in opposition to our university's contemporary values"? (For sources for these quotations, see below in this chapter and chapters 9–10.)

The specific claims about Kroeber's work offered in support of unnaming Kroeber Hall, accepted by many at Berkeley and beyond, are erroneous or unsubstantiated. Yet the actions, choices, and words of anthropologists and linguists over more than twelve decades have led to harm, including understandable anger and pain for many people, especially Indigenous people, both within and outside the academy. At issue, I argue, are impacts of the presuppositions and research choices of memory documentation ("salvage" ethnography and linguistics) as defined by Franz Boas, executed more fully by his student Kroeber than by any other Boasian, and motivated by what the linguist Michael Krauss (1992:8) later called an "urgent [need] to document languages before they disappear." His word *disappear* is critical, and other terms it evokes: *death*, *extinction*, *loss*, and (their precursor) *endangerment*.

While I disagree with many of the specific assertions made by advocates of unnaming, I do believe it was right to unname Kroeber Hall. That name brought pain to those who should feel welcome. In the twenty-first century, an edifice with anthropological tenants need not take its name from an era of extractive, patronizing academic attitudes toward Native people. Monuments have meanings in the present that it can be injurious to ignore.

Kroeber's assumptions and choices expose his intellectual blind spots, as ours will reveal ours. Seeing his clearly today, we can readily imagine other pasts. In an iconoclastic time, I will show, he was an expedient target at a university unprepared to recognize its own foundational, ongoing, systemic contributions to the displacement and erasure of Indigenous people. It also served the interests of non-Indigenous academics to imagine that Kroeber's failings lay in concrete past actions that are easy to deplore rather than in presuppositions and research choices that remain common in 2022. In short, the unnaming of Kroeber Hall represented a serendipitous alliance between activists' desire for salutary change and elites' need to deflect a threatening discomfort.

A PROPOSAL TO UNNAME KROEBER HALL

At Berkeley, a committee appointed by the chancellor evaluates proposals to unname buildings that are named after people who may no longer seem deserving. On 1 July 2020, the Building Name Review Committee received a "Proposal to Un-Name Kroeber Hall" (DKH 1). I will call it the Proposal. Its authors were unnamed and remain unknown, but it came with a letter of endorsement signed by influential campus figures, including both the executive vice chancellor and provost and the chair of the Native American Graves Protection and Repatriation Act Advisory Committee.[4] It was submitted at the same time as proposals to unname two other buildings, and in the wake of an earlier unnaming (chapter 10).

An important backdrop to the unnaming of Kroeber Hall is the history of difficult relations between California's Indigenous people and UC Berkeley. This has many dimensions, including a sense of marginalization among Native students, staff, and faculty, but a focus has been Berkeley's immense collection of ancestral remains (chapter 8). The university is widely recognized as having been slow and obstructionist in returning them to tribes since the 1990 passage of the Native American Graves Protection and Repatriation Act (NAGPRA). This has led to a lack of trust among tribes and even within the university. In 2019, for example, I attended a southern California meeting of UC librarians discussing cultural heritage collections. When I said I thought current Berkeley campus leaders had a more positive approach to repatriation than their predecessors, there was spontaneous disbelieving laughter around the table.

Berkeley discontent with the Kroeber name goes back several decades, mostly driven by the treatment of Ishi, a Yahi man who lived in the UC anthropology museum between 1911 and 1916 (chapter 7). Gerald Vizenor's 1995 play *Ishi and the Wood Ducks* includes a satirical scene, set in Kroeber Hall, in which a Committee on Names and Spaces considers a proposal by Kroeber himself to rename the building Ishi Hall. In 1999, a statement that Kroeber and others' treatment of Ishi was "abhorrent" was endorsed by nineteen anthropology faculty members. A decade later, in 2011, Berkeley cohosted a conference on Ishi; and, in 2012, a campus theater staged a play about Ishi (with Kroeber as a character) that was widely deplored as offensive and for which the theater department apologized. In 2018, the *Daily Cal* student newspaper published a commentary criticizing Ishi's treatment as well as an editorial that urged renaming Kroeber Hall and other buildings named for those who "oppressed and discriminated against people of color."[5] The Proposal itself called Kroeber's research practices "reprehensible," writing that his work "had fundamentally flawed assumptions and was astonishingly detached from ethical standards."

After the Proposal was submitted, comments were invited; 85 percent of 595 comments favored unnaming, including 230 of 264 that were made public (DKH 2). Dozens of public comments criticized Kroeber as "racist"; one referred to his "racist, inhumane pseudoscience." Unnaming was endorsed by the anthropology department faculty (Hirschkind 2020a,b); by student groups, such as the American Indian Graduate Student Association, the Berkeley Native American Law Student Association, and the Graduate Assembly; and by the *Daily Cal,* which stated that Kroeber "studied Indigenous Californians using a starkly racist ideology" (Shok 2020) and "devoted his life to acts or advocacy of racial oppression and subjugation—desecrating and violating Indigenous lands and lives" (Bassett 2020).

Many public comments emphasized repatriation failures. A group of Native students pointed to ongoing impacts (Cesspooch et al. 2020):

> UC Berkeley's administration, students, faculty, and Anthropology Department continue to benefit from stolen land and the genocide of Indigenous peoples. Berkeley's lack of improvement on the repatriation process demonstrates that this is not a distant legacy, but an entrenched and continuous reality. Native students at Berkeley have long voiced these concerns and the proposal to un-name Kroeber Hall and cleanse the campus of celebratory reminders of this past . . . is consistent with a long legacy of Native advocacy.

Their emphasis on repatriation was echoed by the anthropology faculty, whose statement devoted more words to that matter than to Kroeber. In addition to numerous comments from students, staff, and alumni, almost a dozen public comments came from scholars who had published about aspects of Kroeber's work or in areas related to it; most favored unnaming. Two of these were also published as blog posts; the phrase "cancel culture" was used.[6]

A Berkeley policy states: "The legacy of a building's namesake should be in alignment with the values and mission of the university." These values take the form of a list of principles, such as, "We affirm the dignity of all individuals and strive to uphold a just community in which discrimination and hate are not tolerated." The naming policy has an important lacuna; its original formulation referred to a person's "principal" legacy. In either case, the implication is that naming is less about historically situated individuals of the past than it is about what they evoke in the present—their legacies.[7]

One complexity was noted by the task force that established the present Berkeley framework. No honoree, it wrote, "should be expected to reflect modern values in every aspect of their life." For example, it reported that a Yale University committee found that Frederick Douglass's "principal legacies as an abolitionist and an advocate for civil rights overrode some of his problematic statements contrasting African Americans with American Indians."[8] The Yale committee itself pointed out that "interpretations of . . . principal legacies are subject to change" and may vary from person to person: "Determining the principal legacies of a namesake obliges the University to study and make a scholarly judgment on how the namesake's legacies should be understood. Prevailing historical memories may be misleading or incorrect, and prevailing scholarly views may be incomplete."[9] Where misleading memories replace scholarly judgment, decisions about naming may cast more light on the judges than on the judged.

The Proposal identified three actions as showing that Kroeber did not live up to Berkeley's values. First, it said, his "treatment of . . . Ishi and the handling of his remains was cruel, degrading, and racist." Second, "Kroeber and his colleagues engaged in collection of the remains of Native American ancestors, which has always been morally wrong." And third, he "pronounced the Ohlone to be culturally extinct, a declaration that had terrible consequences for these people." On these three criticisms, see chapters 7, 8, and 9, respectively.

The Proposal also raised more general critiques. One was that Kroeber accepted and (in his writing) spread the "myth of the vanishing Indian" (see chapter 2). Another was a metacritique: he "is a hostile symbol to many Native Americans and it is important to remove his name from the building." In other words, the mere connotations of his name today—what it evokes in the twenty-first century, fairly or otherwise—warranted the unnaming of Kroeber Hall.

I evaluate all these critiques below, in the context of Kroeber's work and early UC history. The specific claims itemized above do not stand up to scrutiny, but the general critiques have some validity. As I also discuss, the limitations of early-twentieth-century research practice raise significant questions for linguistics and allied fields in the present.

ALFRED KROEBER

Born in 1876, Kroeber grew up in a middle-class German American household near Central Park in Manhattan. His mother was born in New York to German parents; his father was an importer of European clocks who had come to the United States as a boy of ten. Alfred's first language was German, and he had a German accent when he first went to school at age nine. He described the humanistic German-Jewish milieu of his childhood and schooling as "the carry-over of the Europe of Voltaire" and "the mellow golden sunset of the German civilization of

Kant and Goethe" (T. Kroeber 1970:27). The first book he read was an abridged German translation of *Robinson Crusoe*, and even as a child he was especially interested in linguistic patterns.

Kroeber entered Columbia College in 1892 and received bachelor's and master's degrees in literature. In 1896, he took an anthropology class from a new faculty member, Franz Boas. Adapting methods of classical philology, Boas had students read texts in Indigenous languages of North America to figure out grammatical patterns. Much later, Kroeber (1955–1956) recalled having been "enormously stimulated." Discovering grammatical structure was "fascinating," he added; "Boas' method was very similar to that of the zoologist who starts a student with an etherized frog or worm and a dissecting table." The simile is telling: the "science of man" was about specimens, not people. Yet philological analysis to infer linguistic structure can be satisfying and even inspiring, as it was to Kroeber (and to me ninety years later). Linguistic work, he wrote, "largely steered me into becoming an anthropologist." Kroeber's first research project, assigned by Boas, involved documenting Inuktun (Polar Inuit) language and short texts with several Indigenous people infamously brought to New York by the polar explorer Robert Peary.[10] To this day the texts exist only in manuscript, as in figure 1.3, though English translations of most were published.[11]

As a PhD student in anthropology (figure 1.4), Kroeber did fieldwork in Montana, Oklahoma, and Wyoming and wrote a dissertation on Arapaho art (1901a). He spent the fall of 1900 in California, and moved there in the summer of 1901 for what would be the rest of his life. There he met his first wife Henriette (Rothschild), whom he married in 1906. She contracted tuberculosis in 1908 and struggled with it for five years before dying in 1913.[12] Kroeber married his second wife Theodora (Kracaw Brown) in 1926, and with her raised four children (figures 1.5–1.6).[13] Three children became professors (of history, literature, and psychology); the fourth was a celebrated writer, Ursula Le Guin. Alfred died in 1960, Theodora in 1979, and the four children between 2009 and 2019.

This is not a biography or a full account of Kroeber's anthropological work. It seems useful, all the same, to lay out my sense of his career's arc as it relates to language and the other themes of this book. Oversimplifying, I have come to think of that arc as having four phases.[14]

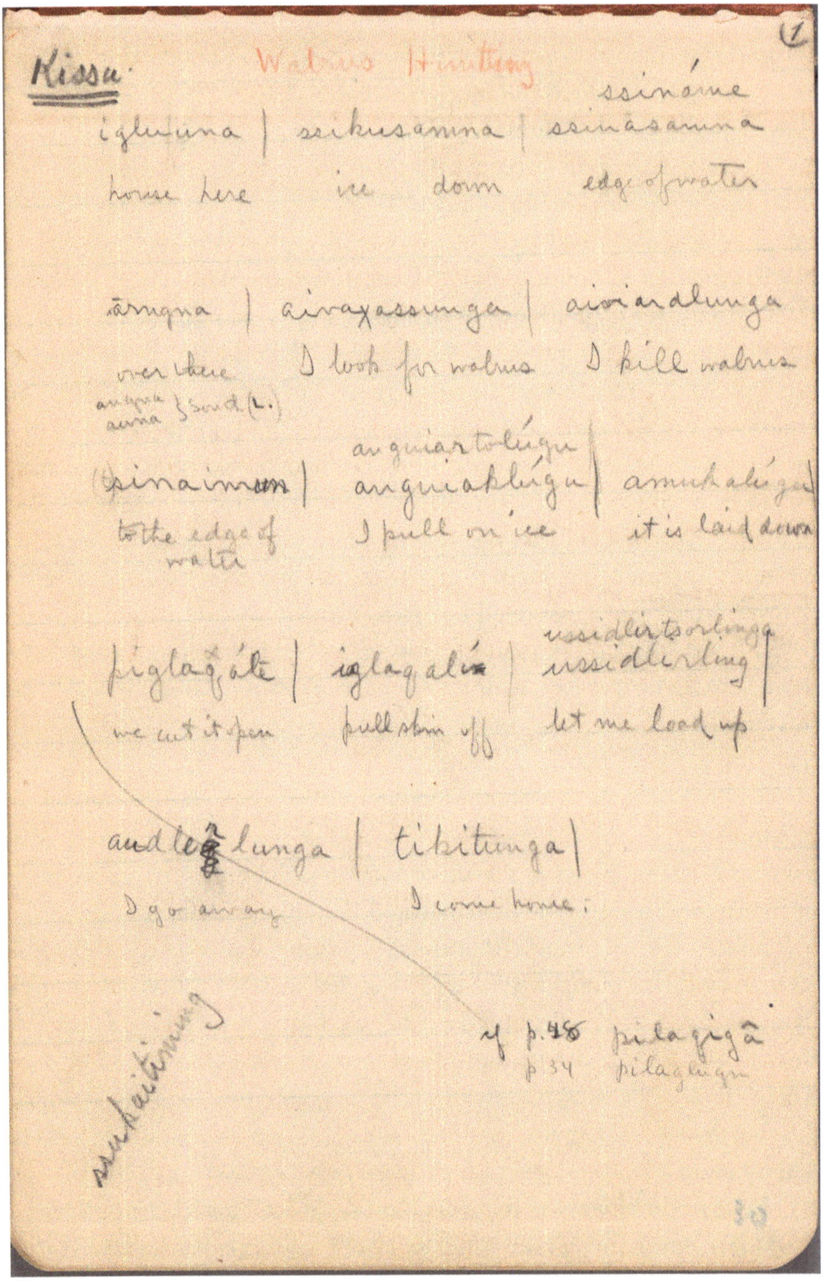

Figure 1.3
Information about walrus hunting, told by Qisuk in Inuktun, October 1897 (ALK Ctn 9:25, p. 1). This was the first Indigenous text that Kroeber transcribed.

Figure 1.4
Alfred Kroeber as a PhD student, 3 December 1899 (ALKFP Box 1).

From 1900 into the 1910s, Kroeber focused primarily on Indigenous California, along the philologically grounded lines of his graduate training. This was the period of most of his California fieldwork, as he documented languages, texts, and cultural practices, analyzing language relationships in order to explain linguistic and cultural diversity. Institutionally, he worked to build an anthropology program and maintain an amicable relationship with its benefactor, maintaining it against serious challenges to his vision.

Kroeber's writing then moved in broader and more synthetic directions, and generally away from linguistic work. Beginning in 1915, he published an influential series of papers that served to demarcate anthropology as an academic field within the social sciences and to highlight what might now be called its anti-racist implications (see chapter 9). A New York sabbatical yielded a book (1919b) on the people of the Philippines; with Zuni linguistics and ethnography and Mexican and

Figure 1.5
Kroeber family, St. Helena, 1931. With Alfred and Theodora were the four Kroeber children: from left, Theodore, Clifton, Ursula, and Karl.

Peruvian archaeology, he also moved beyond California in his firsthand research. Kroeber seems to have been looking for new intellectual and personal centers of gravity during what Theodora Kroeber (1970) called his "hegira," in the wake of the deaths of Henriette in 1913 and Ishi in 1916 (see chapter 7). He suffered at that time also from undiagnosed Ménière's disease, which for several years caused pain and enough vertigo that "onlookers assumed he was drunk" (T. Kroeber 1970:87), and which left him deaf in one ear.

Kroeber's prominent books of the 1920s reflect the first two phases of his career. His *Handbook of the Indians of California* (1925, completed in 1919) is a summation of his research since 1900, informed by the work of many others. His textbook *Anthropology* (1923) gives a sustained argument in favor of cultural relativism and against racist "Nordicism" and a eugenics movement that was popular even among progressive elites (chapter 9).

Though he influenced many students, Kroeber was not a great teacher. The anthropologist Katharine Luomala (1986) recalled an undergraduate

Figure 1.6
Kroeber children playing football, Arch St., Berkeley, November 1932 (ALKFP ALB v. 4). Front, from left, Theodore, Clifton, and Karl; Ursula was the quarterback.

class in the late 1920s. Kroeber had a "charismatic" look, but "strolled back and forth on the platform talking as if to himself. . . . There was no substance. I guess he saved his energies for his books." As a mentor, he is said to have inherited Boas's sink-or-swim style. Cora Du Bois called him a "rather casual advisor" who, asked for guidance in field ethnography, "looked thoroughly perplexed" and eventually said, "Be sure you have a good supply of pencils and note books."[15]

In the 1930s and 1940s, Kroeber's books *Cultural and Natural Areas of Native North America* (1939, completed in 1931) and *Configurations of Culture Growth* (1944a) were concerned with identifying distinctive complexes of cultural elements, what Kroeber (1957) later called *styles*, and with describing the processes by which "cultures" or "civilizations" accrete such elements, a concern already present in his *Handbook* and other work. Institutionally, Kroeber's commitments in this period included a long involvement with the research infrastructure of linguistic and anthropological fieldwork in North America. The sources of research funding had shifted from the individual capitalists and other philanthropists who supported their favorite projects in the 1890s and 1900s to endowments and foundations they created, like the Carnegie Corporation. Kroeber was prominent among the anthropological and linguistic elites who assigned funds and research projects to younger scholars.

In the last part of Kroeber's career, especially after his 1946 retirement, he returned at last to his formative interest in languages and texts. He resumed Mojave fieldwork in 1953 and 1954 (when he was in his seventies), edited a Luiseño grammar, and published a significant series of papers on general linguistics. The late 1940s and the 1950s also saw the formal revival of linguistics at Berkeley; Kroeber was an advocate for creating a new linguistics department that housed a program of systematic California language documentation. Finally, he spent a significant part of this period preparing Karuk, Mojave, and Yurok text collections that would not be published until after his death.

Born ten months after Kroeber died, I am removed in time from what I write about. I can only draw inferences about his and others' intentions and reactions, but the written record masks much that I would like to know. His daughter wrote that he "didn't reminisce" and that "getting his own past out of him was like pulling hen's teeth" (Le Guin 2004b:11). Subtitled *A Personal Configuration*, Theodora's biography is striking for its emotional detachment; it is "not intimate in any sense which would betray Kroeber's lifetime preference for keeping his intimately personal life intimately personal" (1970:viii).

With his "rambunctious" family, as his son Karl Kroeber (2003a:142) put it, Alfred showed a "mischievous sense of humor." With colleagues, he was inclined to be practical and conciliatory. His correspondence is voluminous but emotionally reserved, except when writing to his sister Elsbeth, his daughter Ursula, or an intimate friend like Berna (Rudovic) Pinner, with whom he was gossipy; or when complaining about a bête noir like the eccentric linguist J. P. Harrington, who alienated almost everyone. Kroeber was politically liberal but exhibited what Julian Steward (1973:22) called "extreme conservatism" in institutional matters. Regna Darnell (2000a:262) saw him as a "peacemaker" who urged Boas not to speak out in a cause Kroeber saw as perilous. A doggedly rational person who "shaved with Occam's razor" (Le Guin 1991), he clung to an ideal of scholarly detachment that may now seem either charming (in its bygone optimism) or misguided (given the social impacts of inaction).

A public reserve is not unexpected in someone raised in the 1880s in a middle-class family of recent immigrants; even Kroeber's daughter called him "a Victorian . . . and a bit of a Puritan."[16] To students he could be "mean if he wanted to and very strict," said Du Bois (Seymour 2015:74). Prudishness clouded his judgment—famously, in his evaluation of societies that practice girls' puberty ceremonies, which he called "one slight grade lower in the scale of civilization" (1925:135). In the 1920s, he was censorious of the bohemian lifestyle of his former student L. S. (Nancy) Freeland and her husband, the writer and linguist Jaime de Angulo, saying he would not advise students to visit their Berkeley home without "a very serious warning" because "morally and socially, the milieu was undesirable." Privately he called de Angulo an "unutterable swine," often expressing disappointment that Freeland had left Berkeley's graduate program.[17] (In 1935, he would call her Sierra Miwok grammar "one of the best executed pieces of work in American linguistics, and perhaps the very best expressed one."[18])

Kroeber's record of supporting women was mixed. After meeting his family in 1903, Pliny Goddard wrote him that "I don't understand your attitude toward girls with such sisters as you have" (30 October, ALK Box 16:4). A decade later, regarding a job at the UC anthropology museum, Kroeber told his colleague T. T. Waterman that "women are unqualifiedly barred" (21 May 1913, RDA Box 85). In 1929, he told Elsie Clews Parsons that "if ever Anthropology gets to be prevailingly a feminine science I expect to switch into something else" and that he thought she would too (13 April, RDA Box 118); and in 1932, his brilliantly original student Lila O'Neale was hired not in anthropology but in UC's household arts (later decorative art) department.[19] It is possible to see why George Foster, a student in the 1930s, could say Kroeber was "basically antagonistic to women" (Buzaljko n.d.a).

Yet Kroeber was also an advocate for many women students, beginning with Freeland, who entered the graduate program in 1916.[20] He coauthored papers with his students Anna Gayton, Catherine Holt, Gladys Nomland, O'Neale, and Jane Richardson Hanks, mostly with them as first authors. Hanks recalled his "devotion" and "loyalty" to a "brilliant group of women students" in the 1920s and 1930s, while the Harvard anthropologist Clyde Kluckhohn was said to have "teased" Kroeber "about his women Ph.D.'s" (T. Kroeber 1970:263).[21] Laura Thompson, whose Berkeley PhD was from 1933, recalled in 1984 that "Kroeber certainly created an environment in which women could become anthropologists, a very rare possibility in those days. In fact, I left Harvard and went to Berkeley because of the treatment of women in the Department."[22]

In later years, Kroeber worked to get a Berkeley position for the linguist Mary Haas, who would in the 1950s and 1960s succeed him as the dominant figure in California language documentation.[23] And after he retired, he strongly supported an effort to hire Du Bois, writing that she would be "quite a prize" for Berkeley and was "universally respected . . . as having perhaps the best intellect in her age-group in the profession."[24] If Kroeber could not easily imagine women in his profession during the early decades of his career, his sensibilities seem to have changed by the 1940s, when he was happy that his academic successors might be Du Bois and Haas.

ARCHIVAL LEGACIES

A century after Kroeber and half a century after Haas, many steps led me in turn to California language documentation. I came to Berkeley in 1995 as a historical linguist whose research was based on texts in languages like Hittite and Ancient Greek. My academic heritage was in one of the two founding strands of American linguistics, Kroeber's and Haas's in the other. Three Berkeley experiences changed my path. One was a seminar taught by my colleague Leanne Hinton with two elders who shared their Yowlumne knowledge.[25] In it, I learned how the language differed from earlier descriptions, raising questions about linguistic change in an era of social transformation. A second was exposure to Berkeley's collections relating to the Indigenous languages of California, including extensive materials in my own department. No linguists were studying these; I remember thinking that if our archive instead held Hittite tablets, it would be full of European scholars. A third transformative experience was helping at the Breath of Life Archival Institute (chapter 4), where I witnessed inspiringly creative uses of archival documentation. On their own, Indigenous language learners and activists were engaged in the philological work that many academic linguists seemed to disdain.

My shift to Yurok and (later) Karuk philology was partly an accident, based on personal connections, but it was serendipitous. I would not have started to work with Yurok had it not been for my colleagues Juliette Blevins and Leanne Hinton; nor would I have begun working with Karuk but for Susan Gehr and Ruth Rouvier in the Karuk Tribe language office and my colleagues Alice Gaby and Line Mikkelsen. And I would not have worked with either language were it not for the generosity of many Karuk and Yurok people who welcomed me into their homes and communities.

Yurok is the language Kroeber worked most with, so archival material from this language is especially rich at Berkeley. At first I studied this on its own, as a bundle of decontextualized artifacts. Over time, thanks to students, colleagues, and above all Yurok people themselves, I came to see how rewarding it is to make textual and linguistic description accessible to many audiences, especially those whose parents, grandparents, and great-grandparents created the material it is based on. I had a similar experience a decade later when I began work with the Karuk language. I came to collaborate with Indigenous people from an atypical starting point, the archive, but it has helped me appreciate continuities and changes across more than a century of detailed records in complex, heterogeneous communities.

I have two roles in relation to archival language material. One is that of a contributor and user. As a linguist, I have worked with elders who wished to record their languages and stories for their families and communities, and with learners, teachers, and activists passionately committed to continued language vitality based partly on those records. I also have a broader role as the director of Berkeley's California Language Archive, which began with Haas's and some of Kroeber's collections and has grown over decades of donations from researchers and community members.

When I first became involved with an archive, I was, like most linguists, naïve about cultural heritage in the aftermath of genocide. In 2013, I had a memorable experience when an Indigenous linguist was donating unique recordings of elders speaking her language. She would have digital copies, and we agreed that she could always change her mind and take the originals back; but she was sobbing as she signed a gift form. I have thought about this for a long time, and I believe she was in tears because a colonial institution is able to archive what her own tribe lacks the resources to curate. To secure her heritage, she felt she had to give it up. So her recordings joined the many thousands of Indigenous words, baskets, and bodies that fill the shelves of colonial museums and archives. As Yakima elder Russell Jim said more than thirty years ago (Hunn 1990:67–68), "First the whiteman takes our land, then he takes our fish, now he wants to take our language."

I say all this to clarify my position. My academic life since 2001 has crucially involved Indigenous languages. Like many linguists, I love learning about grammar, vocabulary, and usage and glimpsing connections among languages, texts, and sociocultural patterns. Some of my work involves collaborating with Indigenous teachers, activists, and learners to support language reclamation, often by making documentation accessible and useful. I do this with documentary corpora created in research by Kroeber, his students and colleagues, and their successors over many years. A sympathy for Kroeber thus colors how I write, but it is not always shared by people in the communities whose intangible and tangible heritage he collected.

To state matters bluntly, two framings compete to structure Kroeber's legacy. Each has its narrative. In one narrative, anthropologists and linguists have been part of the apparatus of state-sponsored dispossession and genocide. This is a story of the control and objectification of nonwhite bodies by invaders and their willing or unwitting scientist collaborators, whose consignment of Indigenous people to "extinction" validated the theft of land, ancestral bodies, and cultural patrimony. Where this narrative resonates, it is understandable that Kroeber's name evokes pain.

In another narrative, early-twentieth-century academic and public discourse was marked by virulent racism that some anthropologists and linguists opposed. Kroeber and others sought to show that Native Americans, widely dehumanized as infantile or barbaric, have "civilizations" (his word) as complex and diverse as any, and languages and artistic and cultural traditions as worthy of appreciation and study as anyone's. Indigenous people, traumatized by genocide and marginalized by oppression, seemed to be losing cultures and languages, so Kroeber spent a career recording knowledge he thought would otherwise perish. In this narrative, the records of stories that he wrote down and encouraged others to write down, told by scores of culture bearers in dozens of languages, are an enduring legacy.

This book is my attempt to understand the dissonance between these narratives—between my own sense of Kroeber's legacy and different perspectives expressed, often by people I admire, in recent discourse at Berkeley and beyond. I believe Kroeber intended during his career to help Indigenous collaborators and friends. Yet it is undeniable that many of their descendants, and others in their communities, feel that his work brought harm. Part of what interests me is a disjuncture between intention and impact that can affect any of us, even as we try to be empathetic and mindful toward others.

The unnaming of Kroeber Hall involved judging Kroeber's values, so it is important to try to understand why he made the choices he did. Why did he think his work mattered? What did he feel it was for? His reticence and reluctance to reminisce are obstacles in this context. Kroeber rarely explained the broader goals of his work, apart from dicta to the effect that anthropology promotes "tolerance" (1923:506). In chapter 11, I consider his more personal reflections; I sometimes also view him through the lens of Ursula Le Guin's fiction. The two had long discussions of language and literature. In 1955, for example, she wrote him with questions about his new paper on statistical inferences of linguistic time depth.[26] In the same year, she read a book on literary, philosophical, and linguistic semantics, with selections from Boas, the logician Alfred Tarski, and the linguists Leonard Bloomfield, Edward Sapir, and Benjamin Lee Whorf, among others. Reacting to what she saw as a turn away from cultural interests and toward formalism, she told Kroeber that linguistics was apparently becoming "a self-contained, self-feeding, & conceivably completely abstract science . . . with a *very* narrow basis." He responded that he mostly agreed: for many linguists, "the precision has become an obsessive end in itself."[27]

Stories were a major part of Kroeber's relationship with his daughter. In her childhood, she recalled, he told Native American creation stories "by the campfire, on a dark and stormy night."[28] Later, they talked and wrote to each other about poetry and fiction (and he served as her literary agent). About Tolkien's *The Lord of the Rings* (1954–1955), she wrote her parents in 1956 that she "hardly spoke during the three days" it took her to read its three volumes. It was better than Lord Dunsany "because [it was] longer, more consistent, & more absolutely convincing. . . . Forgive the raving," she eventually concluded, "but how often does one read a new book that one *knows* to be a 'great' one?" Kroeber responded six days later that had just read Tolkien's first volume "with absorption, but with not quite the fascination of Dunsany."[29]

Le Guin's own imaginative writing features prominent characters who do just the kind of language and text documentation that drew her father into his profession. Unlike him, they clearly articulate a set of humanistic values that strike me as central in her oeuvre and his. One such figure is Orrec Caspro, the protagonist of *Gifts* (2004a) and a major character in its sequel, *Voices* (2006). He is a storyteller and collector whose self-description in *Voices* plainly expresses what its author also valued: "Finding what other makers made, speaking it, printing it, recovering it from neglect or oblivion, relighting the light of the word—this is the chief work of my life" (75).

My main argument here is that the "chief work" of Alfred Kroeber's life was to document the words of Indigenous people and find spaces for them to tell their stories. This is his primary legacy in the twenty-first century. At a time of rapid cultural transformation, he and his students recorded narratives, life histories, songs, law, oratory, conversational practices, and systems of geographical knowledge from dozens of communities in California and elsewhere. This unique material has incalculable value today. Kroeber did not anticipate all the uses of what he recorded, but he knew it should not fall into "neglect or oblivion."

My argument is not that Kroeber simply let "the subaltern speak," in Gayatri Spivak's (1988) phrase. This is hardly straightforward, as she has shown. Kroeber's collaborators were constrained by an oppressive colonial system. In that system he had more power, of course, but was himself also constrained in some ways. The cultural and linguistic documentation that he and his collaborators assembled emerged from interactions to which each participant brought goals and presuppositions that were structured by their unequal positions. Reading and listening to what they recorded requires thoughtful attention to the positions and commitments of all participants, not least of which was Kroeber's deeply rooted belief that Indigenous cultural expressions were intrinsically worth preserving.

My argument is also not that Kroeber "saved" languages, stories, or cultures. The outside (white) "savior" trope is demeaning and inaccurate. It is not outsiders but Indigenous people who do the work of relighting their words.[30] Kroeber had his own agendas, and was no savior. But there was enough overlap between his goals and his collaborators' interests for his work to be critical today for many who are reclaiming what he recorded.

A second argument concerns the long process that ended in 2021 with the unnaming of Kroeber Hall. Such moments are in the air in the early 2020s, but this specific process also goes back to the nineteenth-century foundation of a land-grant university by a nation and state that displaced Indigenous people to take their land, devastated their cultures and families, and often tried to end their lives; and to the subsequent anger and pain brought about by university actions of the past fifty years. Changing the name of one building at an institution that still celebrates its colonial project and honors those responsible for colonial depredations was, I contend, a way to deflect attention from self-examination.

ROAD MAP

The rest of this book has four main parts. In part I, "Inventing California" (chapters 2–3), I contextualize Kroeber's work historically, socially, and intellectually.[31] California was "invented" inasmuch as its boundaries correspond to no geological, ecological, or precolonial sociocultural lines. Invaders constructed it for their own purposes; Native people had to choose how to respond to overwhelming outside forces. Inventing California crucially also included the building of institutions like universities and museums, and the removal to them of Indigenous cultural heritage.

In part II, "Indigenous Voices" (chapters 4–6), I write about work with languages and texts. I describe the documentary corpora of sound recordings and written materials that Kroeber and his colleagues and students assembled in their work with Indigenous people throughout California and elsewhere. Their work was novel and created unique resources that are in continual use by Native communities and others today. In facilitating and promoting the language work of Juan Dolores (Tohono O'odham) and Gilbert Natches (Numu), Kroeber also played a role in the beginning of written literature in two Indigenous languages.

Part III, "Native Bodies" (chapters 7–8), concerns Ishi's life in the Bay Area and the collection of ancestral remains in early UC archaeological projects. Key questions concern anthropological and archaeological ethics a century ago and Kroeber's culpability in relation to actions that would be inexcusable if they happened today. Times are very different now, however, and I argue that Kroeber's choices were ethical given the circumstances he faced.

In part IV, "Indian Land" (chapters 9–10), I write about actions Kroeber took in the service of Indigenous land (and other) rights, and I evaluate the assertion that he had an impact on negative government decisions. This is unfounded. I also write about the broader picture of UC relations to Indian land, and rehearse well-known facts about the sources of UC wealth. Here I examine the decision to unname Kroeber Hall, and show how the university used it to avoid discussion of its responsibilities.

Finally, in a conclusion (chapter 11), I reflect on the implications of the Kroeber Hall history for universities and for academic practice in fields like my own, linguistics. Our work is not done: it has hardly begun.

I

INVENTING CALIFORNIA

2

DISPOSSESSION AND DOCUMENTATION

> In the beginning there was no land, but water was everywhere. Sailing around on the water on a sort of a boat were two beings. These beings were the creator & maker. Their names are Wolf & Coyote. Wolf was god the master mind, who had the power to wish or create. Coyote was just the opposite. He was foolish, always causing trouble, and most of the time when Wolf would plan something worthwhile, he would always endeavor to upset Wolf's plans. . . .
>
> Seeing all water, they agreed to make land. So Wolf created a dust on the palm of his hand, and he pour[ed] the dust on the water. Land began to form, and grow bigger. Coyote asked Wolf for more land so he could walk around more, and he urged Wolf to add more land.
>
> —Mose Wayland, "The beginning," 1935

Everywhere in California, Indigenous people tell stories about their world, how and why it is, and how to live in it. In a 1935 oral-history project run by Alfred Kroeber (chapter 5), Paiute elder Mose Wayland told Lee Warlie the story that begins as quoted above.[1] I would not presume to say what it meant to Wayland, but as I now read it, it seems partly to concern the creation of social and ecological balance in domains like birth, death, food plants, and water: balance between the destructive excesses urged by Coyote and the creative work of Wolf. A balance of land and water is especially critical in Wayland's arid Owens Valley. There and elsewhere, Native people nurtured equilibria over millennia before Euro-American people came to despoil them.

The linguistic and cultural diversity of North America posed an explanatory challenge for Europeans and American settlers as early as Thomas Jefferson's *Notes on the State of Virginia* (1787). The challenge was only intensified in California, whose Indigenous language diversity

Figure 2.1
Indigenous California languages. Kumeyaay is at least six languages (Miller 2018); Yokuts, often said to be one language (Silverstein 1978, Golla 2011:147–156), is diverse and may be better described as a group of languages. Map by Hannah Haynie and Maziar Toosarvandani, 2011, colorized by a Wikipedia user.

exceeds that of any comparable area in the western hemisphere. As figure 2.1 shows, California has more than ninety languages; they belong to twenty-one of about sixty North American language families. Its cultural complexity is similarly profound.[2]

Kroeber first came to California in 1900 as a twenty-four-year-old graduate student. In a short-term position at the Academy of Sciences in San Francisco, he collected and cataloged cultural artifacts and worked with several Native communities in California. In August 1901, PhD in hand, he returned to what would be a lifelong position at the University of California, then only a few decades old and rapidly transforming itself from a modest college into a research institution with international ambitions. In California, Kroeber found histories and social realities unlike what he had known growing up in New York, or as a Columbia undergraduate and graduate student, or in his PhD work with Arapaho people.

GENOCIDES AND THEIR AFTERMATH

California underwent two waves of colonial genocide. First, under Spanish rule (1769–1821), Indigenous people along the southern and central coast were brought to forced-labor camps (Franciscan missions) that featured branding, flogging, rape, and stocks. Thousands died of malnutrition and disease in a system whose goal, in Kent Lightfoot's (2005:59) words, was to "transform the population of pagan Native Californians into a peasant class of Hispanicized laborers." Benjamin Madley (2019) has called the missions "California's first mass incarceration system." Indentured servitude and related practices continued after Mexican independence (1821) and after California was ceded to the United States (1848). Resistance was severely punished under all three regimes. At Mission Santa Clara in San José, for example, after the Lakisamne Yokuts rebel leader Yozcolo was killed in 1839, his severed head was displayed in front of the church for two or three months.[3]

Second, beginning in 1848, the gold rush brought hundreds of thousands of Americans to California; miners, ranchers, and others killed and displaced tens of thousands of Native people in areas outside the mission system. Over the next twenty-five years, California's Indigenous population fell from 150,000 to 30,000. Genocide—a term first applied to California by Theodora Kroeber and Robert Heizer (1968:19)—was supported by US and California government policies and funding and implemented by the US Army, volunteer militias, and vigilante bands. The barbarity of its implementation has been well documented.[4]

California is also unusual in that the United States ratified no treaties with the state's Indigenous people; land was seized without even nominal payment. In 1851–1852, eighteen treaties were in fact signed with California Indians, who were then removed from their land, but the US Senate "rejected the treaties and . . . imposed an injunction of secrecy," as Larisa Miller (2013b:39) wrote. In the late nineteenth century, instead of treaty reservations, there were military reservations to which Indigenous people were forcibly removed; conditions were brutal and disease was widespread. As Madley (2016:306–307) described the 1860s, "Confinement to federal reservations was a death sentence for many of the state's Indian people, whether they were starved to death, worked to death, shot, hanged, massacred, or died of sickness there." Others lived in small communities (rancherias) in or near their unceded ancestral land, often working for white people; some tried to pass, or lived in hiding. Indians were mostly not US citizens and had few rights or opportunities in American society.[5] Health care and education were inadequate; languages and lifeways were suppressed; cultural and religious freedoms were denied; economies and families had been shattered.

Early in the twentieth century, philanthropic organizations clearly documented the conditions confronting California's Indigenous people. The nascent Sequoya League described one southern California reservation in a 1901 letter to the US government (Lummis 1901:459):

> The only land which the Indians cultivate—or anyone can cultivate—is of small patches in ravines. Some of these patches are but a few square yards in area. The rest is mountainous, rocky, has some trees upon it, and is suitable only for cattle. . . . There are some patches of open land near the top of the mountain, fit for the growing of grain in favorable years; but the Indians are averse to living up there because of the heavy winter snows. . . . They state, also, that the places with water are already taken up. . . . Why this worthless mountain land was ever reserved for the Indians, we confess our inability to understand. . . . In any event, it is unfit for human occupancy, and inadquate to support human life.

In a 1904 petition, the Northern California Indian Association (NCIA) drew a comparably stark picture (Heizer 1979:111). Dispossession and eviction had left Native people on "worthless tracts" of land:

> Sometimes, as at Crescent City, they have taken refuge upon the ocean beach. Sometimes, as at Seven Mile, Colusa County, on the Sacramento River, they are squatted upon a levee, or, as at Grand Island, also upon the Sacramento,

> ten or twelve families occupy an old cemetery mound three or four acres in extent, outside the levee and frequently subject to overflow, where every turn of the spade brings up the bones of their ancestors, and their only water supply is a well 10 feet deep in this charnel pit.

"Usually no Indian child is permitted to attend a white school," the NCIA wrote, due to "rampant" racism that "shuts off the Indian from all progress and even from justice."

Impacts of genocide, ethnic cleansing, and dispossession were plainly described by Kroeber. Nobody working with Indians "could escape the shattering that their society underwent and listening to tales of their deprivations and spoilation" (1962:58). And a Yurok elder's stories evoked "uncontrollable sobs . . . when his massive frame would struggle and heave for minutes" (1976:162). This was because he "felt sorry for all the people that used to live" in the places he was speaking about, according to Kroeber's interpreter Weitchpec Frank in 1902, and "for the o[ld] man (his father?) who told him the story" (ALK Ctn 12:19, p. 98). His was the trauma of a "holocaust survivor," in Thomas Buckley's (1989:440) words.

In 1906 and 1908, responding to appeals such as those quoted above, Congress allocated a total of $150,000 to buy land for California Indians. C. E. Kelsey, NCIA secretary and director for over a decade, was appointed as California special agent of the Office of Indian Affairs from 1906 to 1913. To prod Congress, Miller (2013a:3) explained, Kelsey had "orchestrated the rediscovery and removal of the Senate's injunction of secrecy from the [unratified] California Indian treaties." In his government role, he arranged to buy forty-five land tracts for rancherias, ideally land that could be farmed. The example of what is now the Blue Lake Rancheria was detailed by the Commissioner of Indian Affairs (Smith 1909:132):

> Of the Indians in Humboldt county, 33 souls constitute what is known as the *Blue Lake Band.* In his efforts to procure land for these Indians, the Special Agent met with great difficulty, owing to the fact that the land of Humboldt county is largely barren ridges surrounding small fertile valleys held at $200 per acre and more. At length, however, he succeeded in obtaining an offer from the Brizzard heirs to sell 29.5 acres of land fairly suitable, and acceptable to the Indians, and this purchase has been authorized at an expenditure of $1500.

Figure 2.2
Robert Spott, Berkeley, 1933 (ALKFP ALB v. 4).

However well-intentioned the program, more than thirty people received fewer than 30 acres, in comparison to the thousands taken from them.

Many communities remained landless, including all those near the Bay Area in central coastal California, and reservation conditions were mixed, so the loss of land remained a central problem and a cause of activism. A 1926 Commonwealth Club of California meeting in San Francisco featured Yurok leader Robert Spott (figure 2.2; see chapter 6).[6] He emphasized what white people had taken (Spott 1926:133):

> In the old time, away back, we had a place where we used to go and pick berries for our winter supply. Then, again, we had a hunting ground where we killed the game for our winter supply. And again, we had a place where we used to go to gather acorns for our winter supply. Then, again, we could go up along the river to where a fishing place was left to us. But today, when we go back to where we used to go for our berries, there is the sign "Keep out." What are we going to do?

> Then again we go to where we used to hunt. You see the sign again, "Keep out. No shooting allowed." All right. We go away. Then again, we go down to where we used to fish. That is taken up by white men. What are we going to do? We cannot do anything.

Indigenous people elsewhere in the state described comparable experiences. In eastern California, Paiute elder Jennie Cashbaugh spoke in 1935 about the American invasion of Owens Valley. Her family was forced to "move off the old home grounds that we thought belonged to us" and live "where nothing could be raised" (ED 154.1):

> All we can see is "no shooting allowed," "no trespassing," what can we do, nothing, but hang our heads in shame and sorrow. For once we had lived & roamed the Valley in peace and harmony but today is selfishness and greed, nowhere to gather the seeds and herbs for medicine and food, we have to eat the white man's food entirely. We get sick the white man's sickness and get white man medicine and our lives is rather shorter than that of the old time Indians lived.

Wailacki-Concow historian William Bauer (2016:102–103) rightly called such treatment "ethnic cleansing." To quote another Paiute elder in 1935, Edith Dewey, Indians "are waiting for a just settlement from the United States for the lands it has taken from them, timber and mineral, reserving forest to rent to some one else for a large sum of money without paying the owner, the California American Indians" (ED 154.1).

At the 1926 Commonwealth Club meeting mentioned above, US and California Indian policies and practices in various domains were described and condemned. From the State Board of Health, Edward Glaser (1926:127–128) spoke about conditions in reservations and rancherias:

> Tuberculosis is a leading disease and cause of death. Quoting,—"a number of middle aged and old couples told us their children were all dead or only one or two living out of a family of 10, 12, or 14, the rest having been killed by tuberculosis during childhood or adolescence." "He sick long time, he cough lots, he get very weak and he died" was a common story.
>
> It has been estimated that fully one-third of the Indians in California have trachoma. . . . In Northern California many of the older Indians are blind or nearly so from trachoma. . . . The communicable diseases find the Indians easy prey and outbreaks of smallpox and diphtheria are not uncommon. Universal among them is malnutrition.

In education, too, circumstances were grim. The goal of US Indian education policy in the late nineteenth and early twentieth centuries was cultural assimilation, if possible through boarding schools (since these removed students from families and home cultures).[7] A federal official explained this in 1885 (Thompson 2013:16):

> These schools strip from the unwashed person of the Indian boy the unwashed blanket, and, after instructing him in what to him are the mysteries of personal cleanliness, clothe him with the clean garment of civilized men and teach him how to wear them. They give him information concerning a bed and teach him how to use it; teach him how to sit on a chair, how to use knife and fork, how to eat at a table, and what to eat. While he is learning these things, he is also learning to read and write, and, at the same time, is being taught how to work, how to earn a living.

Cultural practices were deliberately shorn. A former superintendent of the Fort Mojave School wrote Mojave leader Pete Lambert in 1900, congratulating him on his new position as chief. His letter combined callous recollection and ominous encouragement (Sherer 1966:18):

> My dear Pete, . . . I can remember when I first took you into the Ft. Mohave school and what a time I had in cutting your hair for the first time. I can see now all the old Mohave women standing around crying, while you covered your long hair with your arms and told me that I wouldn't dare to cut that hair off, but the hair was cut in spite of all your efforts and the direful predictions of the Mohave women. I compelled you to have your hair cut off, not because of any objections to the long hair in itself, but merely because the long hair was a symbol of savagery. . . .
>
> When Supt. McKoin asks you to bring him 150 children or any number of children, don't rest either night or day until the Superintendant's request is obeyed.

Some children were kidnapped from their families; corporal punishment was widespread. For speaking their language, Mojave, one former student recalled that "five lashes of the whip" were the penalty for the first offense; another remembered being forced to stand on tiptoes during dinnertime with his mouth on a ring in the wall.[8]

Through such practices, the US education system had a profoundly destructive impact on Indigenous languages. A critical tool of ethnocide was language suppression, whose effects included what the Kenyan writer Ngũgĩ wa Thiong'o (1986) called "colonial alienation." About British rule, he wrote, "The bullet was the means of the physical subjugation. Language was the means of the spiritual subjugation" (9). Before colonization, Gĩkũyũ was the language "of our evening teach-ins, ... our immediate and wider community, and ... our work in the fields" (11). The imposition of English in schools "resulted in the disassociation of the sensibility of [the] child from his natural and social environment, what we might call colonial alienation" (17). For Ngũgĩ, therefore, it was essential to reclaim and revalorize Gĩkũyũ in order to overcome the "imperialist-imposed tradition of contempt for the tools of communication" and "transcend colonial alienation" (28). The same idea often underpins California language activism.

A practical goal of government schools was to train Native people for manual and domestic labor in the Euro-American economy. Schools had a military atmosphere. For example, Frances Hunter (Tule River Reservation) attended Sherman Indian School in Riverside, California during the 1920s and later recalled her experiences (Williams and Tracz 2016:83):

> When we went to school we had to get in line to march to breakfast with the band playing. Just like, you know, how the soldiers do, how they march? Every time, three times a day.... For breakfast, dinner, and supper ... on Sunday, they'd have line inspection, and you'd have to stand there for two hours. [They'd] look at your shoes, see if you'd shined your shoes. See if you've got your clothes all pressed. Some of them used to faint out there.

California schools also featured what Irving Hendrick (1976:168) described as "incompetent teachers, inefficient use of supplies, and poor provision of health, sanitation, and recreation." He noted that a 1923 third-grade final examination included these questions: "Who found America? What is cotton made of? Tell what you know about Eli Whitney. What is fiber? Where do the clouds come from?" A 75 percent score was required to graduate from the third grade.

VANISHMENT AND COLLECTION

Another critical context for Kroeber's work is the "myth of the vanishing Indian," whose manifestations in the American cultural imagination were pervasive.[9] These included written work, from James Fenimore Cooper's

Last of the Mohicans (1826) to Joseph K. Dixon's *The Vanishing Race* (1913), as well as visual representations in many modalities. Edward S. Curtis (1907–1930) began a twenty-volume series with an image "meant to convey . . . that the Indians as a race, already shorn in their tribal strength and stripped of their primitive dress, are passing into the darkness of an unknown future" (vol. 1, plate 1). The financier J. P. Morgan funded Curtis's project, and President Theodore Roosevelt himself justified it in a foreword (vol. 1, xi): "The Indian as he has hitherto been is on the point of passing away. . . . It would be a veritable calamity if a vivid and truthful record of [the] conditions [of precolonial life] were not kept."

The Curtis print in figure 2.3 is representative in the nostalgia it is meant to evoke: the subject is not wearing his real clothes, for example, and Euro-American objects are absent. The photograph was taken near Walker Lake, Nevada, on Agaidɨkadɨ Paiute land. It interests me because Curtis used it to depict a precolonial Paiute artist of his imagining, ten years after Kroeber's work with an actual Paiute artist, Gilbert Natches, whose artistic style was non-"traditional" and whose language documentation reflects linguistic hybridity (see chapter 6).[10]

Vanishment was the intended outcome of US policies in areas like education and land ownership, but Native people did not vanish. They persisted and succeeded. If the year of the Wounded Knee Massacre (1890) was "a cruel, low, painful point," as David Treuer (2019:15) has written, it was "a low point from which much of modern Indian and American life has emerged." In the decades around 1900, change began through the agency of Indigenous leaders; many were active in the Society of American Indians (1911–1923).[11] Influential in California were Euro-American allies like Helen Hunt Jackson, author of *A Century of Dishonor* (1881) and the widely read *Ramona* (1884), and those who led the Northern California Indian Association and Sequoya League, which bought and advocated for land, food, and medical supplies for Indian communities. These organizations were succeeded by Indigenous-led organizations, the Mission Indian Federation (founded in 1919) and California Indian Brotherhood (1926), which were instrumental in securing Native rights and laying the groundwork for reforms such as the right to seek compensation for land seizures.

Still, the vanishment myth was ubiquitous. With it came a desire for artifacts and souvenirs of Native life, influencing academic projects in

Figure 2.3
Edward S. Curtis, "The primitive artist—Paviotso," 1924 (Library of Congress, https://www.loc.gov/item/2002719666/).

at least three domains. One was language and cultural practices. Popular depictions of Indian people featured exoticizing glimpses of their cultures and languages throughout North American colonization. Long before Kroeber came to California, Alexander S. Taylor (1860–1863) published 150 articles on the "Indianology of California" in the *California Farmer and Journal of Useful Sciences*. A typical article includes an Island Chumash vocabulary, place names, and assorted details about physiognomy, boats, and California condor "veneration" (Heizer 1973:40–48). Information about Indigenous lifeways and speech fed an insatiable public hunger.

A second domain was material culture. White people avidly collected objects used in Indigenous ceremonies and daily life. This included outright theft, as well as purchase that could be coercive or at unfair prices. The involvement of wealthy collectors and museums led to a profitable secondary market; even artists who sold their work freely might not see its full market value. In California, some buyers understood their activities as benefiting impoverished weavers, but the basket trade also had the effect of removing objects from their social contexts and disrupting Indigenous cultural practices. At the same time, the vitality of weaving practices was threatened by ecological damage that made it harder to find basketry materials and by American schooling that removed young people from the cultural settings where they could learn to gather and weave.[12]

Archaeology provided a third domain: digging up relics of Indigenous life, notably including ancestral remains buried over centuries and millennia. This also goes back to Jefferson, who excavated burial mounds near Monticello and has been called the "father of American archaeology."[13] In the nineteenth century, where land was taken from Native Americans, amateur archaeologists and other settlers dug for artifacts and human remains; professionals working for museums, universities, and the US government were also involved. In a mania for "skull collecting," to quote Ann Fabian's (2010) book, remains from North America and around the world found their way into museum collections.[14]

One prominent collector was the San Francisco philanthropist Ph(o)ebe Hearst (figure 2.4).[15] She bought art and antiquities from around the world, and sought a museum to house her large and growing collections. In the 1890s, Hearst began supporting UC, which put her on its board of regents. "I should like to organize a regular department of American Indian Antiquities," she wrote to UC president Wheeler (13 August 1901, UCOPAF Box 7). That department later described itself as having been established to "organize . . . several archaeological and ethnological expeditions maintained on behalf of the University by Mrs. Phoebe A. Hearst" (Putnam 1906:2). A local newspaper described her role ("Indian Lore" 1901):

> A department of Indian anthropology will be added to the University of California for the investigation of Indian remains and languages. Mrs. Phebe Hearst is the founder of the new chair and is providing the funds for the

Figure 2.4
UC leaders Benjamin Wheeler and Phoebe Hearst, ca. 1910–1915. Bain News Service (Library of Congress, https://www.loc.gov/item/2014691185/).

> maintenance of the department. The gift comes as the result of an interest she has long felt in the archaeological relics of the former masters of the country, in the investigation of which she has already spent considerable money.

The first (short-lived) US linguistics department was established at UC in the same year, headed by Wheeler. Its first PhD dissertation was by Pliny Goddard (1905b) on an Indigenous language of California, Hupa.

CALIFORNIA MEMORY DOCUMENTATION

Kroeber's teacher Franz Boas (see figure 2.5) was a foundational figure in anthropology. As a linguist, Boas formulated influential principles and parameters of language description, edited the *Handbook of American Indian Languages*, and founded the *International Journal of American*

Linguistics and edited it from 1917 to 1939.[16] Based on collaborations with Charles Cultee, Ella Deloria, George Hunt, and others, he published grammars and texts for several Indigenous languages of North America.[17] And as Roman Jakobson (1944:189) emphasized, Boas's view of phonemic and other structural patterns in language, of which speakers are not consciously aware, came down through his student Edward Sapir into American structuralism. Jakobson implied that cultural phenomena generally exhibit the same "logic of the unconscious" for Boas. An analytic goal was therefore to understand the systems underlying local cultural and linguistic facts.

The 1901 appointment of Boas's first Columbia PhD student at the University of California was arranged by Boas, Hearst, and Wheeler. As "the first Boasian," in Ira Jacknis's (2002) phrase, Kroeber worked in a way that shared many of the assumptions, positive impacts, and limitations of his teacher's research practice. Much of what has been said about Boas thus also applies to what I will call Kroeber's *memory documentation*. Especially thoughtful discussions of Kroeber's work in relation to Boasian ideas are those of Thomas Buckley (1989, 1996, 2002) and Jacknis (2002).

Several ideas and assumptions in Kroeber's work merit special mention. One is *cultural essentialism*. Boas wrote to Kroeber in 1899 that a key goal was finding what is "characteristic of the life and mode of thought of the Indian" (Jacknis 2002:523). Indian people were seen not as historically situated individuals negotiating fraught social worlds in the wake of genocide, but as potential archetypes of timeless cultures whose expressions include languages, stories, songs, ceremonies, customs, and the like. This sprang from the romantic nationalism that also inspired Johann Gottfried Herder's collection of Latvian folksongs and the Grimms' of German folklore; Child's English and Scottish ballads; music by Dvořák and Grieg; and Elias Lönnrot's *Kalevala*, built from Finnish folk traditions. Later American examples included John Lomax's documentation of Texas folk music and Zora Neale Hurston's of African American folklore. As the twentieth century unfolded, of course, a far darker side of essentialism and nationalism became plain.

In the European tradition just mentioned, as early as Herder and still for Boas and Kroeber, language and texts were seen as critical cultural expressions. Kroeber had come to anthropology from literary and linguistic study and averred in 1917 that "my actual work will always be *literature*" (Golla 1984:260).[18] Boas himself explained in 1905 that nobody "would advocate the study of antique civilizations or, let me say, of the Turks or the Russians, without a thorough knowledge of their languages and of the literary documents in these languages; and contributions not based on such material would not be considered as adequate." For Indigenous American cultures, therefore, "literary material" made "available for study" would be "the foundation of all future researches."[19]

A second idea is what Marvin Harris (1968:250) called "historical particularism." An earlier idea, which dominated nineteenth-century American anthropology, was that cultural traits tend to evolve along certain universal pathways, so that societies and civilizations could be ordered according to how far they had progressed. Northern Europeans were often seen as the most advanced by advocates of this evolutionary perspective. Boas argued instead that similar traits can originate in dissimilar ways, depending on cultural context: "The same ethnical phenomenon may develop from different sources" (1896:904). Individual cultural products, expressions, and other traits are therefore not meaningful in isolation; they just "illustrate descriptions" of entire cultures (1887:486), which can be scientifically evaluated only as ensembles.

A corollary of historical particularism is *cultural relativism*. If societies cannot be arranged in an evolutionary scheme, implying a ranking of how advanced they are, then each is in principle the culmination of its own history, and there is no cross-cultural measure of value according to which it is ranked. There is no global hierarchy of more and less advanced peoples, cultures, or languages. Matti Bunzl (2004) has stressed the historical relationship between these ideas and essentialism. "In contrast to the [Enlightenment] conception of a uniform development of civilization," he wrote, Herder and Wilhelm von Humboldt argued that "each human group could be understood only as a product of its particular history, propelled, in turn, by a unique *Volksgeist*" (437). (See chapter 3 of this book for some concrete consequences of historical particularism and cultural relativism.)

Historical particularism as a research program, though liberal and what would now be called anti-racist in its implications, contained within it the seeds of its own undoing. Any school that seems to eschew generalization and encourages the accumulation of particulars runs the risk of appearing to be mere list-making. In California, Kroeber and his students assembled

Figure 2.5
Franz and Gertrude Boas, ca. 1895. Albumen print by J. R. Rockwood (FBP U5-1-8).

inventories of cultural traits for specific tribes and areas. "It may seem to a distant observer," Boas (1920b:314) admitted, "that American students are engaged in a mass of detailed investigations" without broader implications. That observer was not so distant in the end. In a review of Kroeber's *Configurations of Culture Growth* (1944a), Leslie White (1946:78) complained about Boas: "Not only did he fail to see the forest for the trees, he could scarcely see the tree for the branches, or the branches for the twigs. And no two twigs were the same." He thought Kroeber was also overly attached to particulars: he "seems to love facts . . . for their own sake, much as one might love the feel of velvet or the hard, chaste beauty of porcelain"; he "worships at the shrine of induction," though "no amount of mere accumulation of facts will ever produce understanding" (83–84). This question of the reason for documentation also worried Kroeber for many decades (chapter 11).

A third idea, *vanishment*, is a corollary of cultural essentialism. Boas and Kroeber accepted the vanishment conception that was prevalent in

Figure 2.6
Jaime de Angulo, "Boas learns there is a Karankapuwatchimekupitlin Indian still living," undated (Jaime de Angulo Papers, MS 14, Box 7:14, Special Collections and Archives, University Library, UC Santa Cruz). Boas's students Ruth Benedict, Gladys Reichard, and Ruth Bunzel are depicted at the right.

Euro-American society: they believed that the Indigenous languages and cultures of North America were doomed to disappear. Boas stated his view in an 11 April 1901 letter to Zelia Nuttall (Farrell and Hull 2001), suggesting that UC hire one of the young "philologists" he was training, and in an 11 May 1901 letter to Hearst (UCOPAF Box 6:97):

> [To Nuttall:] In California we have an enormous mass of Indian tribes and languages about which we know practically nothing. . . . You are aware that all these tribes are on the verge of extinction, and that it is only a question of a very few years when their languages, and with them their traditions and the records of their customs, will have disappeared.

> [To Hearst:] With the advance of our civilization, primitive customs, habits, and traditions of the natives of our continent are disappearing rapidly, and in many regions the natives themselves are on the verge of extinction. Their

> traditions, their customs, and their physical appearance are the only source from which we can reconstruct the early history of our continent.

Boas's positionality is plain: "we" are European and American, "they" are Indigenous; "we have" their "tribes and languages." His term "primitive" often implied a contrast with "civilized," referring to certain sociopolitical or technological features.

Cultural vanishment did not necessarily mean human disappearance. In a 1911 lecture, Kroeber's colleague T. T. Waterman said that a "wrong impression prevalent in our country is that the Indian has no future, that he is rapidly disappearing." In fact, he continued, "the tribes are increasing steadily and will eventually become a permanent part of the American people, especially in some regions" ("Lectures" 1911). But Boas, Kroeber, Waterman, and others did believe that Indigenous cultures and languages would disappear. Boas's own commitment to what has often been called "salvage" documentation was striking enough to inspire a fond caricature by Jaime de Angulo, who admired Boas and was friendly with him (see figure 2.6).[20]

The vanishment idea is a corollary of essentialism because, while the latter tolerates gradual "organic" changes, it does not admit the kinds of change experienced by colonized Indigenous communities. From an essentialist viewpoint, cultural hybridity and changes in language structure or use (such as domain constriction, interlanguage, and language mixing) can be seen only as steps on a tragic road to extinction.[21] As James Clifford (1988:338) wrote, "The culture idea, tied as it is to assumptions about natural growth and life, does not tolerate radical breaks in historical continuity." In California, according to Kent Lightfoot (2005:211), Kroeber encountered Indigenous people "whose daily lives . . . centered around nontraditional social forms and new kinds of Indian identities." Such communities posed a challenge for an anthropologist with an essentialist view of cultures.

William Sewell Jr. (1999:38) and others have said that the culture idea invites exoticization; a future Berkeley chancellor, Nicholas Dirks, even called it "a colonial formation" (1992:3). Some see a mutually constitutive relationship between Boasian assumptions and assimilationist ideas. "Boas's construction of tradition as unconscious, affective, and inevitably disappearing," according to Charles Briggs and Richard

Bauman (1999:519), "rendered him complicit in naturalizing white control of Native American communities and the ideology of 'assimilation.'" Kahnawake Mohawk anthropologist Audra Simpson (2018:167) was blunter: Boas "worked in concert with a settler state that sought to disappear Indian life and land in order to possess that land and absorb that difference into a normative sociopolitical order." Boas and Kroeber wrote as if assimilation and vanishment were inevitable, but the extent to which they acted "in concert" with settler-state dispossession is another matter. Patrick Wolfe (1999:43) warned against the "crudeness of intentionality" when evaluating the relation between anthropological and colonial thinking; Kwame Anthony Appiah (2020) ridiculed "the extraordinary thesis that Boasian antiracism was an ideology that ultimately propped up a system of subordination."[22] Kroeber did not resist a ubiquitous vanishment narrative, but his role in sustaining it and determining its effects remains to be shown (see chapter 9).

Related to the essentialist and assimilationist assumptions is a constant aspect of Kroeber's discursive posture. His scholarly and popular writings had as their audience his academic colleagues or the broader European and Euro-American public they mostly represented. These people were his unreflecting "we," while Indian (and many other) people remained the Other. Early in his book *Anthropology* (1923:5), he wrote, "It is commonly considered useful for a man to know that Napoleon was a Corsican and was defeated at Waterloo in 1815, but a rather pedantic piece of knowledge that Shi Hwang-ti was born in northwestern China and unified the rule of China in 221 B.C." Kroeber's point was about the arbitrariness of cultural conventions, but his "man" had been brought up in the same cultural and historical context as those among and for whom he wrote. In describing the Yurok traditional prohibition on naming the dead—"a mortal offense, voidable only by a considerable payment"—he similarly expressed both cultural relativism and his Euro-American position (1925:48): "We are wont to think of the hardship entailed by such a law on the unwitting and careless; but the Indian, reared since earliest recollection in the shadow of this regulation, makes no mistakes." Again, "we" are apparently not Yurok.

Late in his career, Kroeber (1945) devised a name for the group among and for whom he wrote. Borrowing a Greek word, he referred to the originally Eurasian "culture aggregate" that is now often called "western" or "global" as the Oikoumenê, an "interwoven set of happenings and products" (9) that have accreted and spread over geographical and social space. This Oikoumenê was crucially a historically situated community, sometimes (in its anthropological role) gazing at a putatively timeless Other.[23]

A fourth assumption distinguishes Kroeber from Boas. To explain the patterns he encountered, Kroeber sought to elucidate their origins. He described languages and clarified their relationships as proxies for the relationships of human populations. Referring to California's Indigenous diversity, Kroeber (1909b:436) explained his view in a public lecture:

> Nowhere in the world are there so many different forms of speech per square mile of territory. A day's journey on foot usually suffices to bring one into a district where the Indian language is different. There are points at which one can stand and draw a circle of forty miles radius which will include within it more distinct families of languages than are spoken in the whole of Europe. . . . The cause of this unexampled multiplicity of languages is the greatest problem that confronts the student of the California Indian, for its solution will do more than anything else to throw light on his origin and that part of his history which is now veiled in obscurity.

By contrast, Boas was sympathetic to diffusional explanations and cautious about genealogical ones, expressing reservations about "the whole theory of an 'Ursprache' for every group of modern languages" (1920a:374). He wrote that "it is not possible to group American languages rigidly in a genealogical scheme in which each linguistic family is shown to have developed to modern forms" (1929:7). While this claim about the exceptionality of Native American languages is now known to be mistaken, it is notable because it was expressed by other contemporary scholars and is echoed in recent (debunked) claims that Australian languages too resist genealogical explanation.[24] Kroeber (1955–1956) himself later wrote about Boas's views:

> Boas was consistently opposed to historical reconstruction, using the indubitable but on the whole minor factor of inter-language influencing . . . as a club with which to belabor reconstruction of ancestral forms from which related languages had diverged. . . . [Indo-European] comparative philology appears not to have entered into Boas' own education. He paid little or no

> attention to it as a model, and remained averse to all genetic problems in American languages, maintaining they were insoluble. . . .
>
> I was obviously so much more prone to compare, classify, and interpret historically in the field of language than was Boas that his influence was unable to restrain me.

For their part, Indigenous people have often pushed back against outsiders informing them about their origins. In the words of Sisseton-Wahpeton Oyate scholar Kim TallBear (2013:202), "We want the power of our stories to shape our lives to be respected and not to be deemed as untruths."

I have described several assumptions and ideas underlying memory documentation: historical particularism and cultural relativism; essentialism; vanishment; and, for Kroeber, diachronic explanation. Memory documentation, then, was a procedure in which languages, stories, songs, and other practices were recorded based on recollection, not observation. Rather than documenting the language use and sociocultural practices he actually witnessed, which almost always showed some effects of Euro-American contact, Kroeber asked people (typically, elderly people) to describe former (ideally, precolonial) times. This method had practical problems, as Samuel Barrett saw during Ecuadorian fieldwork in 1908. In that year, Kroeber turned thirty-two (see figure 2.7), and his student Barrett, three years his junior, received the University of California's first PhD in anthropology. In a 1908 letter to Kroeber, Barrett remarked that Indigenous people along the Río Cayapas could show him "the processes involved in any sort of work that they may be doing. It is quite different from taking a thing on hearsay from some old man who remembers how his great grandfather did it." California "salvage" or "archival" ethnography was "an act of imagination," as Kroeber's student Cora Du Bois put it.[25] Her phrase was admiring, but the imaginative facet of what Clifford (1986) called "ethnographic pastoral" may slip into nostalgia and even fantasy in its depiction of dehistoricized individuals and communities.

In California, based on memory documentation, Kroeber's stated goal was "to reconstruct and present the scheme within which [Indigenous people] in ancient and more recent times lived their lives" (1925:v). His verb was *lived,* his noun *scheme.* This goal had a diachronic component (to explain how languages and societies had changed over millennia) and a structural one (to elucidate their underlying logics).

Figure 2.7
Alfred Kroeber, New York, ca. 1907–1908 (ALKFP Box 1).

The importance for Kroeber of reconstructing change naturally raises the question of how he saw the relation of anthropology and history. Both fields have a diachronic dimension, and Kroeber struggled to characterize the distinction with precision. One example was in a sketch of what would become his *Handbook of the Indians of California* (1925), enclosed with a 1913 letter to F. W. Hodge (26 June, ALK Box 2:14).[26] There, Kroeber outlined what he thought a thorough study of a state's Indigenous people should contain. It would have three main parts: "Ethnology" (his alternative title was "The Indians"); "Archaeology" (or "The Antiquities"); and "History" ("The Indians and the Whites"). The first part includes "bodily type, customs, culture, classification, linguistic and political interrelations, relation to environment, trend of migration, original population, etc." This was the object of memory documentation, corresponding mainly to what we now call linguistics and sociocultural anthropology. In these areas Kroeber felt he had expertise, unlike archaeology and history. The latter included "discovery and exploration, trade and settlement, missionary influences, wars, treaties, land cessions, reservations and reservation life, recent progress, prospects, and in general the relations between the native and the civilized race." With words like "discovery" and "civilized," this is an old-fashioned dossier; and "progress" sounds uncomfortably like the benign goal of philanthropists and progressives.

If the distinction between history and anthropology was about source materials (written documents versus sociocultural observation), maybe it could be maintained for a while. But Kroeber's comments about a part of the world with a longer history of writing exposed a different view. His monograph on Indigenous people of the Philippines ended with a revealing summary of centuries of cultural contact, including successive influences from India, China, Islam, and the Spanish and American invasions (1919b:212–213). "Civilization is more complex than either population or speech," he wrote, "comprising at least half a dozen strains or streams of different source." Among these, "Indian influences are on the whole perhaps the most profound that have affected Philippine civilization," including the transmission of "culture elements" such as the use of iron and certain religious practices. Islam led to the spread of "writing, political organization, some handicrafts," and law among other cultural traits; the Spanish invasion "introduced Catholicism and letters and caused considerable remodelling of economic and industrial conditions." Revealingly, Kroeber then described changes due to the new American regime as "having been remarkably efficient in the direction of bringing the more backward nationalities of the islands nearer participation in contemporary Western civilization; but for that reason fall outside the scope of ethnology." The implication was that anthropology's object was the Other; Western civilization had history. The view that global or Western society was outside the scope of anthropology made no sense and was not adopted in later synthesizing publications. But Kroeber's offhand comment about the Philippines exposed an assumption about timeless, essentialized cultures as the archetypal field of anthropological inquiry. He later made significant contributions to historical study, but his presuppositions guided where he first looked and what he too readily neglected. And his relative neglect of the Indigenous people of the Bay Area itself, compared with his intense interest in less acculturated populations of northwestern and southeastern California, would prove to be a crucial factor in the eventual unnaming of Kroeber Hall.

3

THE WELLHEAD

I want some of these fine things.
—William Randolph Hearst, letter to Phoebe Hearst, 1899

In the public discussion of Kroeber Hall and much talk about Kroeber, it has been taken for granted that the relationship to be critiqued is between Kroeber (or academics generally) and Indigenous people. But this was only a part of what Damon Akins and William Bauer (2021:302) have called the "triangular relationship between philanthropists, academics, and California Indians." In this chapter, I describe facets of that relationship. At the University of California, a program of research on Indigenous cultural heritage was planned, funded, and directed by San Francisco and California Euro-American elites, especially philanthropist and UC leader Phoebe Apperson Hearst. Like the broader educational mission it served and helped constitute, and with many echoes today, this research program was at once extractive and liberal-minded. Both parts of this paradox are visible in the interactions between participants in the triangular relationship.

VERONA

Mission San José was founded in 1797 at the Ohlone place called Oroysom, in what is now Fremont, California, about 30 miles south of Berkeley and 20 miles north of the city of San Jose. In 1809, according to Randall Milliken (2008), over 80 percent of its inhabitants were from Chochenyo-speaking Ohlone communities. Just over a decade later, a plurality of inhabitants (37 percent) were from Yokuts-speaking communities; others came from communities that spoke Chochenyo, Patwin, and Coast, Bay, and Plains Miwok. By 1835, 60 percent of the population

Figure 3.1
Ohlone ("Costanoan") and neighboring languages. Pleasanton and Mission San José are labeled. Cartography by Jackie Honig Bjorkman (Golla 2011:163).

was from Plains Miwok communities. These shifts reflected mortality rates in the mission and active recruitment from ever-broader areas, as more workers were needed and Spanish colonization expanded its reach. See figure 3.1 for the location of Mission San José and the areas from which speakers of Chochenyo (in "San Francisco Bay Costanoan"), Miwok languages, and Yokuts were recruited as laborers. Throughout

Figure 3.2
Indigenous workers in the Pleasanton hop fields, late 1800s. Image courtesy of Pleasanton's Museum on Main (P-0484, from Kolln 1882 album).

their existence, missions like this one had multicultural, multilingual Indigenous populations. Catholicism had been imposed, but traditional practices continued alongside new cultural expressions.

The missions' land-holding role ended with secularization in 1836; their land was given to prominent Mexican families. By law, Milliken (2008:73) wrote, "a mission's Indians were to be given its lands and cattle when it was closed," but the authorities "assessed the Indians as needing none of it." Instead, depending on circumstances, Indigenous inhabitants of Mission San José returned to their homelands, set up new homes in places white people had not taken, or worked as agricultural laborers for the new owners of former mission lands. Figure 3.2 shows some of these laborers.

After California was ceded to the United States and many thousands of people poured in during the gold rush, land conflicts and legal changes led to the reorganization of agricultural work and Indian populations in the area around Mission San José. By 1870, a large Indigenous community lived about 10 miles northeast of the mission, near Pleasanton, at the location of an Ohlone village on the ranch of Agustín Bernal (one of four people who were given mission lands). Because Pleasanton was originally known as Alisal ("alder" or "sycamore"), the Indian community was called the Alisal band. Multicultural and multilingual, like Mission San José, it was "one of the most prominent and important communities of Ohlone Indians from the 1860s onward into the early twentieth century," as described by Rosemary Cambra et al. (2017:48).[1] Oral histories and the reports of outsiders show that people at Alisal continued to retain traditional cultural practices, despite transformations that affected Native Californians everywhere, and that they maintained a network of interactions with family and other tribal members in the Bay Area and the Central Valley.

In 1886, the mining magnate, newspaper publisher, and California senator George Hearst bought about 450 acres of Bernal (former Mission San José) ranch land around Pleasanton. The Alisal rancheria was on that land, which his wife Phoebe inherited when he died in 1891. In the following year, their son William Randolph (Will) Hearst was traveling in Verona, Italy, and passed a courtyard in which he noticed a well with a fourteenth-century wellhead. "Look at that well!" he exclaimed to a companion, and bought it and had it shipped to California.[2] The Veronese wellhead was set up at Phoebe Hearst's Pleasanton estate (figure 3.3), which she named Hacienda del Pozo de Verona (Spanish *pozo* "well"). A train stop added for the Hearst estate was therefore called the Verona Station (figure 3.4); the nearby Alisal community too got the Verona name. Following US government practice (Bureau of Indian Affairs 2001), I will call it the Verona Band (or rancheria).

Living on what had become other people's land in "an assortment of squatters' hovels" (Kroeber 1959:3) that "adjoined a . . . railroad right-of-way" (Bureau of Indian Affairs 2001:44), and working for other people on their farms and ranches, the Verona Band faced precarious circumstances.[3] Maybe they were better off than some of those noted in chapter 2, but they were among the landless Indians whom activists sought to help. Unfortunately, theirs was one of many communities for whom land was *not* bought after the 1906 and 1908 congressional allocations; perhaps BIA special agent C. E. Kelsey thought Hearst land was acceptable. But after a 1916 railway fire that destroyed rancheria houses (Cambra et al. 2017:60), followed by the 1919 death of Phoebe Hearst and 1924 sale of the Hearst property for use as a country club, many inhabitants of the Verona rancheria had to move. Since the 1980s, rancheria descendants have been organized as the Muwekma Ohlone Tribe; the Veronese wellhead itself is now at Hearst Castle in San Simeon.

Between 1880 and 1921, linguists, anthropologists, and others visited the Verona rancheria. Native people generously shared rich oral histories and created invaluable language documentation, complemented by later

Figure 3.3
Veronese wellhead, Hacienda del Pozo de Verona, Pleasanton, ca. 1914. Photographic print by Frederick W. Martin (Martin Collection Box 7, California State Library).

oral histories initiated in the community. In 1904, 1909, and 1914, Kroeber made four one-day visits, mainly recording vocabulary. Figure 3.5 shows María Trinidad Gonzales Reyes and her mother Paula, who lived at Verona and shared their knowledge with Kroeber in 1904 and with the biologist and ethnologist C. Hart Merriam in 1905. Figure 3.6 shows part of a comparative word list Kroeber made in 1904, including numerals (from one to ten) and body parts. The second column is Guaypemne Plains Miwok shared by Paula; the first is Ochejamne Plains Miwok shared by María Celsa Santos, from whom Kroeber also recorded Chochenyo. The fourth column is also Plains Miwok; the third is Northern Sierra Miwok (notably including a Yokuts borrowing as the word for "beard"). Kroeber's documentation was not extensive, but

Figure 3.4
Verona Station, 1904. Photograph by Frances B. Johnston (Lummis 1904:533).

he learned enough to find out what Indigenous languages were spoken at Verona. Among them were Chochenyo, Yokuts, and Bay, Plains, and Sierra Miwok; Kroeber noted in 1909 that Plains Miwok was "the prevailing language" (ALK Ctn 11:12, p. 72).

ANTIQUITIES AND ARCHAEOLOGY

Phoebe Hearst and her son were avid collectors of fine art, from Europe and elsewhere (including painting, decorative arts, and objects like their Veronese wellhead), and of antiquities. As figure 3.7 illustrates, some of the results filled the rooms of Phoebe Hearst's Pleasanton hacienda. A sense of Hearst collecting energy emerges from a January 1889 letter from Will to Phoebe Hearst (GPAHP Box 6:20):

> I want some of these fine things and I want you to have some of these fine things and do you know, my beloved mother, there is a way in which you might get them. . . . Now at this time in the different palaces of Italy several things are to be

Figure 3.5
María Trinidad Gonzales Reyes (left, identified by Cambra et al. 2017:59) and her mother Paula (E-non-na-too-ya), Verona rancheria, 1905. Photograph by C. Hart Merriam (C. Hart Merriam Collection of Native American Photographs, V/21i/1, Bancroft Library, UC Berkeley).

sold that are simply magnificent. In the Balbi palace, Genoa, there is an antique bust of Julius Caesar. If this ever gets into the possession of the Italian government it can never be bought in the world. In the Pallavicini palace, Genoa, is one of the finest Van Dykes I have ever seen. In Pisa is a Guido Reni that is simply lovely. It is his divine and earthly love. Ansiglioni says it is a great time to buy. The people are heavily taxed; the government is nearly bankrupt and cannot buy up these opportunities itself as it has formerly done, and some wealthy American or Englishman will soon step in and taking these chances here and

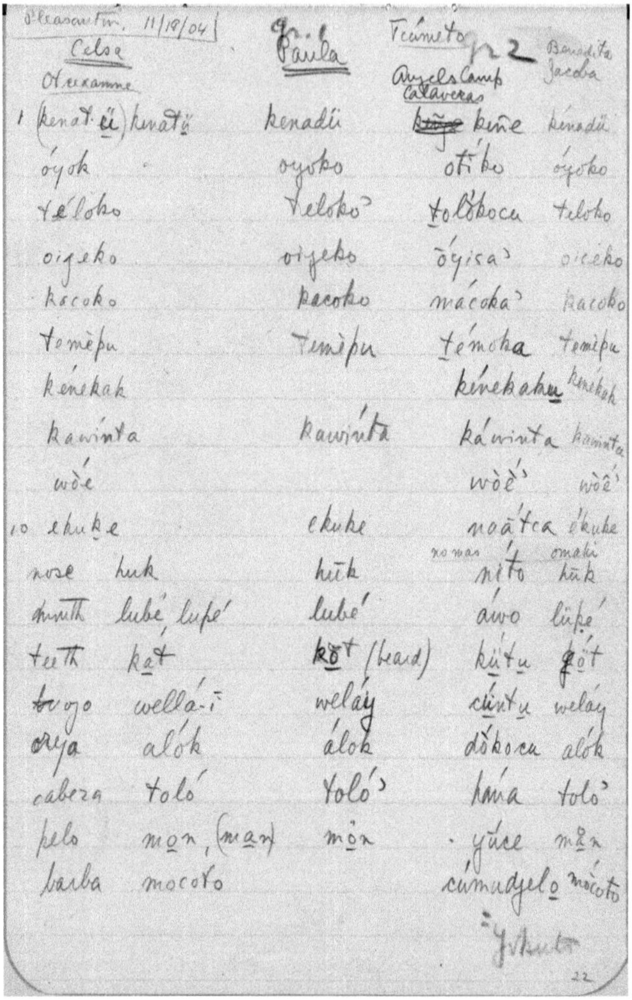

Figure 3.6
Plains and Sierra Miwok vocabulary recorded by Kroeber from four people at the Verona rancheria, 19 November 1904 (ALK Ctn 11:12, p. 22). One of the four was Paula (E-non-na-too-ya, figure 3.5).

Figure 3.7
Phoebe Hearst's hacienda in Pleasanton, ca. 1900. Photograph by G. E. Gould (BANC PIC 1994.002--B, Bancroft Library, UC Berkeley). This picture of the Music Room shows art that she collected, including Native American baskets in the rafters.

> there will have a collection almost equal to that of some of these national galleries. I wish I could be the rich American. I wish you would be.

Later the subject of Orson Welles's *Citizen Kane*, Phoebe Hearst's son was the more obsessive of the two, but both were devoted to the work. Its result was beyond the scale of the Pleasanton hacienda; a museum was needed.

The fin de siècle was an era of ambitious archaeological projects, often conducted in the European and American public eye. Heinrich Schliemann began excavating at Hisarlık (Troy) in Turkey in 1870, and at Mycenae and Tiryns in Greece in 1876 and 1884; Arthur Evans began his work at Knossos on Crete in 1900. In the twentieth century, the Oseberg ship burial was excavated in Norway in 1904–1905; 1906 saw the start of continuous excavation at Boğazköy, site of ancient Ḫattuša and a vast archive of Hittite texts. And in Egypt, after the Napoleonic invasion and the discovery of the Rosetta Stone, a virtual horde of archaeologists came to dig up graves, pyramids, temples, and other monuments; the Egyptian Antiquities Service began exploring the Valley of the Kings in 1883.

Phoebe Hearst began her involvement with archaeology and anthropology in 1895, first directing her patronage to the University of Pennsylvania before shifting it to California in 1898. Her interests were wide-ranging, but she gave special attention to Egyptology. She toured Egypt (figure 3.8), cultivated relationships with Egyptologists like George Reisner, funded archaeological work, and collected avidly. Figure 3.9 shows a 1902 party she hosted for Reisner and 150 guests, with palm trees and a lecture by Reisner; Alice Fletcher called it "a wonderful spectacle" (Mark 1988:287). It recalls a ball Hearst held in 1895 in Washington, described by Alexandra Nickliss (2018:287–288) with quotations from contemporary news articles:

> Guests were dressed in colonial era gowns, and servants wore the costumes of "Moorish slaves, gorgeous in crimson velvet suits, embroidered in gold," and heads crowned with "fantastic turbans of rich silken stuffs," one newspaper noted. Hearst "wore a Colonial dress of gray striped satin, brocaded in roses," and trimmed in "rich old lace." Diamonds and rubies were draped around her neck.

In 1899, soon after Phoebe Hearst's first trip to Egypt, her son was also there and wrote about what her projects could yield (GPAHP Box 6: 31–32):

> The Egyptian government allows anybody who will excavate at their own expense to take away a large quantity of the antiquities found. It struck me that if you wanted to supply the Egyptian room of your museum that this was a good and cheap way. You are sure to find interesting stuff and you may find really important stuff, New Papyri, Missing Kings, &c.

He added subsequently, "In Egyptology as in everything else the great idea is to do something new and 'sensational' and not laboriously potter over what has been done before."

Hearst was collecting for herself, but also for what she described as her museum at the University of California. This is why she established and fully funded its anthropology department and museum, hiring its faculty and staff. She also sponsored major UC archaeological research

Figure 3.8
Phoebe Hearst (back row, center, on a camel) visiting the Sphinx and the Pyramid of Khufu (the "Great Pyramid" of "Kheops") at Giza, Egypt, January 1899 (PAHMA 15-18884).

Figure 3.9
Illustration of Phoebe Hearst's "Egyptian night" at her Pleasanton hacienda, celebrating Egyptological research by George Reisner for the University of California. *San Francisco Examiner*, 19 September 1902 ("Historic Splendor" 1902).

and antiquities purchases.[4] In Egypt, these included a cemetery of the eighteenth and nineteenth dynasties at Deir-el-Ballas (near Luxor); predynastic cemeteries at Ballas; a predynastic and a late New Empire cemetery at El-Ahaiwah; and eleven cemeteries at Naga-ed-Der from the predynastic to the Coptic periods. If European Egyptology was "the handmaid of imperialism, in a manner that Caesar would have recognized and applauded," as Toby Wilkinson (2020:3) wrote, Hearst's investment called forth a California avatar.

Hearst's Egyptian expeditions also yielded exceptional papyrus collections, including the Hearst Medical Papyrus and the Tebtunis papyri. The published edition of the former is dedicated "to Mrs. Phoebe Apperson Hearst, who, in the interest of the University of California, has borne for five years the entire financial burden of scientific expeditions in Peru, North America and Egypt" (Reisner 1905:iii). The sources of the UC Tebtunis collection include mummy cartonnage made (as a kind of papier-mâché) from discarded documents. This was removed from fifty human mummies unearthed in 1900 at Umm el-Baragat and many crocodile mummies. Papyri preserve ancient literary works, historical records, and other documents.

From Italy, Hearst purchased for her museum "the contents of seventeen Etruscan and Graeco-Etruscan tombs" from southern Etruria, a "group of ten stone sarcophagi . . . from the neighborhood of Musarna" (an Etruscan settlement), and a "large collection from the [ancient] cemeteries of Orvieto."[5] In Peru, she sponsored excavations by Max Uhle that included an Early Chimú cemetery (before 700 CE), "rich tombs of the Inca period" (Rowe 1954:8), and cemeteries and burial caves from various periods around Cusco, among other contexts; Uhle sent Hearst detailed reports (Protzen and Harris 2005). In California itself, UC excavations around the turn of the century that were sponsored by Hearst were Philip Mills Jones's Central Valley and Channel Islands excavations and the Bay Area shell mound excavations by John Merriam, Nels Nelson, and Uhle (see chapter 8).

NATIVE CULTURAL HERITAGE

Phoebe Hearst was finally both an individual collector and a sponsor of museum collections of Indigenous North American art and cultural artifacts. Her dual role was well known. Native art figured in her home (figure 3.7), as emphasized in an admiring contemporary description of her "great entrance hall" (North 1900:594): "Navajo blanket and serape lend their lawless colorings, quaint Indian baskets stand for savagery, Spanish chests and rare old cabinets give suggestion of history." Derogatory stereotypes like "lawless" and "savage" would have seemed commonplace to white readers. The description also shows that a contrast between "history" (where Europeans act) and a timeless, essentialized present (where Native Americans are situated) was prevalent in public discourse and not a peculiarity of Boasian thinking or Kroeber's writing.[6]

Since Hearst's interests were widely publicized, she was deluged with offers of Indian art (GPAHP Box 67:28). A typical 1901 letter was from a "dealer in Indian, Mexican and California curiosities" in Santa Barbara. He told Hearst about a woman who "has a very valuable collection of Indian Curios which herself & husband have collected during the past years, while stationed amongst the army posts." She was once advised "that the collection would be cheap at 2000^{\underline{00}}$ & she has since added a number of things." It was a "*priceless* collection," he stressed. A resident of Portland, Oregon, wrote in 1905, "Have been informed that you are collecting rare Indian baskets to be exhibited in the proposed Museum at Berkeley. I have a valuable and rare old basket which I should like to dispose of." A 1910 letter offers a Navajo blanket made with red cloth "from the coats of British soldiers," one of "only about three . . . in the U.S." A 1912 letter from Philadelphia offered 265 baskets, mostly from California, adding, "I also have a large collection of ethnographic objects of the North American Indians for sale, nearly 2000 specimens, the majority good, old pieces." Such examples give a sense of activity in a trade that involved individuals, dealers, institutions, and wealthy collectors.

Most inquiries to Hearst came from white people in possession of Native art, but an unusual appeal came from a Washoe woman, Daisy Washington (figure 3.10). At the age of five, perhaps an orphan, she had been enrolled in Stewart Indian School near Carson City, Nevada, one of thirty-seven students in its first class in 1890.[7] In her first months there, a mumps outbreak infected 90 percent of the students, according to Samantha Williams (2022:29); some fled. Bonnie Thompson (2013:7) described Stewart Indian School in these years, decades before the Indian New Deal, as a "repressive and exploitive" institution where students were

Figure 3.10
Daisy Washington, undated. George W. Ingalls Photograph Collection, ca. 1869–1915, photCL 275, fld. 5 (20), Huntington Library.

punished for speaking their own languages and trained "to become part of a subservient working class." The government, Washoe elder Steven James told Caitlin Keliiaa (2012:20–21), was "after our customs and language" and built the school to "separate the kids from their parents." Some students were taken from their families by force. Many did not go home during an entire academic year, and many were sent to work for white people during the summers; a significant number ran away. Washington herself was sent to work for the family of Nevada banker, mining magnate, and former state senator Evan Williams from September 1898 through June 1899.[8]

In 1899, Washington entered Haskell Institute, the government boarding school and college in Kansas (now Haskell Indian Nations University), where she was secretary of a literary society, a journalist, and a student in domestic art and science and the commercial department. She spoke about her chosen profession in a graduation oration (1908:4):

> The pupils here realize, now as never before, that they cannot always be dependent upon the government; that sooner or later they must be thrown upon their own resources. . . . The success that others of our race have achieved and are achieving, should also be an inspiration to all.
>
> An occupation should not be chosen with the thought of getting a mere living out of it. We should choose with the purpose of gaining the higher things of life, those things that will mean advancement to ourselves and to our people. I have chosen stenography as a means of making a living, not because I think there is nothing better, but because I consider it a worthy occupation, and a stepping-stone to wider fields of life. I realize more and more what it must mean to go out into the world to win my way unaided.

These comments highlight two facets of what the US government hoped to accomplish through its Indian education system. First, Indian people were to be taught skills that would enable them to work in the Euro-American economy, outside their own societies; eventually they would not be "dependent upon the government." The goal was independence through assimilation—in other words, benignly intended cultural destruction. Second, much as the Spanish mission system had trained Indigenous people for agricultural work under European direction, the American system mostly presupposed a limited set of work options. Even students with literary inclinations were channeled into practical ("worthy") occupations.

After her student years, Washington worked at Haskell and then back in Nevada as a clerk and stenographer at Stewart beginning in January 1910. In May 1912, she visited California for a ten-day YWCA conference at Phoebe Hearst's Pleasanton estate; Hearst became a major YWCA supporter.[9] A tent city was built for three hundred attendees from UC, "Stanford, the San Francisco branch, the Indian school at Carson, Nevada, and Mills College," according to the *San Francisco Call* ("Y.W.C.A. Host" 1912). An allegorical masque concerning "the forces that influence a maiden to choose her life's work" was described by the *San Francisco Chronicle* ("Masque" 1912): "Each of the nations personified by the students passes in turn, ending with America." The nations pose in figure 3.11. Draped in a US flag, "America" is flanked by two "North American Indian" women wearing Native blankets; one of them was Washington.

Figure 3.11
"Congress of nations," 1912 YWCA conference, Phoebe Hearst's estate. Left to right: Spain, Persia, Japan, Russia, "North American Indian" (Daisy Washington), "America" (with a US flag), "North American Indian" (Gertrude Shaw, also from Stewart Indian School), Sweden, Turkey, Norse, China, Japan. *San Francisco Examiner*, 24 May 1912, p. 13.

Afterward, reports were delivered by various participants, including Washington. "We have had to give up all our old traditions and to adopt those of the white race," the *Chronicle* quoted her as saying. "We thank you for your religion . . . and we hope to prove to you some day that we have a soul that is as good and true and as capable of as much good as if we had been born with a white skin." This is difficult to read. The *Chronicle* took it as an "appeal for forgetfulness of race and for help," as Washington no doubt meant her white audience to do. But her polite assertion that Indigenous people "had to" accept new ways (rather than choosing them) and are not inferior to Euro-Americans can also be interpreted as resistance—a style of Indigenous survivance in white spaces.

At the end of the conference, according to Will Hearst's *San Francisco Examiner* ("Hacienda camp" 1912), the participants "sang to Mrs. Hearst the song that has served as an expression of love and respect so many times in the past week: 'Mrs. Hearst, Mrs. Hearst, we are singing praises, praises ringing; For we have never found your equal. Mrs. Hearst, here's to you.' "

Disease remained a problem at Stewart when Washington worked there, especially measles, trachoma, and tuberculosis. By 1912, the main school building "had fallen into complete disrepair" under "a mediocre and corrupt superintendent," and a visitor reported that "teachers and employees were all in misery" (Thompson 2013:69–71). In 1913, Washington left Stewart and moved to San Francisco. A letter written in the fall of that year shows how a talented, thoughtful Indigenous woman felt she should address Hearst (3 October 1913, GPAHP Box 67:28):

> Dear Mrs. Hearst:
>
> Please pardon me for taking up a little of your valuable time.
>
> You may remember me when I tell you that I am one of the Indian girls who had the wonderful privilege of attending the Young Women's Christian Association Conference held on your estate a year ago last May.
>
> I have been in San Francisco since February of this year. I gave up my position in Nevada because I wanted to get employment in the city, where I could see more of the outside world. I have been employed regularly by a public stenographer. I like my work very much and my experiences in the city, but I find it hard—very hard—to meet expenses.
>
> While in Nevada, I purchased from my people—the Washoe Indians—between thirty-five and forty baskets. They are indeed very pretty, and I have thought that if I could sell them, it would be of help to me. I have, therefore, inquired among different people and store-keepers, but they offer me so little for other Indian curios I have that I could not let them go. For this reason, and knowing that you realize the value of baskets, such as I have, I write to ask if you know of any one who would like to purchase these. Probably you could tell me of someone here in San Francisco whom I could call upon. . . .
>
> I wish to tell you, humble as I am, that I have many times been thankful for the great privilege of having gotten a glimpse of your lovely home, grounds, etc., and above all, of the beautiful life of one of our country's most generous women.
>
> Humbly yours,
> Daisy Washington

Washoe baskets were prized by collectors; according to Marvin Cohodas (1979:8), Washoe weaving from 1895 to 1935 was "one of the most important artistic movements" in Native American art history. One can only speculate about the feelings of someone who felt compelled to sell objects of her own cultural patrimony—"to give up all our old traditions," as she had said in 1912. It is all the more disturbing that the buyer was Hearst, whose wealth was partly from mining in and around Washoe land.[10] The pattern in this and other instances was that profits from land and resource theft were used to strip cultural heritage from those whom the invaders' devastation had left with few choices.

Washington wrote again to Hearst a few years later, apparently in 1918, reminding her that she had bought "some baskets" and that Washington had then been unwilling to part with "a piece of bead-work" that "has been a source of pleasure to me."[11] Subsequently, Washington wrote, she had contracted tuberculosis, had had to quit her job, and had lived in the YWCA "for a year and a half." She had been advised that she "was failing" and that it might help her to "go to the country." With her "meagre savings . . . about used up," she asked if Hearst might buy the beadwork piece so Washington could afford to leave the city. Unfortunately, there is no record of Hearst's response (if any).

Hearst and Washington died within a few months of each other. Hearst died at the age of seventy-six on 13 April 1919 at her Pleasanton hacienda, where she had contracted influenza in December. Her death prompted academic mourning: UC "canceled classes so that faculty and students could attend the cathedral funeral" (Nickliss 2018:422). Washington died at the age of thirty-six on 28 July 1919, also in Alameda County (she had not managed to leave), and is buried in the Old Stewart Indian Cemetery, Carson City, Nevada.

The location of the baskets Washington sold Hearst is unknown, but more than two thousand Native American baskets collected by Hearst and others, including more than two hundred Washoe baskets, are held by Berkeley's anthropology museum. In 2018, I attended an open house at the off-campus facility where they are stored. Dozens of Native people were present; museum staff were eager to help them locate objects and study the artistry of their families and communities. When I went outside, a friend was crying there because she could not bear it any longer in the "basket prison." Many Indigenous people say baskets used for their intended purposes are living. What are they when shelved in a secure climate-controlled warehouse?

HEARST AND KROEBER

The relationships among Kroeber, his colleagues, and their patron Hearst have been studied by several scholars.[12] It was Hearst who, with input from friends and other university leaders, planned UC anthropological and archaeological work, fully funded it, and recruited its major figures. By the 1903–1904 academic year, the faculty included Kroeber, linguistics PhD student Pliny Goddard, classicist Alfred Emerson (teaching Greek art and classical archaeology), paleontologist John Merriam (teaching the "Geological History of Man"), and Max Uhle and George Reiner. Merriam was an assistant professor, Emerson was a lecturer, and Goddard and Kroeber had the lowest rank as instructors. As "Hearst Lecturers" in "Peruvian Archaeology" and "Egyptology," respectively, Uhle and Reiner had no teaching duties and instead engaged in field research for the UC collections.

During its first seven years, the UC anthropology department was entirely funded by Hearst, who provided more than $230,000 (more than $7 million in 2022 dollars) throughout that period (Long 1998:232). A 28 February 1902 report (RDA Vol. 1) indicated that she had thus far spent $90,104. Expenses included a collection purchase account ($5,927), academic salaries, and research funds for seven scholars: $27,805.80 for Reisner, $17,262.09 for Emerson, $9,908 for Uhle, $125.70 for Merriam (California archaeology), $7,057.25 for Philip M. Jones (California archaeology), $1,500 for Kroeber, and $350 for Goddard.[13] Funds were provided in advance; researchers asked Hearst for special funding as needed and reported to her solicitously.

The head of the anthropology department (and museum) was Frederic Ward Putnam, nominally a full professor. His involvement was mostly in absentia because he also held a full-time position at Harvard, but he was an active chair of an advisory board for most of the first decade of the 1900s. He and UC president Wheeler made programmatic decisions until late in that decade. In their leadership roles, it was Wheeler and Putnam (1902) who publicized the new Ethnological and Archaeological Survey of California and made "a special appeal" to the public for Indigenous cultural artifacts and related information, including the location of burial sites:

> Hundreds of Indian objects are found annually, which if carefully labelled as to where and how found and sent to the university, would . . . aid in the settlement of many important questions. . . . Information relating to the location of caves, shellheaps, old burial places, ancient village sites, and scattered fragments or survivors of nearly extinct tribes, is earnestly solicited, that such may be investigated by the [anthropology] department and may be correctly recorded on its ethnological and archaeological maps of the State.

The public responded. For decades, Indigenous remains were sent to the university by non-Indigenous Californians who intentionally robbed burial sites, or found remains in construction projects or on the ground (often, abandoned by grave robbers).

During his first decade in California, Kroeber's UC position and work faced two existential crises. The first and major one came after a year, and resulted from a clash of goals. Hearst wanted a focus on the museum and public education, with lectures for San Francisco society; Kroeber preferred a research focus on linguistic and ethnographic documentation. This was the local version of a national conflict, described by Regna Darnell (2000b), between two models of anthropology. One was an older, museum-centered model, associated with Lewis Henry Morgan's evolutionary view of societies. According to this view, Euro-American people were at a higher level than others. Museums organized by artifact type could then show the evolution from "primitive" to "civilized" for each type, ratifying elite assumptions. A newer model, favored by Boas and his students, centered academic (research and teaching) departments that integrated linguistics and sociocultural anthropology alongside collecting objects. In line with historical particularism, this emphasized the accomplishments of diverse societies. A recognition that "unlike causes produce like effects" led Boas (1887) to what was then a novel conception of museum organization:

> We have to study each ethnological specimen individually in its history and in its medium [i.e., social and geographical context]. . . . By regarding a single implement outside of its surroundings, outside of other inventions of the people to whom it belongs, and outside of other phenomena affecting that people and its productions, we cannot understand its meaning.

As Ira Jacknis (1988:79) has emphasized, this new organization indexed "a transfer of anthropological interest from the external form to an artifact's *meaning*" in its cultural context.[14] When the UC anthropology museum opened to the public in 1911, it had separate rooms for distinct cultural areas (California, Egypt, Peru, etc.), each presented in similar fashion in its own terms; see figures 3.12–3.13. Even within the California Room, collections were organized by area rather than type of artifact (see figure 3.14).

Figure 3.12
California Room, UC anthropology museum, 1907. Photograph by Alfred Kroeber (PAHMA 15-4206).

Figure 3.13
Graeco-Roman Room, UC anthropology museum, 1907. Photograph by Alfred Kroeber (PAHMA 15-4210).

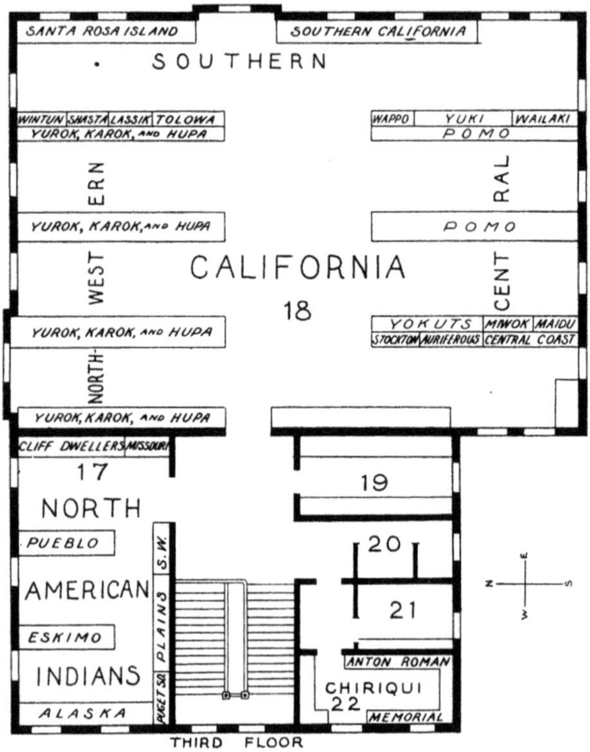

Figure 3.14
Floor plan, California and North American Indian Rooms, UC anthropology museum (Putnam 1906:7).

Alexandra Nickliss (2018:259) has suggested that Hearst "shared Morgan's racial and anthropological views, which in turn influenced her vision for . . . the new department and museum of anthropology she was hoping to establish." As with her other philanthropic projects (e.g., kindergarten and the YWCA), Hearst's anthropological vision had a moral aspect. Kroeber's commitment to ethnography did not suit that vision well, and Hearst "did not like Kroeber," according to the anthropologist Alice Fletcher's biographer Joan Mark (1988:287). Fletcher, a friend of Hearst, was offended by Arapaho stories collected by Kroeber because some were obscene; Boas (1936:138) thought Fletcher "wanted to know only the ideal Indian, and hated what she called the 'stable boy' manners of an inferior social group." On Hearst's behalf, Fletcher called Kroeber "unsatisfactory." In September 1902, Hearst tried to have him fired, suggesting that Putnam and Wheeler replace him with the botanist and ethnologist William Tufts Brigham, head of Honolulu's Bishop Museum. "If Mrs. Hearst stops the work," Fletcher threatened, "this will be a loss to science that ought not to be allowed to occur."[15]

Kroeber may have been given notice. G. J. M. E. d'Aquin, the anthropology department secretary (business manager), told Wheeler on 26 September 1902 that Hearst "does not for the present wish to fill" a vacancy associated with "[Dr.] Kroeber formerly of our Department" (RDA Vol. 1). The day before, d'Aquin had written to Kroeber that he wanted to discuss "an important matter" with him—presumably his termination. Their discussion, like the conversations Kroeber and Wheeler had, is not reported, but Kroeber did not leave. Within a few months, in fact, he replaced d'Aquin as department secretary and assumed more responsibility. Conflicts with Hearst were resolved or at least patched up; she continued to support anthropological work. Kroeber learned that he must engage with museum work and its collections of specimens. The linguistic and ethnographic research he preferred would continue (linguistics was completely absorbed into anthropology in 1906), but not at the expense of other areas.

Much later, in giving advice to his younger colleague T. T. Waterman, then at the University of Washington, Kroeber reflected on his early UC experience (20 January 1920, RDA Box 55):

> Anthropology is always going to get the short end of every deal for at least another generation except where it is specially endowed or where it helps to make a showing in a Museum. You might as well make up your mind to that and saw wood. Trying to buck the line too hard merely makes them stiffen up. I was a long time learning that in my contacts with Wheeler. As soon as I stopped harrassing him, he became exceedingly friendly. Your authorities are almost certainly like those everywhere else. Men in administrative positions are bound to be similar. They appreciate enthusiasm and ambition but too much dunning makes them react as towards a book agent. Your work is going to be kept back for a number of years. If you produce results, whether in students or otherwise, with small expenditure and in spite of handicaps, you will in time get a larger share of what you want and ought to have.

Kroeber's own research goals were not aligned with museum work, but he learned that publications and the success of the museum would give

UC anthropology what it "ought to have." He was a practical institutionalist.

A second clash has been described by several scholars.[16] Its backdrop was the financial collapse of 1907, which created uncertainty about Hearst's future support of UC anthropology; in the end she did not withdraw support, but did greatly reduce it. Budget cuts often exacerbate conflicts, like one that had emerged between Kroeber and his colleague Pliny Goddard (UCOPAF 21:68). On 21 December 1907, Goddard sent Wheeler a peremptory letter without explanation: "Unless the ideals governing the research work of the Department of Anthropology and the standard of its publications are material[ly] raised, I do not care to remain a member of it." Wheeler consulted Kroeber and evidently mollified Goddard, but the conflict simmered.

By 1909, Goddard had received an outside offer and made new requests. One complaint was that his annual salary was $200 lower than Kroeber's. He was also unhappy with the organization of the anthropology department and the prominence of museum work, writing on 9 February 1909 that the department should ideally have one person teaching ethnology and another who "should be a biologist in order to present the physical side of man properly," and implying that he himself should be freed to write up his mainly linguistic research: "I do not seem to be particularly needed here." Goddard's advocacy of physical anthropology was supported by paleontologist John Merriam and opposed by Kroeber. The disagreement remains ill-defined, expressed fully only in person, but Goddard apparently saw his linguistic work as scientific, in contrast what he called Kroeber's "ethnographic" approach. Goddard, whose PhD was from Wheeler's short-lived linguistics department, was an innovator in phonetics who had published an overview of experimental methods (1905a) and a study of Hupa phonetics (1907).

Two weeks later (22 February), Goddard suggested instead that the anthropology department be split, and that he should join a renewed linguistics department. An advantage of his proposal, he said, was that he "would no longer be held to the large field of Anthropology" by those "who think it strange if I confess ignorance on some point of physical anthropology or archaeology. I should be able to confine my reading to linguistic subjects."

The conflict puzzled Wheeler: "Whatever Dr. Goddard thinks Dr. Kroeber does not think, and vice versa," he told Hearst (8 April 1909, UCOPAF 21:68). Kroeber argued successfully against the scheme advanced by Goddard, who resigned soon afterward. There were no other US linguistics departments in 1909; the professionalization of linguistics was in the future. Kroeber told Hearst that since Goddard's successor "will no doubt be able to sympathize more heartily with the Museum as such, closer cooperation should result than has existed heretofore, with the consequence, in some ways at least, of greater efficiency of the Department." The first draft of this letter said instead "closer cooperation than has existed between Professor Goddard and the rest of us" (21 May 1909, ALK Box 2:5). Goddard was replaced by Kroeber protégé T. T. Waterman.

The two conflicts were simultaneously about academic boundaries and competing conceptions of "culture." The boundaries at stake were between an academic department and a museum, and between anthropology and linguistics; contested cultural questions involved evolution versus relativism, and whether language is an inextricable part of culture. It was the Boasian approach, emphasizing ethnographic field research (including linguistics) as a key component of cultural relativism, that proved successful and came to characterize UC work led by Kroeber.

Throughout these years, Kroeber was attentive to Hearst, a UC regent who was funding his research and from whom UC had hopes of a major endowment. Putnam also wrote to her, but his long, conversational letters treated her as an equal, including expressions of friendly affection from him and his wife. By contrast, Kroeber's reports were obsequious. A typical letter included this paragraph (26 July 1904, GPAHP 43:10):

> I am sending to your London address by this mail copies of two papers published at the University on the studies which I have been able to make for our Department through your generosity. I am glad of this occasion to express to you once more my thanks for the opportunity of doing this work, the importance of which to later times, and its present urgency if it was to be done at all, you have so broadmindedly seen; and I trust that the results may in some degree meet your expectations.

Kroeber saw linguistics as a central part of his research program, likely to be of particular interest to a patron. A 5 June 1903 letter summarized the findings of a new article (ALK Box 1:3):

> I am pleased to be at last able to send you the first result in print of my work for you at the University, a joint paper by Dr. Roland B. Dixon and myself on the Indian languages of California. . . . The upshot of it is to bring some system out of previous chaos by a classification of the languages of the state. In the course of the investigation we have secured information as to the structure of sixteen linguistic families, increasing the total number thus known in North America more than twenty five percent.

A 3 January 1913 letter mentioned a sequel: "You will be interested to learn that, working in collaboration with Dr. Dixon of Harvard University, I have discovered that many of the supposedly distinct languages of the California Indians are connected." He explained that their research "not only recasts our knowledge of the linguistics, but puts the entire prehistory of California in a new light" (GPAHP 43:10).

But for the most part, Kroeber's correspondence with Hearst was about the maintenance of her collections and the organization of her museum. He was invariably upbeat. On 11 May 1906, he wrote that the outcome of the recent San Francisco earthquake (which did relatively little damage in the museum) "will be not only a better San Francisco but a greater University" and "that the realization of this will not be a long distant hope of the future, but a matter of a very short time." All who work in "your own special Department of the University," he said, "are ready to put our shoulder to the wheel in whatever way you may think best" (GPAHP 43:10).

Solicitous correspondence continued even after Hearst limited her support. Kroeber described his awkward position to Boas (4 March 1913, FBP):

> Mrs. Hearst since 1908 has made a generous annual allowance for the maintenance and care of the Museum, but as this is a fixed amount we can not appeal to her for further contributions. On the other hand, her connection with the department renders it impossible at present to ask other people for financial assistance.

Yet he continued to flatter her, as on 12 September 1911: "Let me express to you my sincerest thanks for your generosity in the matter of the totem-pole. It is only another instance of your devotion to the University" (GPAHP 43:10).

Figure 3.15
UC anthropology museum, San Francisco, October 1911. Photograph by S. M. Grow (PAHMA 15-5390).

For the October 1911 public opening of the anthropology museum (figure 3.15), the two prepared carefully (Hearst to Kroeber, RDA Box 13):

> [22 September] I have thought it might be well to have some light refreshment, tea, coffee, bread and butter and cakes, no ices no hot food excepting the tea and coffee. Have you some place there where these refreshments could be served? Also, some place where the tea and coffee might be prepared?
>
> I hardly think music would be proper on such an occasion, as the people will most likely prefer to talk freely, but if you think otherwise and would, for any reason prefer to have music, let me know and I will make the necessary arrangements.

> [25 September] I think the large office with the two smaller connecting rooms should do very well for the refreshments, and the small gas stoves will answer for the tea and coffee.
>
> I do not favor the idea of receiving in the large Egyptian Hall. I think I can decide where I will stand after I go to the museum on the afternoon of the Reception.

SECOND SECTION **Oakland Tribune.** CLASSIFIED PAGES

VOL. LXXVI. OAKLAND, CALIFORNIA, THURSDAY EVENING, OCTOBER 5, 1911. NO. 46

1000 GREET MRS. HEARST IN NEW MUSEUM

FINEST ANTHROPOLOGICAL EXHIBIT IN THE ENTIRE UNITED STATES IS GIFT OF GENEROUS WOMAN TO THE UNIVERSITY OF CALIFORN'A

History of the World From Time of Dark Ages Is Told in Display, Which Is Seen by Hundreds

MRS. PHOEBE A. HEARST

DEATH ENDS A DAUGHTER'S VIGIL

For 12 Years Miss Teubnor Kept Watch at Mother's Bedside.

During the Entire Period She Never Stepped Foot Out of Doors.

OAKLAND GIRL IS AMONG MISSING

Fifteen-Year-Old Ruth Griggs Leaves Home and Disappears.

Mother Alleges That She Was Detained at Home of Hulgerras.

PLANS FOR TAFT'S RECEPTION LAID

Line of March Across Bay Is Given Out: Banquet Committee Swamped.

FORMER OAKLAND MAN TO MARRY

Harry Seward Van Dyke Will Wed Society Girl of Minneapolis.

GEORGE F. HERR WINS PROMOTION

Appointed General Passenger Agent of Line by Western Pacific.

CONVICT AUDIENCE ATTEND 'THEATER'

Full-Fledged Performance of Play Is Given at San Quentin.

ISLANDS BELCHED FORTH BY OCEAN

Sea Captain Tells of New Land Formed While Crew Looked On.

31 PERSONS SENT TO ASYLUMS IN MONTH

MARY E. SMYTH ESTATE IS VALUED AT $37,600

MISSING BOY FOUND IN RELATIVES' HOME

Burglar Waits for Woman to Return

Robs Householder of Jewels and Flees at Her as She Cowers in Terror.

New Army Officers On Way to Islands

More Than Score of West Point Graduates on the Transport.

Auction Sale!

BIG SPECIALS ON FISH TOMORROW FRIDAY

WASHINGTON MARKET

Ninth and Washington Streets

Figure 3.16
"1000 Greet Mrs. Hearst," *Oakland Tribune,* 5 October 1911.

Hearst was the hostess at an invitation-only reception. The newspaper account in figure 3.16, with its casual exoticization of Native people, expressed the presuppositions of Euro-American readers in describing the museum's collections (including contemporary Indigenous artifacts) as "food for the brain of he who likes to delve into the shrouded mysteries of the past."

On 8 March 1912, Kroeber wrote Hearst about damage to a painting: "I am only sorry that you should have anything of the kind called to your notice. I sincerely trust you will not hesitate at any and all times to give me any instruction regarding the disposal of specimens in the museum that you see fit" (GPAHP 43:10). His style underscored the unequal relationship between the philanthropist who sent her son to Harvard, and favored Harvard-educated men like Brigham, Putnam, and Reisner, and the grandson of German immigrants whose father could not afford Harvard.[17]

Later that year, for Hearst's seventieth birthday, UC honored her at a public celebration attended by students and faculty. A full-page feature in Will Hearst's *Examiner* detailed the grandees present, their speeches, the music, and even the ovations. One speech was by UC President Wheeler (1912):

> In the older days of this university a little company of scholars fed the flame of learning here, in a bare and humble precinct. But your eyes beheld the vision of a broader day. . . . From all lands have you gathered here the sculptured stone, the pictured clay, the metal hand-enwrought, and the fabric all interwoven with symbol and tradition—things which tell the story of how men have lived their lives through the changing ages.

Wheeler's characteristically florid address directly linked the university's "broader day" to Hearst's collecting prowess, among other munificence.[18]

In sum, the collection and display of global cultural heritage, including the heritage of the state's Indigenous people, was a project of California and San Francisco elites, among them especially Hearst. It was implemented at the state's new university by Goddard, Kroeber, the paleontologist Merriam, the archaeologists Reisner and Uhle, and others in the first decade of the twentieth century. What roles did Kroeber have in this project?

THE "TRIANGULAR RELATIONSHIP"

The people discussed in this chapter epitomize paradoxes that can easily embrittle good intentions within a destructive system. Most of them meant to create satisfying lives while benefiting society as they saw it. The wealthy philanthropist Phoebe Hearst thought she was improving the world with gifts to progressive educational and social causes, helping women and others who were disadvantaged. The middle-class Boasian scholar Alfred Kroeber believed he was contributing to the common good by documenting languages, stories, and practices that he (sometimes correctly) thought would otherwise never be recorded. The Washoe teacher and stenographer Daisy Washington found her work not only personally rewarding but uplifting for her people; and those who lived at the Verona rancheria seem to have found value in their generosity to inquisitive visitors. But the system that encompassed all of them and so many others who made lives in it was one that transferred cultural wealth from Native people and communities to the archives, museums, and other display cabinets of Euro-American elites, replacing it with a paternalistic philanthropy that dispossession and land theft had rendered necessary.

From a systemic perspective, individual magnanimous intentions may not matter. The Martinican writer Aimé Césaire (1972:33–34) famously castigated "goitrous academicians," ethnographers, and "chattering intellectuals" (to name a few) as "tools of capitalism, all of them, openly or secretly, supporters of plundering colonialism." For him, "whether personally they have good or bad intentions . . . is entirely irrelevant to the social implications of the evil work they perform as watchdogs of colonialism." Césaire's critical perspective has many advocates today and raises several questions for my purposes. Did Kroeber do "evil work" on colonial guard duty? How do we assess a colonial academician's actions and choices? And, shifting our attention to Kroeber's university, which has announced that his views are opposed to its "contemporary values," how do we interpret that evaluation? In the next three chapters, to begin answering these questions, I discuss what Kroeber's work actually was.

II

INDIGENOUS VOICES

4

DOCUMENTARY LEGACIES

My actual work will always be literature.
—Alfred Kroeber, letter to Edward Sapir, 1917

Kroeber considered himself an anthropologist, worked in an anthropology department, mostly published in anthropology journals, and is mainly remembered as an anthropologist. But he began his career in an era when the disciplinary boundaries between anthropology and linguistics were blurry, he sometimes published in linguistics journals, and he served as president of the Linguistic Society of America. In this chapter, I review his language work. With changes in anthropology near the end of his life and afterward, a major part of Kroeber's legacy is centered not in that field but in his documentation of languages and stories—work that would today count as linguistics, folklore, or linguistic anthropology. His theories of culture, culture areas, and culture change are now mainly of historical interest, but the documentary corpus he built in collaboration with Indigenous people, students, and others is of immeasurable value for the present and future.

Kroeber's language documentation also formed the basis for significant contributions in language typology and historical linguistics. In typology, his analyses of noun incorporation (the kind of noun-verb compounding found in words like *babysit*) initiated a still-active debate about whether that phenomenon is fundamentally morphological or syntactic.[1] In historical linguistics, his contributions lie in two broad areas. One is language relationship. He and Roland Dixon elucidated the relationships and primary groupings of California languages—most importantly, identifying the putative Hokan and Penutian language families, proposals that remain controversial.[2] Kroeber's work on the subgrouping of Northern Uto-Aztecan (1907b, 1909a) and Yuman (1943) was also foundational in those fields. More than any other researcher, he mapped the relationships among California's many languages and language families.

Less widely appreciated is Kroeber's role in statistical historical linguistics, an area that has grown exponentially in the last two decades.[3] It is no longer possible, as it was even a decade ago, to read historical linguistics journals without encountering analyses of language relationships and linguistic time-depth using statistical and computational methods. Current methods are drawn mostly from biological cladistics, but this general line of work in linguistics goes back to Kroeber's statistical phylogenetics, itself an outgrowth of his statistical analyses of cultural features.[4]

Beyond these academic impacts, while Kroeber was a Euro-American writing from and for his Oikoumenê, his work elevated the knowledge, histories, perspectives, and status of Native people. I will discuss this under several rubrics, focusing on Kroeber's own documentation, his support for recording oral histories, his long-term collaborations with Indigenous people, and his impact in multiple language areas. In this and the next two chapters, I argue that Kroeber's work with Indigenous languages and texts is a central aspect of his legacy, and that he did that work in ways that gave space to Indigenous voices.

LANGUAGE AND TEXT DOCUMENTATION

Kroeber's documentation of texts led to English-language collections of traditional narratives and other texts originating in nine different languages:

- Arapaho-Atsina: *Traditions of the Arapaho* (Dorsey and Kroeber 1903), "Gros Ventre Myths and Tales" (Kroeber 1907a)
- Cheyenne: "Cheyenne Tales" (Kroeber 1900)
- Colorado River Numic: "Ute Tales" (Kroeber 1901b)
- Inuktun (Polar Inuit): "Tales of the Smith Sound Eskimo" (Kroeber 1899)
- Karuk: *Karok Myths* (Kroeber and Gifford 1980)
- Mojave: "Seven Mohave Myths" (Kroeber 1948b), "A Mohave Historical Epic" (Kroeber 1951b), *More Mohave Myths* (Kroeber 1972), *A Mohave War Reminiscence, 1854–1880* (A. Kroeber and C. Kroeber 1973)

- Wiyot: "Wishosk Myths" (Kroeber 1905b)
- Yuki: "Yuki Myths" (Kroeber 1932b)
- Yurok: *Yurok Narratives* (Spott and Kroeber 1942), *Yurok Myths* (Kroeber 1976)

All these publications present the voices of Indigenous people, if through translation and organized by interpretive logics that can be criticized.[5] Still, for example, Robert Heizer (1975:119) called the historical account in *A Mohave War Reminiscence* "one of the most human documents ever published about California Indians."

Bruce Mannheim and Dennis Tedlock (1995:5) have described the abandonment of text collection in mainstream anthropology:[6]

> There was a time when the same anthropologists who worked on producing ethnographies also worked on text collections, but that came to an end when American cultural anthropology was diverted from its course by British social anthropology, which tended to treat the utterances of natives as falsehoods. . . . The collection of texts fell to other field-workers whose concerns were narrowly linguistic and who increasingly pursued their careers in academic departments separate from anthropology.

Kroeber's documentary work in the Boasian philological mode came to occupy a place between disciplinary niches. Out of the mainstream, it is easy for anthropologists to ignore. But Kroeber's lack of technical expertise (and a lack of interest in the analytic questions that came to concern linguists) meant that his linguistic descriptions were not precise enough for many purposes as linguistics became more specialized and sophisticated—more "obsessive" about "precision," as he himself put it (chapter 1).

Mannheim and Tedlock's implication that text collection might have thrived in the "narrow" pastures of linguistics was too optimistic. Since the professionalization of the field in the 1920s, the structuralist and generative linguistic movements have led American linguists to a preoccupation with the theoretical implications of language data, rather than the discursive uses of language, the role of language in communities, and the texts that languages encode. Texts have been seen as manifestations of language, not as constitutive of it. Between 1960 and 2000 (and later), many linguists who recorded and published texts felt themselves marginalized in their field. (See chapter 11 for additional discussion.)

As the study of language and languages, linguistics depends critically on information about a wide range of languages. Collecting such information has always been a part of the field, whether through notes, sound recordings, other instrumental data, or electronic records. Linguists documenting the languages of North America and elsewhere have always assembled documentary corpora. But only in recent decades has it become common to conceive of such corpora as the basic objects of *documentary linguistics*, defined by Anthony Woodbury (2011:161) as "the creation, annotation, preservation, and dissemination of transparent records of a language."[7] These are the basis for scientific research, humanistic inquiry, and cultural and language reclamation in their communities of origin.

One of Kroeber's enduring legacies is a consequence of his emphasis on precolonial linguistic and social practices. He assembled a corpus of notes on and recordings of a wide range of traditional narratives, ceremonial and other texts, songs, and information about Indigenous languages of California and elsewhere. But documentation as such was downplayed in at least one obituary. At a time when linguists felt pressure to make their work relevant to theories of language, Dell Hymes (1961:6) wrote somewhat defensively that "Kroeber's empirical work was never data-gathering for its own sake." Today, when documentation is again valued, it is possible to give Kroeber's work its due.

Based on the documentary corpus he assembled, Kroeber published sketches of eight California languages and linguistic overviews of Washo, Yokuts, and the Chumash and Ohlone languages; analyses of Arapaho and Yokuts dialectology; phonetic studies of Kumeyaay, Marshallese, and Mojave; and an innovative report on a Zuni child's language learning.[8] Most of these were the first studies of their kind for the languages in question.

Committed as Kroeber was to language documentation, he was not an exceptional linguistic analyst. His grammatical descriptions were mostly short, and longer ones like the 1907 Washo grammar lacked the detail and rigor associated with linguists like Edward Sapir, whom Kroeber called "a wizard on language" (to Boas, 21 September 1907, FBP). Kroeber himself never wrote a grammar of the Indigenous language he knew best, Yurok, despite promising one as early as 1909. A dramatically framed news article about a lecture in that year (figure 4.1) reported that he was "actively

CALIFORNIA INDIAN TONGUE MOST PERFECT IN WORLD

Language More Comprehensive Than Greek or Latin, Discovers Dr. Kroeber, Philologist.

Figure 4.1
Headline about a public lecture (*San Francisco Examiner*, 8 August 1909, p. 13).

engaged in compiling a grammar of the language of the Yurok Indians" and that he said, perhaps referring to Yurok, "While the grammatical structure of the Indian language is of the most complex and involved nature it is nevertheless the most perfect of languages." This quotation is probably garbled: I doubt that Kroeber would have called any language "perfect," though he might have said that some grammatical features were perfectly suited to a language's environment.[9] In any case, Kroeber did not finish the promised work; half a century would pass before the publication of a Yurok grammar by R. H. Robins (1958).

In addition to written documentation, Kroeber made more than a thousand sound recordings with speakers of at least thirty languages, including twenty-four languages of California.[10] These are the earliest recordings of each language, including the only ones of at least two (Huchnom and Yawdanchi Yokuts). They stand out among early field recordings, as Ira Jacknis (2003) noted, by including not only songs but many spoken texts. The latter include traditional narratives, ceremonial recitation, prayers, oratory, historical narratives, and descriptions of traditional law. With few exceptions, the voices are those of Indigenous people.[11]

The full collection has more than 1,700 other recordings made by Kroeber's students and younger colleagues, and has recently been digitized through an optical scanning process developed at the Lawrence Berkeley National Laboratory (see figure 4.2).[12] These recordings are actively used in cultural reclamation projects. They are "the only recordings we have to hear how we sounded," Tongva artist and language activist

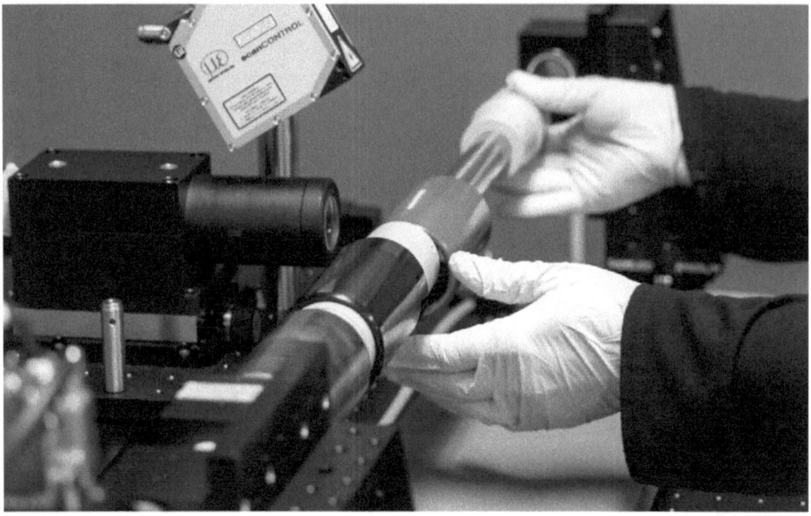

Figure 4.2
Three wax cylinders being mounted for scanning in Project IRENE. A camera faces them; a laser guides rotation and movement. The rightmost cylinder is a recording of Singing Jack (Mono) made with E. W. Gifford in 1926; the middle cylinder is a recording of Gilbert Natches made with Kroeber in 1914. Photograph by Jami Smith (Hoban 2018).

L. Frank Manriquez said (Gehr 2013:101), referring to early recordings of the Indigenous language of what is now Los Angeles. Similarly, according to language activist Louis Trevino, the Rumsen recordings that Jacinta Gonzalez and Maria Viviana Soto made with Kroeber in Monterey in 1902 are "especially precious to us" (Tobin 2017).

The overall scope of Kroeber's documentary corpus is broader than almost any other US researcher's. His notes on more than forty Indigenous languages are available at Berkeley and widely distributed to Native stakeholders; a few items are at the American Philosophical Society and the Smithsonian. The languages and the language families they belong to are listed in table 4.1. Kroeber's work was often carried out through fieldwork, especially in his first years in California. But memory documentation used interviews rather than observation (or participation), so his work was also partly done when Native people visited the Bay Area. Interview methods have limitations, even for studying language; it is impossible to document conversational practices and other socially conditioned aspects of usage in isolation. Nevertheless, a lot can be

Table 4.1
Alfred Kroeber's linguistic and cultural documentation. Abbreviations: UA = Uto-Aztecan, YU = Yok-Utian. Asterisks (*) mark languages from outside California. A small proportion of Kroeber's notes are at the American Philosophical Society (Parsons 1880–1980, Pitkin 1884–1980) and the National Anthropological Archives.

Achumawi	*Arapaho-Atsina (Algic)
*Assiniboine (Siouan)	Cahuilla (UA)
Chemehuevi (UA)	*Cheyenne
Chimariko	Chochenyo (YU)
Barbareño Chumash	Chumashan
Coast Miwok (YU)	Eastern Pomo
Esselen	*Hopi (UA)
Hupa (Dene)	*Inuktun (Polar Inuit)
Karuk	*Keres
Kumeyaay (Yuman)	Luiseño (UA)
Maidu	*Maori (Austronesian)
Maricopa (Yuman)	Mojave (Yuman)
New River Shasta	*Nlaka'pamux (Salishan)
Nomlaki	Numu (UA)
Patwin	*Quechua
Rumsen (YU)	*Seri
Serrano (UA)	Shasta
*Shoshone (UA)	Sierra Miwok (YU)
Southeastern Pomo	*Tohono O'odham (UA)
Tolowa (Dene)	Tongva (UA)
Wappo	Washo
Wintun	Wiyot (Algic)
Yana	Yokuts (YU)
Yuki	Yurok (Algic)
*Zuni	

learned about vocabulary and grammar from interviews, still the standard methodology for many linguists.

An example of serendipitously occasioned documentation was Kroeber's work with two Indigenous people in March 1909, when Fred Wadzese (Bannock Numu) and James Brown (Shoshone) were among a group of San Francisco visitors from Utah. Working with them for apparently at most a couple of days, Kroeber recorded basic vocabulary and grammatical paradigms in their respective Uto-Aztecan languages (ALK Ctn 9:4). This led to an article clarifying dialect relations in the Numic branch of Uto-Aztecan (Kroeber 1909a). When Brown wrote to

Kroeber about that article, Kroeber responded, mentioning the planned San Francisco world's fair (28 February 1911, RDA Vol. 13):

> I am glad that you are all O K and that everything is going well with you. Remember that if you ever travel as far as San Francisco again, our Indian room here is ready for you and that we will be glad to let you have the use of it without charge. I wish very much you could make the trip and pay us a visit. . . . There is not much new here except that we are going to have the big Fair in 1915, as you no doubt know. If you cannot make the trip here before then, you must certainly try to come in that year because there will be a great deal to see and lots doing. If you will write me and tell me where your regular address is, I will be glad to send you another copy of the little paper on the Shoshone language you ask for. But I do not like to send it if it may get lost in the mails and never reach you.

UC's anthropological collections had been moved to San Francisco in 1903, occupying a Romanesque building (figure 3.15) at the "Affiliated Colleges" of medicine, dentistry, and pharmacy (now UC San Francisco). Some employees lived there, and it had a room (mentioned by Kroeber to Brown) regularly used by Indian visitors. As discussed in chapter 3, this building opened as a public museum in October 1911.

Another correspondent was Pedro Encinales, a Salinan man who came to San Francisco to work with Kroeber's PhD student J. Alden Mason for a month before Christmas 1910 (Mason 1918:4). On that visit he also interacted with T. T. Waterman and with Kroeber, who afterward corresponded with him. A letter of 28 February 1911 (RDA Vol. 13) answered a query about prints of certain photographs:

> Dear Friend:
>
> I was very glad to get your letter of February 14 and to know that you got there all right and that everything is going well with you and your family. We are the same here and both Mr. Mason and Mr. Waterman were very glad to hear from you and asked me to send you their regards. I have not forgotten about the pictures of the old Missions. We got them from the photographer some time ago but have not had time to paste them up on cards, and I wanted to send them to you in good shape. I hope before the end of the week we will have time to mount them up and will then send them to you at once.
>
> With best wishes and regards to you and all your people, and hoping to hear from you whenever convenient, I am

As ever your friend,
[signed:] A. L. Kroeber

P.S. Do not forget that if you ever come up here on a visit, whether you are alone or have any of your family with you, we will be glad to have you make use of your old room in our building and of course there will be no charge for it.

In the following sections, I describe Kroeber's work with speakers of five languages: Karuk, Luiseño, Yuki, Yurok, and Zuni. Other examples discussed in chapters 5–6 are Mojave, Numu, and O'odham. All are distinctive for their breadth, their personal dimensions, and the richness of the resulting text corpora.

KARUK

The Karuk people live along the middle Klamath River in northern California; their language is an isolate (unrelated to any other language).[13] Ten of Kroeber's field notebooks (from 1901, 1902, and 1923) preserve Karuk linguistic and cultural documentation, including ten Karuk-language creation stories; most of the stories were published in English translation, and none in Karuk. One narrative was dictated by Martha Horne, and seven more by one of her daughters, Julia Bennett. In 1904, Kroeber hired another daughter, Jeannette Horne (then living in San Francisco), to create a notebook of vocabulary and sentences. After Pablo Tac's early-nineteenth-century Luiseño work in Rome (discussed below), it is among the oldest extant examples of writing by an Indigenous Californian in their own language.

Kroeber's work with Bennett is illustrated in figure 4.3, the first page of a transcript of a narrative about a young woman from Thúfip, the Yurok village (Requa) at the mouth of the Klamath River. This text has not been published in English or Karuk. After the formulaic opening *uknîi* (often beginning creation stories), the narrative begins like many Karuk stories: *káan kun'áraarahitih* "they lived there," referring to the young woman's family. This page has a word not recorded elsewhere in Karuk, *voonfunich-vaan* "suitor(s), wooer(s)," which is derived from the verb *vôonfur* "take a wife in half-marriage, working for her father" with the suffixes *-iichva* "in play, pretense" and *-aan* (agentive)—literally, "one(s) who pretend(s) to marry." The last two lines show a unique collocation, *púxay fâatxay* "not

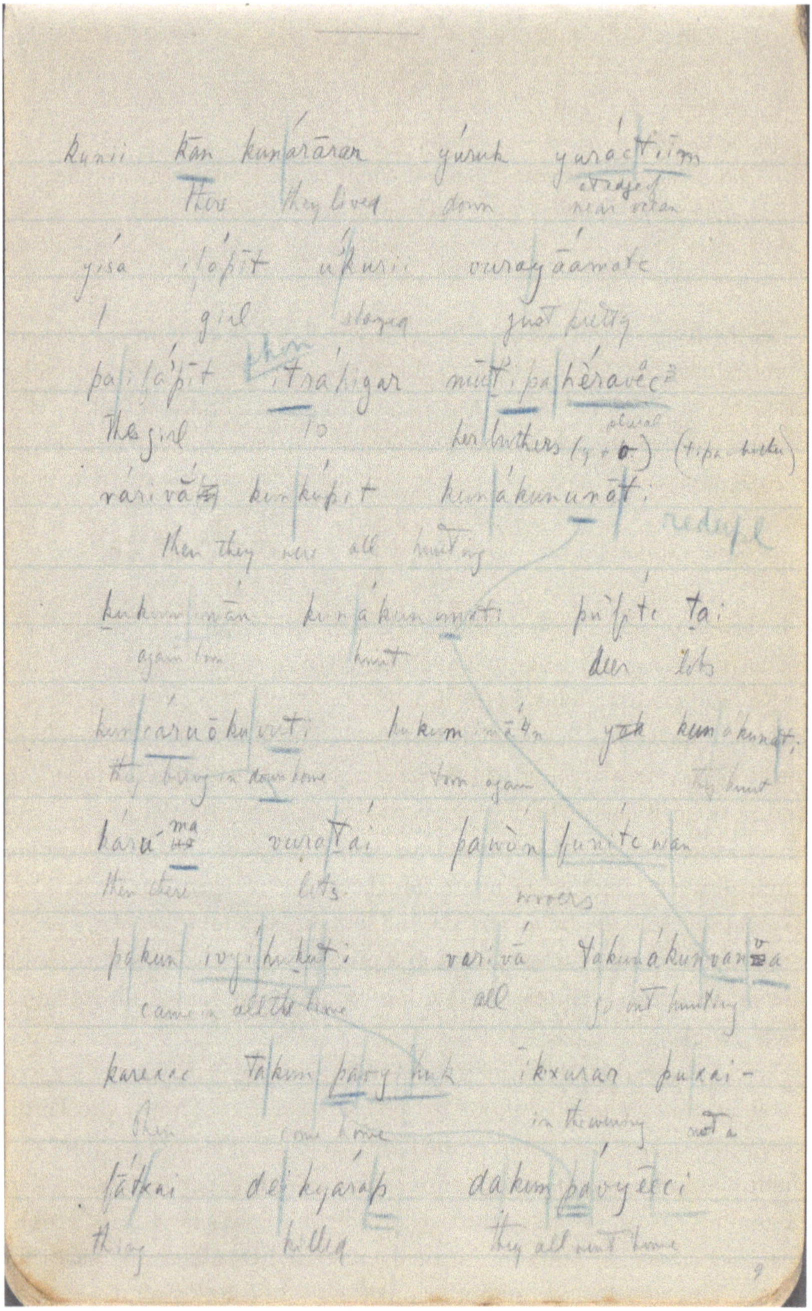

Figure 4.3
A page of Kroeber's transcript of a Karuk narrative dictated by Julia Bennett, 20 June 1902 (ALK Ctn 12:18, p. 9). Blue pencil marks were added later as Kroeber analyzed the language.

a thing, nothing at all," with a negative particle *-xay* reinforcing both parts of what is today a single word, *púfaat* "nothing" (*pu-* "not" + *fâat* "something"). This pattern has not been attested since the 1950s, when a dramatic instance was recorded from Chester Pepper (Bright 1957:254): *púxay vúraxay amkúufxay* "there was no smoke," with *ámkuuf* "smoke," the discourse particle *vúra*, and three cases of *-xay*.

Figure 4.3 also shows significant phonetic details. These begin with the first word, formulaic *uknîi*, which Kroeber spelled *kunii*. In the next line, he wrote *ú'kurii* for *úkrii* "she sat, lived, stayed." Both examples show a process, today not written in Karuk orthography, whereby an initial-syllable *u* is partly or entirely transposed across a following *k*. And in Kroeber's *ú'kurii* and *ifápīt* (line 3, for *ifápīt* "young woman"), the apostrophe indicates a lengthening process that regularly affects intervocalic consonants after accented vowels.[14] Two words show palatalization (*y*-insertion, informally) after certain consonants preceded by *i* or *y*: in *ikxúrar* "evening," it is marked by a raised dot after *k*; *téeykárap* "(he did not) kill (it)" is written *deikyárap* with an added *y*. Kroeber's notes contain the earliest evidence for this process, recorded only variably in recent speech. Finally, spellings like *yísa* for what is now *yítha* "one" show that the Karuk change of the dental sound [s] to interdental [θ] (as in English ***th**in*) had not yet happened.[15] Kroeber did not share the prodigious phonetic gifts of some of his contemporaries, but his transcriptions reveal much of value.

Karuk documentation associated with Kroeber and those he influenced, such as his student L. S. Freeland, has been valuable in language reclamation. Vocabulary they recorded is included in a dictionary published by the Karuk Tribe; information from their notes is used in Karuk language teaching.[16] Stories and cultural information that Kroeber and his protégés recorded have also contributed to cultural reclamation.[17] For example, one of the stories Julia Bennett dictated to Kroeber involves the larval coastal giant salamander, called *thúfthaam*, or *púfpuuf* in its adult form.[18] This is a "focal species" for land restoration, according to the Karuk Tribe (2020). As a "spiritual being" that "monitor[s] spring and creek water quality and quantity," *púfpuuf* "has its own prayer in ceremonies related to how humans . . . can maintain balance in riparian systems." The restoration of Indigenous language, stories, and cultural and ecological practices is integrated here and throughout California.

LUISEÑO

North of San Diego in southern California are spoken the Luiseño and Acjachemen (Juaneño) languages, part of the Takic branch of Uto-Aztecan, a family spread across the western United States, Mexico, and Central America. Precolonial Luiseño and Acjachemen were likely a network of dialects varying from village to village, not sharply demarcated languages, but dialectal and social organization were transformed by the Spanish invasion and missionization at San Luis Rey and San Juan Capistrano. The first linguistic description of Luiseño was written by Pablo Tac, an Indigenous person who was born in 1822 and taken from his home in 1832. From 1834 until his death in 1841 he was a student in Rome, where he wrote a Luiseño grammatical sketch and partial dictionary that remained unpublished for ninety years.[19]

Kroeber got involved with Luiseño because of Philip Sparkman, whom he called "a gaunt, pale, red-bearded Englishman—lonely, quiet, and studious in habits." Sparkman had settled at Rincon, 50 miles from San Diego; there learned to speak Luiseño "perfectly," according to a Luiseño acquaintance; and drafted a dictionary and a grammar.[20] To transcribe the language he developed his own English-based spelling; discerning "a strong likeness between Latin and Luiseño in the declension of nouns" (26 August 1902, ALK Box 28:2), he cast his grammar in a Latin mold. Kroeber and Sparkman began corresponding in 1901; after Sparkman was killed in 1907, his Luiseño manuscripts came to Kroeber. An ethnographic paper appeared in 1908, but it took decades for work originating from Sparkman's drafts to result in a published grammar and dictionary.[21]

In 1904, Kroeber visited Rincon for Luiseño documentation; there, he mainly worked with Feliz Calac, a fluent speaker and gifted analyst of the language.[22] In San Francisco five years later, they recorded instrumental phonetic data and retranscribed and translated "about every stem and at least some part of every paradigm and set of illustrative sentences recorded by Sparkman" (Kroeber and Grace 1960:3). For some years the work languished, but Kroeber returned to Luiseño in the 1930s, and again after he retired. In the 1950s, with funding from the Wenner-Gren Foundation, a collaboration with linguistics student George Grace and Luiseño people Leonidas Calac, Willy Calac, Johnny McDowell, and Cornelia Ward allowed the completion of Sparkman's grammar.

The grammar begun by Sparkman and written by Kroeber and Grace is distinctive most of all because of its diachronic depth: unlike most grammatical descriptions of Native American languages, it presents a record of documentation across more than a century, including frequent citation of information from Tac. This has allowed analysts to describe grammatical changes, such as a striking reorganization of the system of sentential particles identified by Sandra Chung (1974:305–307). The Kroeber and Grace book was also the first published grammar of a Takic language (after Tac's sketch), setting the stage for a series of others beginning in the 1960s.[23] As such, though different in analytic style from a conventional linguist's grammar, it played an important role in identifying and describing the central grammatical categories of the Takic languages.

Luiseño is now among the best-described California languages. In addition to the Sparkman grammar and a linguistic overview by André Malécot (1963, 1964), Luiseño elder and language teacher Villiana Calac Hyde published an exemplary pedagogical volume in 1971, working with a UC San Diego team, and a 1,400-page text collection two decades later in collaboration with Eric Elliott (Hyde and Elliott 1994). The lexical material collected in the Sparkman-Kroeber project was incorporated into Bright's short 1968 dictionary, mainly aimed at comparative linguists, and into a monumental (1,863-page) dictionary of Rincon Luiseño by Elliott (1999), whose cultural and textual detail makes it a model for many communities.

YUKI

Yuki belongs to a small language family, Yukian, whose other member is Wappo. Several dialects of Yuki are spoken in the Eel River drainage and along the coast in what is now Mendocino County north of San Francisco. Near the end of his life, Kroeber (1958b) wrote an account of his earliest work with Yuki. In Covelo on the Round Valley Indian Reservation, he spent a month from December 1901 to January 1902, documenting Yuki language and cultural practices with Ralph Moore. Moore was only a couple of years older than Kroeber but was knowledgeable about language and the kinds of precolonial cultural patterns that interested Kroeber, having learned from his grandfather and others of the same generation (Kroeber 1932b:905). Their collaboration continued in San Francisco in March 1902:

> I found lodgings for him two or three blocks away [from Kroeber's lodging], and most meals we ate together. When I had to go to the university, or other business, he went to neighborhood restaurants with which he had become familiar, attended nickelodeons, or otherwise saw sights or amused himself. . . . The bulk of our work [for two weeks] consisted of recording songs and interlinear translating of narratives.

Moore's 1902 visit was the subject of a full-page feature in the *San Francisco Call*, "An Indian Who Gave Our College Professors Pointers." It quotes his skepticism about sound recording: "I didn't come here to talk into no horn. I come to teach the professors."

Kroeber and Moore met for language work later in 1902 and again in 1910, 1912, 1923, 1927, 1931, and 1932; and they maintained a friendly correspondence, discussed in detail by William Bauer (2003:153–170). Their work yielded a corpus of twelve notebooks, mainly containing linguistic information, Yuki-language text transcriptions, and translations of Yuki texts, as well as a significant amount of phonetic data that could be used for scientific or language-reclamation purposes. Figure 4.4 shows a significant page from a narrative Moore dictated in 1902. This page was omitted from an archived photocopy, so the first five sentences of the 423-sentence narrative were left out of an eventual published edition.[24]

On publishing a book of sketches of some California languages (Kroeber 1911d), Kroeber wrote to several consultants who contributed information for the volume, including Moore (22 May 1911, RDA Vol. 13):

> I am sending you the book which the University has just published for me. In that you will find about 50 [sic; actually 36] pages given up to an account of the grammar of your language. I thought you might be interested in looking this over. Very likely you will find some mistakes and if so, I hope you will not be bashful, but will let me know what they are. I do not suppose you remember my system of writing very well, but as I have always translated the Indian words, you can tell by the meaning what the Indian words are. You will see that the grammar of your language runs from page 348 to page 383. This little sketch is only the beginning and, as you will notice, I have printed only the very beginning of one of your stories and all the others you gave me are still waiting to be put in shape to be published. I am hoping to get around

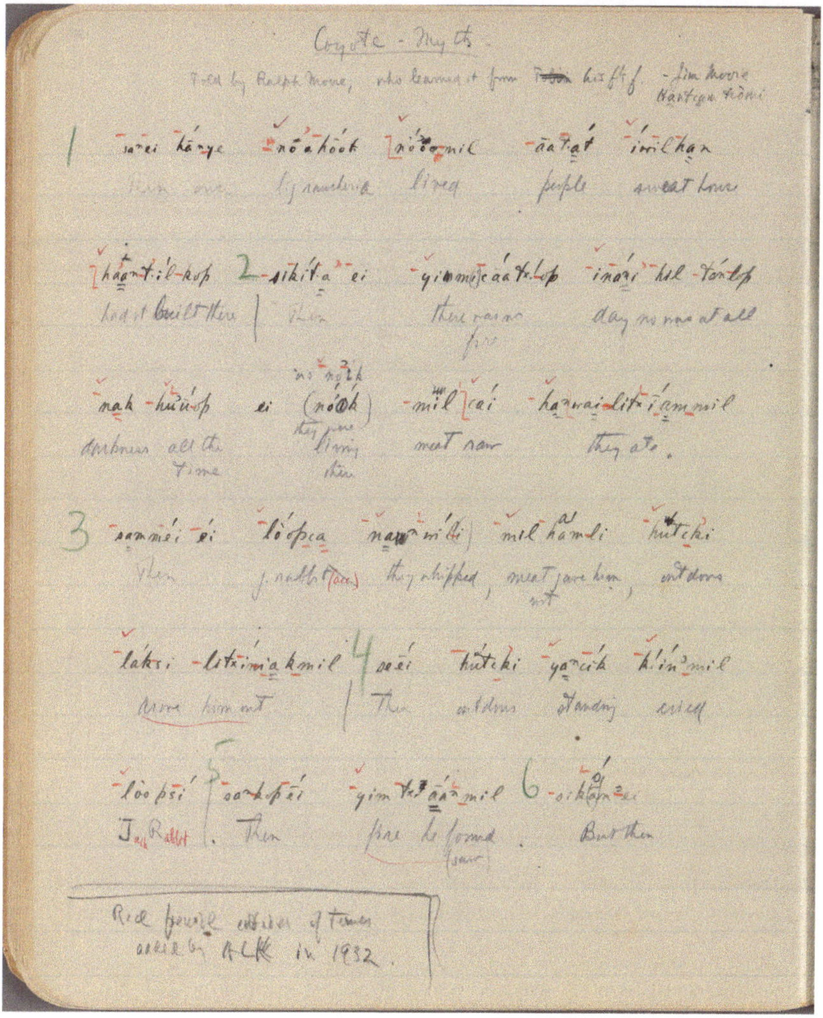

Figure 4.4
Yuki "Coyote Myth" dictated by Ralph Moore to Kroeber, 1902 (ALK Box 40:1, facing p. 59). The first five sentences of a 423-sentence narrative were transcribed on this page.

to this work one of these days and rather expect that before I get through with it I will have to have the assistance of a Yuki. So, when the time comes, if you are still on deck and ready to make the trip to the city once more, I will be glad to send for you. Meanwhile I hope that all goes well with you and should be pleased to hear from you.

Figure 4.5
Ralph Moore and Alfred Kroeber, Berkeley, 1 June 1927 (ALKFP Box 2).

The photograph in figure 4.5, taken at Kroeber's house, is from Moore's 1927 visit to Berkeley.[25] In the end Kroeber did not "get around to" preparing Moore's Yuki-language texts for publication. The work was only finally completed in a 650-page volume by Uldis Balodis (2016), with a thorough grammar and almost two hundred pages of text transcriptions.

The last fluent first-language speaker of Yuki passed away three decades ago, according to Victor Golla (2011:190). In 2016, Berkeley's documentary corpus of Yuki material (largely created by Kroeber and Moore) was used in a language reclamation project by a Breath of Life Institute participant from Round Valley described by Leanne Hinton

(2018:455). Recent years have also seen community and high-school Yuki language classes in Covelo, based on information derived from archival sources.

YUROK

A member of the Algic language family, Yurok is spoken in northwestern California along the Klamath River from Weitchpec to the river mouth at Requa, and south along the coast (see figure 4.6). It is the language to which Kroeber devoted the most energy over his career. In the first decade of the twentieth century, with more than thirty elders, he made more than two hundred sound recordings of songs, narratives, and other texts (about seventeen hours in all). From 1900 to 1941, he filled thirty-six notebooks with information about language and cultural practices and dozens of stories (in Yurok and English) shared by dozens of Yurok people of several generations.

Kroeber often visited Yurok land. He recalled in 1921 that he had lived in Weitchpec "half a dozen times, once or twice for a month or more. I used to know all the inhabitants and every shack and tree and trail in and around the village."[26] His first Yurok work took place in September 1900, when he was employed by the California Academy of Sciences. A two-week trip to northwestern California afforded him six days of Yurok linguistic and cultural documentation around Weitchpec and Requa (ALK Ctn 12:7–9). As his main duty on behalf of his employer, he also bought seventy-eight ethnographic objects (such as baskets, cooking implements, and nets) for the academy's collections. These objects, later destroyed in the 1906 San Francisco earthquake, cost $78.80 in all. Other expenses included $5 each way for a shipboard berth between San Francisco and Eureka (September 10, 27), $1 for a night at a hotel in Blue Lake (September 11), 25¢ for dinner in Trinidad (September 25), 15¢ for a shave (September 26), and a total of $12.75 to five Yurok people from whom he recorded language, cultural information, and texts (in English). These were Weitchpec Frank (September 16, 18, 20), Julia Wilson (September 17), Obie (September 19), William Johnson (September 20), and Captain Spott (September 23).[27] Over the next seven years, Frank was Kroeber's usual "interpreter and vademecum" (Kroeber and Gifford 1949:133), recording a few elders for him with the cylinder

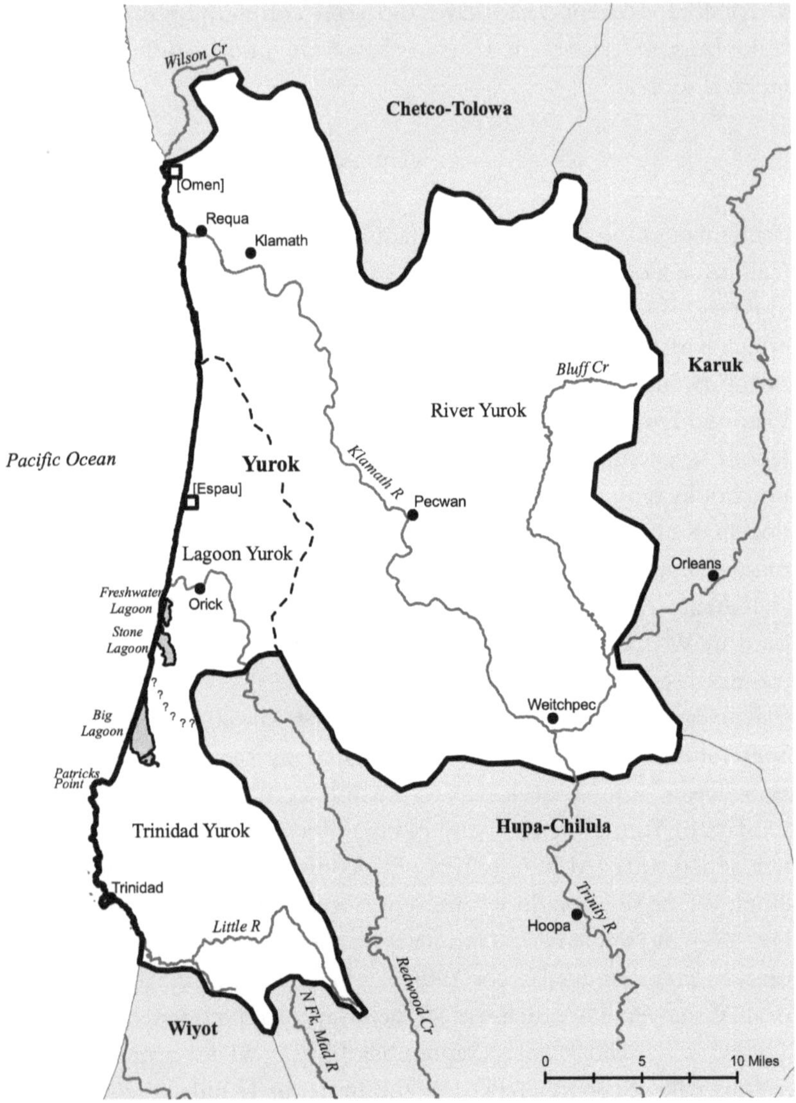

Figure 4.6
Yurok territory and dialects. Cartography by Jackie Honig Bjorkman (Golla 2011:66).

recording apparatus and coming to San Francisco to help him transcribe and translate Yurok sound recordings.

In the 1920s, Kroeber spent summers near Orick in a ramshackle cabin above the ocean. Yurok elders Laura and Robert ("Orick Bob") Johnson were his neighbors and friends there. "I bring [Laura] oranges and cake," he wrote Berna Pinner, "and they give me surf-fish" (28 July 1924, ALK Box 3:7). Theodora Kroeber (1970:158) recalled that Alfred and Bob "fished, hauled driftwood, talked, and worked at recording the Yurok language and whatever other aspects of Yurok life occurred to Bob." The cabin was just north of Freshwater Lagoon at Seeegonoy (Lookout Point), so Alfred was called *Seeegonoy meweemor* "old man of Seeegonoy," and Theodora (in her twenties) was playfully called *Seeegonoy 'o perey* "old woman of Seeegonoy."[28] With Bob in 1927, Kroeber recorded vocabulary in several domains, such as the words for the kidneys and umbilical cord (nowhere else documented) and coastal directional and geographical terms. Examples are coastal names of the four winds: *'ue-perwery* "south (literally, downcoast)," *hehlkeek mew'* "east (literally, inland) wind," *pueleek 'ue-mew'* "north (literally, downstream) wind," and *tewolew mew'* "west (literally, ocean) wind."[29]

Kroeber's documentation of Yurok language, texts, and cultural practices is so rich that it is hard to pick out just a few of its most important features, even excluding his collaboration with Robert Spott (discussed in chapter 6). Here I highlight four features that interest me.

First, because Kroeber's documentation was far more substantial than earlier BIA survey work, like that of Jeremiah Curtin (1889), and predated later work by fifty years, he recorded patterns that were regularly used in his day but documented poorly or not at all in later work. A simple example comes from a common Yurok verb: *'new* "I am called," *k'ew* "you are called," and so on. The first consonant is an agreement prefix, but an ending that would also agree with the subject is absent. Such endingless forms normally correspond to longer forms of the same meaning. For this verb, however, longer forms were not documented from the 1950s on, nor used or volunteered by the last generation of fluent first-language speakers. But Kroeber's corpus has many examples, such as *'newolek'* "I am called," confirmed around 2004 with *'aawokw* Georgiana Trull. "That's right," I recall her saying, about a Yurok word that might not have been spoken for decades.

Numerals provide another case. Yurok is well known for its elaborate inflection of numerals, depending on the meaning of what is counted.[30] Sixteen categories were identified by R. H. Robins (1958:87–91) and later researchers. Numerals up to "five" are shown here for four categories:

- Animals: *kerhtery'* "one," *ner'er'eryhl* "two," *nerhkser'eryhl* "three," *cher'erner'eryhl* "four," *merueh termerwer'eryhl* "five"
- Flat things: *kohtok's, no'ok's, nahksok's, to'onok's, merueh tomowok's*
- Round things: *kohtoh, no'oh, nahksoh, to'onoh, merueh tomowoh*
- Sharp things: *kerhterpee', ner'erpee', nerhkserpee', ter'ernerpee', merueh termerpee'*

Other categories are for people, boats, bushy things, trees and stick-like things, snake-like things, houses, days, times, sacks full (of a substance), arm's lengths (measuring depth), finger-joint spans (measuring dentalium lengths), and miscellaneous objects.

Kroeber's earlier corpus adds information of two kinds. He recorded more categories, including dentalium strings, woodpecker scalps, and daily ordinals ("the Xth day/night"). Focusing on usage, not just the formal properties linguists often describe, his work also yields detail about the meanings of numeral categories. For instance, the numerals for boats are used for wagons and other conveyances (Kroeber 1911d:423–424); presumably, they are appropriate for cars, trucks, and other such vehicles. This is important because many Yurok people are proud of their language's numeral system and value using all its resources, in a way they perceive as authentic. Some describe its implied categories as expressing a distinctive worldview. They are well aware of the inevitable impact of English, but prefer if possible to minimize that impact in culturally emblematic aspects of language. The fullest possible description of the traditional numeral system and its uses is therefore a desideratum for language reclamation.

A second feature of note in Kroeber's Yurok corpus is its broad dialect coverage. As seen in figure 4.6, Yurok is spoken along the Klamath River and the coast (and in a wide diaspora today). Kroeber transcribed vocabulary and grammatical patterns at many villages along the river, and along the coast with speakers from Orick (as noted above), Stone Lagoon, and Trinidad. The Yurok spoken on the Klamath is homogeneous dialectally, but there are major differences from place to place on the coast.[31] Americanization was so intensive there that coast dialects were spoken by few people even in 1900; by the 1950s, when hundreds of people on the river spoke Yurok, only scattered coast vocabulary was remembered. Kroeber's documentation shows that Coast Yurok has many idiosyncratic word forms (e.g., *nihks-* for *nahks-* "two") and sound patterns, such as the regular insertion of a vowel in words like *hohokuem* "tobacco" (river *hohkuem*) and *kohochew* "six" (*kohchew*), of interest to families with coast heritage.

Third, Kroeber's sound recordings of Yurok include not only songs but also sixty-four spoken texts, made with twenty-two people from 1902 to 1909.[32] Ethnographic fieldworkers in the early twentieth century often recorded songs, which could not be transcribed in the field, but rarely made significant collections of recorded speech. Kroeber's corpus of spoken Yurok recordings is the largest such collection of its era. Durations range from two or three minutes to over a half an hour, in the case of Dave Durban's death purification medicine and Juanita's brush-dance medicine, both from 1907. Most narratives were published in English (Kroeber 1976), but not in Yurok, and nonnarrative texts were also recorded; one of the latter is discussed in chapter 5. Some of the stories are no longer told in Yurok, while many of the medicine texts pertain to activities still practiced locally.

Texts dictated or recorded by women make a fourth notable aspect of Kroeber's Yurok documentary corpus. He worked mainly with men, to be sure, and Victorian gender assumptions informed his research (chapter 1). When he worked with women, he mainly asked about what he thought were women's matters. He also stacked the deck against any semblance of gender balance in *Yurok Myths*, which omits narratives from six women mentioned only in an appendix; at least two other women dictated texts he did not classify as myths. In all, at least eleven Yurok women shared texts with Kroeber in the first decade of the twentieth century. Two who merit special mention are Mary Marshall and Trinidad Jim's wife.

Marshall (figure 4.7) was a trilingual Hupa, Yurok, and English speaker who had a Yurok mother and a Hupa father, married a Hupa man, and lived in Hoopa. In a part of California famous for multilingualism and for cultural interactions and convergence among speakers of three unrelated languages—Hupa (Dene), Karuk, and Yurok (Algic)—she stands out as the only person, as far as I know, who has ever shared texts in more than

Figure 4.7
Left: Mary Marshall and two sons, Hoopa, 1904 (1999.07.2979, Humboldt County Collection, Cal Poly Humboldt Library). Right: Captain Spott, 1907, commercial postcard sent from Catherine Goodwin to Kroeber (18 November 1910, RDA Box 12:3).

one of them. In 1901 and 1902, she dictated nine of the fifty-one Hupa texts published by Pliny Goddard (1904). Working with Kroeber in July 1906, she dictated two Yurok texts that she had learned from older (male) relatives: the medicine text for the Kepel fish dam and a long text for purification after contact with a corpse.[33] In 1927, Marshall also dictated three other Yurok texts to Edward Sapir (Berman 2001), and shared with him extensive Yurok grammatical information. But it is her (unpublished) purification text that is especially significant, not because of its length but because there are two other texts of the same nature in Yurok as well as one that Marshall herself dictated in Hupa (Goddard 1904:351–359). The three Yurok versions differ, but Marshall's Hupa and Yurok versions are similar in most details. They invoke the spiritual inhabitants of the same places along the river. The invocations are also the same. Goddard translated the Hupa as follows:

> The people are afraid of me. I do not have a fire where the others have their fire. I have a fire by myself. And besides, what the rest eat I do not eat.

> Furthermore, I do not look at the world. So much my body frightens them. I am telling you that you may be sorry for me.

Marshall's Yurok text is parallel. Among dozens of Hupa, Karuk, and Yurok narratives that tell the same or similar stories, this is the only case of parallel texts that may be described as Hupa-Yurok translation.[34]

Trinidad Jim and his wife (whose name was not recorded) were staying in Pecwan on the Klamath River when Kroeber worked with them in 1907. She was born at Stone Lagoon on the coast; language she shared is the fullest information about coast Yurok. In that dialect, she recorded on fourteen cylinders a historical account of an 1860 raid by Dene people on a Yurok village at Stone Lagoon, and of the kidnapping and subsequent escape of one of the survivors. It is a rare captivity narrative in a California Native language, and a window on northwest California Indigenous history in the years after the US invasion.[35]

I have described Kroeber's Yurok corpus in detail because it has many layers, and I know it well. What did Yurok people themselves think at the time? Views surely differed, but letters to Kroeber offer a glimpse. A 1903 letter from Weitchpec Frank mentions many deaths in a smallpox outbreak ("fourteen of the Mad River Indians have died so they are about cleaned out") and the elders' desire to see Kroeber: "All the old fellows was asking about you and was very much pleased when I told them you were coming next month" (9 April, ALK Box 31:28). Others were also aware of his connection to the "old fellows," including Catherine Goodwin, a Yurok woman who worked with Kroeber to transcribe many sound recordings. She sent Kroeber a postcard when Captain Spott died in 1911 (figure 4.7): "your old friend *Spot* died Oct. 20. He was ill only three days. He [was] only one of the many that have died[,] as many as three a week." As discussed in chapter 2, the health and living conditions of California Indians were precarious.

Memories of Kroeber that eventually crystalized were mostly positive. Florence Shaughnessy (born in 1902) might not have met him, but knew well many people who knew him, and later said that he "came early, *he always had time*, he was loved."[36] Margaret Marks wrote in 1930 to tell him that the Yurok Indian Club, a Bay Area organization of Yurok people, had chosen him as an honorary member "in recognition of your effort to preserve the history and lore of the California Indians" (6 May 1930, RDA Box 99). And after Kroeber died, Mary Gist Dornbeck, executive secretary of the Council of California Indians, circulated to its members an appreciation based on her memories of his Yurok work (15 December 1960, ALK Ctn 12:32):

> It was soon after the turn of the century when I was a very young person that he first attracted my attention. . . . Dr. Kroeber stayed with my family several summers at which time, I came to know of his interest in Indian ethnology and ethnography. When my family sensed his inspired enthusiasm to learn all there was to know about the present and past history of Indian people, they, as well as others, gave him their moral support and help in getting interpret[e]rs to enable him to get the direct and correct information from the older Indians who could not speak English.

She concluded by calling him "our friend and in later life, our greatest hope for long delayed justice" (a reference to the Indian Claims Commission case discussed in chapter 9). As Yurok activist and cultural leader Joy Sundberg commented (Platt 2011:46), "I don't put Kroeber or any of those anthropologists down, because there's lots of things that would not have been documented if it hadn't been for him to come up and interview these people." See also chapter 6 on Kroeber's work with Alice and Robert Spott.

Today, Kroeber's Yurok documentary corpus is used in both language pedagogy and linguistic research.[37] To the example of numeral classifiers mentioned above, I will add one example. Listening to stories is an important part of Yurok language education, and learning to retell them; one pedagogical practice is to have students memorize and repeat a recorded story verbatim even before they know what all the individual words mean. But the corpus of recordings includes some from the 1950s and earlier in which words that normally begin with *h* sometimes instead have *l*. The exact distribution of this pattern, otiose by the 1960s, is recoverable only from Kroeber's corpus.[38] Understanding it has been helpful in knowing why early stories sound as they do, and in retelling these stories to new audiences.

ZUNI

Zuni is an isolate language spoken at Zuni Pueblo in New Mexico. In the summers of 1915, 1916, and 1918, Kroeber engaged in cultural and linguistic documentation at Zuni, partly collaborating with the anthropologist Elsie Clews Parsons. It was his first fieldwork outside California since moving there in 1901. His wife Henriette had died in 1913, and he spent the 1915–1916 academic year in New York, visiting Zuni en route in each direction.[39]

Zuni was a site of fascination for anthropologists and other outsiders in the nineteenth and twentieth centuries. A statement made by Kroeber typifies this view ("Zuni Life" 1916): "The Zuni Indians are living still in the sixteenth century. I should never have dreamed that aboriginal life could still be going on in America so totally unaffected by modern civilization." This was either naïve or a deliberate simplification: Zuni lifeways in 1915 had many distinctive elements, sometimes leading to perceptions of an "intact" culture; but Zuni people, like all twentieth-century Native Americans, participated in a changed world and had to negotiate realities created by US colonialism. Still, Kroeber's interest in precolonial patterns is clear.[40]

In 1915 and 1916, Kroeber lodged with the family of William Lewis, then governor of Zuni Pueblo. His wife Margaret later shared her memories with Triloki Pandey (1972:330). "I am willing to eat beans three times a day," Kroeber told her when they met. "Will you accept me to live here for the summer?" As she recalled, "I thought he was so cute that I agreed to rent him a room." Via fictive kinship, he was then referred to locally as her mother's brother.[41] Pandey added that she "remembered Kroeber as a friendly man who was always helpful to her. While she went to teach school, he used to carry her one-year-old son on his back to the boy's grandmother's house." That boy, future Zuni governor Robert Lewis, was the subject of Kroeber's "The Speech of a Zuni Child" (1916c). One of the earliest studies of language learning in a minoritized community, it described vocabulary change over two months, phonological substitutions and word truncations, and the early emergence of intonation, among other phenomena.

In the year after Kroeber's first summer at Zuni, he corresponded briefly with Flora Zuni (with whom he had worked on language and texts). "We are wishing [that] you come soon," she told him on 2 February 1916.[42] "I think the Zunis like you very much. They always talk about you. We miss you very much, hope you [miss us] too."

William Lewis recalled Kroeber in a song that Parsons told Kroeber he had "inspired at Zuñi—no doubt the greatest compliment ever paid you"

(11 May 1917, ALK Box 25:2). Lewis sang and then spoke it, Margaret translated, and Parsons wrote down the Zuni and a telegraphic translation:

South fathers, south clouds,
rain touches [i.e. falls]. Road catching up.
He [Kroeber] appeared.
You oriole learn [to] talk Pima, Santo Domingo.
[Kroeber speaks:] "Your tale is pretty and your way of living."
Ground wet till [spring].

These words highlight Lewis's sense that Kroeber understood language and stories as central parts of culture. Lewis's son Robert expressed a similar understanding fifty-five years later, in his introduction to a book of stories (Zuni People 1972:vii): "Stories . . . that symbolize these [Zuni] ways have kept us together so long."

Kroeber's Zuni documentation yielded a corpus of twenty-seven notebooks as well as methodologically pathbreaking publications on anthropological topics, including a paper on historical inference from pottery fragments and a monograph on kinship, social structures, and urban geography. Yet apart from the language-acquisition paper noted above, the language and texts that Kroeber recorded have languished. This is partly because he saw his work as superseded by Ruth Bunzel's fieldwork, beginning in 1926, which led to a short grammar and many published texts.[43] Kroeber's position in California also means that his notes are not an obvious source of information about a language of New Mexico. The Zuni corpus he assembled has not been used in language reclamation or by scholars; as far as I know, scholars have not even mentioned its existence.[44]

This corpus is nonetheless significant as the earliest extensive record of Zuni language and texts. It has several noteworthy features. First, Kroeber recorded generically diverse stories from different tellers a decade before Bunzel, who wrote in her own collection that "the only material in the Zuni language previously published has been ritual text" (1933:vi). While unpublished, Kroeber's 1915–1918 corpus includes songs and two dozen stories: traditional creation stories, historical narratives, and life experiences. Some of the creation stories are variants of stories recorded elsewhere in English. For example, the seven-page story "Coyote & Raven" (dictated in 1915, probably by William Lewis's father), is a variant of "The Coyote and the Ravens Who Raced Their Eyes," published by Frank Cushing (1901:262–268). And "Salt-Lady Story" (also told in 1915, probably by Lewis's father) is a short (three-page) version of a well-known, culturally significant story.[45] In the telling transcribed by Kroeber, two war gods enabled Zuni people to get salt by killing Cloud Swallower and an anthropophagous cow that did not want people to get salt; "from then on Zunis got salt." But after young men and women who went to get salt behaved disrespectfully, Ma'l Oyattsik'i (Salt Woman) went far from Zuni. "Now when I stay here nobody will treat me badly," she said, explaining how Zuni Salt Lake came to be 50 miles south of Zuni. It is a sacred place for Zuni people and others, Winona LaDuke wrote in describing a proposed coal-mining project that would have devastated the lake. She quoted a cultural leader: "When Zuni Salt Woman got angry and left, she taught us a lesson. We should learn from that." Indigenous activism was successful in this case: the project was cancelled.[46]

It is also striking that several of the Zuni narratives Kroeber transcribed involved personal experiences, not precolonial traditions. For example, on 25 June 1915, Luisandachu told a story about his mother. She and another girl were taken by Navajos while carrying water from a well, put on horses, and brought to a place north of Fort Defiance, Arizona. After a year the other girl "died of homesickness" and the teller's mother began a lengthy, circuitous return to her Zuni home and family.[47] The corpus also features stories about experiences of hunting and warfare.

Another feature of Kroeber's Zuni documentation is that it included greetings and other conversational language (for a selection see figure 4.8). This is unlike most work by linguists, who have usually focused on areas of special research interest, like verbal morphology and clause subordination. Even anthropologists in the memory-documentation style often ignored discursive practices critical for ordinary life—how to talk to children, greet friends, tell jokes, and the like.[48] Presumably Kroeber's Zuni documentation included these because he was participating in a family's daily routines.

Its many toponyms are a final notable feature of Kroeber's Zuni corpus. His notebooks contain not only numerous maps of Zuni streets and houses but many pages listing the names of landscape features and villages, including former habitation sites. For example, a single page of notes from 20 June 1915 has the names of seventeen creeks or washes.[49] The first

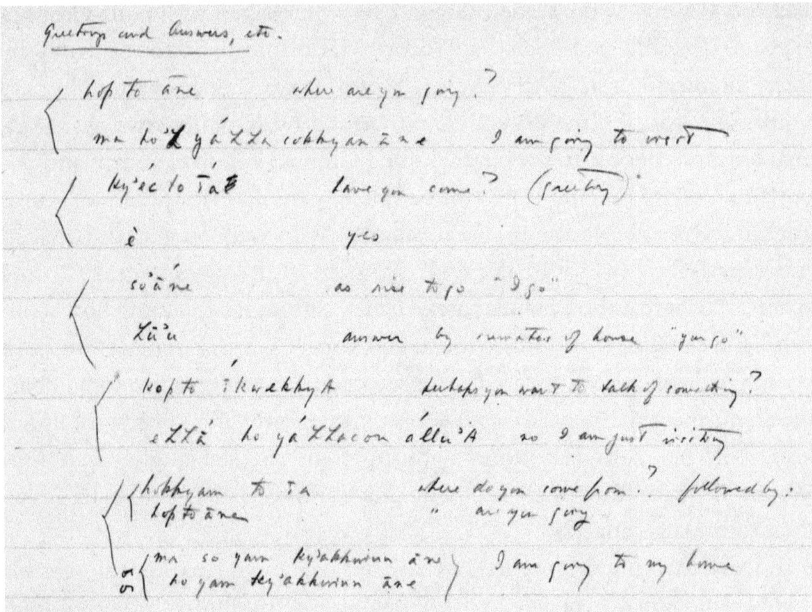

Figure 4.8
Selected Zuni "Greetings and Answers, etc." transcribed by Kroeber in work with Luisandachu, 24 June 1915 (ALK Ctn 13:37, p. 11).

three are representative in also identifying locations: *wimmayā akwenne* "wash that Gallup road follows for ca 10 miles, comes into Zuni river ca 1 m. below here, this side of hattsināwe"; *hé'icukktákkwenne* "wash this side [of] Peach Orchard, W of N of here"; and *LáwuLLiákkwenne* "creek heading W of Van de Wagon ranch, flows into Zuni river below here." The toponyms recorded by Kroeber could contribute to Zuni cultural reclamation projects, which for many years have creatively centered Indigenous geography.[50]

STUDENTS

In addition to the kinds of linguistic and cultural documentation described above, Kroeber led students and younger colleagues to do similar work. As a result, there are substantial documentary corpora for languages throughout California and beyond (see table 4.2). This collective legacy of Kroeber's protégés goes well beyond that of his teacher's, because Kroeber was at a public university in the western United States, unlike Boas, and was aware of a duty to record its Indigenous languages and cultures.

Kroeber's impact also went beyond just anthropology and linguistics. As discussed by John García (2001), Kroeber influenced the ideas and methods of his undergraduate student Milman Parry. Famously called "the Darwin of Homeric studies" by H. T. Wade-Gery (1952:38), Parry transformed the study of oral literature as a classicist and folklorist, tracing intricate compositional processes and emphasizing how creativity emerges within a traditional system.[51] Though he majored in Greek, Parry took anthropology classes and was part of what Robert Kanigel (2021:50) called "a group of students, faculty, and hangers-on centered around two Berkeley anthropologists," Kroeber and Robert Lowie. His ideas were first expressed in a University of California MA thesis (1923) that emphasized the oral traditional nature of Greek epic in almost Herderian language. Downplaying the role of individuals and expressing a cultural essentialism like that of Boasian anthropology, he wrote that "the [Greek] race was the artist" (1971:428). Later, Parry sent Kroeber a copy of his doctoral thesis (1928) and wrote of feeling a "personal" connection; and he made a point of seeing Kroeber when he visited Berkeley in 1935, shortly before his own untimely death.[52]

Kroeber's influence was primarily local in his first decades in Berkeley, but with the professionalization of linguistics in the 1920s he came to have a critical national role in organizing Native American language research. In the 1920s and 1930s, the Boasian goal of language and text documentation was nationalized, so to speak, by the creation of a Committee for Research in Native American Languages.[53] Managed in effect by Boas and his students, especially Kroeber and Sapir, its first stated purpose was "to collect data on those languages which are near extinction." A major aspiration was to ensure that all North American languages were documented. Kroeber's correspondence throughout this period includes many letters and even telegrams about which languages were most urgently in need of documentation and which students should be sent where; national professional elites were self-consciously organizing the research activities of students at a range of universities.

Finally, in the 1950s, Kroeber was actively engaged with the work of Californianist students and other young scholars in a new department of

Table 4.2
North American documentation by Kroeber's students and younger colleagues, including only cases where notes or recordings are accessible at Berkeley and contain language, linguistic anthropology, or songs or texts. Work by those who were not Kroeber's protégés is excluded, as is work by students whose documentation is now elsewhere. Most material listed is part of a single collection (ED).

RESEARCHER	LANGUAGE(S)
P. E. Goddard (PhD 1904, faculty 1901–1909)	Hupa, Kato, Mattole, Nongatl, Tolowa, Wailaki, Western Apache
Samuel A. Barrett (PhD 1908)	Coast Miwok, Klamath, Modoc, Nomlaki, Numu, Pomoan languages, Wasco, Yuki
T. T. Waterman (BA 1907, faculty 1910–1921)	Kumeyaay, Luiseño, Lushootseed, Makah, Otomi, Sahaptin, Tubatulabal, Yana, Yurok
Juan Dolores (chapter 6)	Numu, Tohono O'odham
J. Alden Mason (PhD 1911)	Mutsun, Salinan, Tohono O'odham
E. W. Gifford (curator and faculty, 1912–1955)	Colorado River Numic, Eastern Pomo, Hupa, Karuk, Mono, Sierra Miwok, Wiyot, Yavapai
L. S. (Nancy) Freeland (PhD student 1916–)	Eastern Pomo, Karuk, Nisenan, Shasta, Sierra Miwok
Paul Radin (faculty 1918–1920)	Wappo
Grace Dangberg (BA ca. 1919)	Washo
Lucille Hooper (MA 1920)	Cahuilla
Gladys Reichard (visiting PhD student 1922–1923)	Wiyot
Anna Gayton (PhD 1928, faculty 1948–1965)	Mono, Nisenan, Yokuts
Ronald Olson (PhD 1929, faculty 1931–1956)	Bella Bella, Haisla, K'wak'wala, Tsimshian
Paul-Louis Faye (PhD 1930)	Cupeño, Maidu
Cora Du Bois (PhD 1932)	Tututni
Isabel Kelly (PhD 1932)	Coast Miwok, Colorado River Numic
Charles Voegelin (PhD 1932)	Tubatulabal
Erminie Wheeler-Voegelin (MA 1931)	Tubatulabal
Abraham Halpern (PhD student 1935–1936)	Quechan (Yuma), Pomoan languages
Omer Stewart (PhD 1939)	Pomoan languages
George Foster (PhD 1941, faculty 1953–1979)	Huchnom, Yuki
Arden King (PhD 1947)	Maidu
William Elmendorf (PhD 1949)	Twana
William Hohenthal (PhD 1951)	Tipai
George Grace (researcher 1951–1952)	Luiseño
Mary Jean Kennedy (PhD 1955)	Karuk, Kashaya

linguistics, where a tradition of language documentation that he brought to California in 1900 continues in the twenty-first century. Though retired, he was a founding member of that department. He advocated for the establishment at Berkeley of a Survey of California Indian Languages to record information about the state's languages and publish a series of dictionaries, grammars, and texts. At the same time, Kroeber was organizing Karuk, Luiseño, Mojave, Yokuts, and Yurok text and language materials for eventual publication—a kind of work that would be his primary legacy.

"GATHERING OUR WORDS"

In November 2008, I was visiting a Yurok elder in Hoopa. Our purpose was language documentation, but I knew he was in poor health and I would probably not see him again. I wanted to spend time with him because of an emotional connection I felt too shy to express. I have felt connections with all six Yurok elders I was privileged to work with between 2001 and 2013, but each evoked a different emotional resonance. It sounds oddly unemotional to put it this way, but with *'aawokw* Glenn Moore I felt a scholarly or intellectual bond, as if what connected us was curiosity about his language, how it was patterned and used, and what it expressed about Yurok lifeways. Kind to a younger, ignorant visitor, he was more interested in writing and reading Yurok than most other fluent speakers; and he was committed to getting things right. Glenn was an authority on place names, boats, and vocabulary of direction and location, among other topics. We were recording language for places and travel:

> *Pechkue soonekw laas.*
> A trail (*laas*) goes upriver (*pechkue*).
> *Wee'eeet 'o tepon' s'e'goh.*
> There's a madrone (*s'e'goh*) there (*wee'eeet 'o*).
> *Weet 'o telohpekw laas.*
> The trail forks there (*weet 'o*).

Only from Glenn were the Yurok verbs *soonekw* "it (a path) goes (in a specified direction)" and *telohpekw* "it (a path) forks" ever documented, and the syntactic constructions they are used in. From his discourse, it is also clear that Yurok deploys positional verbs, like *tepon'* "it (a tree or vertical object) is rooted (or fixed in place)," in existential constructions where the copula is used in English.

On that day a younger Yurok visitor had dropped by and was asking a lot of questions during our recording session. This was fine with me; my sense of such situations is that I am an outsider, and should defer to the choices of community members. But eventually Glenn got testy, and told his visitor to stop interrupting. I remember what he said, insistently: "*This is real important.*" I felt awkward then, unsure if it was so important, and thinking that Yurok people should have priority. Yet Glenn had made time for me, and obviously did feel that our work was critical.

I did not ask Glenn why he felt this; I let it pass. What I now believe is that he knew that what we did was for the long-term benefit of his people. Forced by colonialism and bigotry to set aside much of their language, they would eventually reclaim it. Researchers like Kroeber—like me—imagine an idealized benefit to "scholarship" or even "humanity," but our Native collaborators have often had a different perspective.

Why did Indigenous people choose to work with Kroeber and other anthropologists and linguists? Perhaps there are as many combinations of reasons as there were individual circumstances. Usually we cannot know the details now, a century or more later, but the documentary record affords glimpses. Sometimes a reason was financial, since Indigenous consultants were compensated for their time.[54] In her 1905 correspondence with Kroeber (ALK Box 18:27), Jeannette Horne (mentioned above) wrote about Karuk language work as a kind of job to be juggled with other employment. Other people described emotional satisfaction in the work. In his January 1902 Rumsen language notes, Kroeber wrote, "Maria Soto said she would dream of me because she had talked to me in the old language" (ALK Ctn 9:12, p. 41). I take that to express her pleasure in speaking a language she no longer regularly used.

In many cases, as I found with Glenn and other Yurok and Karuk elders, Indigenous people have worked with linguists or anthropologists in order to preserve knowledge for their communities. This is illustrated by a comment made by Kroeber's student George Foster (2000), recalling work in the late 1930s with Yuki elder Eben Tillotsen, who told him, "I want you to make sure you get this right because my children and grandchildren are going to know about this only if they read what you write." Foster observed, "I thought he had a very far-reaching view of the role of the anthropologist." Tillotsen understood that documentation was for his descendants, but an anthropologist had no clue.

A similar sentiment was expressed in 1980 by Middletown Rancheria elder James Knight, recording Lake Miwok with linguist Catherine Callaghan (Luthin 2002:340): "I'm putting what they told me a long time ago onto the tape.... My friends and relatives can listen and say, 'Yes, this is true.'" Indigenous culture bearers, as Herbert Luthin (2002:504) wrote, "have a keen sense of posterity when it comes to the work they do."

In 1901, given the vanishment idea, Kroeber cannot have thought his documentation would benefit Indigenous people. Even in 1959, when he expressed pleasure at a major accomplishment of Native American activism (chapter 9), he surely did not imagine the linguistic and cultural revivals that would follow his death. But he would probably have been pleased by the use of documentation he had helped create. In an undated letter, Theodora Kroeber told Ursula Le Guin about "a rather nice experience" Alfred Kroeber was having. The sound recordings he had made some fifty years earlier on wax cylinders were being transferred to tapes for easier access. In the newly revived linguistics department, "the sharp, highly trained specialists are working with Pa's invaluably early stuff.... It is exciting and a tremendous satisfaction to him" (ca. 1958, UKLG Box 65:5). This was not Indigenous language reclamation, but Kroeber would surely have been just as satisfied if he had lived long enough to witness that too.

Above I quoted Yurok elder Joy Sundberg: "There's lots of things that would not have been documented if it hadn't been for him." Others have expressed the same view. In discussing Mataviily's prescriptions for living, Mojave elder Robert Martin (1972), who had himself worked with Kroeber almost twenty years earlier (figure 5.3), mentioned Kroeber's early work:

> If it [Mataviily's advice] were printed, [it] would undoubtedly make a book as big as our bible ... but it has never been written, for in the day, the Mojave had no written language.... Dr. A. L. Kroeber saved fragments of tiny pieces of the long, long cycle of stories and songs, but as yet the cycles have not been translated and revealed to us. We know some of the words, but not the meanings.... The knowledge of Mojave, Mataviily['s] advice would have been lost had Mataviily not provided ways to preserve it.

Martin went on to speak about medicine men as keepers and interpreters of Mojave wisdom. One of his points was that in a historical era when this was threatened by anti-Indigenous educational and social policies, Kroeber "saved fragments" for later reclamation by those with cultural authority.

Ethnocidal forces had complex impacts. The linguist Mary Haas, who took a Berkeley position in 1943 and went on to direct the Survey of California Indian Languages until she retired in 1977, later recalled her language documentation in British Columbia, Louisiana, and Oklahoma in the 1930s (Markel and Haas 1984). The elders she learned from "couldn't understand" why she "would come and show an interest in their language when their own grandchildren wouldn't or their own children wouldn't." She added, perhaps with rose-tinted memory, that "they were only too happy to talk to you and tell you everything that they could remember, and teach you the language. They were always delighted." I take it that younger people were experiencing colonial alienation as an impact of genocide and ethnocide; elders hoped outsiders could help them preserve knowledge for posterity.

What Haas and Kroeber recorded now returns to communities. Tunica documentation created by Sesostrie Youchigant with Haas in the 1930s has been the basis for an active language reclamation program.[55] In California, writer and tribal leader Greg Sarris (2022:11) of Graton Rancheria described using similar material: "We offer prayers in languages we are relearning; we listen to songs found on wax cylinders in museums and university libraries." An excellent Patwin grammar by Lewis Lawyer (2021) is derived from the twentieth-century work of Kroeber and others. In celebrating this book's publication, the Yocha Dehe Wintun Nation Tribal Council called language "the basic building block of identity" (Holder 2021):

> This is as true now as it was back in the time when forces were seeking to exterminate our people by requiring our ancestors to attend schools where speaking Patwin was forbidden. This book represents a monumental step forward in reclaiming Patwin from those dark times, and we are thankful to the many people who have worked hard and risked much to keep ours a living language.

Documentary corpora also constitute cultural-heritage repositories whose full aesthetic and expressive significance is realized only in their

Figure 4.9
At the 2018 Breath of Life Archival Institute, language activists, learners, and teachers studied field notes and other material held in UC Berkeley archives to reclaim information about their languages. Photograph by Scott Braley.

original language, since culturally salient linguistic systems do not always survive language shift.[56]

Language is a central part of cultural revitalization for many activists. The American invasion was "like an apocalypse," in the words of Yurok language teacher James Gensaw Sr. (Hinton 2022:279). It left "a lot of deep wounds," he said. "It's not something that can be fixed in one generation or two generations. I think that all of us are working toward that healing. And I think the language plays an important role in that healing process." Gensaw's insight recalls Ngũgĩ wa Thiong'o's (1986:28) view that language use helps "transcend colonial alienation."

One family of reclamation projects is the Breath of Life model, developed in the 1990s as a collaboration between the Advocates for Indigenous California Language Survival and linguists at Berkeley, especially Leanne Hinton. Its motivation has been described by one of its creators, L. Frank Manriquez (2013): "We were trying to read and understand diacritical marks, working alone day in and night out. We were looking for language understanding, knowing that in the language we would find our people."

At Berkeley's Breath of Life Archival Institute, language activists, learners, and teachers spend a week working on their languages with material from the documentary corpora of Kroeber and his protégés and successors (see figure 4.9).[57] Two dozen language communities were represented in May 2022. Chochenyo cultural and language activist Vincent Medina (2014) eloquently described his experience at an earlier institute:

> The miraculous occurred when our sleeping language was reawakened. The words were relearned from those old archives, the dust was wiped away. The songs and voices of our ancestors were heard on those wax cylinder recordings, and the language became alive, nudged into consciousness and heard again. The words were given a second chance at life, and this is for me what the Breath of Life conference is about.

Esselen leader Louise Ramirez (2008–2009) said she "began thinking about my native language in 1997 with a Xeroxed copy of anthropologist Alfred L. Kroeber's notebook number 26. I felt so good reading those words, knowing that my ancestors could hear and understand me." Similarly, Rumsen artist and language activist Linda Yamane described using the notes of Kroeber and his contemporaries to learn her language (Hinton 2022:199): "It's not just words on a piece of paper, but it's saving something from the past that connects with people now." As Karuk language activist and teacher Crystal Richardson told me in 2020, referring to documentary collections at Berkeley, "We're gathering our words so we can take them home and use them with our families."

5

LANGUAGE AND LAND

> "Now I will show you how to speak. I want you to talk like this," he [Mastamho] said to the Chemehuevi. "I want you to speak like this," he said, and gave their language to the Walapai. "And I want you to speak like this," he said to the Yavapai. But he gave nothing to the Mohave as yet. Then he said: "Now it is all made. I have prepared it. You can go, you Walapai, and scatter into the mountains there. You need not go into one place. You can go all about, for I have made springs everywhere. You can live in one spot, and when you want to live in another you can do so. You Chemehuevi can do the same, and you Yavapai too. But I will do differently for the Mohave. They will have everything along the river: whatever grows there will be theirs."
>
> —Jo Nelson, Mastamho narrative, 1903

In October-November 1903, Kroeber's Mojave friend and interpreter Jack Jones visited San Francisco with elder Jo Nelson. On 16 October, Nelson told in Mojave (and Jones translated into English) a long creation narrative; an excerpt is shown in the opening epigraph.[1] Its themes have also been expressed by other Mojave people. In 1967, Robert Martin said the creator "gave men everything, even the language—told the people how to talk" (Crawford 1967:32). More recently, the creator's words were recounted by Llewellyn Barrackman (Peterson 2014): "I'm going to select you as my chosen people, and I'm going to put you along the river, and I'm going to call you *Pipa Aha Macav*." Barrackman translated this as "people who live along the water"—in the words of Mojave poet Natalie Diaz (2020:46), "the true name of our people, given to us by our Creator who / loosed the river from the earth and built it into our living bodies."

Accounts such as Nelson's would have informed Kroeber's sense of the links among language, land, and identity among California cultures.

Certain land along the Colorado River is said to belong to the Mojave people, who speak the Mojave language; other lands belong to other people, who speak their own languages. Such a relationship between Indigenous people and their lands was also emphasized by Yurok leader Robert Spott, and would have been a point of discussion in many communities that Kroeber visited.

In this chapter, I describe two aspects of Kroeber's documentary legacy that go beyond just language. One is the large number of Indigenous oral histories collected under his supervision, including accounts of daily life in the nineteenth and early twentieth centuries. The other is his copious documentation of Mojave, Yurok, and other place-names and their social meanings. What links these culturally significant aspects of Kroeber's legacy is how they emerged from storytelling. Kroeber's commitment to text documentation—recording stories—made space for Indigenous people to talk about what mattered, even if it was not what Kroeber might have meant to ask about. In the cases discussed here, this led to a rich corpus of first-person accounts of lived experience and detailed maps of the Indigenous landscape.

RECLAIMING HISTORY

Reclaiming History is the subtitle of a book by Wailacki-Concow historian William Bauer, *California through Native Eyes* (2016), which tells a striking history by animating and contextualizing stories from a remarkable documentary resource. In 1935–1936, Kroeber sent three students to different areas of California, where they worked with the State Emergency Relief Administration (and after August 1935 the federal Works Progress Administration) to hire Native people to interview elders in their communities. Participants were paid 50¢–75¢ an hour, often working thiry-hour weeks.[2] Kroeber secured the funding and planned the project, whose goals were "to provide as much relief as possible to Indians who need it"—especially elderly people, he wrote—and "to have them do work which will be genuinely useful" (9 April 1935, RDA Box 134). The students (each organizing the work of up to forty participants) were to send him progress reports every other day "at least for the first couple of weeks" (13 June 1935, RDA Box 134), and did indeed correspond with Kroeber about many details throughout the duration of the project.[3]

One student, Abraham Halpern, went to the Fort Yuma Indian Reservation in southeastern California for documentation of Quechan, a sibling of Mojave. Kroeber told the government that such work "saves for permanent preservation the vanishing data on the history of part of the native American race," knowledge that "passes irrevocably if not now recorded in writing." The Quechan Tribal Council chairman indicated that elders "are extremely reticent toward divulging secrets, and feel that they have all too often been betrayed by research students," but that tribal leaders "are deeply concerned in seeing the primitive language and traditions preserved." At Fort Yuma, Halpern documented Quechan language and texts and taught community members to do the same. The younger participants whose work he coordinated and mentored variously focused on topics like mesquite vocabulary, the names of mountains and geographical features, and basketry language. After two or three months, the council expressed its "enthusiasm" and asked that the work be continued.[4]

Halpern's work did continue, though the program funding it ended; he wrote a PhD thesis about Quechan at the University of Chicago. And it was a lifelong interest, even after Halpern left anthropology and linguistics. In 1976, almost forty years later, he returned to begin a new community-based documentation project with dozens of elders. Published outcomes of this collaboration include three significant collections of Quechan texts.[5]

Two other students, Frank Essene and Frederick Hulse, went to eastern and northern California to arrange oral histories and ethnographic interviews. These yielded thousands of manuscript pages whose contents were determined and written down by Indigenous people. They document creation stories and traditional narratives; precolonial lifeways, including dances, hunting, food collecting and preparation, and travel, and changes after colonization; Indigenous language, especially the names of places, animals, and plants; and memorable experiences ranging from the happy (children, family life, celebrations) to the traumatic (killing, ethnic cleansing, rape). They have informed historical analysis and have been used by communities repatriating knowledge.[6] Many await detailed study.

Here I focus on stories from Paiute and Shoshone elders in Owens Valley. Some of them spoke Timbisha Shoshone, but most spoke what linguists call Mono, whose eastern dialect is Owens Valley Paiute (see

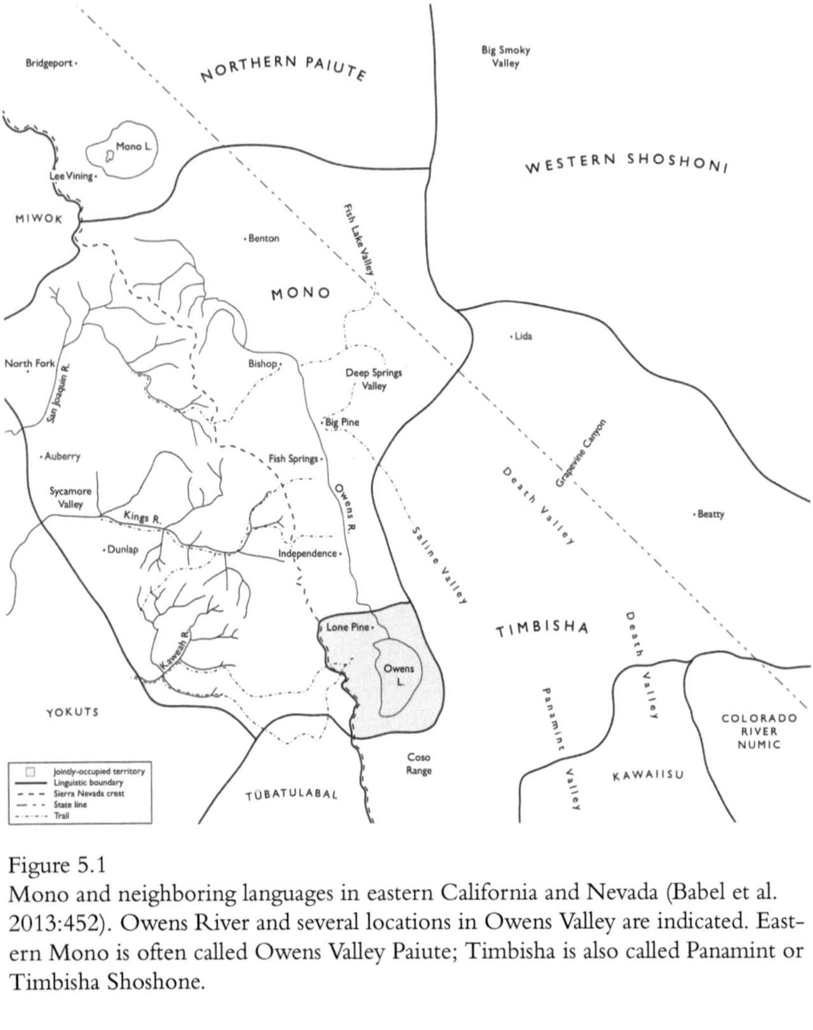

Figure 5.1
Mono and neighboring languages in eastern California and Nevada (Babel et al. 2013:452). Owens River and several locations in Owens Valley are indicated. Eastern Mono is often called Owens Valley Paiute; Timbisha is also called Panamint or Timbisha Shoshone.

figure 5.1). Those who translated and transcribed their stories were often family members. Topics were suggested, from "Myths and Legends" to "when the old men were young," but the details were up to participants. Unlike work that mainly answers questions of interest to anthropologists and linguists, what emerged in this project was a record of what community members chose to share. Its eighty-six notebooks (6,211 pages) constitute a unique documentary corpus, complementing the contemporary anthropological canon.[7]

The contents of these notebooks are mostly creation stories, other traditional narratives, and descriptions of sociocultural practices. Language itself was even the subject of a creation story, told by Hank Hunter to Philip Buff, about a "stranger who gave the Indians in this valley their language" (ED 208.4). The stranger arranged that "Paiute is heard" from Round Valley (a dozen miles east of Bishop) to Lone Pine; starting at Owens Lake, "the language of the Shoshone Indians is taught." He was "not yet satisfied" and "decided some change ought to be made, so he begins to divide the Paiute Indians of this valley" into dialects. Therefore "the pronunciation of some words is different" in Round Valley, Big Pine, and other places to the south. In short, Hunter told Buff, the stranger "said that the Indians throughout the valley will not talk their language the same. According [to] the Indians, he was the linguist of his time."

Stories are a central part of the life revealed in the corpus. Mary Cornwell and Jim Jones vividly depicted the space and time afforded to story telling as a social activity:

> [Cornwell, ED 213.2:] When we decided where we would stay for the winter, the men would get together to make a large hut. Here everyone gathered to listen to the stories told by the elders. All the children would listen. Stories were told all during the winter.

> [Jones, ED 211.1:] Some times these stories were so long that it took two or three nights to tell them. It did not matter if the person who told the story were a man or woman, but it must be some elder person. I used to listen to these stories as the rest of them, and to the one that is to tell the story. He was not to be paid in money, but food, usually pine nut gravy with some sort of meat to go with it. This he would eat whenever he grew hungry from telling the stories. And then begin in telling his story on. There in the middle of the one room there was a fire going so everyone would be warm. These storytelling gatherings were held quite often in this one large room throughout the winter until early spring.

Mary Harry said that "a person should not tell legends to youngsters in the summer" because rattlesnakes "might bite them." Stories should be told in the winter when snakes are hibernating (ED 213.3).

Narratives of life experiences also make up a substantial part of this corpus. Twenty-nine elders told such stories, which range in length from a single page to Jim Jones's four-notebook autobiography.[8] Jones and some other elders in 1935 were children before the most intense conflicts with American settlers and soldiers in the first half of the 1860s. They began their life stories with childhood memories of precolonial lifeways.

Food and its preparation were salient in such memories. One elder's story began, "I, Mary Cornwell, was born in Mono County, somewhere near Crooked Creek, in Long Valley. I grew up eating what I was fed" (ED 213.2). She went on to name some of her main childhood foods. A notable food practice, detailed by her and by Jennie Newlan (ED 213.1), was gathering and preparing Pandora pinemoth caterpillars.[9] This appears prominently at the outset of Jones's biography (ED 211.1):

> I was born at Pague Who [*paggwihuu*] (Fish Stream) in Long Valley, Mono County, California. The Indians there lived mostly on fish, pine-nuts, and piegue [*piagü*]. The piegue is a large worm that lives on the bull-pine trees. The people gathered these worms in the summer about the time the sun goes south again [the solstice]. . . . My father and mother dug trenches about three [feet] deep around the trees. When the worms get fat they come down from the trees. Then they are trapped in the deep ditch around the tree. We gather them up and throw them into a willow basket. A big fire is made and spread out to make the ground underneath hot. The women pour the worms into the hot ashes. This kills the worms. They are covered with hot ashes and left there for a while. We take them from ashes. When they [are] cold the women clean all the ashes, sticks, and dirt from them. A winnowing basket was used for this. They are stored in a large hole and are covered with pine needles. Late in the fall, we go back there and dig up our worms. They are cured and ready to eat during the long cold winter. My mother cooked these worms in a pot made of clay.

Hulse wrote dismissively about such childhood memories (to Kroeber, 14 July 1935, RDA Box 74): "The old people repeat, again and again, that in those days there was enough to eat, and that it tasted good—it's rather pitiful." From a student more interested in physical anthropology, this shows a lack of awareness both of how quotidian details organize experience and of the impact of the destruction of Indigenous foodways.

Many of the oral histories in this corpus were structured by family, social relations, and social networks within and outside of Owens Valley. The nineteenth-century Paiute social landscape included caring for the elderly, orphans, widows, and neighbors and relatives in need.

For example, Mamie Gregory told Esther Checo about a frail old woman whose daughter carried her on her back and fed her, and who was later bedridden and aphasic (ED 212.11). Others shared childhood experiences of losing parents to illness, injury, or winter weather, and being raised or taught by other relatives. Such stories reinforce social values and norms of caring.

Dee Lacey began the "Story of my Life" (ED 212.7) by speaking about the illness and death of her mother. Afterward, Lacey's father used to take her fishing. He stunned small fish with a "certain kind of weed" that he mashed, and the two would gather fish floating on the surface. The "ladies [would] come over and put the fish in a basket and take them home," mashing or mixing them with seeds for "a big party." Or her father went out to pick certain insects that "live on green grass." The young ones they would eat; the old ones he would dry for winter. In the summer they would go into the mountains to fish and gather certain larger insects. Throughout Lacey's story, she emphasized activities that looked forward to the whole year and that brought connections with family and other community members.

Other stories documented relationships far beyond Owens Valley. For example, Jim Jones captured an eagle as a pet (ED 211.1):

> I caught this one young little baby eagle one day when his mother eagle was off hunting. I climb up on the high cliff to where the nest was. About the time I reach the nest she must saw me from far off and she made for me. I already got the little baby eagle. The mother eagle charge at me few time. She flew very close to my head few time, but she didn't hit me. I manage to get down to the ground with the little eagle in my arm.

Jones fed it rabbits, squirrels, and lizards that he himself caught.

> I tied him up when he got big. He used to stay around the house. When he saw me coming he know I had something for him to eat. He make noise like any other bird when you going to feed. Then me and my folk started for west. I took my eagle and keep him in basket. Just like my mother would to her little baby or any other woman would do to her baby. And I pack this eagle on my back. This eagle was fully grown by this time and he was quite [a] load to pack, but sometime my father would pack him.

Their trip west ended on the other side of the Sierra Nevada, where Jones's father asked him if he wished to sell his pet. He decided to do so;

Mono people valued eagle feathers. Jones also learned that Mono people went as far as the ocean for dentalium and other shells. Paiute people thus took part in social and trade networks that spanned the width of California; growing up included learning about these.

Enculturation patterns continued under colonial rule. Willie Goodale was born in 1866, after the worst atrocities in the US treatment of Paiute people. He told Guy Milton (ED 210.5) about a childhood in which cultural values were learned in a life centered on the waters of Owens Valley:

> When I was a young boy my father taught me to swim by carrying me on his back across the river. [He taught me] to be kind to everyone. My father took me down to the slews, which are now dry, and located east of Fort Independence & the aqueduct. There I was taught to fish and gather oysters during the spring, then early in the fall we made our camp in the mountains, hunting deer. My father left me home because I was still small. We stayed in the mountains long enough to kill two or three and dried them for the winter. Then we came to back to Fort [Independence]. The white soldiers were here then. My father used to chop wood for them.

The Los Angeles Aqueduct (completed in 1913) diverted water from Owens Lake and desiccated a valley that Paiute people had cultivated and irrigated for centuries. A verdant marvel became a parched realm of sagebrush.

The first nineteenth-century white people in Owens Valley inspired only occasional anecdotes in these narratives. For example, John Alston's "Old Happenings at Deep Springs Valley" (told to his grandson Roy Bacock, ED 151) began with the story of a white man who came one winter and cannibalized his dead traveling partner's frozen body before later freezing to death himself. This stands out as a lurid tale of depravity—the traveler offered human flesh to the Paiute people, though he could instead have asked them for food—perhaps highlighting what it meant to live outside social norms, or foreboding what was to come.[10]

The Owens Valley invasion was brutal even by US standards.[11] The gold rush brought miners to the area in 1859, followed by ranchers whose cattle destroyed Paiute food and intricate irrigation systems. If cattle died from eating wild parsnip, Indigenous people might take the meat; occasionally they killed livestock for food. Then, as Jim Jones told Billy

Williams (ED 211.4), the invaders "became angry and begin to make war on us. Also by this time there kept coming into the valley more white people." Mattie Bulpitt explained to Lee Warlie (ED 154.5):

> The Indians were very friendly. . . . Nearly all plants that produce seed were the Indians' food, from the little seed to the taboose [*tüpüsi*, a tuber (Lawton et al. 1976:33–36)], yet they never complain when they see these horses and cattle roam over them; they used to irrigate these fields. Eventually the white man begin to tell the Indian what to do. They told them not to pick the seed, and he says that seed they pick from plant will not make them grow, and when they go out to irrigate their seed beds, the white man says don't take any of the water.

Later, she said, white people were "using force to keep the Indians from harvesting the seed," and finally they "told the Indians where to go."

Dorothy Cragen (1975:56–57) has described what can only be called genocidal policies and practices in Owens Valley. The commander of US forces at Fort Independence in 1863 instructed soliders to "shoot on sight and show no mercy." Soldiers were sent out to destroy all food that Indian people were storing or cultivating. In May 1863, four men from one company "destroyed 300 bushels of seeds (pine nuts and taboose) cached in the vicinity of Bishop Creek, and they kept no count of the number of Indians killed." And Mary Harry was not alone in recalling that soldiers would rape Paiute women when they encountered them (ED 205.1)—a government-sponsored terror campaign.

When soldiers came to one village, Charlie Wrinkle told Esther Checo (ED 212.9), the chief asked "why they had come to the village. The soldiers said they come to kill them." On another occasion, according to Dave Yandell (ED 154.6), Indigenous people were marched to a natural mountainside enclosure near Owens Lake:

> Here they rounded them into this place, and there they huddle[d] together, not knowing what to do next. Then the soldier[s] spread out to cover every escape. At the signal from the officer in charge [they] fired on the huddle[d] group of Indian, men and women. At the first volley they howled with pain, but volley after volley were fired on them. They shrieked in death agony. Others ran here and there seeking refuge, then in desperation they ran toward the firing soldier[s] and broke through [the] firing line and escaped. Many escaped and many more were slaughtered.

The vast majority of the violence was intentionally and systematically perpetrated by the invaders, but there was also violence in reaction. "White people were not treating the Indians right and the Indians finally got tired of it," as John Shepard put it. Once, he told Roy Bellas (ED 212.3), a group of "warriors" came to George Stephson's house. They knocked "to ask the woman for something to eat." When she locked the door, "the Indians got mad. They set a fire to the cabin and went away." Mrs. Stephson and two children died. When Stephson found their burned bodies, he went in search of the culprits. He could not catch them, finding instead an unrelated group: "an old man carry[ing] his grandchild, two women and one young boy." Stephson and his associates shot and killed the old man and his grandchild. The boy started to run away, but the white men grabbed the women and told them "to call the boy back, for if they don't they will get killed." One was his mother, who obeyed, telling her son he would not be harmed. When the boy came back, Shepard said, "the white man shot him [in] front of his mother. The boy died." The women were released.

The most infamous US action in Owens Valley was the forced removal of more than nine hundred Indigenous people to Fort Tejon and the Sebastian Indian Reservation in San Joaquin Valley.[12] This brutal 225-mile march took eleven days in July 1863, in the middle of the summer; many died en route, some escaped, and 850 people reached the destination. Over the next couple of years most or all returned home, hiking across the Sierra Nevada (or perishing in the attempt). All this history figures in many narratives.

Indian people were tricked into removal. News was circulated that they should come to Fort Independence, where the United States was going to make peace and give them land, food, and clothing. Several years of conflict, killings, and destruction of land and property had created desperate circumstances. Many felt they had no choice; others did not believe the American promise. For example, Mary Harry's family met "to discuss if they were to . . . settle at Fort Independence, and receive food, clothes, etc. . . . They discussed their plan and said that they would stay here" (ED 152.4).[13]

Those who went included Jim Jones's family (ED 211.4). They had few resources: "After all of our food and homes burned to the ground by these white soldiers there was nothing left for us. We had to do the best we could digging roots, seeds and the other wild food which we know." An Indigenous ally of the military, José Chico, urged them "to go down to the fort and sign up our names, so that we shall have our own land to live on. That we would be given food and clothing." But at Fort Independence about a thousand Indian people were disarmed, put in a corral, and surrounded by armed guards. Then, said elder Susie Westerville, they knew they would be "driven away from their home, a home which they lived in for generations" (ED 208.2). Jones remembered Chico saying that the "white soldier[s] want to take all of you people to better country" with good clothing and good food. These promises sounded fine, but "Chico lied. We didn't know him. I am sorry we didn't kill him. He put us Indians in awful trouble. Our old men and women died of hardship on the desert."

When the march began, Westerville said, the "line of men and women and children strung out for two and [a] half mile[s] long." Jones recalled that "some of the people start crying, tell one another they going kill us." They did not fight because "the soldiers might start killing women and children." Some escaped. For instance, according to Westerville, "the whites drove the Indians through a swamp where tule plants and marshes were thick. In that place dozens and dozens of Indians hid among the tules in the marshes laying in the water under plants seen in swampy places."

For those who could not escape, the journey was brutal. Mattie Bulpitt recalled that "we were all scared to death" (ED 154.7):

> I stayed right with my mother and run along side of her. Sometimes my parents would have to carry me on their backs when I got tired. So it was no fun for me. Some women folks lost their babies. They didn't have time to stop to bury them, so they just leave it on top of sage brushes, left it there to the coyotes. My grandmother was killed then because she couldn't go any further. She was very tired. . . . So she got sort of weak and tried to cry for pity but the soldiers shot her and stab her with their swords and left her there to die.

Rape was routine, according to Jones:

> When night would come they stop us for the night. . . . Some of the soldiers would take the young women to their wagon houses and sleep with our young women. If the girl don't want to go the soldiers would drag her anyway. We was all afraid to say any[thing] or start anything. . . . The soldiers

> do lot dirty things to us people. I will never forget. I could not under[stand] English or talk English [at] that time.

Once, John Shepard told Roy Bellas (ED 212.2), soldiers stopped at a homestead. After talking with a young settler couple, a soldier "came over where the Indians were" and gave the settlers a "young Indian girl" before resuming the march. What was perhaps the same event was also recalled by Sam Newland (Steward 1934:437): "We met a white man at his ranch who wanted to adopt an Indian orphan. We gave him a child of six or seven years."

The authorities were not well prepared for the new arrivals. Needless to say, the promised utopia was a mirage. It left some positive memories, to be sure, like camping "among oak trees," absent in Owens Valley, and "the first watermelon I ever tasted and I sure enjoy it" (Ben Tibbits, ED 152.3). But many experiences recalled by survivors seventy years later were traumatic. They lived in fear of being shot or relocated again, according to Westerville, who witnessed disease and death when "measles broke out among the poor Indians." Many died "without receiving a single treatment." Feverish, some "would run and jump into the lake nearby to cool their bodies" and "instead would meet death." Every day, she said, "wagon loads of dead bodies were hauled away." Even as the exaggerated memory of a terrorized child, this was surely grounded in truth.

Devastating as the American invasion was, many narratives in this corpus focused on creativity, persistence, and connection. An example is the life story of Mary Harry told to Tom Stone (ED 152.4). She was born in Chalfant, 14 miles north of Bishop, but grew up at Oasis in Fish Lake Valley, near the Nevada border, where her parents moved after her grandfather's death "to forget their elderly relative." As a girl, she learned about basketry from her grandmother and her mother, with whom she went gathering:

> She never liked the idea of others gather[ing] more than she does. She tr[ied] her best to get more than others. Her idea was to race and beat the others. And later she learn[ed] to make her own baskets of all kinds. At first her grandmother taught her how. But however she learn[ed] soon. She thought it was [a] high honor to help [her] mother gather seed and make baskets.... Later when she became older she was then able to make her own baskets.

She became a well-known weaver (see figure 5.2 for one of her baskets).

Figure 5.2
Mary Harry, twined basketry hat (PAHMA 1-26991).

As noted above, Harry's family avoided the forced march to Fort Tejon. After the upheaval of the 1860s, they "used to hear of the events that went on in different parts of the valley. Then later on Mary and her family migrated to Deep Springs where her husband work[ed] at the Deep Springs Ranch, for a man named Gilbert, and he was very kind to Mary & her family." In subsequent years they lived in Big Pine and Fish Springs. They had "a wagon and horse," and later went "back to points in Fish Lake Valley to gather Indian foods." Harry's account ended on a positive note: "At present she still lives in Big Pine, still in good health, and her son is at Giroux Ranch in Fish Lake Valley. Her age is probably nearing the century mark, but she has some bright years ahead of her yet." She died six years later, in 1942. Hers is just one of many rich life stories documented through Kroeber's 1935–1936 project.

Overall, three aspects of the documentary corpus created in this project seem especially significant to me. One is its scope. The Owens Valley part of the corpus alone has six thousand manuscript pages created by dozens of Indigenous people. The "same" cultural practices, historical events, and traditional narratives appear in multiple versions, from multiple points of view, and with details absent in other sources.

A second is the inclusion of information about life and language since colonization. Some historical events have been mentioned above; others include the deadly 1872 Owens Valley earthquake, which was larger than all but one later California quake and was recalled in several oral histories. As for language, some oral histories included incidental Indigenous-language vocabulary or even word lists. For example, Esther Checo recorded five pages of Timbisha vocabulary from Charlie Wrinkle (ED 212.10, pp. 66–70). Included are many terms for objects ignored in memory documentation but important for daily life in the 1930s (e.g., "clock," "clothes line," "frying pan," "needle," "radio," and kinds of clothes). Some are in Jon Dayley's (1989) Timbisha dictionary (e.g., *kottoonnümpu* "stove," *siiya* "saddle"), but some are not (e.g., "chaps," "phonograph").

A third compelling aspect of this corpus reflects its Native authorship. Kroeber and others of his era described cultures as trait assemblages, often disassembling them into inventories: child-rearing, creation stories, food, hunting, kinship, magic, toponyms, weaving, and so on. Studies of Paiute culture used the disassembled-inventory style despite being based on information from many of the same elders who participated in the 1935–1936 project, describing the same cultural traits.[14] But in the corpus of stories in their own voices, Indigenous people made their own meaning to depict their cultures and experiences.

For example, as noted above, food and its collection and preparation played a role in many stories of childhood. Typically identified were the parents, grandparents, or others from whom practices were learned. These stories are also replete with accounts of caring for others in the community, and year-round planning for bitter winters (the Owens Valley floor is 4,000 feet above sea level). Such planning included travel for multiple purposes, which meant interacting with a dispersed set of people. Narratives like Jim Jones's about a pet eagle thus reinforce the sense of obligation in broader social networks. Even stories of amoral or immoral white people (a householder who refuses to offer food, a cannibal, outright killers) underscore relational norms by exposing deviation from them. In short, as I read them, the stories in this collection are often about the social worlds of their tellers and the moral networks that connect individuals. These add meaning, a glue, often absent in early ethnographic dissection.

NAMING YUROK LAND

In northwestern California, Yurok toponymy is well known from T. T. Waterman's *Yurok Geography* (1920). Based on work by Kroeber and Waterman, this book catalogs more than a thousand names of places, including locations in the natural world, habitation sites, and houses (households), with detailed discussion of overall patterns. Extensive additional information is present in J. P. Harrington's notes, while Kroeber and Waterman recorded further toponyms after the completion of the latter's book manuscript.[15] An expansion and modernization of the book would serve cultural reclamation. Many names fell out of use during the twentieth century, as elsewhere in North America, but toponymy remains of great local interest. Today, when many Yurok people do not speak their language, one of the first things students learn is how to name the villages their families come from.

I illustrate the Yurok toponymic repertoire from Kroeber's field notes. His consultants named and mapped dozens of locations, especially on the Pacific coast, near Rek'woy (Requa) at the mouth of the Klamath River, and at Wechpues (Weitchpec) near the upriver boundary of Yurok land. These include all the Yurok villages, such as 'O Rek'w (Orick) and Rek'woy, both of whose names mean "(at the) river mouth," and others like Chahpekw and Wehlkwew, whose names are opaque. Consultants often shared explanations of names and associated cultural information. Common formal elements in Yurok toponyms include the locative preverb *'o*, usually with a verb ("where such-and-such happens"), and the iterative infix *-eg-* or one of its allomorphs, indicating a habitual property.[16]

Many names are based on landscape features. Names like 'O Chaahl in this list are in common use, and even 'O S'o is documented as the name of another place elsewhere (Waterman 1920:B63):

- Ha'aag 'O Kloh "where rock overhangs" (RS, 1933, 12:34, p. 6)
- 'O Chaahl "where it's sandy" (RS, 1933, 12:34, p. 42): a house in the village of Wehlkwew on the south side of the Klamath River mouth
- 'O Menuel' "where water backs up" (RS, 1941, 12:41, p. 14): the village at the mouth of Wilson Creek, north of Rek'woy
- 'O S'o "where it's red-brown" (JW, 1907, 12:23, p. 37), opposite the mouth of Blue Creek, so called "because [of] a reddish slide near top" of the hill

- 'O Teekwteekwohl "where there's a lot of sliding" (RS, 1940, 12:39, p. 49): a house north of Rek'woy, "so called bec[ause] close to lake, sand washed or caved sometimes near to house"

Some natural characteristics other than visual appearance are reported:

- Ha'aag 'O Chweeegeen "where a rock speaks" (RS, 1941, 12:41, p. 25): an "overhanging rock with echo"
- 'O Sue' "where it splashes" (RS, 1941, 12:41, p. 24): a rock one "can walk out to at low tide," so called "because spray when high tide surf hits concave front"

An animal or plant may be a place's salient characteristic:

- 'Er Lergerh "where there are potatoes" (GM, 1902, 12:18, p. 78): an ocean rock (False Klamath Rock) with "Indian potatoes in abundance"
- Hee'nk'elohl "at the white oak" (MJ, 1902, 12:18, p. 62)
- Hlmeyep'eer 'Wo-'Ol' "rattlesnake house" (RS, 1939, 12:47): "a big rock [at Serperh] where there is a rattlesnake den"
- Kego'sneg 'O Leguuek "where there are seagull babies" (RS, 1941, 12:41, p. 24): a place where seagulls nest
- K'err' 'O Chyeguuek'w "where crows sit" (RS, 1941, 12:41, p. 14): a bluff overlooking False Klamath Cove

The names above are mostly *environmental*, in the typology of David Harris and Gary Holton (2018:128), "describing the geographic, environmental, or biological features of a place."

Other names index various sociocultural practices. They are *functional*, describing the use of a place:

- 'O Leeegoo "where they holler" (RS, 1941, 12:41, p. 25): a "rock [people] stood on & hollered from, praying aloud"
- Pekwon 'O 'Elew "where acorn-pounding baskets hang" (RS, 1939, 12:38, p. 2): an "acorn ground, uphill from Kep'el-Sa'a in a gully"
- Tmery 'We-Roy "cut-off, half-way creek" (RS, 1941, 12:41, p. 25), so called "because in salmon ceremony can't eat fish caught below, is the dividing line" (at Rek'woy along the Klamath River)
- Wenchokws Hehlkue 'O Legem' "where women go inland" (RS, 1933, 12:34, p. 15), an ocean rock north of the Klamath: "Women who did not like long sea-voyage, or feared passing Klamath bar, walked

ahead to here, embarked there. . . . Always calm in rough weather at this rock."

Sociocultural exigencies can lead to dense toponymy. In 1939, Robert Spott identified adjacent spots on the Klamath River at Wechpues, and the rock that separates them (12:36, p. 6):

- Mewolep' 'O Wegesah "where the dance officiant bathes": a "little eddy between 2 rocks. No profane swimming there, though there is just above."
- 'O Kegep "where they swim": the ordinary swimming place, a section of the river just upriver from the preceding
- 'O Teguuek "where they dive": a "rock from which [they] jump off to swim," separating the two preceding areas of water

Locally dense toponymies are also documented at Rek'woy and Chuerey (Trinidad), among other places.

A routine question in place-name documentation is whether an expression is a conventionalized toponym or a nonce descriptive term. Kroeber's and Waterman's consultants regularly gave explanations of names, as is unnecessary for descriptive terms.[17] Further evidence of conventionalization is that the same terms were reported by multiple people.

Many places are named after events that happened in the era before humans came into the world:

- Ch'uy 'O Sreyr' "where a digging stick slid" (GM, 1902, 12:18, p. 85): "A digging stick escaped from two women who were taking out brodiaeas from the top of a rock and it left a mark where it slid down the face of the rock" (13:2)
- Huueks 'O Rek' "where children sit" (Waterman 1920:E76), a boulder in the river: "Some owls once carried off some children and sat them here. They . . . finally turned into rock."
- Pahtekws 'O Tek "where a storage basket sits" (WF, 1901, 12:13, p. 57): "a rock, hollow on top," which was "thrown there by someone at Kenek"
- Poykoh 'O Lepon "where they left a pan" (GM, 1902, 12:18, p. 85): "You can see the rocks now, where they left it; it stands from in the water, high up"

- Wohkelo' 'O Tep "where a pepperwood stands" (12:41, p. 25): this rock "used to be a very small pepperwood (is green patch there)"

Despite their environmental aspect (they often explain the look of a place), such names cannot be seen as purely descriptive terms.

Referring to places on the Columbia plateau, Eugene Hunn (1996:18) wrote, "What gets named in Sahaptin are *places where things happen*, places where people fish, gather roots and berries, hunt, and camp." He argued that "plotting the distribution of named places in Sahaptin is one means to appreciate the ecological niche occupied by local Indian peoples." This ecological account is valid for Yurok as far as it goes, but Yurok place-name are also associated with prehuman events, the creation of the world, and spiritual and imaginative life. Perhaps an apter characterization is J. J. Egli's, as paraphrased by Boas (1934:9): "Geographical names, being an expression of the mental character of each people and each period, reflect their cultural life and the line of development belonging to each cultural area." Similarly, Andrew Cowell and Alonzo Moss Sr. (2003:384) have described Arapaho patterns as "specific indigenous modes of naming and thinking about the landscape, with a particular cognitive basis in the culture." The corpus of Yurok toponyms is more than a gazeteer: it is a cultural atlas whose entries index a world of salient meanings.

The use of directional terms in Yurok place-name illustrates the link between cognition and cultural experience. Yurok lacks cardinal direction terms analogous to English *north*. As in many languages of the Pacific coast, riverine orientation terms are instead used for spatial reference: upstream, downstream, uphill, downhill, and across the water. Such systems have been described and analyzed in language typology and cognitive psychology.[18] The Yurok system itself was briefly portrayed by Kroeber (1925:15): "A house has its door not at its 'western' but its 'downstream' corner. A man is told to pick up a thing that lies 'upstream' from him, not on his 'left.' " Such terms pervade Yurok toponymy, as in the following examples:

- Kenek Puel "downstream from Kenek" (CS, 1901, 12:10, p. 62): a village
- 'O Chepor Won "above 'O Chepor (a village at Bluff Creek)" (WF, 1902, 12:15, p. 88): the "name of Sheldon's Butte"

- 'O Men Heepuer "a little downstream (i.e., upcoast) from 'O Men" (RS, 1941, 12:41, p. 14): a village
- Serperh Heekoh "across from Serperh" (WF, 1901, 12:13, p. 49)
- Serperh Pech "upstream from Serperh" (CS, 1901, 12:10, p. 60): a village site
- Wehl Heepech "a little upstream from Wehlkwew" (RS, 1933, 12:34, p. 42): the upstream house at Wehlkwew

Smaller settlements are routinely named as "across," "downstream," or "upstream" from larger ones. "Above" them are gathering, hunting, ceremonial, and spiritual places in the hills.

Yurok toponyms thus structure key facets of sociocultural experience; learning them would be a pillar of enculturation. A Berkeley child in 2022 grows up with schools named after King, Muir, and Washington and streets like Oxford, San Pablo, Shattuck, and University, echoes of Europe and non-Indigenous America (including descendants of settlers and enslaved people). Parts of the city are called North, South, and West Berkeley. On Yurok land, Indigenous toponyms reinforce a very different cognitive and sociocultural map. Its effects can be inferred from testimony elsewhere in western North America. For example, in 2008, Nicholi Carltikoff Sr., Olga Balluta, and Okzenia Delkettie spoke about Alaskan toponyms in their language, Dena'ina (Evanoff 2010:15): "Everywhere you go, it brings back memories of what happened there. It's like markers of all the places and what we did, you think about what happened there and who was there before."

TRAVERSING MOJAVE LAND

In southeastern California lie the Mojave Desert and Colorado River. Along what Kroeber (1925:726) called "this enormous Nile," he began documenting the Mojave language in 1900. Like Quechan, Mojave is part of the Yuman family; Kroeber worked with this language in two periods.

In the first period, from 1900 to 1910, Kroeber recorded texts, songs, and a range of linguistic and cultural information. The corpus that emerged in this period includes seventeen notebooks (ALK Ctn 10:6–22) and 653 sound recordings, and is reflected in relatively early publications.[19] Kroeber's first Mojave work was with Jack Jones in

Needles, California, on 27 November 1900; he visited Mojave land again in March 1902, March and June 1903, and April 1904. Jones first came to San Francisco in October 1903 with elder Jo Nelson. Kroeber's letter describing the travel logistics highlights the complexity for those with little experience outside their land (12 October 1903, ALK Box 1:5). "I have arranged for your transportation," he began, "and you can start just as soon as you are ready. Go to the Ticket Agent in Needles and tell him your name and he will give you two tickets, one for yourself and one for the old man. He will also give you a paper, or ticket, for two beds on the train, one for each of you. Don't pay anything for your tickets or beds." Kroeber went on to explain how to get food on the train, when and where to get off, and what to do in case of emergency: "I enclose also a letter. Carry this with you, and if you want anything, or want to know anything, show it to people and it will tell what your business is." Everything seems to have gone well.

Jones returned in November 1905 with Aspa-saqam, and in December 1910 with Achora Hanyava. These visits yielded sound recordings, articulatory and acoustic phonetic data, and documentation of texts. Most of the texts were transcribed in English, but selections from four narratives were recorded in Mojave; two are on eight cylinders each, and two others have a few minutes recorded. These are the earliest recorded stories in Mojave, and are unpublished, though partial transcripts made by Kroeber and Jones (as in figure 5.4) will aid future researchers.

Kroeber's second period of Mojave work followed his 1946 retirement. He then spent considerable research time on Mojave, including historical studies based on stories he had recorded and three small volumes of narrative texts in translation (two published in his lifetime, one posthumously). When *Seven Mohave Myths* was published, he sent copies to the Fort Mojave Indian Tribe, the Colorado River Indian Tribes, and the sons of three of his collaborators from four decades earlier (November 1948, ALK Box 4:6).[20]

In preparing *More Mohave Myths* (1972), Kroeber revisited Mojave land in 1953 and 1954 to document toponyms and related information (ALK Ctn 10:23–24). "These were his last field trips" and "immensely rewarding to him," according to Theodora Kroeber (1972:vi):

> To spend the hours and days needed to retrace and identify as far as possible (and it is possible to an amazing degree) the routes, overnight stopping

Figure 5.3
Robert Martin (Mojave), Alfred Kroeber, and Pete Sherman (Mojave), near Parker, Arizona, 10 February 1953. Photograph by Cherie N. Gregoire (Kroeber 1972: Plate 9a).

> places, and sites mentioned in the song cycles—places that are the scaffolding of the dreamed tales Mojaves tell. Some of the tales are wholly grounded geographically. . . . On the desert and on the river Kroeber and his companions followed the dreams, mapping them as minutely as they could.

Figure 5.3 shows Kroeber and two of these companions, Robert Martin and Pete Sherman.[21]

As Theodora Kroeber indicated, places and their names, the river and desert landscape, and paths through that landscape are highly significant in Mojave culture. Ethnonyms dominate the early pages of Alfred Kroeber's first 1900 notebook with Jack Jones; the first place named is Huukyámpve, the Needles, a group of pinnacles southeast of the city (ALK Ctn 10:6, p. 12). On the sixteenth page, Kroeber recorded the word *'ath'ii* "salt," followed by information about Salt Song performance. According to Jones, one man sings through the night, using a gourd rattle, and accompanied by two or three women; "the rest listen."

There are dozens of Mojave song cycles, each with up to two hundred songs in a narrative frame. A performance alternates between singing and the telling of what Kenneth Stewart (1983:65) called "mythological episodes." These explain how the founder of its song cycle came into being, traversed the land, naming its features among other actions, and was eventually transformed "into an animal or a landmark" (Kroeber 1925:756).

Each stop on the narrative journey has its songs; stories and songs often come in dreams, and singers may say they saw what they describe. One elder explained in 1903 that he had dreamed an 'Aqaaq Song cycle in utero: "Crow said to me, 'When you sing, use this (gourd).' " He added, "Dreamed this when never born yet. If I had been born when dreamed this, I would forget it."[22] In the narrative era, the world had not reached its present form. "When the mountains were not yet made," Jack Jones said in 1900, "the Mohaves came into this country" (ALK Ctn 10:6, p. 32).

The story of Nyuuhayv dictated by 'Aspa-saqam and translated by Jones in 1905 (Kroeber 1948b:27–36) highlights the role of places and their names in Mojave song cycles. The narrative itinerary features about three dozen stops (with a hundred songs), ending at 'Avii Suukwily, Black Mountain:

> She went eastward two steps and stood there. "The name of this place is Amaṭ-ya'āma," she said. Then, standing there, she threw Otšôuta's skull far south, nearly to Yuma. "I want it to become a rock," she said. Then it became the rock called Avi-melyekyête ['Avii Malyakyet, Picacho Peak].
>
> . . . She was thinking about her own body. "I wonder what color I shall be: white or blue or yellow? Well, I will turn black. I shall be a rock, but all will know me, that I am Nyohaiva [Nyuuhayv]. My name will be Avi-soqwīlye. All will know that rock and that it is Nyohaiva."

Nyuuhayv turned into "a black rock as large as a house on which soqwīlye hawks nest" (Kroeber 1972:144). Another rendering of the same part of the story is partly transcribed in figure 5.4.

A Mojave Salt Song narrative with twenty-five episodes was dictated in 1910 by Achora Hanyava, translated by Jones, and published in English six decades later (Kroeber 1972:34–40). A typical episode is the twelfth:

> Now the two started north from there. As they walked, a little thing like a grasshopper came in front of them and sat there. Whenever they reached him, the grasshopper flew up and settled ahead of them. "If you keep doing that, I am going to give you a name, so everybody will know you," they said. "I call you Hunye-kampute-avunye-kwekatšinatše."

A map by Achora Hanyava shows the Salt Song route, one of several narrative itinerary maps he drew by hand in 1910. At its center is 'Avii Kwa'ame, Spirit Mountain. As detailed by Kroeber (1972:149), the counterclockwise journey begins at 'Aha 'Avulypo, where Mataviily died

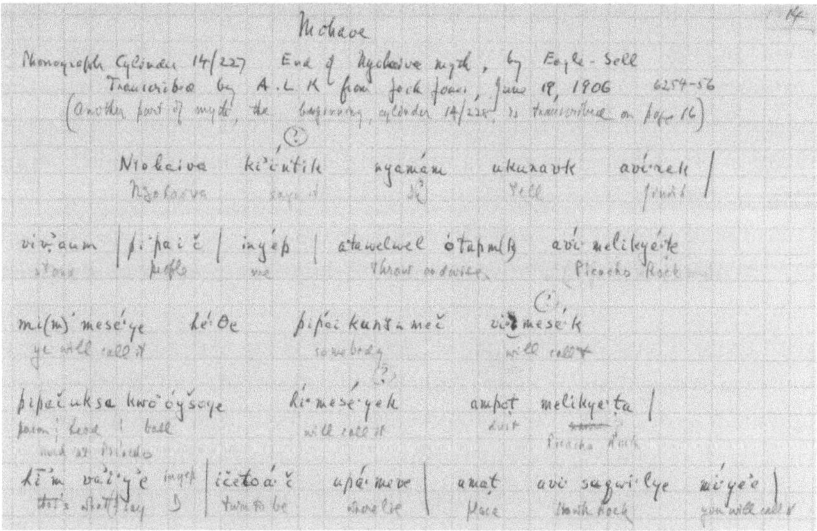

Figure 5.4
Part of a transcript of the Mojave Nyuuhayv creation story (CLA Kroeber.002, p. 14). 'Aspa-saqam recorded this version in 1905 (CLA 24-799); it corresponds to the end of the version published in English by Kroeber (1948b:34). The recording was interpreted by Jack Jones and transcribed by Kroeber in 1906, and recopied by Kroeber in the 1950s.

(see chapter 11). This is the starting point for many Mojave song cycles. The Salt Song journey ends at (Hi)me-kuvauve, where the protagonists think about the death of Mataviily:

> "When I cry and my tears drop on the ground they will be salt." There was no mountain then, no rock, only sand. As they stood there, they said: "I think I will become rock and the rock will be salt. . . . You will see a high mountain, all salt."

Mojave narratives other than the song cycles are also grounded in place. In March 1902, for example, Inyo-kutavêre told part of a heroic epic; it was rendered in English by Jack Jones, and published by Kroeber (1951b). Arthur Hatto (1999:13) called this "a Mohave counterpart to the *Iliad*, the *Nibelungenlied*, the Old Irish *Cattle-raid of Cooley*, the *Roland*," and several other texts from around the world, writing that Kroeber "interpreted it in ethnographic detail never attained with any other oral heroic epic" (136). Significantly, of all the epic narratives known to Hatto, this tale about Mojave migrations "is the most given to the naming of places and itineraries" (99–100). Kroeber (1951b:71) expressed the suspicion that even in 1902 nobody had "learned and reëlaborated a version of the migration legend in several decades. If this is a fact, it was the very last of the crop of aged migration dreamers that I encountered at Needles about 1900 to 1905."

As noted above, Kroeber's Mojave fieldwork in 1953 and 1954 focused on place-name and narrative itineraries. His last (posthumously published) Mojave volume included a long list and explanations of toponyms, with more than a hundred names (1972:135–154). At around the same time, partly based on Kroeber's earlier publications, Judith Crawford documented scores of toponyms and related information throughout her work with several Mojave elders (Brown et al. 1967–1972). Some of the narratives she recorded also reflect the sense of place Kroeber encountered. An example is Satakoot Kuunaavch, the story of Satakoot.[23] As told in 1968 by Robert Martin, it begins with the origin of Maricopa and other Yuman people:

> From 'Amat 'Avii Kwa'ame they started coming, coming, coming,
> Maricopas, Quechans, Mojaves, Kumeyaays, Cocopas, coming, coming.
> To 'Amat 'Avii Kur'utat [Whipple Mountains or Peak] they came.
> With the Mojaves was traveling a young girl, traveling with them.
> [She, Satakoot, said:] "I won't go farther.
> This is the end of my land."

Leanne Hinton and Lucille Watahomigie (1984:3) wrote that 'Avii Kwa'ame is "a sacred place to all the tribes. Yuman oral tradition names Spirit Mountain as the source of human emergence from the earth."

The whole Mojave landscape is culturally important. Community members interviewed in 1986 expressed "a widespread feeling for the overall sacredness of the Mohave Desert" and "a strong feeling of stewardship for those same lands."[24] The poet Natalie Diaz has also described the meaning of toponyms (Shook 2020:13):

> We live on our Mojave homelands and see the land's stories all around us. We don't name things after the white men who "discovered" our land—we name things for what has happened there, the ways we interacted with the land in that place. For example, here, Pach Karawhe (the Man of War) tried to lift the mountains but dropped them, and now the peaks are crooked and

> Mojaves are fallible; here is 'Avii Hukyaampve, where Pach Karawhe taught the people, many of whom were still in their animal form, to shoot arrows and other arts of war; here is 'Aha Kulooh, or the name for where our California village is located now, and it tells you that before the dam was built, this is where the river broke loudly against the bank.

Other Indigenous people in the region have similar artistic and cultural traditions. For instance, the Salt Song cycle also describes the Chemehuevi landscape. "Knowledge of the system was kept in song and stories," Fowler (2009:104) wrote, "and gave the mental maps to be handed down through generations." She added that many songs and stories have fallen into disuse, their toponymy forgotten, and that recovering them from early sources would benefit Indigenous communities. Kaibab Paiute elder Vivienne Jake called Salt Songs "a cultural and spiritual bond between the Nuwuvi people and the land" (Musser-Lopez and Miller 2010).[25]

Mojave elder Robert Martin said almost fifty years ago that "no one tells about Mataviily now" (Crawford 1972:111). In the 1990s, Betty Barrackman emphasized the significance of Mojave stories and songs: "If we don't preserve these songs they won't be remembered by anyone. It's important for the children to know how we came to be Mohaves, especially the creation stories" (Klasky 2000). Mojave people have since worked actively to reclaim their language and songs.[26] A key resource for that work is the documentary corpus of toponyms and geographical information created by earlier generations who shared their knowledge with Kroeber.

RECLAIMING LAND

In California and elsewhere, recent years have seen more and more cases of Indigenous land reclamation as a result of activism and work by tribal nations. Sometimes this means returning land to its original owners, or it can mean acknowledging their right to determine land uses. On the northwest California coast, the Wiyot Tribe has reclaimed most of the former Gunther Island in the city of Eureka—perhaps "the first city in the United States to unconditionally return land to its original owners," according to David Helvarg (2020). After the land was returned in 2019, the island was given the name of its precolonial Wiyot village. It is now Tuluwat Island.

Also in 2019, the Wiyot Tribe advocated successfully against an industrial wind-turbine project at a prayer site in the southern hills of Wiyot land. Elder Cheryl Seidner spoke out publicly: "You would not sell your mother. We cannot sell our earth" (Canter 2020). The project was to be on Bear River Ridge, which the Wiyot call Tsakiyuwit; a "Protect Tsakiyuwit" banner was carried at the head of a December 2019 march and rally. This name was itself recovered from documentation created by Kroeber in 1902 work with Wiyot elder Blue Lake Bob.[27]

In September 2021, also on the northwest California coast, the former Patrick's Point State Park was renamed Sue-meg State Park following a request from the Yurok Tribe.[28] The Yurok word Suemeg (alternatively spelled Suemeeg) is a traditional name for the point, well known to Yurok people. Restoring its name in this public context, according to Rosie Clayburn, director of the Yurok Tribe's Cultural Resources Department, "gives a more balanced and just world for not only Yurok children but to all children" (Wear 2021). The California State Parks systems has since embarked on a signage project for several parks on the north coast, displaying Native toponyms alongside English names. These are often reclaimed from early documentation; an example is 'E'goo (Waterman 1920:K4), a beach just north of Trinidad Head, managed by the state as Trinidad State Beach.

As these examples indicate, place-names resonate powerfully in asserting land ownership or custodial authority. Kroeber did not anticipate this, but he certainly grasped the importance of names. His documentation of Yahi and Zuni toponymy was copious, for example, in addition to the cases discussed in this chapter, including Mojave geography. According to Dell Hymes (2000), Ursula Le Guin remembered "helping her father calculate the distances and sites mentioned in the [Mojave] song-cycles, places that are the scaffolding of dreamed narratives." This was probably during her student years in the late 1940s or very early 1950s. And toponyms resonate in her poesis, from *A Wizard of Earthsea* (1968) to *Always Coming Home* (1985, 2019). Asked in 1968 to write "a fantasy novel for younger readers," Le Guin (2018:ix) later recalled, "The first thing I did was sit down and draw a map. I saw and named Earthsea and all its islands. I knew almost nothing about them, but I knew their names. In the name is the magic."

In the memory-documentation style, Kroeber himself asked about the names of places. His lack of fluency (and the absence of recording technology that was not cumbersome) made it impossible for him to learn how toponyms were actually used, other than in the narratives he recorded or transcribed. From his documentary corpus it is therefore impossible to envision research like that of Keith Basso (1988) for Western Apache, exploring the implications of discursive choices in this domain. But Kroeber did facilitate a remarkable statement about place-names and Indigenous land ownership, more than a century before current reclamation work. It is part of a seven-minute sound recording made in 1907 by Yurok elder Domingo Jack (usually called Domingo).[29]

Domingo's recording was prompted by questions about land use and described gathering, hunting, and fishing rights traditionally associated with specific families in the area of Wechpues (called Weitchpec in English). A Yurok verb that he used frequently is *megetohl,* literally "look after" or the like, but used to refer to owning or taking care of children, pets, land, and so on; I leave it untranslated.[30] Domingo began with the information Kroeber must have asked about:

> *Weesh ho son' 'o Wechpues. . . .*
> This is how it was at Weitchpec. . . .
> *To' wee' megetohlkwee' k'ee hlkehl 'o Wechpues.*
> The land was *megetohl* at Weitchpec.
> *Mekwtegen ho 'wernerger'ermerhpue'.*
> At Mekwtegen they would set snares.

Mekwtegen is the location of a fishing rock a mile or two downriver from Weitchpec (Waterman 1920:G8). Proceeding upriver, Domingo's account identified places and the households with rights at each of them.

Near the end of the recording, Domingo shifted to the present day:

> *Kwelekw weet skewok kee 'nekcho', kwelekw weetue' ho son'.*
> This is actually what I want to tell you (folks), this is how it was.
> *Nuemee skuy' soo nee megetohlkwee' k'ee hlkehl.*
> This land is very well *megetohl.*
> *Kelew poy 'ee ma 'ap sonowow'.*
> You (folks) got to be in charge.
> *Nee yegolue', "Kwelekw neemee ho megetohlkwee'."*
> You (folks) just said, "It wasn't *megetohl.*"
> *K'ee reeek'ew tue' neekee ko'see megetohl, neekeechyue 'ok'w 'wewolek'. . . .*
> But along the river everywhere is *megetohl*, everything has a name. . . .
> *Neemee heepuereesh nee me'womechok'w weesh 'ee nue 'wer'erkerh. . . .*
> One doesn't come from downriver to net fish. . . .
> *Tue' kem wee' sonowok' k'ee sloowehl 'wegohkue'. . . .*
> And it's also like that gathering wild oats. . . .

Kem wee' sonowok' k'ee woomehl 'wohkue'. . . .
It's also like that gathering acorns. . . .
Tue' kelew nee yegolue', "Neemee megetohlkwee' 'o k'ee hlkehl."
You (folks) just said, "This land isn't *megetohl*."
Kwelekw 'ochkeech megetohl k'ee ko'see 'o k'ee hlkehl.
But actually everywhere in this land was *megetohl.*
Peesh tue' weet keech kee soo 'nekchek'.
And that's what I can tell you now.
Weet soo skewok kee 'nekchek'.
That's what I want to tell you.

Breaking the ethnographic frame to address Kroeber's people, who invaded Yurok land, Domingo played on the senses of *megetohl*, a verb that conflates the meanings of English *own* and *take care of.* The invaders said nobody owned the land, but Yurok people took care of it all, and named it all.

This example underscores a feature of Kroeber's documentation. He thought of himself as an objective researcher, recording for posterity information about the past. Perhaps it was for this reason that while Domingo's account of land rights informed Kroeber's account of Yurok law (1925:20–35), he never wrote about what Domingo said he wanted to tell white people. I wish I knew whether this just did not suit Kroeber's preconceptions about his own work, or if its political dimension made him uncomfortable. For Kroeber's interactions with Domingo and other Native interlocutors, even those who were his friends, were colonial encounters. And these interlocutors were not just participating in research: they were speaking to their descendants, or in some cases to Kroeber's people. Domingo's speech was an assertion of Yurok sovereignty, presaging what Indigenous people would say more than sixty years later at Akwesasne and Alcatraz: "You are on Indian land."[31]

6

COLLABORATIONS

I believe that more and more of our work will be done by Indians.
—Alfred Kroeber, letter to Edward Sapir, 1913

In the letter quoted in the chapter epigraph, Kroeber was reflecting on writing systems for Native American languages in connection with an American Anthropological Association committee on practical orthography (Golla 1984:78). He advocated using only the symbols found on typewriter keyboards because he envisioned, inter alia, that Indigenous people with no specialized training or tools would ("more and more") write and type texts themselves in their own languages, rather than dictating them to researchers like himself. It must have seemed obvious that fluent speakers of a language, if they know how to write all its sounds, can transcribe it faster and more accurately than anyone else.

Kroeber was no doubt also aware that he did not have a superb ear for phonetic detail, even before his midlife Ménière's disease; literate Native people would be able to record their own speech better than he could. Early in the twentieth century, the elders with whom he recorded language and stories were often illiterate. Even younger people did not learn to write their languages in American schools; on the contrary, they were routinely punished for using them. In this context, a significant aspect of Kroeber's career was his commitment to teaching Native people to write in their languages.[1] If the future he predicted to Sapir did not come to pass in his lifetime, he at least helped lay a foundation for that day.

In this chapter, I explore a set of relationships Kroeber had with younger people from Native communities, collaborations in which he supported and publicly acknowledged their work. From 1909 to 1949, his relationships with Juan Dolores, Gilbert Natches, and Robert Spott were critical for documenting O'odham, Numu, and Yurok languages, cultures, and historical experiences. Indigenous people have always been central participants in American linguistics and anthropology, but they were not often given public credit for their work in the early twentieth century. Kroeber's choices are notable because white outsiders usually took credit for work produced in intellectual collaborations with Indigenous people.[2]

JUAN DOLORES AND O'ODHAM

Juan Dolores (figure 6.1) was born about 1880 on Tohono O'odham land in Sonora, Mexico; his first language was O'odham. As a child he lived in Sonora and near Vav-Givulk (Baboquivari Peak), Arizona, where his parents moved to enroll him in US schools. He learned English at the Tucson Indian School, where he and other students were regularly whipped and were sometimes punished with bread-and-water rations for days or imprisoned in a room without light. Dolores's later schooling was at the Teller Institute in Colorado and at the Hampton Institute, a primarily Black college in Virginia. After graduating from Hampton in 1901 and spending an additional year there in a postgraduate business course, he led an itinerant life in the west.[3]

Dolores met Kroeber in 1909, leading to collaborations with him and other anthropologists and a friendship with Kroeber and his family that would last until Dolores's death in 1948.[4] In the 1930s and 1940s, Karl Kroeber (2003b:136) recalled, Dolores was "a frequent visitor to our home here in Berkeley and annually spent his vacation at our summer place" (in Napa Valley). The Kroeber family would go "in June as soon as school was out," Ursula Le Guin (2004b:14) wrote; they "settled in and set up the packed-dirt croquet court, and Juan—a killer croquet player—always got there in time for his birthday." His room there was still called "Juan's Room" decades after his death, according to Le Guin; several Kroeber family snapshots featured his croquet playing.

Dolores worked at the University of California for many years, may have been its first Indigenous employee, and was almost certainly its first Indigenous researcher.[5] (According to UC records, he was first a regular "employee" in April 1912.) Between 1909 and 1926 his UC work alternated with jobs in California, Oregon, Nevada, and Arizona as a teamster and skilled laborer. At UC, he was hired intermittently for language

Figure 6.1
Juan Dolores, 1911. Photograph by J. Alden Mason (ALKFP Box 1).

documentation in 1909 and 1911–1913; as a guard in the anthropology museum between 1911 and 1916; as an anthropology research fellow for the 1918–1919 academic year; and as a museum guard, janitor, and preparator from 1926 to 1936. Dolores's 1926 return to UC was prompted by health problems that made it harder to get other jobs and by a wish to continue "that [language] work I started with you [Kroeber] some years ago" (25 February 1926, RDA Box 49).

In 1936 and 1937, Dolores managed a government-funded research project at the University of Chicago, focusing on the lives of Mexican immigrants in Chicago. In these years, Kroeber reached out to multiple

US government officials to try to get Dolores a job doing O'odham language work (such as literacy training). For example, on 14 May 1937, he wrote to BIA commissioner John Collier asking if the BIA could support Dolores. Collier replied a few days later that "we have something rather specifically in mind for him in the event we do not receive too much of a set back in our appropriations" (ALK Box 13:15). Whatever this was, it did not come to pass, and Dolores resumed a permanent UC position as a preparator in the anthropology museum later in 1937. He retired as "senior museum preparator" at the end of June 1948, a few weeks before his death at Vamori, Arizona, in the Tohono O'odham Nation. With him when he died were his nieces, who buried Dolores by his brother and sister (Rosaria Vavages to Kroeber, 22 July 1948, RDA Box 49).

Dolores's linguistic sensibility was in evidence at a young age, as was his lifelong ironic style. In a memoir written in O'odham and edited and translated by Madeleine Mathiot (1991), he described being in an Arizona classroom with older students (312–313):

> I discovered a way to make my companions laugh as I listened to Miss Grant. Whenever she said an English word that was almost like a[n O'odham] word, I would whisper that word to them in O'odham. This was very funny in O'odham. The women would try not to laugh but sometimes one of them could not control herself and she would just burst out laughing. I was delighted. I was constantly listening for words that would sound funny in O'odham.

Native languages were suppressed in government schools. "They did not allow us to speak O'odham," Dolores wrote (Mathiot 1991:309); punishment was severe for students who did speak their languages.

After his Arizona and Colorado student years, Dolores (1901a,b, 1902) published three short articles as a Hampton student. One was based on an address to the Nineteenth Lake Mohonk Conference of Friends of the Indian, a meeting of white philanthropists. In it, Dolores quoted what an elder had said at a meeting among his people (Dolores 1901a:76):

> We go into Mexico to learn the Mexican songs and prayers, and when we return home we sing and pray. Now, are we a better people than we were years ago when we sang our own songs, when we spoke to the Great Spirit in our own language? We asked then for rain, good health and long life; now what

> more do we want? What is that thought so great and so sacred that cannot be expressed in our own language, that we should seek to use the white man's words?

In context this was a polite rebuke of the assimilationist program of his hosts. Dolores's lifelong project of writing and documenting the O'odham language was also in turn a response to this elder's rhetorical question. And it was through Dolores's eventual collaboration with Kroeber that he learned to write O'odham and became, in the romanticized formulation of Dean Saxton and Lucille Saxton (1973:iii), "the first writer of his people's legends."

It is unclear how Dolores and Kroeber met, but it was a fruitful encounter. Dolores made twenty-eight O'odham sound recordings in 1909, and worked with Kroeber on documentation. One of Kroeber's notebooks has vocabulary and grammar, with some cultural information and a text; one has short text transcriptions; a third is from 1911, when Dolores began writing O'odham, and focuses on phonology. Over the years, Dolores created a major corpus of O'odham writing in his own hand, including his own tellings and retellings, English translations, linguistic and cultural notes, and transcriptions of stories and songs shared by elders. The latter were based on more than fifty sound recordings those elders made with him; fourteen more recordings of Dolores himself were made in 1928, 1932, and 1933. Unfortunately, it is hard to be precise about the scope or contents of Dolores's manuscript corpus, since it is divided among archives in Berkeley, Philadelphia, and Tucson; it includes multiple versions and copies of some texts; and individual texts are not always clearly identified. In any case the corpus has thousands of manuscript pages; only some of it has been published.[6]

Dolores's O'odham work led to publications before and after his death. During his lifetime, he was the author of four papers about his language.[7] Two were descriptions of aspects of grammar, prepared in collaboration with Kroeber and J. Alden Mason but with Dolores as sole author; one was a contribution to Kroeber's Festschrift, on nicknames; and the last was a methodologically innovative analysis of color terms. This last, in collaboration with Lila O'Neale, emphasized how the O'odham-language color palette is embedded in its cultural and environmental contexts. All these works were the first published linguistic studies of O'odham, prior to a grammatical sketch by William Kurath (1945).

In 1947, Dolores submitted O'odham texts to a new monograph series, edited by Carl Voegelin, whose first volume would be a collection of Ho-Chunk (Winnebago) narratives edited by Paul Radin (1948). Kroeber suggested Dolores's corpus as another volume. Dolores wrote Kroeber that "Voegelin want[s] to see my manuscript before he makes up his mind. They have agreed to publish Paul Radin's Winnebago; after this mine will be next, if Voegelin agrees" (26 July, ALK Box 13:15). Dolores worried about orthography and the publication of his full text corpus: "When you think it is good enough I can then let him . . . take all, not let the little ones get left behind." In response (31 July, ALK Box 4:2), Kroeber encouraged Dolores to send "the stories written out clean the way you had them a couple of years ago." Kroeber would add an orthography key "and everything would be ready for the printer, as soon as Voegelin gives the word." Dolores submitted a manuscript in 1947 and worked on orthography with Kroeber and Voegelin as late as June 1948. Apparently Voegelin decided not to publish the texts as submitted. In a letter to Kroeber, after describing transcriptional questions raised by a recording Dolores had recently made, he said he would return the manuscript: "The problem is much too complicated to publish without extensive and sensitive commentary" (9 July 1948, ED 134.8.1). Perhaps he meant that the texts would require a technical scholarly apparatus. This was not to be: Dolores died on 19 July 1948.

After Dolores's death, others wrote two books based on his work. One was Mason's 1950 O'odham grammar. Undertaken at Kroeber's suggestion, this book almost entirely depended on Dolores. Dolores accompanied Mason on the latter's sole fieldwork trip "of a few weeks" in 1919, which Mason said was "mainly to get some impression of the phonetics" (3).[8] Otherwise the grammar is an analysis of Dolores's text corpus. Over the years Dolores often inquired about its progress, but the typescript was not done until 1947; the book was published in 1950, after Dolores's death. A second book was an O'odham story collection edited by Saxton and Saxton (1973), whose 350 pages of text are mostly from Dolores's corpus (without Voegelin's "extensive and sensitive commentary"). Mason and the Saxtons contributed substantial analytic and editorial labor, but Dolores was not named as an author, as he had been in his work with Kroeber. Extractivist authorship norms and Dolores's death have partly obscured his foundational contributions in O'odham grammar and narrative.

Figure 6.2 is an early page of Dolores's O'odham writing that illustrates two notable orthographic choices. One has to do with what constitutes a basic unit of sound, the other with what constitutes a word. The O'odham sound system distinguishes what Albert Alvarez and Kenneth Hale (1970) called "sharp" and "mellow" stop consonants. In their orthography, adopted by the Tohono O'odham Nation, the sharp stops are *p, t, c, k* and the mellow ones *b, d, ḍ, j, g*; Mason's spelling was similar.[9] The sharp consonants are phonetically preaspirated in non-word-initial position, Alvarez and Hale explained (94); the mellow consonants are not.[10] They judged preaspiration an automatic phonetic effect of the consonant it was associated with, and did not write it.

Unlike Alvarez and Hale, Kroeber (1913:243) treated preaspiration not as a consonant effect but as a vowel feature, referring to a "class" of vowels that are "sonant and aspirated, represented by following h."[11] In line with this view, both Dolores and Kroeber wrote preaspirated sharp consonants with an *h*, as *hp, ht, htc, hk* in contrast to mellow *p, t, ṭ, tc, k*.[12] Mason (1950:7) too noted preaspiration as a phonetic effect, but treated it as an effect of the stop.[13] He was probably influenced by his prior work with the closely related Tepecano language. There he also described two contrasting series, *b, d, g* and *p, t, k*, writing that the latter "entirely lack aspiration when initial, intervocalic or when the second member of a consonantal combination" (Mason 1917:317–318) and are not preaspirated in final position, but postaspirated. In O'odham, therefore, Dolores used spellings like *ha'**ihtc**uh* "something" (figure 6.2, line 6) and *ko**hks*** "the old woman" (ED 134.1.1, pp. 33, 36); the same words are now spelled *ha'**ic**u* and *g 'o**ks**.*[14]

The difference between the orthographic practice of Dolores (and Kroeber) and that of Mason (and others) was a difference between two ways of writing a language's sounds. Should sounds be spelled more phonetically (transparently reflecting pronunciation) or more phonologically (reflecting their place in the structure of the language)? Like many American linguists of the generation after Kroeber, influenced by Edward Sapir and Leonard Bloomfield, Mason preferred to omit predictable aspects of pronunciation and transcribe structurally similar elements identically.

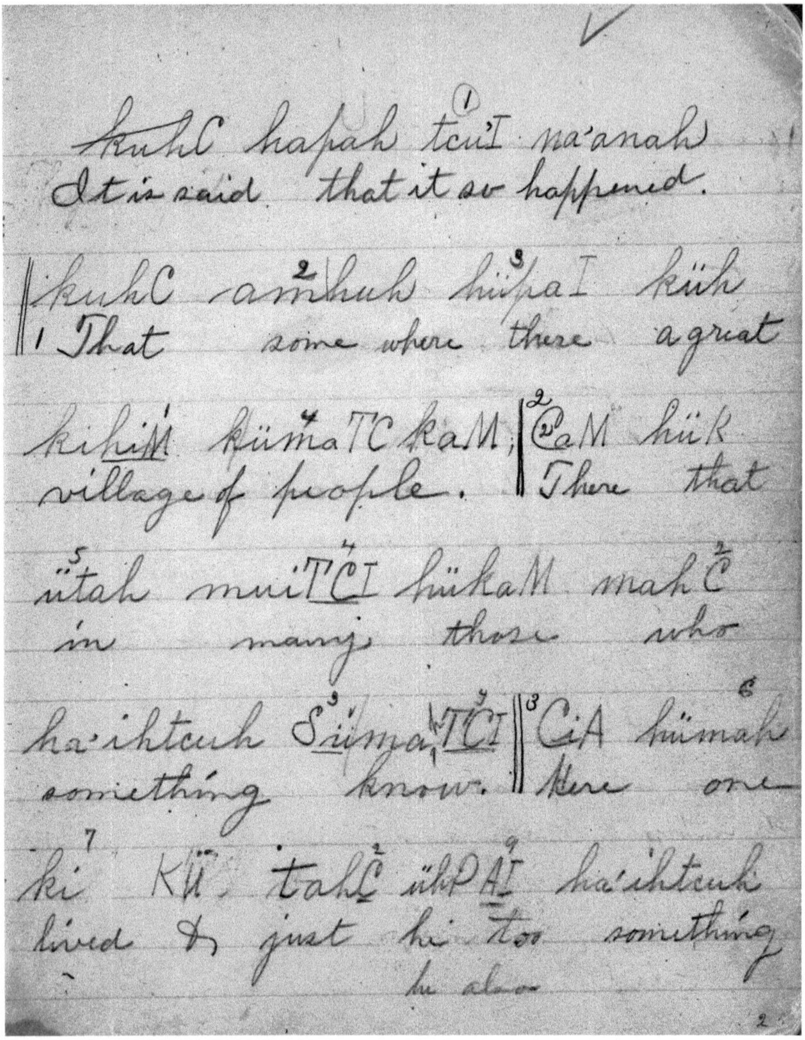

Figure 6.2
Juan Dolores, beginning of an O'odham story about wind and rain, 1911 (ED 134.1.5, p. 1). The phrase written *hük ütah* in lines 3–4 is one of several that embodies two notable orthographic choices.

To Dolores, plainly, this made no sense: preaspiration was noticeable and therefore should be written.

Another notable orthographic choice concerns wordhood. Dolores and most others have written a variety of unaccented adverbs and particles as separate words.[15] Mason had a different view. In analyzing a language, he wrote, "the determination as to what constitutes a 'word' . . . should be attempted only after long acquaintance has familiarized the student with its spirit. In Papago, as in many languages, the criterion for the native feeling seems to be the accent" (15).[16] According to this phonological definition, unaccented elements are part of the word they adjoin or depend on. Mason thus treated elements like the negative particle *pi* and the punctual auxiliary *t* as part of the verb they ordinarily precede (much as one might treat English *n't* as part of *hasn't*). But sometimes they are "separated from the verb stem by nouns, adverbs, and other words." This again led Mason to a practice derived from his prior analysis of Tepecano. There he wrote long sequences as single words, like *kumticiampöp·túk·u·*R "then they simply thus stung him" (Mason 1917:379). He extended this to O'odham (1950:15):

> To consider these [unaccented elements] as necessary parts of the verb produces, as it did in Tepecano, long verbal complexes with nominal incorporation, such as, for example, *ku-'tc-se-we'ho-'pi-ha'i'tcu-wo-'ca'i-ñel*, "Will we really be able to see nothing?" This is, literally: That-we-(uncertainty)-true-not-anything-will-some-see. Dolores, probably correctly, insisted that such complexes are phrases; he broke his sentences into shorter "words." For instance, he wrote the above sentence *kutcs wüho piha'itcu wo ca'i nül.*

But since Dolores did not write accent (whose position is predictable) and Mason himself had limited exposure to O'odham beyond Dolores's written texts, he was effectively guessing about wordhood—and contradicting Dolores's own ("probably correct"!) "native feeling." Short instances of the contradiction are in expressions like Dolores's *pi wühhoh* "not true" (ED 134.9, p. 25, now *pi veho*), written *pi-weho'* by Mason (45); and *hük ütah* "in that" (figure 6.2, now *heg 'eḍa* with a postposition *'eḍa* "in"), written *he'*G*-'eḍa* by Mason (37). Given here is a longer example in Dolores's spelling and word-by-word translation (ED 134.1.5, p. 34), followed by modern spelling:

maC aM kih K tcukI TC hüwühLI
that there lived the rain and wind
maṣ 'am ki: g ju:kĭ c hevel
"(The hummingbird arrived) there where the rain and wind lived."

Mason would have combined the first three words as one, and the next two ("the rain") as another.[17]

Dolores came by his sense of wordhood early in his language work. In one of his earliest letters to Kroeber, he recounted a dream that came after finishing a 2,873-word story late one evening (16 March 1911, RDA Box 11):

> That night [when] I went to sleep, I saw words appearing on the wall, like [a] moving picture show. First a word would go clear across the wall and then automatically arrange itself into two or three words. Sometimes there would be only one letter and under it would be two or three English words. When I awoke, I said this is no dream. It is the correct way of writing the Indian language.

Kroeber had a similar practice in his 1911 transcriptions with Dolores. He wrote *nap' do hūk dju'huk'* (ED 134.7.1, p. 25) for *Napt o hu: g cuhug* "Will you eat meat?" Mason would have combined both *g cuhug* "the meat" and the sequence of *n-apt* (question particle + auxiliary), future *o*, and *hu:* "eat."[18]

Dolores's analytic differences with Mason were not mere spelling details. His choices in writing the two series of O'odham stops, for example, provide a counterpoint to Sapir's (1933) famous study of native-speaker orthographic practices. Sapir described cases where Indigenous people learning to write their languages avoided spellings that correspond well to pronunciation (expressing phonetic detail) in favor of those mirroring phonological patterns (which may seem more abstract). Subsequently, at least since Kenneth Pike (1947), linguists involved in orthography design have often argued for systems with a unique representation for each phoneme or phonologically distinctive element. Yet for O'odham, Dolores initially used a system that underdifferentiated phonemes in word-initial position (spelling mellow and sharp stops identically, e.g., as *t*) but wrote phonemically identical sharp stops differently depending on pronunciation (e.g., *t* initially and *ht* elsewhere).[19] The preaspiration is perceptually quite salient.

Words are typically both phonological and semantic-syntactic units, so the two approaches to wordhood also highlight an analytic problem. If a language has a mismatch whereby a semantically or syntactically heterogeneous group of elements shares some phonological feature (like a single accent), a complex decision must be made. Like many researchers following structural discovery procedures, Mason preferred to use phonological criteria in defining words. Dolores based his choices on (implicit) semantic and syntactic criteria.

After meeting and working with Mason, Dolores expressed displeasure in a series of letters to Kroeber in 1919, culminating on 26 December (RDA Box 49), when he said he had known all along "that Dr. Mason would never do the work satisfactory to me" and that he (Dolores) had agreed to let Mason write a grammar based on his corpus only because he thought Kroeber wanted that. "How does anybody know how to write a word unless he knows how that word is pronounced?" he asked, alluding to Mason. "How does anybody know the true meaning of any Indian expression (a phrase, in a sentence) unless he knows the language?" His questions index the two main differences between his practice and Mason's.

Kroeber was away from Berkeley but later responded with a characteristic attempt at peace-making (9 March 1920, RDA Box 49): "I realize there is something in your point and I will put it to Mason in the best way I can." Acknowledging that Mason might view O'odham through a Tepecano lens, Kroeber promised to "try to see to it that you get a crack at everything he does before publication." After all, he wrote, "Mason will realize as much as anyone that the basis of all his Papago work is what you have done."

As noted above, Mason's O'odham grammar was not published until after Dolores died. Meanwhile, during the years when he had jobs away from the university (1919–1926), Dolores continued to work on texts. He and Kroeber exchanged many letters; he wrote about his siblings' poor health, his own health and money troubles, and his longing for a home and role among his people. At the same time, an enduring whimsy pervaded his writing. As early as 1911, for example, Dolores wrote about how a linguist should think about O'odham grammatical "rules" (10 May, RDA Box 11):

> Allow me to suggest, that whoever makes the rules for the Papago language, he or she must take into consideration the great difference in the climate of

> southern Ariz. and Berkeley. You see, I was thinking that many things which grow in Berkeley could not grow in southern Ariz. The climate I think could make anything grow in Berkeley, I believe, I grew some the time I was there. The hot weather has taken me back to about 150 lbs now. For this reason I am compelled to think very seriously, whether the rules now growing on the college grounds (there among the beautiful grass, trees, and flowers, and the nice sea breeze blowing over them every day) could not be too tender, and when exposed to that hot and dry climate of Ariz., get sun burned, change its color, [d]ry up, lose its flexibility, it[s] elasticity and break. What a great sorrow this would bring to me, for I am doing the best I can to help nurse your rules. I suppose the ground where you have planted, those rules must be fertilized with Papago language, so I'll stop here, and start [writing] another [O'odham] story.
>
> The fertilizer that I have is perhaps not the best to be found in Ariz., but it is the best I have, and there is only a little more, and I might as well give you the rest.

This final intimation of mortality was typical of Dolores's style. Sometimes he included aperçus about Mason (2 August 1920, RDA Box 49):

> Some day when we are all well, I'll build a house and then I'll send you that invitation. I am in no hurry about building that house, and if you want to come out next summer I'll find somebody to board us, and we'll sleep in the open, look at the stars, and talk Papago until your tongue gets tired flying up and down trying to make that ṯ or Mason's ḏ. In day times, when you are not working on the Papago language, it will be a good exercise to go out and help me chop trees, dig stumps, or if it rains we'll plant corn, beans and do all kinds of stunts you never done before. While doing the above named exercises, we will at the same time puzzle out the meanings of Papago phrases. Papago words I mean. Dr Mason takes a whole phrase and calls it a word, because he can't understand why any part of an unpronounceable collection of syllables should have any special meaning.

Mason's view was not that the parts of words lack meaning but that words are phonological units. Dolores's misunderstanding shows how obvious it must have seemed to him that meaningful units are words.

Later, Dolores mainly wanted Mason's work completed (RDA Box 49). "I am sure [it] is good enough to all who don't know the Papago language," he wrote on 23 August 1921, going on to "wish him good luck but more speed, so I can see the work finished before I depart to some other sphere." On 31 October 1922, he wrote to ask about Mason. "My health is good," he said, "but my teeth are getting bad, and I suppose when I can't eat, I can't live. I must be nearing the time when I shall have to take a trip to some other planet, so hurry up Dr Mason, I want to see his work before I go."

After Dolores returned to UC in 1926, correspondence with Kroeber was mainly just when one of them was out of town. For example, Kroeber wrote to encourage publication of a set of texts that Dolores had prepared in English (16 April 1927, RDA Box 49):

> I looked over your stories and liked them very much. I would advise you not to turn them over except for cash. . . . If you do not sell the stories outright, I would suggest that you write as many more as you can in the same way, and I will try to get them placed for you as a book under your own name. . . . You have a somewhat new way of writing them which is different both from the way scientists have written Indian stories in English, and which is also different from the way literary people write them. It is this new way of presenting them that I think might make them go.

Subsequent letters indicate that Kroeber sent copies of some stories to New York publishers or editors, whose reactions were mixed. The book described by Kroeber was never published, though it may have evolved into the volume that Dolores submitted to Voegelin in 1947.

Dolores was close to Kroeber and his family for more than twenty years. In 1925, when Dolores was hospitalized in Los Angeles with chest pain and an infected foot, Kroeber feared tuberculosis, corresponded with Dolores and the hospital, and sent money. Back in Berkeley, Dolores had a standing invitation at the Kroeber house "every Thursday evening" (Kroeber to Dolores, 18 October 1927, RDA Box 49). Dolores gave Christmas presents to the Kroeber children, like a bow and arrows to four-year-old Karl (22 December 1930, RDA Box 49): "I hope he'll not be trying to shoot his play mates. The arrows have no points but I imagine Carl will not be hunting mountain lions and the arrows will be good enough to play with." Decades later, Le Guin (2004b:16–17) recalled Dolores's first sojourn at the Kroeber summer house, in "the summer I learned to walk" (1931):

> This infant would stagger over to Juan and say "Go-go?" And whatever he was doing, writing or reading or talking or working, Juan would excuse himself

Figure 6.3
Juan Dolores, undated photo sent by his niece Rosaria Vavages to Alfred Kroeber in 1948 (TKQP).

> and gravely accompany me across the yard and up the driveway on a great journey of a hundred yards or so, I holding on to him by one finger.... I know which finger it was, the first of his left hand, a strong, thick, dark finger that entirely and warmly filled my hand.

Dolores's relationship to Kroeber was salient also to Silva Beyer, an anthropology student who married Dolores in 1935 and lived with him in Chicago. After they separated in 1937 and he returned west, she wrote Kroeber that "you ... are far more significant to him than I had become" (15 June 1937, ALK Box 13:16).[20] Echoing Beyer's observation, Dolores's niece Rosaria Vavages wrote Kroeber in 1947 that her uncle "has told me . . . how he feels that your family is his family too" (16 April, TKQP).

Dolores's later years brought challenges. A 1940 workplace fall damaged a shoulder and caused "permanent loss of vision" in one eye (Dolores to Kroeber, 27 July 1940, RDA Box 49). In November 1947 (RDA Box 49), Dolores was mugged, badly beaten, and left unconscious outside his home in Oakland. The Kroebers were at Harvard and Radcliffe but came home for the winter break. Dolores visited then, as Le Guin (2004b:17) remembered:

> He was tired, and old, and sad. I was too ashamed and shy to show him my affection. I didn't know I loved him. . . . I see Juan now, a gentle, intellectual man, living in exile and poverty, licensed by bigotry to be a prey of bullies—the world was full of such people in the 1940s. It is full of such people now. I wish I had had the sense to take his hand.

Dolores spent several months recuperating, less than a year before he died.

Dolores's legacy is the corpus of texts and other materials he assembled from 1909 to 1949. This has already structured the trajectory of O'odham language study and linguistics, but more remains. Keiko Beers (2020) drew on that corpus to analyze twentieth-century language changes, noting that O'odham educators "expressed an interest in these particular texts as potential resources for culturally relevant school curriculum" (113). Dolores "began the work of producing . . . a written literature" of his language, as Dean Saxton, Lucille Saxton, and Susie Enos (1983:v) put it. The US Indian education system did its best to beat his language out of him, while Kroeber made space for him to write O'odham and worked to help him disseminate what he wrote.

GILBERT NATCHES AND NUMU

In northeastern California, northern Nevada, eastern Oregon, and southern Idaho live people who speak the Numu language, also called Paviotso, Paiute, or Northern Paiute (to distinguish it from Southern Paiute).[21] Like O'odham, this belongs to the Uto-Aztecan language family. Kroeber got involved through correspondence with an Oregon doctor, Walter Marsden, who had learned to speak the language well, had assembled a collection of texts, and was writing a grammar.[22] When he died in 1913, his widow Clara sent his manuscripts to Kroeber, who expressed an interest in seeing them published. But as he put it to her, this would mean "getting a Paiute Indian to come down here" to check the transcriptions (7 October 1913, ALK Box 2:15).

Kroeber's first attempt to do this involved Captain Dave Numana, a Kuiyuidɨkadɨ Paiute (Pyramid Lake, Nevada) elder who came to San Francisco in October 1913, when he was around eighty years old. Numana then recorded a historical account of the American general John Fremont, also dictating one or two Paiute narratives and sharing vocabulary in work with both Dolores and Kroeber.[23] But he was apparently unable to help with the Marsden text material.

Gilbert Natches (figure 6.4) was a landscape painter and musician from a prominent Kuiyuidɨkadɨ Paiute family in Nevada. His artistic talent was recognized as early as his days at the Stewart Indian School (which Daisy Washington also attended a few years earlier; chapter 3). The school newspaper reported, in April 1901, "Gilbert Natches, one of the boys in the Fourth grade, is quite an artist. The blackboards in his schoolroom are seldom left untouched with his artistic work."[24] As an adult, Natches exhibited his work in Reno and San Francisco. The drawing in figure 6.5 was probably shown in San Francisco; it eventually came into the possession of Berkeley anthropologist Robert Heizer, who donated it to the University of Nevada in 1970.

A Nevada minister who supported Natches's artistic work facilitated an introduction to Kroeber. In 1913 and 1914, Natches came to San Francisco to promote his art and work with the Marsden Numu language material. The 1914 visit lasted three months, from October through December, included an exhibit of twenty-one of his drawings at the UC anthropology museum, and was the subject of a *San Francisco Chronicle* feature.[25] Again it proved impossible to make substantial progress with the Marsden texts. Instead, Natches created an exceptional documentary corpus.

Natches's Numu language materials include sixty-nine recordings of songs and stories; a notebook and folders with transcriptions, sentences, and vocabulary; and other material. An article by Natches (1923, edited by Kroeber) presented several of the texts in cursory form, and one was recently published in a linguistic edition by Tim Thornes (2020), but the bulk of the material remains in archives. Natches wrote much of it down

Figure 6.4
Gilbert Natches, Washoe County, Nevada. He holds crutches; his right leg had been amputated in 1907 after a train accident. Undated photograph by Lorenzo D. Creel (UNRS-P2710-0156, Special Collections and University Archives Department, University of Nevada, Reno).

himself after learning transcription from Kroeber, so this was also the first body of Numu texts and vocabulary written by a Paiute person. Like Juan Dolores, Gilbert Natches began a written literature for his language.

Excluding spoken explanations of songs, Natches's Numu language corpus includes a dozen texts:

- Bird story (transcript 10.5–8, 10.41)
- Conversation with a cat (24-2306; transcript 10.36, 15.65–66 = figure 6.6; translated H21)

Figure 6.5
Gilbert Natches, "Pyramid Lake," 1914. Watercolor drawing. NC 533, Special Collections Department, University of Nevada, Reno (Bandurraga 1990).

- "Cottontail" (24-2288; transcript 10.19–30, 15.7–11, 70–76)
- Coyote and mouse (published N256–257; translated H31)
- Coyote at the dance (transcript 10.17; translated H30)
- Dove story (24-2264; transcript 10.8–10; translated H37)
- Flint and coyote (24-2289; transcript 10.13–14, 15.85; translated H35)
- Frog and moon (24-2265; transcript 10.1; published N256–257)
- An incident (transcript 10.4, 44; published N258–259)
- "Owl" (24-2287; transcript 15.68–69; published N256–259, Thornes 2020)
- Short conversation (transcript 15.40)
- "The star story" (24-2296; transcript 10.15, 15.81–83)

Seven of these were recorded. Most are short; the longest is the "Cottontail" story, recorded on three cylinders and almost seven minutes long.[26]

Four facets of the corpus show its interest. The first is technical, concerning a process whereby the initial consonant of a root or suffix sometimes changes depending on what precedes it. The specific elements triggering this "consonant mutation" must be learned.[27] In *kaupa*

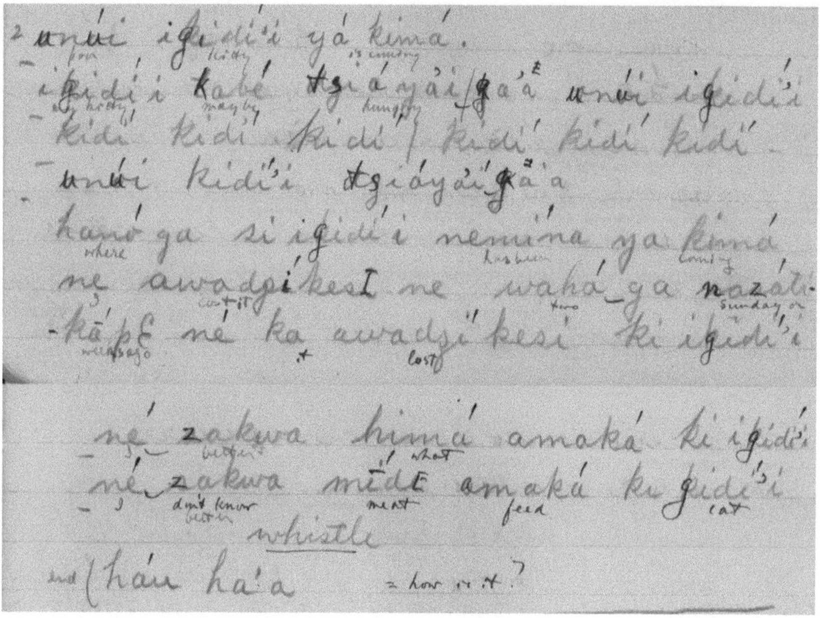

Figure 6.6
Gilbert Natches, conversation with a cat, transcribed from his own 1914 sound recording (CLA 24-2306), ca. 1914 (CLA Marsden.015, pp. 65–66). Kroeber's corrections and glosses were added in ink.

"leg," for example, *k* undergoes mutation after the prefix *i-* "my" (*igaupa* "my leg"), but not after the same vowel in a compound (*huupikaupa* "wooden leg," with *huupi-* "wood"). The phonetic difference between *k* and mutated *g* is salient to any language learner or non-speaker, but Natches ignored it. In his transcription in figure 6.6, he regularly wrote *ikidi'i* "my cat" with the same *k* as in unprefixed *kidi'i* "cat." Just as regularly, Kroeber changed it to *g*. This difference between what Kroeber heard (the pronunciation *igidi'i*) and what Natches perceived (the linguistic units *i-* + *kidi'i*) recurs throughout the corpus. Listening with a fluent speaker's ears, Natches did not attend to mutation any more than English speakers attend to the difference between the quite distinct *t* realizations in *sit* and *sitter*. His spellings expressed his intuitive understanding of grammatical structure rather than simply rendering pronunciation.[28]

Second, the Numu words that Natches chose to record went well beyond basic vocabulary and traditional cultural terms. His notebook includes four pages of "New Words for New Things" (CLA Marsden.015, pp. 59–63), all of them English loanwords like *puuka* "book," *saakɨsi* "circus," *kudupaa* "crowbar," and *sɨtobɨ* "stove," to name a few. In the compendious dictionary by Sven Liljeblad, Catherine Fowler, and Glenda Powell (2012), some of these words can be found (like *puuka*), some are recorded in slightly different forms (like *sɨtoba* "stove"), but others (like "circus" and "crowbar") are absent entirely. Yet all these words are fully adapted to Paiute phonology according to systematic patterns; they are integrated in the language. Numu words always end in vowels and lack consonant clusters, so vowels were added to English words beginning with clusters or ending with consonants. Between *s* and a consonant, *ɨ* was regularly inserted (*sɨtoa* "store," *sɨtobɨ* "stove"); after most word-final consonants, *ɨ* was added (*kaapɨ* "cap," *sɨtobɨ*), but *i* was added after *s* (*kaasi* "cars," *saakɨsi* "circus"). These and other rule-governed patterns reveal how English was indigenized. And the vocabulary itself—the "New Words" that Natches chose to document (like *kudia* "corral," *ládɨ* "lard," *sɨtopaipɨ* "stove pipe," and *tainopɨ* "suspenders, tying up")—shows what contemporary Paiute people needed to talk about.

Third, Natches's manuscripts are enriched by drawings that illustrate vocabulary. Perhaps the most interesting are in figure 6.7, showing parts of the *toibɨ* "cattail, *Typha latifolia*," a marsh plant with many uses. In the word *toibɨ*, *-bɨ* is a suffix; its root *toi-* is found in several of the other words, including *toikwammu* "cattail rhizome(s)," *toitɨna* "cattail root(s)," and *toipitakwa* "cattail base, stalk."[29] These terms are known from other sources, but two others in figure 6.7 are not.[30] One is *toitɨ*, which Natches glossed "new shoots." The other is *toikaa* "cattail cone," referring to the distinctive pistillate (female) flower; *kaa* or *akaa* means "cone" (as in *tɨbakaa* "pine cone"). According to Catherine Fowler (1990:71), the term *tsimaa* refers to cattail spikes "containing both male and female elements," that is, both the seed-bearing pistillate flower and the pollen-bearing staminate (male) flower. But these parts of the flower spike look different, have distinct functions, and are used differently in food preparation. It would be surprising if they were not distinguished linguistically. Natches's drawing plainly shows his understanding that *toikaa* refers to the female cattail flower and *tsimaa* to the male flower.

Finally, Natches's corpus has a personal character. On one recording, after singing a song, he explained that his family sang it for his father

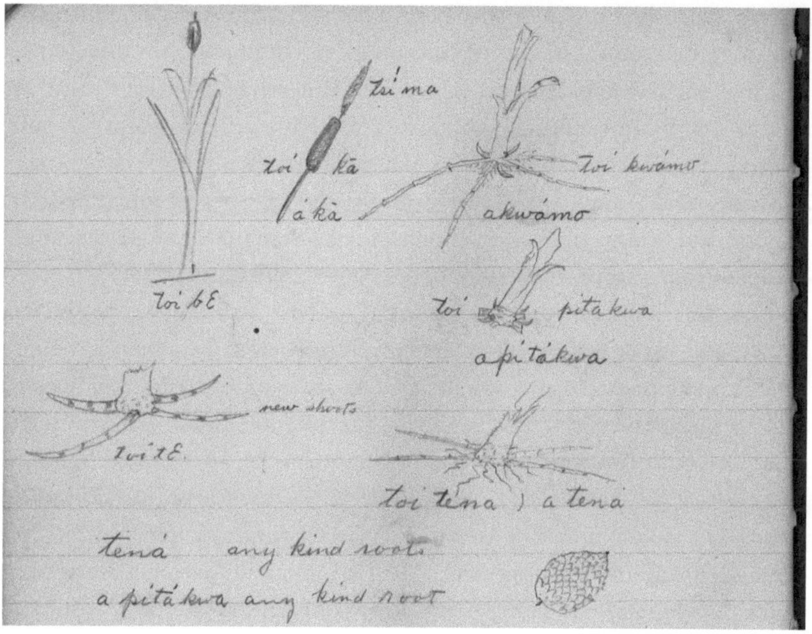

Figure 6.7
Gilbert Natches, cattail drawings and Numu vocabulary, ca. 1914 (CLA Marsden.015, p. 94).

when he was sick: *nanikuwɨdɨ tu'ihanano nɨmmi nikuwɨyaina, su mina pizayaina* "whenever we sang the song, our father became better."[31] On another (transcribed in figure 6.6), he performed a dialogue with a cat: *ikidi'i tabɨ(a) ciaya'iga'a* "it looks like my cat is hungry," he said; the cat responded with (Natches) meowing.[32] Still others included new musical forms: a waltz on the harmonica; a Christian hymn sung in Shoshone; and two popular songs on Native American themes, Billy Murray's 1904 "Navajo" and Mills and Chattaway's 1907 "Red Wing," whose melodies Natches played on a bugle.[33] No other collection of sound recordings that Kroeber or his protégés made with Indigenous people had this diversity.

The documentation Gilbert Natches assembled was no mere reflection of Kroeber's memory documentation. It was a body of work that expressed Natches's own choices, creative interests, and linguistic sensibilities, opening a window on his early-twentieth-century multicultural world. I also perceive a broader resonance between his language work and his art. In each field, outsiders with essentialist presuppositions sought to depict a vanished precolonial world. This was a focus not just of memory documentation but also of Edward Curtis's photographs, like that of the imagined Paiute artist in figure 2.3. But while Natches's paintings depicted scenes of cultural significance for Kuiyuidɨkadɨ Paiute people, they used new styles and tools to express his contemporary perspective. His music also drew on multiple traditions, his speech integrated the English and Numu languages, and his stories were both modern and fully Indigenous. In short, his legacy belies naïve essentialism.

Natches's life was not easy. His right leg was amputated after a 1907 injury, and his vision deteriorated significantly over the years. Kroeber's 1915 correspondence documents that he had arranged for Natches to "go to the University clinic regularly for treatment" and tried to make sure he would continue to consult a BIA physician in Nevada. Without treatment, UC doctors said, "it will be only a question of time until he becomes totally blind. The treatment is exceedingly simple and the cost in medicine absolutely nominal."[34] In 1916, Natches wrote Kroeber that he made a "pretty bad living here" and asked if more language work was available. In 1917, he said that his eyes were "too weak for drawing" and he was broke: "I wish you could help me . . . try to sell my drawing[s] & send me [some] money!"[35] His correspondence with others in later years also indicated "the rather desperate straits the artist found himself in," according to Peter Bandurraga (1990), "as his eyesight failed and the Bureau of Indian Affairs from time to time cut off his government allowance. The latter consisted of $10 per month in groceries doled out at the reservation store, with which Natches supported his mother, his sister, and himself." He died in 1942 at the hospital of the Stewart Indian School, where he had been a student forty years earlier.[36]

Gilbert Natches evidently valued his collaboration with Kroeber. Two decades after that work, the anthropologist Saul Riesenberg met and became friendly with him. Riesenberg was a Berkeley graduate student who supported himself in a job with the Railway Post Office that took him regularly to Lovelock, Nevada. There, in 1940, he filled a notebook with English-language Paiute stories Natches shared; some are versions of stories in the earlier Natches corpus.[37] Riesenberg reported an anecdote from his visits:

> One day he startled me by saying, "You know, I wrote a paper with Alfred Kroeber on Northern Paiute verbs, and I've lost my last copy; can you get me

> one?" Only half-believing him I went to see Kroeber when I got back from that trip. . . . Kroeber gave me a reprint, and I brought it to Gilbert the next trip, and found myself unable to do any work with him for the next hour, because Gilbert sat there oblivious of me, holding that paper about an inch from his nearly blind eyes, while the most beatific smile hovered over his lips the whole time.

Why did Natches choose to document his language, making recordings and writing down stories, sentences, and words? There is no way to know for sure, but his obvious pleasure may suffice as an explanation. In the Pyramid Lake Paiute Tribe, his work has an impact more than a hundred years later. The Kooyooe Tukadu Numu Yadooana (Pyramid Lake Language Program) has described Natches's work as "invaluable" for their ongoing language revitalization and preservation efforts, which include transcription, analysis, and digitization of his manuscripts, recordings, and stories. In their words: *Oo Ki Nasumoowakwatatu* "he will never be forgotten."[38]

ROBERT SPOTT AND YUROK

Kroeber's interpreter and a consultant in some of his first Yurok work was Weitchpec Frank. Frank's children Alice (figure 6.8, born 1879) and Robert (figures 2.2 and 6.9–6.10, born 1888) were adopted by his sister and brother-in-law at Requa, by the mouth of the Klamath River. Frank's brother-in-law, Captain Spott (figure 4.7), was a knowledgeable cultural leader whose work with Kroeber included sound recordings of significant narratives and other rich cultural and linguistic documentation. His adoptive children, Alice and Robert (Frank) Spott, were a young woman and a boy on the periphery of Kroeber's interactions when he first came to Yurok land in 1900. Both eventually became friendly with him, writing letters like this one from Robert (2 September 1908, RDA Box 11):

> Now I am thought drop you a few lines to you and like to know how are you getting along. I [am] hoping you are well. Hoping these few lines will reach you in [best] of health. For it leaves me in best health every day and I am working in the cannery. Also everybody are getting [a]long well as ever. And all of your friends in Klamath River are well. Also I like to know if you are coming this way some time this [year] before winter. Mr. [i.e. Captain] Spot[t] send[s] you his best regard.

Figure 6.8
Alice Spott Taylor, Requa, California. Undated photograph (1999.24.0363, Roberts Collection, Cal Poly Humboldt Library).

> How is Mrs. Kroeber? I [am] hoping she [is] well.
> I am going close you with my regard.
> I remain as ever.

Kroeber did not visit Yurok land between 1907 and 1923. This period saw the deaths of his wife Henriette (1913, after five years of illness) and Ishi (1916), as well as work with Dolores, with Ishi, in Zuni, and on broader anthropological questions. Based on Spott family memories, Francesca Fryer (1995:166–167) described Kroeber's return to Yurok land: "When Alice Spott and Alfred Kroeber met for the first time after all those years . . . they flung their arms around each other. Both were crying." It might not have been exactly so, but his reunions were no doubt emotionally significant. Fifty years later, Theodora Kroeber (1976:xvi) recalled, "When I went upriver with Kroeber, his old Yurok friends, recognizing him as our canoe came close, hurried to greet him, often to embrace him, the rush of words, his and theirs, coming first in Yurok."

Figure 6.9
Alfred Kroeber and Robert Spott, 1939 (PAHMA 15-19477).

Figure 6.10
Ursula Kroeber and Robert Spott, Berkeley, 1933 (ALKFP ALB v. 4).

Robert Spott served in the US Army during World War I, receiving the Croix de Guerre for bravery in France; in California, he was an advocate for Indian rights and cultural heritage.[39] Off and on for a decade (1933–1943), he and Kroeber worked together in Berkeley, St. Helena, and Requa (Spott's home at the Klamath mouth). This yielded a coauthored monograph and notebooks full of linguistic, cultural, and historical information copied down by Kroeber (ALK Ctn 12:34–40). Knowledge that Spott chose to share about child language and ceremonial speech usages was reported in a paper published after his 1953 death (Kroeber 1960b), but the bulk of this documentary corpus exists only in manuscript.

Spott and Kroeber's 1942 book *Yurok Narratives* has a logic and texture that are unique in California. It includes eighteen stories about nineteenth-century Yurok people, several from earlier generations, and more than a dozen narratives of the time before people came into the world. The collection expresses Spott's interpretation of Yurok cultural values, each story embodying principles he decided to convey. In recounting historical events, he contextualized individuals' actions by explaining whether they accord with Yurok law and what consequences each would have for other people or families. Kroeber added commentary, including some from Spott, but the latter's choices and explanations provided the book's enduring interpretive system.[40]

Each of Spott's narratives of prehuman times "emerged . . . from discussion of a folkway" (Spott and Kroeber 1942:vi). For example, "The old dog" (235–237) was told to Spott by James Mennow, and by Spott to Kroeber in August 1940. It concerns a young man who cared for his infirm dog so much that he would not marry until he found a woman who promised to care for it equally. But things changed after they had a child, and one night the dog appeared in a dream:

> *'Er'gerrk 'er 'we-chkeyek' weehlkwo' 'ue-megokw 'we-tegerew.*
> When he slept in the sweathouse, he dreamed that his dog talked.
> *"Keetee knokseechek', mehlkwehl tkeektkekoh."*
> "I'm going to leave you, (because) she keeps jabbing a stick (at me)."

In the end the young man shot the dog, mistaking it for a deer; this was the origin of white-rumped deer. Spott told this story to Kroeber while sharing Yurok teachings regarding dogs (ALK Ctn 12:39, pp. 73–83).

Similarly, Spott first told "The inland whale" (224–226) to Theodora Kroeber, who recalled, "I took no notes, the story having come to Robert's mind apropos of his saying something about bastards."[41] Its protagonist is a *kaamuueks* (a bastard, literally "bad child") whose mother has been disowned by her family; the whale also calls herself a *kaamuueks* and lives in a lake on a mountain whose name, 'O Kaa "where there is something bad," indexes her status.[42]

Kroeber has been criticized for focusing in his work on precolonial practices and neglecting experiences of genocide, dispossession, and survivance. Yet Spott's focus was similar in the stories that comprise *Yurok Narratives*. Most of the book concerns events after 1850, but not one narrative treats the actions of white people or Indian experiences as a result of the American invasion. Instead, with the invaders lurking on the periphery, as it were, Spott's stories are about social and cultural relations among Indian people, and how they reflect Yurok norms and values. A short narrative about a Shaker doctor is not about her nontraditional medicine practices but about practices relating to payment for healing. A long narrative about a Wiyot ceremony is about the ceremony itself, not the catastrophically destructive impacts of white people in heavily settled Wiyot land, forcing Wiyot people to give up their ceremonies for over a century.

An alternative interpretation is that Spott knew what Kroeber wanted to hear, and was accommodating him. Spott himself was quoted as saying, about anthropologists, "don't give people what they can't understand."[43] But reading the published book and the notes it is based on, I am impressed by Spott's own presence as a researcher, seeking to understand the cultural implications of traditional stories and individuals' historical choices. As Thomas Buckley (1987, 1989) has perceptively discussed, Spott was a reflective narrator whose telling expressed a search for meaning. His collaboration with Kroeber was fortuitous, inasmuch as the same kinds of stories interested them both, rather than somehow one-sided.

I do not mean to imply that Spott lacked concern for Indian rights. His attention to problems facing Native people and his record of advocacy are clear. My point is that his analytic and reflective side resonated with Kroeber's memory documentation. For *Yurok Narratives*, an impact of the American invasion was that Spott was led to find this resonance with an outsider.[44]

Like Dolores, Spott became a Kroeber family friend and spent summer vacations with them (see figures 6.9–6.10).[45] He encountered many anthropologists, and reportedly said that they "looked at [you] like you were a bug."[46] But he evidently got along well with Kroeber, whose daughter later recalled him vividly (Le Guin 2004b:18–19):

> I often felt uncouth around Robert Spott. He had tremendous personal dignity and authority. . . . Robert was grave, serious; we took no liberties with him. . . . I can still blush when I remember myself rather unusually holding the table, chattering away breakneck, telling some event of the day, and being abruptly silenced by Robert. I had far exceeded the conversational limit proper to a well-bred Yurok girl, which I imagine may be a word or two. Robert laid down his fork and swallowed, and when I paused for breath, he spoke to the adults on a subject of interest to adults.
>
> . . . There is a photograph of my father and Robert, one listening, the other telling, with lifted hand and faraway gaze. . . . Robert and Alfred talked together sometimes in English sometimes in Yurok. It was perhaps unusual for the daughter of a first-generation German immigrant from New York to hear him talking Yurok, but I didn't know that. I didn't know anything. I thought everybody spoke Yurok.

Le Guin kept a copy of the photograph in figure 6.9 "on or near my desk most of my adult life" (email to Joan Berman, 2 February 2015). In Kroeber's notebooks from his work with Spott, I see the relationship of telling and listening that Le Guin named. Spott's curiosity and desire to teach guided their collaboration as much or more than Kroeber's research questions.

FOUNDATIONS

Dolores, Natches, and Spott were not Kroeber's only sustained Indigenous collaborators; others were Ralph Moore (chapter 4), Jack Jones (chapter 5), and Ishi (chapter 7). But his collaborations with Dolores and Spott lasted longer than others, and all three were authors or coauthors of publications based on the work. Kroeber arranged these and could easily have taken sole authorship, as many linguists do even today. These collaborations also yielded collections of stories that reflected not Kroeber's purposes but the individual goals and interests of three Indigenous tellers. Their academic interlocutor gave them the space and tools to say what they wanted in their particular styles. Each created a foundation of stories for his community.

Dolores bequeathed many stories, in his own voice and recorded from elders. Hundreds of pages of creation stories and traditional narratives are included, as well as his own lengthy memoir—a rare, early autobiography written in an Indigenous language. Other historical texts he wrote down are "Events of the Mexican War in 1904" (in O'odham) and the English-language biographies of Sawe Nnuhwe (also concerning conflict with Mexicans) and Antonio Lopez.[47] Dolores recorded and transcribed not only the words of dozens of songs but O'odham-language speeches (ceremonial oratory) in the call for rain from two elders.[48] Transcribing his own stories and songs and stories from others, he also supplied extensive linguistic detail (especially on word meaning and usage) and information about cultural, geographical, and historical context. His sixty-page telling of one creation story was followed by six pages of notes like this (ED 134.1.15, p. 62): "The race track is that open space, under the mountain, on the west side. There are no trees on this land, and [it] is level. The distance is about 50 mi[les] or more." His transcription of a creation song (ED 134.4.E) added the comment that one word is used "only in baby language. It means, Come along." In the song, he explained, the earth doctor was "speaking to the earth as if it is his child, holding it by the hand [as] he pull[s] it along, saying Come along." It would be fair to describe the entirety of Dolores's work as an O'odham cultural atlas from the late nineteenth and early twentieth centuries.

Natches grew up surrounded by English as well as the Numu language; engagement with American society was an important aspect of his family history. As discussed above, he was especially interested in crosscultural connections—in art, language, and music that drew on Indigenous and European traditions. The documentary corpus he created is a witness to Indigenous linguistic and cultural creativity and evidence that change and self-assertion are not at odds.

For his part, Spott explained that Yurok has terms for two kinds of story. A story is called a *chpeyuer'* if "it has a foundation . . . from the places where it happened. Without such a foundation, a story is called *'er'gerp*."[49] An *'er'gerp* is any story or news. A *chpeyuer'* implies a link between language and land; it is a story about what happened in specific named places. Such stories explain the world. (They are also literally told with care: *chp-* means “careful”[50]). The last story in *Yurok Narratives*, for example, explains why Captain Spott used to address *mer'wermerys 'ue-mey'* “daughter of the headwaters” when he set out on an ocean voyage: “You crossed without paddle from Mer'wermery to Wohpekw. Lend me your boat,” he would say to her. “This is it. I shall have no trouble from the ocean.”[51] The story told how the daughter of the headwaters sat in a boat with no paddle and traveled downriver, through the breakers at the mouth of the river, across to a sandy land on the other side of the ocean, home of *wohpekws 'ue-mey'* “daughter across the ocean,” and eventually back home. It explained why people did as they did, where they did it. “Every story should have a foundation,” Spott said in 1941 (Erikson 1943:270); “explain where something began and came from, and if you do not know the foundation, do not try to teach.” His goal was to understand and teach the origins and purposes of Yurok cultural practices, on Yurok land and in Yurok waters, through the stories that explain them.

III

NATIVE BODIES

7

ISHI'S CHOICES

> To know him was a rare personal privilege, not merely an ethnological privilege. I feel myself that in many ways he was perhaps the most remarkable personality of his century.
> —T. T. Waterman, "Ishi," 1917

One of the twentieth century's best-known Native Americans was the Yahi man called Ishi. Born in the 1850s or 1860s, he lived in hiding for years before walking into Oroville, California, in August 1911. He and other Yahi people had interacted with white settlers, but newspapers spread the story of a "wild Indian" who spoke no language others knew; gawkers thronged. Kroeber's colleague T. T. Waterman came to Oroville, learned that Ishi spoke Yana, and brought him to San Francisco. Ishi chose not to divulge his name, and was referred to by an Anglicization of the Yana word for "man."[1] He was an object of scrutiny and fascination during his lifetime, and has been the subject of articles, books, and films in the decades since Theodora Kroeber's extremely popular book *Ishi in Two Worlds* (1961).

The words "Yana" and "Yahi" are Anglicizations of the word for "person" in the language now called Yana and in its southernmost dialect. The Yana language was spoken before colonization in the Sierra Nevada foothills of northeastern California. Yahi land lies in the southern part of Yana territory, in the Deer Creek and Mill Creek watersheds, between Lassen Peak and the Sacramento River in northern California.

From September 1911 until his March 1916 death from tuberculosis, Ishi lived in the UC anthropology museum in San Francisco, and for a summer with the Waterman family in Berkeley. The museum housed other employees (archaeologists and caretakers) and Indian visitors; Kroeber himself had lived there after the 1906 San Francisco earthquake.[2] Ishi

ISHI, THE LAST ABORIGINAL SAVAGE in AMERICA

THE nameless aborigine, whom the anthropologists call Ishi for convenience, was discovered in a slaughter house near Oroville on August 28 in the act of stealing meat. He is a man about 60 or 65 years old, and was garbed in a canvas shirt when first discovered. For five or six days he was lodged in the Oroville jail, while Indians of all the surviving tribes were brought in as interpreters, none of whom could make themselves understood. Prof. T. T. Waterman of the University of California visited him September 1, and concluded that he was the last survivor of the tribe of South Yanas, supposedly extinct. Then Sam Batwee, a North Yana, was sent for, and with some difficulty they conversed upon Ishi's past, his identity and the fate of his fellow tribesmen. According to his story, he has been alone for many years, but it is believed that he was one of four Indians, the last of the Deer creek branch of the South Yanas, driven out of a thicket by surveyors in Tehama county some months ago.

Following Professor Waterman's visit, Ishi was brought to San Francisco, and has since been lodged at the Anthropological museum south of Golden Gate park, where Professor Waterman and Dr. A. L. Kroeber have taken records of his speech and, with the help of Batwee, have learned as much as possible of his history and of the customs of his people.

He is still living at the museum, gradually adapting himself to the marvels of a civilization with which he was never in touch, and has so far been a gentle, affectionate, timid old man, the least civilized and yet the most harmless barbarian in the world.

Figure 7.1
Newspaper coverage of a visit to the Orpheum Theater (*San Francisco Call*, 8 October 1911, p. 4). Front row (left to right): Ishi, Sam Batwi, and performer Lily Lena. Back row: Henriette Kroeber, Alfred Kroeber, T. T. Waterman, and Grant Wallace.

participated in Sunday afternoon cultural demonstrations in his first seven months, including activities like flint knapping and net weaving; worked on language, texts, and songs with Kroeber, Waterman, and (in 1915) Edward Sapir; and was employed as a "Museum Helper" (Waterman's term) or "factotum" (Kroeber's).[3] He had an active social life until he fell ill in August 1915. His last months were spent in the museum and next door in the UC hospital. After his death, an autopsy was done, against his known preferences and Kroeber's insistent wishes; his cremated remains were interred locally. As extensively discussed, most importantly by Orin Starn (2004), Ishi's brain was not cremated, and was reunited with his ashes only in 2000, in a tribal burial in northeastern California.[4]

Figure 7.1 typifies contemporary news coverage that was variously patronizing, dehumanizing, or racist; newspapers delighted in showing Ishi in "modern" settings like a theater or automobile. Referring to a mummy collected in Phoebe Hearst's Peruvian excavations, a piece in her son's *Examiner* mirrored public attitudes in describing two "specimens" at the museum ("University Folk" 1911):

> One was the huddled, dried figure of a Peruvian man, dead no one knows how many thousand years, the hair matted and tangled over the skull, the features still plain and the legs and arms the size of pipestems. What kind of soul looked out of those eyes in life? . . .
>
> The other was alive and smiling, with the same dark skin and the same black, coarse hair. This was Ishi, the Deer Creek Indian captured in the Sacramento valley, recently, and now a captive at the Affiliated Colleges where, as the last of his tribe, he is being studied by the professors with intense interest.

Kroeber encouraged the publicity, only sometimes pushing back. An article associated with figure 7.1 was so demeaning, with Grant Wallace (1911) calling Ishi an "abysmal brute," that Kroeber published a response. "There is nothing undeveloped" about Ishi, Kroeber (1911c) wrote. "He has the mind of a man and is a man in every sense."

Figure 7.2 shows Ishi with Joseph K. Dixon, author of *The Vanishing Race* (1913). An impresario of assimilation, Dixon enlisted the likes of Andrew Carnegie, William Randolph Hearst, John D. Rockefeller, and Theodore Roosevelt in support of a proposed American Indian Memorial in New York, a monumental statue he described as "a witness of the passing race to all the nations of the world as they come to our shores" (Barsh 1993:96). Dixon organized a 1913 "expedition of citizenship," touring the country in a special train car and cajoling Indian communities into pledging loyalty to the US flag. Figure 7.2 features a Haida totem pole (PAHMA 2-10723) that was erected in 1870 at Skedans, Haida Gwaii (Queen Charlotte Islands, BC), collected by Charles F. Newcombe, and secured for the museum by Phoebe Hearst (see chapter 3). Whatever Ishi thought about this moment (probably he was being polite to a visitor), the enculturation of Native people and display of their cultural heritage are at the surface.

Ishi's story is often understood as an instance of the colonial captivity and exhibition of Indigenous people. Damning evidence, it would seem, is Kroeber's press announcement in Ishi's second month in San Francisco of "the wild Indian Ishi being on exhibition . . . this Sunday afternoon" (13 October 1911, RDA Vol. 13). Certainly, the fact that Ishi and other Native people were subject to BIA decisions meant that he lacked liberty. Coco Fusco (1994:146–147) included him in a

Figure 7.2
Joseph K. Dixon and Ishi at the UC anthropology museum, 1913 (NAA Photo Lot 24 SPC Misc Historical Unid Portraits Objects 01279200).

centuries-long list of " 'aborigines' on display" who "served as proof of the natural superiority of European civilization, of its ability to exert control over and extract knowledge from the 'primitive' world, and ultimately of the genetic inferiority of non-European races." A *Daily Cal* editorial described Kroeber as "penning up" Ishi and "studying him until his death" (Shok 2020); Lumbee scholar David Shane Lowry (2021) said Ishi was "imprisoned within the University." Even Berkeley's anthropology museum recently asserted that his position there "resembled indentured servitude."[5] Understandably, given all this context, the "Proposal to Un-Name Kroeber Hall" summed up Ishi's treatment by Kroeber and others as "cruel, degrading, and racist." But the evidence, as I will show, does not support this perspective.[6]

BEFORE 1911

Ishi had survived a genocide that was especially brutal for Yahi people and their neighbors. To the south was the 1863 Konkow Maidu Trail of Tears; to the north, violence against Yana people included the massacre of three hundred people at an 1864 ceremony.[7] Yahi land alone endured more than a dozen massacres from 1850 to 1871, with more than two dozen victims in several cases. Many people (usually women and children) were also abducted in these assaults, and brought to reservations or kept as servants. In the 1871 massacre, four ranchers killed about thirty people who had taken refuge in a cave. "The last known large-scale massacre of California Indian people," according to Benjamin Madley (2016:335), it was described in gruesome detail by a local man: "In the cave . . . were some Indian children. Kingsley could not bear to kill these children with his 56-calibre Spencer rifle. 'It tore them up so bad.' *So he did it with his 38-calibre Smith and Wesson revolver*" (Waterman 1918:150, emphasis original).

By the turn of the century, only a few Yahi people were still living. They had taken refuge near an abandoned village above Deer Creek. They did not live "traditional" lives: their communities and broader networks had been destroyed, much of their land had been taken, and they were in danger from but partly dependent on white people. In 1908, a surveying party encountered them and they fled, abandoning their encampment; many of their possessions were stolen.

In the following years, Kroeber and Waterman tried to contact these Yahi people. Waterman spent almost two months looking in 1909 and 1910, but saw only traces. In March 1911, Kroeber wrote to the Commissioner of Indian Affairs, encouraging "the Indian Office to obtain further information about these Indians and if possible to bring them in and care for them." In this letter, he expressed concern for their welfare.[8] The land they occupied was unforgiving; unable to use traditional fishing and gathering places, they sometimes took food or livestock from settlers to avoid starving. Kroeber emphasized that "they are likely at any time to commit thefts which will so incense the neighboring whites that a chance encounter with the latter may result in fatalities for the Indians." He also noted what researchers might learn. Kroeber (1911a:550) explained in a popular piece, distinguishing as usual between history (studying recent events) and anthropology (studying "ancient" cultural practices):

> These people must preserve, besides their language, many entirely aboriginal beliefs and innumerable native customs and practices. . . . A record of their wanderings, their vigilance, their traits and habits, would appeal to the historian, while a knowledge of their ancient institutions and traditions, preserved from purely aboriginal times into the Twentieth Century, would be a rich mine to the ethnologist and anthropologist of the future.

Kroeber's revealing, no doubt unwitting metaphor was that anthropology is like mineral extraction.

At the request of the BIA, Kroeber also wrote to BIA California special agent C. E. Kelsey (13 April 1911, RDA Vol. 13):

> I believe that if the necessary arrangements were made with the ranchers in the vicinity, the Indians could probably be induced to come in, or at least to open negotiations when next somebody meets them. I hardly imagine that the tract which they particularly inhabit has ever been taken up, so that in such an event it might be feasible to place them legally upon the land which they occupy, with the probable result that they would stop stealing and would themselves enjoy a fair measure of security, without any undue complications or change in their mode of life.

Kroeber's idea that Yahi land should be set aside for Yahi people continued after Ishi came to Oroville.

SAN FRANCISCO AND BERKELEY

Ishi appeared in Oroville hungry and with short hair that signified mourning (figure 7.3). Kelsey sent Waterman a telegram: "There is no objection to taking wild Yana to San Francisco" (2 September 1911, RDA Box 14). Publicity and crowds surrounded Ishi. A front-page San Francisco newspaper article had Kroeber calling him "the most uncivilized and uncontaminated man in the world to-day" ("Untainted Life" 1911), plainly expressing his interest in precolonial cultures and languages.

Following the lead of Kroeber's letter to Kelsey, Waterman said publicly that Ishi and the United States must enter into a treaty relationship, since Ishi's people had never ceded their land.[9] The *Oroville Daily Register* headline was "President and Senate to Make Treaty with Aborigine"

Figure 7.3
Ishi in Oroville, 4 September 1911. Photograph by John H. Hogan (PAHMA 15-5404; see also Burrill 2011:172–173).

(1911), while another newspaper suggested that Ishi might be given "a plot of land . . . in the Deer creek canyon where his forefathers hunted and trapped" ("Sideshows" 1911). Juan Dolores heard about this and wrote to Kroeber that he (Dolores) ought to "hide someplace" in the Arizona mountains (10 September 1911, RDA Box 11): "When you find me, tell [President] Taft or somebody, that they have to make a treaty with me. I think that will be the only way I can get some good place to stay the rest of my life." The BIA refused to consider a treaty with Ishi, of course, insisting that he was a legal ward of the US government.

Kelsey and Sam Davis, a BIA representative who visited Ishi in San Francisco, wrote separate letters in September 1911 to the Commissioner of Indian Affairs (C. Kroeber and K. Kroeber 2002). Davis suggested eventual placement with a Yana person, Sam Batwi (whom Ishi disliked[10]) and Kelsey wrote similarly:

> [Davis: Ishi] is wholly incapable of protecting himself if left to drift back to the wilds, as he would doubtless commit some act sooner or later that would bring him in conflict with the law. Neither is he a proper person to

> leave to the charity of the county or local community. I suggest, therefore, that . . . arrangement be made with Sam Batwee or some other Indian of the community to look after him and provide him with food and raiment. I think Batwee would do this for a few dollars a month, say about seven dollars, and it would be the kindest arrangement that can be made. After a year or two he would doubtless be able to look after himself, or become a member of the band and live as they do.
>
> [Kelsey:] They have quarters at the museum for visiting Indians, which are more comfortable than most Indians have at home. The Indian says he is willing to stay there with Mr. Waterman. How long he will remain in this frame of mind we can not tell. . . . I am inclined to think that he could be placed with some of the few remaining Indians of the Yana stock, most of whom are near Redding. I think some of the Indians there would take care of him for five or six dollars a month. He might learn to work so as to support himself, in time, though he may be too old for very much physical labor.

Kroeber described himself to Erving Ackerman as Ishi's "guardian" (26 March 1912, ALK Box 2:12), meaning that the BIA had temporarily ceded its role to him. This was paternalistic; maybe Kroeber should have refused to work with the BIA. But it is unclear that the US government would have made good choices for Ishi. Kelsey was instructed by BIA officials to inquire, "first, [as] to the possibility of training him [Ishi] to conform, at least to a reasonable degree, to the customs of civilized life; and, second, as to the possibility of training him for the performance of simple manual labor" (27 October 1911, RDA Box 14). He might, in other words, have been subjected to a rapid, adult-education version of the US Indian schooling system described in chapter 2.

What did Ishi himself want? In considering the last five years of Ishi's life, Les Field (2005:83) posed the key questions:

> Was Ishi treated as a living exhibit of primitive culture, the last example of a vanquished Indian world, on display at the museum for both a voyeuristic public and a data-hungry anthropological community? Or was Ishi instead a willing, conscious participant in co-creating a new life for himself in San Francisco, a life that afforded him comfort, dignity, friendship, and personal satisfaction?

Despite Field's "or . . . instead," the answer may be "yes" to both questions. Given a full menu of options, few would choose to live in a museum building, even in what Elizabeth (Pope) Davis (1973) recalled as "a small, sunny room," so it is understandable that some writers have perceived Ishi's condition as akin to captivity. Yet Ishi stated a preference to live there, not on a reservation or with other Indians unrelated to him, as the BIA would otherwise have arranged. Evidence comes from half a dozen sources.[11] BIA representative Davis reported in 1911 that Ishi "evidences a desire to remain with his new acquaintances rather than expose himself to those unknown." In the same year, Kroeber wrote, "For a time I believed that he was unhappy, but when Batwee asked him if he would rather live with the white men or the Indians he said he preferred to stay where he was." In 1912 he quoted Ishi's statement to Batwi: "I want to stay where I am. I will grow old here, and die in this house [the museum]." And in a 1914 letter, Kroeber wrote that Ishi "has been self-supporting for over a year, serving as assistant janitor and general helper about the Museum. . . . He has been free to return to his old home and manner of living ever since being with us, but much prefers his present condition." Waterman wrote that Ishi "never wished to go back to the wilds, naturally enough, for there was nothing to go back to. He had however, to be reassured repeatedly that we had no intention of sending him back." And Saxton Pope commented, "When asked if he wanted to return to the wilds, he replied that he did not, because everybody was dead, only evil spirits inhabited the places of his former pursuits, and there was not enough food to eat there."

A final indication that Ishi felt comfortable where he was comes from the correspondence of Kroeber and his Yuki collaborator Ralph Moore. After a San Francisco visit, Moore wrote, "Tell Ishi that I still sing his song yet" (4 February 1912, RDA Box 22). Kroeber's answer, maybe referring to a picture of a Moore family member, was that Ishi "did not get nearly so excited about that as about the photograph you carried around in your pocket" (10 February). Moore responded in turn (13 February) that he told people in Round Valley that Ishi was "a nice singer." A woman there wanted to see him and said Moore should "bring him back home with me" next time. Kroeber replied (25 April) that Ishi "did not get very excited" about that: "You might say to her that she can give you her picture to send to Ishi [and] may be he will know better." All in all, Ishi seems to have been clear about his preferences.

In a letter to Kroeber from Pyramid, Nevada, Dolores also reflected on Ishi's situation (12 October 1912, RDA Box 21). Kroeber had sent photos, and Dolores wrote that he "was very glad to look at my friend Ishi. Just now, I can say that Ishi is in a better place than this place where I am today; should any accident happen to him, I am sure he will be well taken care of." Prompted by a heavy-machinery accident his brother had had, Dolores detailed some of "the many abuses which the working men get sometimes." His point was that Indian people often led precarious lives.

Ishi lived in San Francisco rather than Berkeley, where the university was mainly located and many faculty lived. This was not only because the museum had sleeping quarters where employees already spent the night, but also because "dark-complexioned individuals were not always welcome" in Berkeley, as Kroeber (1958a) later put it. Berkeley was a residential suburb and would in 1916 be one of the first US cities to institute zoning laws meant to exclude people of color.[12] Kroeber himself lived in San Francisco and clearly thought that Ishi would feel more comfortable there.

UC Berkeley's anthropology museum has asserted, as noted previously, that "Ishi's position at the Museum resembled indentured servitude." Readers can evaluate the resemblance for themselves, but it is worth adding that Kroeber's interest in hiring Indigenous people as docents and in other roles was not restricted to Ishi. Dolores did such work, as noted in chapter 6, and Kroeber also (unsuccessfully) offered his Mojave friend and interpreter Jack Jones a job in the museum "explaining some of the Indian things to people who come to see them" (14 December 1911, RDA Box 13). It would pay less than interpreting, he wrote, but the position would last longer and Jones would have no expenses. "I think you would like the job," Kroeber wrote, "because you know how to get on with white people and how to talk to them and they would take to you." Kroeber understood the museum not as a place of mutual cultural exchange, but as a site where white Californians learned about the Greek, Egyptian, and Peruvian pasts, and about Native American cultures, assumed to be heading to another past. One can admit this limitation while also respecting the impulse to employ Indigenous people and create contexts where they were acknowledged as bearers of valuable knowledge.

Ishi's demonstrations at the museum ended after seven months. Noting the "somewhat spectacular use that has been made of the collection," Phoebe Hearst wrote President Wheeler on 25 April 1912 that she was "disturbed that so much has been made of Ishi, who seems to have been rather too fully exploited. That particular mixture of anthropology and the show business may have swelled the number of visitors, but if so I hope a fair proportion of those who came to stare remained to study."[13] Her complaint was not about Ishi's treatment, but that it was undignified for her museum to promote cultural demonstrations. These were "spectacular," like circus acts, not edifying. Wheeler conveyed the sentiment to Kroeber. In response (20 May), Kroeber acknowledged that "we have driven close to the edge in exploiting the Museum." A museum with a central location and modern conveniences "could have afforded to be more dignified," he said, adding that Ishi's demonstrations were ending that month.[14]

Ishi's Bay Area life mixed documentation of language and sociocultural practices, general museum work, and a variety of activities in his free time. He never learned much English, apparently by choice, but communicated successfully enough. His friends included academics and their families, like Edward and Delila Gifford, at whose house he sometimes spent weekends (Foster 2003:97); museum colleagues like Dolores; and others in San Francisco.[15] Ishi had two cats, and he wore a coat bearing as many as forty lapel badges with the slogan "Votes for Women."[16] Davis (1973) remembered that he loved going to movies—one of the few things he spent money on apart from necessities.

A colleague and fellow museum resident, archaeologist Nels Nelson, dictated reminiscences of Ishi in 1962 for Theodora Kroeber (TKP Box 10):

> Ishi and I saw each other probably every day from about the middle of December 1911 until June 1st 1912. During that time we lived in the University of California Museum of Anthropology in San Francisco. From this building we could see a little of San Francisco Bay, the Golden Gate, and a stretch of the Pacific Ocean.
>
> We could communicate hardly at all by word of mouth, but we exchanged many ideas by sign language and demonstrations. . . . I took him on several walks west and southwest of the city to show him the various kinds of native trees, brushes and flowers in order to find out what he knew about them as useful for food or any other purposes. We also frequently visited Golden Gate Park, partly to show him imported and cultivated trees and flowers as well as the caged animals in the small zoological park.

> ... Ishi also showed me how he chipped arrowpoints, spearpoints and knife blades from flakes of flint, obsidian (volcanic glass) and ordinary window glass of various thicknesses. The museum's Sunday visitors were invited to the assembly hall where while I told them what little I knew of his life's story, Ishi was kept busy with his flint chipping, the result of which was finally held up for them to see....
>
> Ishi was a good marksman with the bow and arrow and after my departure, Dr. Saxton Pope, in the adjoining medical building, encouraged him to experiment with bow and arrow making.

Pope (1920:186–188) himself wrote that Ishi "was remarkably talkative, rambling off into stories, descriptions, humorous episodes, and many unintelligible tales.... He was a particular favorite with all small boys." One such boy, Fred Zumwalt Jr., shared his memories in 1962 (Zumwalt 2003):

> I would wait for him on the corner of 11th Avenue and Lake Streets so that I could look down 11th Avenue and see him get off the street car. Usually he would see me and start waving while still a block away—once across the street he would pick me up like a sack of potatoes and carry me into the garage where he would remove his shoes, casually give me a present, and greet Jerry, my King Charles Spaniel and Billy, my pet chipmunk. Billy would immediately run up his arm as soon as he opened the cage and dive into Ishi's shirt where he rode around all day—when it came time for Ishi to put him back in his cage Billy was usually sound asleep in a pocket somewhere. Jerry adored him too but was not permitted to go on our walks since he was too noisy and would frighten birds. Our walk would then begin by a trip to the kitchen for a handout of cookies, bar chocolate and jerky.... Our next point of call was the garden where Ishi examined the progress of slips that he brought from time to time. One of the gardeners in Golden Gate Park gave him slips of roses and fuch[s]ias which he brought to my mother and were planted. He was always pleased to see his gifts growing.
>
> ... I can recall one afternoon when we both lay nose to the ground smelling the earth from different places around the lake so that I would learn how to tell one place from another by scent alone. Then Ishi drew an outline of the lake and marked from where each sample came.

Many similar memories came to Theodora Kroeber from readers of her book (TKP Box 10). Dorothy Stevens knew Ishi when she was about ten, regularly played jacks with him, and wrote, "I felt I had lost a real friend when I heard he had died of tuberculosis." Another correspondent remembered the dolls Ishi had carved for her and a friend, and another wrote that "when he walked by our home on his way to visit Mr. Poyser [the museum janitor], we took his hand and walked with him. He stopped and pressed a blade of grass between the sides of his thumbs and made a whistle."

Dental students occasionally paid Ishi to make casts of his teeth. Herbert Samuels had been a student in the 1910s and remembered Ishi's teeth ("as near a perfect denture as I have ever seen") and companionship. When Samuels was eating lunch with a colleague, "quite often Ishi would stroll over to us. There would be greetings and we shared a sandwich or piece of cake with him. He expressed considerable liking for coconut layer cake."

Two of Pope's children themselves recalled Ishi well. Elizabeth (born in 1903) met Ishi first when she was eight and spent time with him throughout his San Francisco years. Ishi told her many stories, she later said (Davis 1973), for example about Coyote; and he came to dinner at the Pope house "many, many Sundays—it seemed like every Sunday." She also remembered "the last time I saw him. It was a few days before he died, and he was so very thin, and frail. I held his hand, and couldn't help just burst[ing] into tears. But he was very brave and stoic about everything, although he knew it was the end, and gave no sign at all."

Elizabeth's brother Saxton Jr. (born in 1902) also had many memories of Ishi (Pope 1972).[17] "Father and Ishi were hunting rabbits," he said about a San Francisco picnic, for example, "and they made calling sounds. I don't remember that they got any. . . . I think it was generally agreed that Ishi's skill and results were the better at short distances and father better at long." He also accompanied his father, Ishi, Kroeber, and Waterman on a trip in Yahi country that involved documentation of place names and traditional practices. The boy remembered parts of that trip:

> Ishi did swim with me and he had a very curious method. It was a series of short underwater dives, not very deep. Meanwhile, I held on to his hair, which I was able to hold even when he was underwater, and downstream we merrily went, and it was very cold water. I was able to swim at the time of the excursion or lesson, but not very well. . . . Ishi was in high good spirits on the trip, and I think a good example of that was my swimming lesson. He told of great hunts, and he laughed with enjoyment often. . . .

> What did not strike me at the time as unexpected certainly does now: how after such a life and such early experiences he could ever have trusted a white man again. His adjustment, however, was not without its complexities. On his excursions into the Yana country, on several occasions he heard his mother and sister calling when no other member of the party could hear them; and presumably they weren't there.

Ishi had to be persuaded to go, according to Theodora Kroeber (1961:205–206), but apparently he mostly enjoyed himself in the end.

The elder Pope (1920:178–186) depicted a man who enjoyed visiting the university hospital (next to the museum): "He came to the women's wards quite regularly, and with his hands folded before him, he would go from bed to bed like a visiting physician, looking at each patient with quiet concern or with a fleeting smile that was very kindly received and understood." Other accounts confirm this. According to one newspaper report ("Ishi Is Second Nurse" 1912), when Ishi and Kroeber were scheduled to go to a lecture, Ishi could not be found. Kroeber "searched all through the [hospital] building and at last heard his voice lifted in a chant in one of the private wards. Going in he found Ishi sitting at the bedside of a woman patient and singing his very best in an effort to cheer her up." And in a 1962 letter (TKP Box 10), H. H. Gaston recalled undergoing surgery in March 1915: "Dr Saxton Pope performed the operation and as you know Dr Pope and Ishi were close friends. Ishi used to come through the ward every morning with the Dr. and he spent some time visiting with us." Ishi was himself in the hospital later in that year. Adelaide Weihe Strange (1976) remembered going with her grandmother to visit him there, when she was seventeen or eighteen years old, and seeing that a friend had given him a record player on which he was listening to marches by John Philip Sousa.

Not all reports portrayed the docile figure that might suit the white imagination. In two 1962 letters to Theodora Kroeber (TKP Box 10), Esther K. Watson recalled seeing "much of him" in 1915 when she was a summer student taking a class from Waterman. She met Ishi on campus ("work[ing] on arrowheads etc. as he sat under a pepper tree at the corner of the anthropology building"), at the Waterman house (see figure 7.4), and on an outing to a shell mound site. There they found "bones and broken bits of pottery," and Watson remembered that "Ishi was not happy with the experience; he seemed to be an unwilling

Figure 7.4
Left to right: T. T. Waterman, his daughter Helen, Ishi, and family friends in front of the Waterman house, Berkeley, August 1915 (T. T. Waterman photograph collection, 1907–1919, PH Coll 434.13, University of Washington Libraries, Special Collections, UW 41053). Ishi lived with the Watermans from June through August 1915.

member of the expedition, doubtless because he did not enjoy disturbing these relics of by-gone days."

The contradictions are encapsulated in Pope's account: Ishi locked his door in the museum at night because of mummies, other human remains, and their possessions; nevertheless preferred to sleep there, where it was warm, rather than in a canvas house outside; and "was very thrifty and saving, and looked forward to the day when he could buy a horse and wagon" (1920:186). This statement by a friend implied that Ishi felt agency. The Proposal to Un-Name Kroeber Hall for its part adopted a depersonalizing narrative, suppressing Ishi's agency, by reporting that his "white benefactors" gave him "a janitorial position to earn pocket money" (DKH 1).

Kroeber developed a strong personal attachment to Ishi, according to his wife and daughter and by his own account. He himself wrote that Ishi "thoroughly endeared himself to all with whom he came in contact" (1925:343–344), while Theodora wrote that Alfred "loved Ishi" and throughout his own life "was unreconciled to the waste and loss in a life [Ishi's] so rich" (T. Kroeber 1963a:4).[18] She was more forthright privately. In a letter to a friend, she said that Alfred "would not, could not, 'reminisce' about Ishi" because of what Ishi's death evoked, not long after his first wife's 1913 death following her struggle with tuberculosis. Theodora summed it up: "*Five* years of agony for him and Henriette—this barely over, and then Ishi's illness—the same one."[19]

Kroeber could be extractive and paternalistic. Some of his letters show a disturbing emphasis on research goals. In April 1915, after Ishi was briefly ill, Kroeber wrote that "the moral is to get from him what we can while he is well instead of trusting that he will last indefinitely" (Golla 1984:186–187). Yet less than a year later, when Ishi was dying, Kroeber famously wrote to Gifford from New York to discourage an autopsy and, following Yahi practice as he understood it, to insist on cremation. (T. Kroeber 1961:234, Heizer and T. Kroeber 1979:240). His language was uncharacteristically emotional:

> As to disposal of the body, I must ask you as my personal representative to yield nothing at all under any circumstances. If there is any talk of the interests of science, then say for me that science can go to hell. We propose to stand by our friends. Besides, I cannot believe that any scientific value is materially involved. We have hundreds of Indian skeletons that nobody ever comes to study.

When Kroeber returned in August, not only had an autopsy been done, but Ishi's brain had been preserved. Instead of cremating it and interring it with Ishi's ashes, Kroeber sent it to the Smithsonian Institution, an unsentimental and apparently disrespectful choice contradicting his letter to Gifford.[20] Nancy Scheper-Hughes (2003:115) perceived this as "an act of disordered mourning," while Clifford (2013:126) suggested that "Kroeber may have felt there was no way, any more, to do the right thing for his friend." Whether explained by psychological or structural constraints, as betrayal or a nod to science, this last ambiguous action epitomizes much of the larger story.

Near the end, Waterman wrote frankly to Kroeber (25 March 1916, ALK Box 31:23): "The poor old Indian is dying. The work last summer was too much for him. He was the best friend I had in the world, and

I killed him by letting Sapir ride him too hard, and by letting him sneak out of lunches." Kroeber and Waterman often referred to "the Indian," not "Ishi" (which was after all not his name); the mention of lunches means Waterman thought he should have eaten more. Whether or not this is medically plausible, it seems natural to feel guilt. Orin Starn clearly articulated the contradictions (Day 2016): "On the one hand, they used him as a scientific discovery. On the other hand, they deeply loved him."

DOCUMENTATION

By all accounts, Ishi took great pleasure in sharing his language, songs, and cultural practices. His volubility was emphasized by Kroeber in preparing Sapir for his 1915 visit to Berkeley: "You will find Ishi bursting with mythological, ethnological, tribal, and geographical information, which he is delighted to impart, but he may need a little training before he will dictate connected texts slowly enough for writing" (Golla 1984:188). Afterward, Sapir reported that "my work with Ishi is by far the most time-consuming and nerve-wracking that I have ever undertaken. Ishi's imperturbable good humour alone made the work possible" (Golla 1984:194).

Two strategies were employed to try to overcome the problem that Ishi spoke too fast for easy transcription. One was sound recording. Ishi's cylinder records include over 150 cylinders of songs and spoken narrative, procedural and informational content; they were added to the Library of Congress National Recording Registry in 2010.[21] The longest text is the Story of Wood Duck, on fifty-one cylinders (two hours and fifteen minutes), but Ishi's speech rate and style still make transcription challenging.

A second strategy was to teach Ishi to write Yana, as Juan Dolores earlier and Gilbert Natches later learned to write their languages. A folder in Kroeber's papers documents this apparently unsuccessful attempt, though its label "Ishi Reading lessons" is a mistake by Theodora Kroeber or an archivist. What it contains are not reading but *writing* lessons, meant to teach Ishi how to write the sounds of Yana. Its centerpiece is a booklet whose pages mostly have Yana words that share a syllable; each word has a picture suggesting its meaning. For example, the page in figure 7.5 has two words with the syllable *si*; the preceding page has four words ending

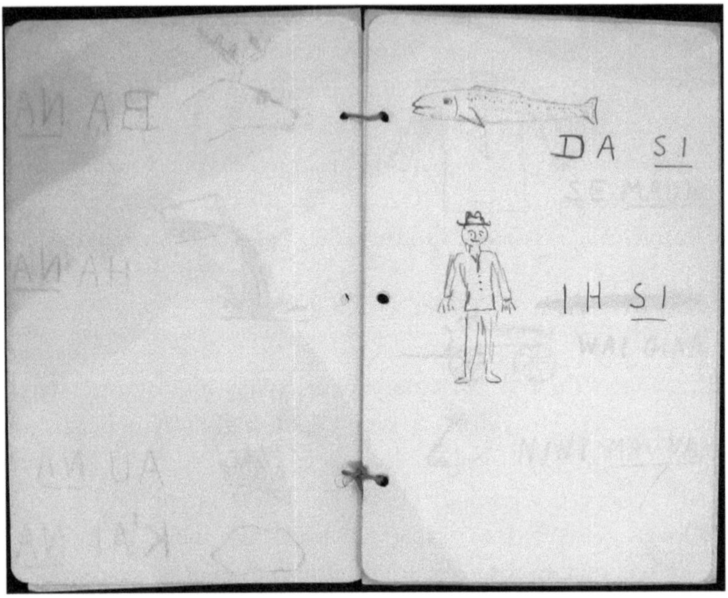

Figure 7.5
Ishi's "reading" (actually writing) lessons notebook (ALK Ctn 17:33). Vocabulary: *daasi* "salmon," *hisi* = Yahi [(h)ihṣi] "man."

in *na*. In any case, there is no record that the project interested Ishi, whose speech endures today only in words recorded by others.[22]

Ishi's language documentation yielded a significant corpus through his work with Kroeber, Sapir, Waterman, and Gifford, mainly in 1911–1912 (his first year in San Francisciso), in spring 1914 (during the expedition to Yahi land), and in summer 1915 (with Sapir). He recorded a total of sixty-seven songs on fifty-five cylinders.[23] Linguistic transcriptions include texts, grammatical information, and vocabulary ranging from nouns and verbs to botanical and geographical terminology. With Sapir he dictated five traditional narratives, transcribed in "approximately 13,000 words," as counted by Victor Golla (2003:217). With Waterman in 1911 he recorded and dictated six texts, including the Story of Wood Duck mentioned above (partly transcribed by Waterman in three notebooks, ED 35.1–3) and five nonnarrative texts:

- Information about the fate of the dead (recorded on twenty-eight cylinders, 72 minutes, partly transcribed in one notebook, ED 35.4)

- Information about girls' adolescence ceremony (recorded on seven cylinders, 18 minutes, fully transcribed, ED 35.5, pp. 8–30, 40–43)
- Information about earthquakes (recorded on one cylinder, transcribed, ED 35.5, pp. 31–34)
- "Description of fishing" (recorded on two or three cylinders, not transcribed)
- "Salmon information" (dictated in four notebook pages, ED 35.5, pp. 35–38)

Ishi's documentary corpus also includes one or two dozen pages of lexical elicitation with Waterman, forty-five pages of lexical and grammatical elicitation with Sapir, and dozens of pages of notes by Kroeber and Gifford.[24] More technical parts of Ishi's corpus include musical transcriptions of some of his songs and phonetic data from his speech.

Kroeber's work with Ishi is especially rich in geographical documentation, including many scores of place-names with carefully drawn maps, information about places and the people who lived there, and ways of talking about place. The example in figure 7.6 shows directional vocabulary shared by Ishi in April 1915. At the bottom of this manuscript page, a map shows a variety of trajectories from the anthropology museum at Parnassus Heights in San Francisco. Directions are labeled in Yana and glossed in English. This is interesting as a rare record of how an Indigenous directional system is used outside its place of origin. Significantly, Kroeber translated *tinji* (#5) as "due W[est]" and "downstream" and *teenauna* (#10) as "N[orth] E[ast] N[orth] = upstream." Sapir glossed the same words as "west" and "east," respectively, based on other work. He also glossed *tinjamna* as "north" (Kroeber's #9 "N, across Golden Gate") and *tintpa* as "south" (#4 "S[outh] W[est] S[outh]"), identifying *tin-* as a "stem for cardinal points."[25] Sapir understood the Yana system as one based on cardinal directions, while Kroeber knew it might have the riverine aspect he had encountered in Yurok. In Yahi land, where waterways like Deer Creek and Mill Creek flow from east to west into the Sacramento River, upstream is east. From San Francisco, one source of water flowing into the bay is more north than east, but it is still called *teenauna*.

On the next sheet in the same folder, Kroeber recorded Ishi's terms for wind directions. A general word for "wind" is *ju'k'alla*; the related verb is *ju'k'aalsi* "the wind is blowing." Both are based on a root *ju-* "wind

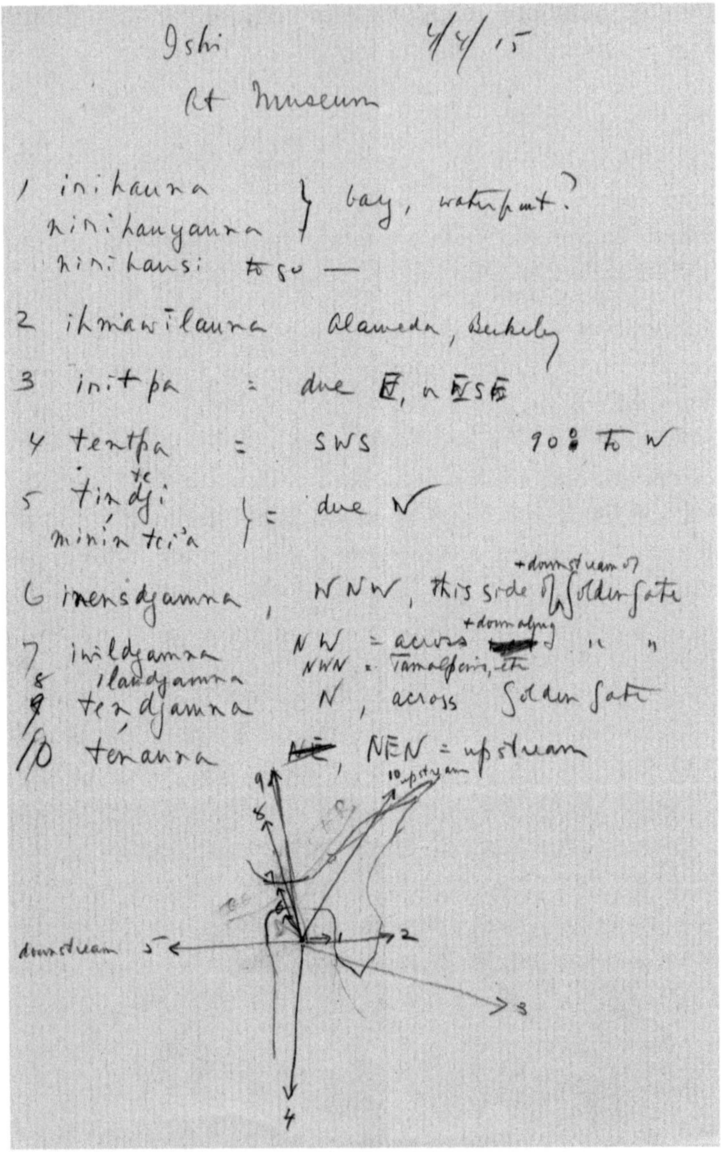

Figure 7.6
Yana terms for directions in the San Francisco Bay Area, written down by Kroeber with Ishi, 4 April 1915 (ALK Ctn 17:29). The origo is in the UC Museum of Anthropology at Parnassus Heights in San Francisco.

blows" and a suffix *-k'al.*[26] Specialized terms, each formed with the root *ju-* and a directional suffix, index four of the directions in figure 7.6:

- West wind: *juhxaujuusi* "it's blowing from *tinji*" (#5, directional *-xauju*)
- North wind (*juhgamna*): *juhgamsi* "it's blowing from *tinjamna*" (#9, directional *-gam*)
- East wind: *jutkiisi* "it's blowing from *teenauna*" (#10, directional *-tki*)
- South wind: *juhwajuusi* "it's blowing from *tintpa*" (#4, directional *-waju*)

These are significant linguistically and for their broader implications.[27] Despite the many terms in figure 7.6, Ishi volunteered just four terms for wind directions. They include verbs ("wind is blowing in some direction") and nouns ("wind from some direction") and thus constitute a paradigm, suggesting that these are the basic Yana directional categories, whether the "east" and "west" terms index cardinal directions or waterways.[28] The basic system determines even local reference: in a story, a bird sitting on the left side of the head of someone facing east says *darigamsit'oo'* "I will look down from the north," that is, "from your left."[29] People use directional language to map and navigate their land. In sharing this knowledge, Ishi offered a key to the Yahi landscape and to the many toponyms he also shared.

ISHI'S LEGACIES

Over decades of stories about Ishi, the Yahi man has been a palimpsest on which viewers write their own stories about Indigenous experiences and relations with white people. Highlighting how these images and perspectives had come to replace the actual man, the Anishinaabe scholar Gerald Vizenor (1994:126) called Ishi "a simulation," one who "posed at the borders of the camera, the circles of photographers and spectators, in the best backlighted pictures of the time."[30] In "haunting" photographs, James Clifford (2013:133) has written, "the man seems somehow present and absent."

Ishi became famous in 1911, and again in 1961 with Theodora Kroeber's book about him. Alfred hardly wrote about Ishi, reluctant to revisit an emotionally difficult time, but he shared information with Theodora. When her book manuscript was done, he told Ursula Le Guin that it was "a remarkable text" (10 July 1959, UKLG Box 129:7): "It will be authentic but also exciting. Above all she has felocity, I would say. Felocity of word, of approach, of continuity with modulation." His invented word was apparently a blend of *felicity* and *ferocity*.

Readers of Theodora's book included Ella Deloria, the Yankton Sioux writer who was also an accomplished anthropologist and linguist.[31] Deloria sent Kroeber what she herself called a "fan letter" (28 December 1961, TKP Box 11). It offered her praise as "an ethnographer of Dakota culture and language" as well as a more personal reaction:

> As an Indian, I am thrilled and, at once, also proud, with a touch of regret that our people are so confused today. I can't quite explain my feelings. But I do take this "wild" (?) primitive Indian as a symbol of the inherent qualities in our people's former life (I have known Dakotas in the past who would have reacted exactly like Ishi), and of course as an even larger symbol of such qualities in mankind universally as long as their native integrity remains unmarred.
>
> To have made this fact plain, not by a conglomerate of details of a culture, but by presenting *a life* so objectively yet so understandingly, is indeed, to my mind, the achievement to struggle for. . . . May I add that the Sioux "intellectuals" all acclaim the story too? As well they might.

Her "conglomerate of details" meant precisely the kind of work published by anthropologists like Theodora's husband Alfred.

The Proposal to Un-Name Kroeber Hall forcefully criticized Kroeber's treatment of Ishi. Some responded with defensive approbation; a former student said Kroeber "rescued [Ishi] from jail and gave him shelter, a job, respect" (DKH 2). Others had a different view. In an article supporting the Proposal, four Native students wrote about the resonances of Ishi's UC experience (Cesspooch et al. 2020). His story was "all too familiar" to them:

> When we think of Ishi, we think of ourselves. We think about our grandparents and the ancestors we lost to genocide. We are reminded that institutions such as UC Berkeley were not made for us or our ancestors. We consistently have to present ourselves in white spaces to succeed and survive, not only for ourselves but for our communities that continue to be adversely impacted.

Each generation thus sees in Ishi someone other than the Yahi man himself. He evokes the presuppositions of all who encounter his memory, shaped as we are by our different individual experiences.

There is no direct evidence of what Ishi wanted for himself in his San Francisco and Berkeley years; there are only reports from those who mostly thought they were his friends and benefit from a positive story. But what evidence there is points in one direction: on balance, he liked his life at the museum. He faced "a narrowed freedom created by colonial violence," as Clifford (2013:107) described it, but within that inescapable context, he had agency, made choices, and planned a life. While his friends could be paternalistic (or protective, as they might have said) and were interested in his unique knowledge, their actions were not (as the Proposal declares) "cruel, degrading, and racist." On the contrary, they seem to have afforded him space to make his own decisions and to carry them out.

Critiquing a seemingly endless fascination, William Bauer (2014b:50) has suggested moving on. "People have searched for Ishi not necessarily to learn more about Ishi," he wrote, "but to inform their own understandings of the world. . . . Perhaps it is a good time to stop hunting Ishi and let him rest." Bauer's critique is on point, but I believe there is a way to talk about Ishi's legacy that respects his choices.

From what has been reported of his San Francisco and Berkeley life, it seems plain that while he may not have relished cultural demonstrations to impassive spectators, Ishi loved teaching. He enjoyed showing children and students how to appreciate the world, sharing cultural practices with friends, and telling about his land and lifeways. As Kroeber put it, he was "bursting" with knowledge he was "delighted to impart" and wanted others to learn. Despite his backlit image, his voice is clear in recordings and writings, in stories he chose to tell his friends and colleagues. We honor Ishi by continuing to tell them and learn from them.

Factors making it hard to appreciate Ishi's legacy include his choice not to use the written word or to learn English fluently. Hearing his voice on his terms rather than anyone else's therefore means attending to Yana, the language in which he recorded stories and shared knowledge. But if we try to do so, then at least two areas open wide.

One area is geography. In 1984, some of the land where Ishi had lived was set aside as what the US government calls the Ishi Wilderness.[32] This is land that Kroeber and Waterman said should be given to Yahi people; instead, it is for hikers and hunters. An imagined association between Ishi and "wild(er)ness" goes back to the August 1911 day he walked into

Oroville. Both Alfred and Theodora Kroeber accepted the association: he called Ishi "the last wild Indian in the United States"; her book's subtitle is similar.[33] That he used the term at all may be surprising, given that he often referred to Indigenous California "civilizations" and defended their cultural intricacy. But he distinguished "cultured" or "refined" Indigenous populations from those he called "wild." The latter, as he apparently saw it, were smaller, nomadic groups living on the periphery of larger, settled "civilizations" like those of Hupa, Karuk, Maidu, Mojave, and Wintu people (Kroeber 1925:128, 343, 889). In any case, Le Guin (2004b:29) dispatched the fantasy:

> Ishi was not wild. He did not come out of the wilderness, but out of a culture and tradition far more deeply rooted and soundly established than that of the frontiersmen who slaughtered his people to get their land. He did not live in a wilderness but in a dearly familiar world he and his people knew hill by hill, river by river, stone by stone. Who made those golden hills a wilderness of blood and mourning and ignorance?

"To Natives," Damon Akins and William Bauer (2021:195) have written, "the area was not a wilderness. It was the land."

Ishi shared some two hundred Yahi toponyms with Kroeber and Waterman, including the names of camps, villages, creeks, springs, mountain peaks, and other landscape features.[34] A "wilderness" named after Ishi perpetuates the idea that precolonial Indigenous people lived in "the wild." His teaching could instead be honored by restoring the age-old names of places in Yahi civilization. Table Mountain (upriver on Mill Creek) could again be called Waamatiwi; and in Lassen Volcanic National Park, Lassen Peak and Brokeoff Mountain could be known as Pulpulli and Buskuina, respectively.

A second area is narrative. A Yana creation story is a *maumaiyauna*, literally "teaching, telling."[35] Ishi called the people in such stories *c maumaiyauna*, which Sapir tentatively glossed "the story, mythological people" (ED 68.5, pp. 23–24). Ishi's *maumaiyauna* "focus on the rhythms of daily life" more than other narratives in Yana or other Native American languages, according to Herbert Luthin and Leanne Hinton (2003a:348), making him "a storyteller unlike any other . . . in the traditional oral canon of Native America" (351). For example, his introduction to one story has fourteen food preparation scenes, some of them lengthy, as well as "four hunting scenes, four firewood-gathering scenes, and seven eating scenes—not to mention three arrow-making scenes" (333).

Luthin and Hinton also argued that Ishi's interest in scenes of daily life was reflected in a linguistic detail of his narratives. Yana has a verbal aspect marker *-'andi*, which serves to move the discourse reference time forward and is sometimes translated "now" or "then." It was typically used by other storytellers at the beginnings of narrative episodes, in effect demarcating and summarizing them. But in Ishi's stories, *-'andi* is frequent even in other contexts. In the following short excerpt from a creation story translated by Jean Perry (2003:280–292), *-'andi* appears in three of five sentences, each naming an activity the story people undertook to get food:

C jo'la' c maumaiyauna.
The story people ate.
Bairuyau'andi'.
Then (*-'andi*) they went hunting deer.
Juwa'c'iru'andi'.
Then (*-'andi*) they went hunting small game.
Galaahiru'andi'.
Then (*-'andi*) they went fishing.
Tuusin'aigambati.
"It will be like this," they said.

By depicting the three activities as temporally distinct, Ishi drew attention to each in turn rather than just relegating them to the background.[36]

Quotidian activities are often presupposed by other storytellers, whose real or imagined audiences may be quite familiar with the details. Instead, like the Owens Valley life stories discussed in chapter 5, Ishi's narratives emphasized food preparation and other practices structuring daily life and social relations. In teachings shared with friends and colleagues, Ishi described an ordered life before the US invasion and asserted a distinctive set of cultural values.

What Ishi emphasized in *maumaiyauna* was echoed in what he taught children. His skill in archery and in making bows and arrows, for example, was also part of his pedagogy. In a 1962 letter to Theodora Kroeber (TKP Box 10), Fred Zumwalt recalled that Ishi "made me a small bow and arrows with which he taught me to shoot lizards, a willow seine for catching minnows and soft rabbit skin moccasins with the fur on the inside. We spent hours calling quail and wild ducks and stalking rabbits." And arrow making is a preoccupation in Ishi's narratives, especially the Story of Lizard, beginning with its first sentences:

> *Hiri', heebil' k hiri'mauna.*
> He made arrows, he was busy with his arrow making.

From the details in this narrative, Luthin and Hinton (2003b:296) remarked, "one can almost learn how to make arrows."[37]

Edith and Frances Bepler learned another kind of food gathering. When they were young, Edith later wrote, they lived near the UC anthropology museum and "became friends" with Ishi (Yates 1988).[38] Sometimes he would pass their house on his way to the grocery store:

> He would sit on the curb outside our home to remove his hated shoes, and if we saw him, we'd ask mother if we may join him. When yes, we'd run out and each take one of his hands and go happily down the middle of the cobbled street. Then one day he taught us how to pounce on grasshoppers in the vacant lot across the street from our home. We'd clutch them in our little fists, then open them slowly for Ishi. He would pull off the hind legs and pop the body into his mouth. I can still recall the sound of his crunching them.

The origin of this food was also part of Ishi's creation narrative:

> *Jau'ati juurik'u.*
> It is said they (the story people) made grasshoppers out of snow.

Sapir's manuscript has a note that they also made acorns out of rain.[39]

Ishi taught children far more than just finding food in the natural world. As quoted earlier, Zumwalt recounted Ishi's interest in growing flowers. He also described learning how to nurture butterfly cocoons (2003:15):

> One day [Ishi] returned with a few pieces of grass [or milkweed?] to which were attached butterfly cocoons. We put them in a glass jar in my room and over a short period of time watched them break open and the butterflies emerge. As soon as the sun had warmed and dried them, Ishi put them on the balcony to fly away to enjoy their freedom.

Ishi was showing his young friend how to care for the world, somewhat as he himself might have learned when he was young.

In short, I am struck by the common themes in Ishi's interactions with children; his cultural demonstrations for friends, colleagues, and museum visitors; the Yahi geographical knowledge he shared; and the stories he told in Yana. An observer schooled in other traditions might have the impulse to separate work from social life, relations with San Francisco children from those with academics, and cultural work from language documentation. A holistic assessment would instead see all these activities as articulating Ishi's sense of cultural values—literal and metaphorical *maumaiyauna*. To acknowledge this legacy would respect Ishi's agency and choices.

Ishi's stories flow one into another. My impulse as a philologist is to treat them as discrete artifacts—to "entextualize" them, in Richard Bauman and Charles Briggs's (1990) term—but the actual documentary record is often continuous. For example, the Story of Lizard begins (as above) with the arrow making that frames the narrrative. Yet Ishi told it after a creation story that ends with the same activity, transcribed by Sapir on the previous manuscript page:

> *Bairu'moyol'andi.*
> Now they went to hunt deer.
> *Hiri'gati.*
> It is said he (Lizard) makes arrows.
> *Gi't'ap'pausiwa.*
> They were taught.

The two stories have been published as separate texts, but the verbal echo is unmistakeable as one narrative follows another.[40] A *maumaiyauna* may conclude, but Ishi's teachings do not stop.

8

ANCESTORS

> "If Indians die, where will [they] go?" the *'woogey* said. "[They] will go under ground. [They] may not leave them outside of ground; [they] have to bury them. So [it will] be done to them."
>
> —Johnny Shortman, 1902

At Wehlkwew by the Klamath River estuary on 14 September 1902, Johnny Shortman spoke in Yurok (translated by Weitchpec Frank) about the origin of death.[1] Those who lived in the world before human beings, the *'woogey*, were preparing the world. After determining that people should die, the *'woogey* arranged practices relating to death. One such practice is the burial of the dead. Some others practice cremation, but Yurok people have traditionally interred the dead. A cemetery (*koweesh-tewohl* "fence place") is often surrounded by sticks like a picket fence. Families clear weeds from cemeteries annually—in late spring, according to Robert Spott, in *kohchaawech*, the sixth month of the Yurok calendar (ALK Ctn 12:35).

To disinter the dead seems barbarous, but it is what archaeologists have long done. More than 125 years ago, the president of the American Association for the Advancement of Science, Daniel Brinton (1895:244), said with reference to past generations, "We rifle their graves, measure their skulls, and analyze their bones; we carry to our museums the utensils and weapons, the gold and jewels, which sad and loving hands laid beside them." Today, as Berkeley anthropologist Rosemary Joyce (2015:169) put it, "there is still a great need for anthropologists engaged in excavating human remains to find a standpoint from which to articulate why this peculiar practice of ours is not gruesome."

Berkeley's anthropology museum holds thousands of skeletonized bodies and body parts taken from burial sites in the nineteenth and twentieth centuries, including Native American sites excavated while Kroeber was in charge (1909–1946). South America, Europe, Africa, Asia, and Oceania are represented as well, and many artifacts buried with people are included.[2] A 1990 law, the Native American Graves Protection and Repatriation Act, mandated repatriation of bodies and cultural items taken from US graves, subject to conditions; a California NAGPRA was enacted in 2001 and significantly revised in 2020. Yet repatriation from Berkeley has been slow, and the university widely perceived as uncooperative or obstructionist. Its failure to return remains continues to be a source of pain for Native people whose ancestors lie in storage boxes on the Berkeley campus.

NAGPRA legislation was the result of Indigenous advocacy and activism in the 1970s and 1980s, the work of Native scholars, and efforts by organizations like the American Indians Against Desecration (founded in 1980).[3] The broader context of Indigenous activism includes the American Indian Movement (founded in 1968) and the occupations of Alcatraz Island (1969–1971) and Wounded Knee (1973). In 1970, according to Tony Platt (2011:128), California became "the first state in which a grassroots organization," the Northwest Indian Cemetery Protection Association, "was created to specifically halt the desecration and looting of cemeteries." In 1971, the California legislature temporarily banned any excavation of Native burial sites other than those abandoned for more than two hundred years.[4] The social movements of the 1960s were also a critical backdrop.

Repatriation has been fraught. More than twenty years ago, Standing Rock Sioux scholar and activist Vine Deloria Jr. (1997:212) could write with characteristic acuity that UC Berkeley "still considers the reburial issue simply a minor political squabble that has nothing to do with religious and cultural beliefs." A decade later, Ted Howard, cultural resources director of the Shoshone-Paiute Tribes of the Duck Valley Indian Reservation, called repatriation "a human rights issue" (Paddock 2008). He added, "All we're asking for is to be treated fairly." UC Berkeley chancellor Robert Birgeneau then accused university critics of a "campaign of vilification" and expressed concern "about the damage done to possible educational opportunities for Native American people." He may not have intended this as a threat, but it did not ameliorate relations. "It's always going to be a trauma for us," wrote Charlene Nijmeh, chairwoman of the

Muwekma Ohlone Tribe, whose ancestral land includes Berkeley (Koseff 2020). "It really comes down to regaining our culture that we were robbed of—connecting to what was lost."

Times are changing. California governor Gavin Newsom (2019) has formally apologized on behalf of the state for the "violence, maltreatment, and neglect California inflicted on tribes." The state auditor issued a report that was critical of UC repatriation practices, especially at Berkeley. Its subtitle was blunt: "The University of California Is Not Adequately Overseeing Its Return of Native American Remains and Artifacts" (Howle 2020). Administrative changes beginning in 2019 led to guarded optimism among some who are eager to see repatriation of ancestors to all tribes that wish to have them returned, while others remained skeptical.[5] Important changes made to the California law in 2020 also made it easier for Native American tribes to make successful repatriation claims.

Kroeber's name was not traditionally raised in repatriation discussions, but the "Proposal to Un-Name Kroeber Hall" laid out a case (DKH 1). He "personally engaged in excavating grave sites," it said, "directed the work of others in this regard, and built a repository for human remains exhumed by academic researchers and government agencies." Its judgment was unflinching: "This has always been wrong and is also now illegal. Few actions conducted at our university in the decades that followed Kroeber's work are of similar enduring negative consequence or constitute such an incredible breach of ethics."

In fact Kroeber did not run US excavations and initially discouraged new archaeological research in California, though for scientific rather than ethical reasons.[6] But he excavated in Latin America and was engaged with California projects, especially at the shell mounds along the San Francisco Bay coastline that were being razed by urban development. In a few cases, he sent students or museum employees to excavate in California or nearby. It is fair to ask about Kroeber's understanding of such work.

Taken at face value, the Proposal's moral assertions have serious implications. If "excavating grave sites . . . has always been wrong," as it insists, archaeologists today must abandon many practices and their employers should repudiate them. To mention just one university, recent Berkeley research has included excavation of human remains and funerary objects at sites on three continents: Palenque, a Classic Maya city in Chiapas, Mexico; medieval Villamagna, Abruzzo, Italy; Late Bronze Age Aidonia,

Greece; and Bronze Age Tel Megiddo, Israel. Creative research focuses on burial sites and previously excavated funerary objects from Pharaonic Egypt.[7] This work has been praised at Berkeley, not condemned.

Archaeological projects in collaboration with local communities now also involve excavation and even biological analysis of human remains. In east Africa, Elizabeth Sawchuk et al. (2019:6240) reported a study of burial practices circa five thousand years ago by Lake Turkana, Kenya, with permission from "the people of Turkana County." In Vanuatu, Matthew Spriggs and David Reich (2020:2) described DNA analysis of skeletal remains in a Lapita Culture cemetery, undertaken with "the full support of the traditional Eratap village landowners and chiefs." As part of a long-term collaboration between the Metlakatla First Nation in British Columbia and researchers at the University of Illinois at Urbana-Champaign, John Lindo et al. (2016) reconstructed immunological changes associated with colonization by comparing genetic data from twenty-five living people and remains of twenty-five individuals who lived between circa 6,260 and 1,036 years ago.[8] In California, Tsim Schneider et al. (2014:195) described the excavation and analysis of remains of 163 people at a Napa County site "in cooperation with representatives of the Mishewal Wappo Tribe of Alexander Valley." And a study by C. L. Scheib et al. (2018) of ancient DNA from California and elsewhere in the Americas, reconstructing likely population relationships, included analysis of recently excavated Ohlone ancestral remains in collaboration with the Muwekma Ohlone Tribe. In California and elsewhere in the United States, such work now ordinarily occurs only in limited circumstances, as when a construction project unearths a burial; Native monitors then play a key role. Still, in the United States and elsewhere, archaeologists and biological anthropologists routinely do what the Proposal deemed "always wrong," often with the close involvement of Indigenous participants or collaborators.[9] What is at issue is precisely when such work is ethical or unethical, and how the relevant contested boundaries are constructed and change over time.

WHY DIG?

Archaeology offers a key source of knowledge about the human past, alongside oral or written histories and inferences from language and biological data. The field now incorporates non-extractive methods, such as surveys, satellite imaging, and ground-penetrating radar, but material dug out of the ground still exposes what histories do not tell and shows how stories about the past serve purposes in the present. For example, archaeological data from the centuries after the end of Roman control of Britain contradicts later stories of invasion by "Anglo-Saxons" who subdued or expelled Britons to claim their new land. Instead, Germanic settlers and Romano-British indigenes engaged in complex, mutually beneficial interactions that were eventually forgotten or did not serve the ideological goals of elite foundation narratives.[10]

Often enough, archaeology reveals pasts whose very memory has also been buried. The Minoan polities of Crete in the second millennium BCE were barely known before early-twentieth-century excavation. That work uncovered new forms of writing, Linear A and B, the latter of which was ultimately deciphered as an early dialect of Greek. It also exposed sophisticated artistic traditions and a long-lasting sociocultural world whose details and changing interpretation continue to inspire discussion and analysis. As often in archaeology, evidence from mortuary practices and artifacts plays an important role. Precisely because the dead are so significant for their families and communities, evidence of this kind opens a unique window on ancient social lives.[11]

Biological data from ancestral remains can also help answer significant questions about human history. The study of ancient DNA in particular allows a previously unimaginable level of precision. For instance, archaeogenetic analysis has shown that central Europe underwent a significant population replacement during the early third millennium BCE with the first appearance of individuals with ancestry from the Pontic-Caspian steppe.[12] The estimated population replacement (at least 40 percent) has been interpreted as supporting a linguistic model of early Indo-European language spread from the steppe into Europe, in contrast to other models.[13]

Ancient DNA evidence can be used to identify relationships between individuals as well as community-level demographic patterns. In an archaeogenetic study of 244 individuals living in southeastern Iberia over a period of two thousand years, Vanessa Villalba-Mouco et al. (2021) showed that Copper Age genetic stability was followed in the Early Bronze Age (ca. 2200 BCE) by the arrival of a large population with steppe ancestry, at the same time as cultural changes visible in the archaeological record. And since multiple individuals at each site were studied, some could be identified as the children, parents, and siblings of others. In a broader analysis, Villalba-Mouco et al. also found population-level patterns they interpreted as evidence of patrilineal social structures. Archaeogenetic evidence helps answer questions about how people lived as well as where they came from.

A century ago, DNA was unknown and archaeogenetics was inconceivable. Analysis of osteological data was its precursor. Physical anthropologists believed that anatomical traits that were observable in skeletal remains and significantly determined by heredity could be used to infer likely relations between populations or even the ancestry of individuals. As an analytic tool, such methods have outlasted scientific belief in the reality of "races."[14] Osteological data is still critical in forensic work. For example, the noted forensic anthropologist Phoebe Stubblefield (2011) used statistical analysis of cranial measurements from several control populations to show that remains found on a university campus in 2007 were those of a Black person whose body was likely used as an anatomical teaching specimen in the nineteenth century. Her work to identify remains from the 1921 Tulsa race massacre (in which her aunt's house burned down) has used similar tools. As Stubblefield put it (Rose 2021), "If we get enough of your skull, we can, with fair reliability, assess your ancestry."

Physical anthropology was therefore potentially relevant for Kroeber's goal of understanding the ancestry of Native American populations. A typical point of uncertainty concerned the early occupants of Lovelock Cave (discussed below), about 100 miles northeast of Reno, Nevada. Local Paiute people were reported to have said in the 1910s that the Lovelock Cave inhabitants were not Paiute. Rudimentary osteological measurements led L. L. Loud and M. R. Harrington (1929:32) to identify differences between the Lovelock Cave people and contemporary Paiutes and to suggest "admixture" with "brachycephalic Sierra Nevada peoples" as an explanation. While their brief remark is hardly convincing, the point is that biological data was used then, as it often is now, to help establish diachronic relationships among individuals and populations.

UC ARCHAEOLOGY IN 1901

When Kroeber came to the University of California, its archaeological programs included the excavation and collection of artifacts and ancestral

Figure 8.1
Proto-Nazca ceramic bowl decorated with hummingbirds, excavated by Max Uhle from a grave at Ocucaje, Ica Valley, Peru, with funding from Phoebe Hearst (PAHMA 4-4652).

remains in California, South America, Europe, and Africa. These efforts were organized and subsidized primarily by Phoebe Hearst, whose interest in collecting fine art and elite cultural artifacts did not match Kroeber's sense of the mission of anthropology. In 1902, as discussed in chapter 3, their differences almost got him fired. His own "interests were in ethnology and linguistics," as he later told UC president Wheeler (2 March 1909, ALK Box 2:4), but in his UC role he "worked, as impartially as I might, for the furtherance in an equal degree of archaeology and physical anthropology." Despite preferring a California focus, he "did not work against" the collection of ancient Egyptian, Italian, and Peruvian artifacts, "but for it."

Figures 8.1–8.3 show material collected from human burials under UC auspices around the time of Kroeber's move to California. Figure 8.1 shows a Proto-Nazca ceramic bowl, one of thousands of objects taken from early Peruvian graves as part of Max Uhle's UC archaeological research. As Uhle summarized that work in 1901, "I discovered at Ica [Valley] five civilizations, three of which may be considered new."[15] One was Proto-Nazca, "an ancient civilization whose remains alone would have deserved a visit." In figure 8.2 is an otherwise unknown part of an ancient Greek play, probably Sophocles' *Inachus*.[16] Removed from a human mummy excavated in Egypt in 1900, it is now part of Berkeley's Tebtunis Papyri archive, the largest US papyrus collection. Figure 8.3 shows a stela from the tomb of Wepemnefret, a son of the pharaoh Khufu

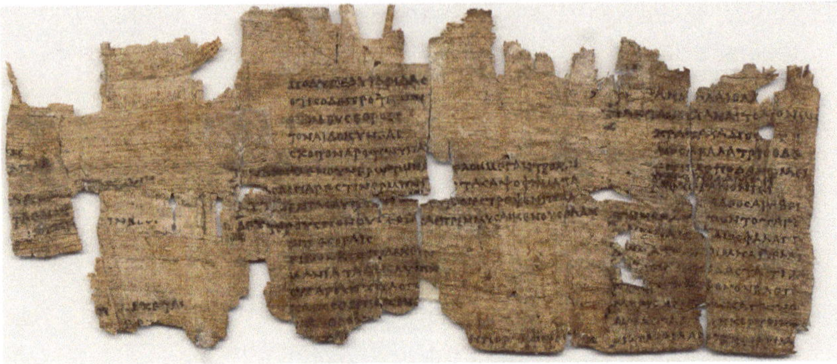

Figure 8.2
Papyrus fragment, probably of Sophocles' *Inachus*, removed from a human mummy excavated in 1900 at Umm el-Baragat, Egypt, in a UC expedition funded by Phoebe Hearst. PTebt. 692 (selection), Bancroft Library, UC Berkeley.

Figure 8.3
Stela of Wepemnefret. Limestone slab, Giza necropolis tomb 1201 (PAHMA 6-19825). The stela depicts Wepemnefret and lists his name and titles, provisions for the afterlife, and linens included in his burial. It was set in the tomb face and walled over.

("Cheops," reigned ca. 2589–2566 BCE). Wepemnefret may have been involved in constructing the Pyramid of Khufu (figure 3.8, the "Great Pyramid of Giza"), in whose shadow he was buried. Said by one scholar to be "the best preserved example of Old Kingdom painted low relief" (Smith 1963:3), Wepemnefret's stela was removed in 1905 during George Reisner's excavation for Phoebe Hearst. It and other objects from the same cemetery made their way to the UC anthropology museum.

Objects like those in figures 8.1 and 8.3 were put in graves and tombs by the family, friends, and associates of the deceased. Papyrus fragments as in figure 8.2 were used to encase the bodies of the dead and are removed today through processes that are often destructive. The presence of such objects in libraries and museums contravenes the intent of those who long ago deposited them. But Phoebe Hearst, the "rich American" whose son urged her to "buy up . . . opportunities" (chapter 3), had a program typical of her era. The collection and metropolitan exhibition of cultural treasures from "antiquity" was assumed to be a public good. Whether the context was a Scandinavian ship burial, an Egyptian pyramid, or an Inca cemetery, ethical doubts about unearthing the ancient dead were not voiced in academic or elite Euro-American circles.

California archaeological projects supported by Hearst when Kroeber came to UC included the excavation of Bay Area shell mounds and the work of Philip Mills Jones at places such as Santa Rosa Island, whose Indigenous inhabitants had been removed in the nineteenth century. It had been used as a sheep ranch for several decades before Jones arrived in 1901. On 28 March, according to his journal, he was at a cave near the south coast. It was "the oldest camp I have yet seen," with bone fragments "sticking out from loose soil filling" (Jones 1956:209). On that day, "29 bodies [were] removed: probably more, but all are comminuted and fragments of burned and unburned bones lie together." Overall, during Jones's short tenure working for Hearst (1900–1902), he took thousands of objects and ancestral remains from Santa Rosa Island, sites near Stockton (Jones 1923), and elsewhere. All made their way to the UC anthropology museum.

At the same time, throughout California, agricultural and construction work and urban development routinely exposed Indigenous burials. These were regularly reported in newspapers, whose many brief accounts offer a glimpse of the treatment afforded the Native dead. This was sometimes respectful.[17] As early as 1897, when "many human skeletons were found" during Marin County roadwork, the bodies were "interred in the county cemetery" ("Indian Skeletons" 1897). And in 1904, laborers excavating a ditch near Cedarville in Modoc County found five Indian skeletons, which "were carefully carried to another place and reburied" ("Workmen" 1904).

More often, newspapers reported and even relished disrespectful treatment. In 1907, Los Angeles sewer excavators unearthed a "skeleton, evidently that of an Indian, . . . four feet beneath the surface." They kept working, according to a local newspaper, "tossing out the pieces of the skeleton, as though they were accustomed to finding human bones in the city streets" ("Indian Skeleton" 1907). Road workers did the same three years later in Greenbrae, Marin County. "Six Indian skeletons" were uncovered by men who "tossed them to one side." One of the workers was quoted: "Indian bones make bum roads. We throw them all in a heap as we come to them" ("Workmen" 1910). In 1918, a different style of disrespect was shown by a man who was digging on his land in the Piute mountains east of Bakersfield when he found skeletonized bodies presumed to be Indigenous. He brought them "to the Board of Trade rooms" in Bakersfield, "where they will be on display for those interested" ("Digs Up Ancient Grave" 1918).

Large numbers of bodies were sometimes encountered.[18] In 1908, John Cadoni was ploughing a field when he uncovered a mound "bristling with Indian skeletons" in Ross Valley, Marin County. John Wetel was hauling sand in 1909 and "uncovered about 20 Indian skeletons in a sand knoll" in Hanford, Kings County. In 1916, workers digging for a canal near Oroville uncovered the remains of eighteen Indigenous people. And in 1908, after workers digging under a Shasta County hotel found the remains of twenty-two Native people, the *Sacramento Bee* ended its report with a dehumanizing joke: "Nearly every person in Coram got a souvenir of some kind and it can be said truthfully that several homes in Coram have skeletons in their closets."

This is the context in which UC researchers first engaged in California archaeology. It is worth bearing two perspectives in mind, with empathy for both. One is what many archaeologists have believed, then and more recently: development and looting were destroying history, and it was better to keep artifacts and ancestral bodies in a university than to discard them or keep them privately where they would not contribute to understanding. The other perspective is a fair counterpoint: After people have chosen to bury their loved ones and possessions, how is collecting them for a state-owned museum different from storing them in a settler's closet?

BAY AREA SHELL MOUNDS

A conspicuous feature of the built landscape along San Francisco Bay from precolonial times through the nineteenth century was what have come to be called "shell mounds" because of their many mollusk shells. Survey work by Nels Nelson (1909) under the supervision of UC paleontologist John Merriam identified more than 425 such mounds; the earliest is more than five millennia old, predating the pyramids of Egypt. Some were abandoned centuries ago; others were used until the Spanish invasion, and even in the nineteenth century as Indigenous refugia, as described by Tsim Schneider (2021). In precolonial times, Lightfoot (1997) argued, some served as ceremonial and sociopolitical centers. They "would have provided ideal points of aggregation on the landscape," Lightfoot et al. (2011:75) wrote; "groups could periodically come together for mortuary practices, ceremonies, feasting, and food gathering and processing."

Early in the twentieth century, initially with funding from Hearst, excavations at several shell mounds were undertaken by Merriam and the archaeologists Uhle, Nelson, W. E. Schenck, and L. L. Loud. Artifacts and human remains by the thousands came to the UC anthropology museum. Prominent examples near the UC campus are the Ellis Landing, Emeryville, and West Berkeley mounds.

At Ellis Landing in Richmond, north of Berkeley, excavations by Nelson under Merriam's direction in August 1906 and February 1908 yielded artifacts, sixteen human skeletons, and data about multiple strata. The 1908 dig involved sinking a deep shaft "to obtain some clue to the culture conditions represented in the strata below sea-level" (Nelson 1910:359). In July-August 1907, Nelson also collected artifacts and ancestral remains when "a large part of the mound" was removed by the landowner. Nelson's work was disadvantaged by "three to four teams of horses moving about" (372), but he recovered 265 artifacts ("with an additional half-dozen remaining in the hands of the workmen") and 126 human skeletons. Within six years, urban development and agricultural mining had completely leveled the mound. "It seems a pity," the *San Francisco Call* lamented, "that such a wonderful evidence of the habits of our ancestors is to be effaced forever by the onward march of civilization, and that the sacred burial place of the past ages should give way to city lots" ("Old Ellis Mound" 1913). The phrase "our ancestors" is notable.

The Emeryville shell mound is near Berkeley by the mouth of Temescal Creek and was known already in the nineteenth century as a site of burials. Ancestral remains were found there in 1896, for example, during ground leveling "near the Oakland trotting park at Shell Mound station." As reported by the *San Francisco Chronicle* ("Find Relics" 1896), "Professor Merriam was sent for," and the remains of at least four people were unearthed and taken to UC. Merriam, later a major supporter of eugenics research, was said to be convinced that a skull found in this excavation "belongs to a very low order of man. The brow is two or three inches lower than in ordinary man and the cheek bones are decidedly more pronounced than in Indians of the present day." His comfort with evolutionary racism contrasts notably with Kroeber's approach to human diversity.

In 1902, Merriam and Uhle excavated more systematically at the Emeryville shell mound with Hearst's "ample financial support" (Uhle 1907:2). Further work was undertaken in difficult circumstances twenty-two years later. In October 1924, Jack Broughton (1999:27) reported, "the Pacific States Construction Company arrived at the Emeryville Shellmound with the task of leveling it." The land had been leased to a company "whose sulfur plant had for some time encroached on the northern extreme of the mound." The landowner let UC archaeologists sort through material "placed in trucks by steam shovels, hauled a short distance where it was dumped and spread" with a scraper, according to Schenck (1926:165). Many artifacts and adult skeletal remains were found; smaller objects and infant remains were probably destroyed by the industrial process. Early in the following year, the UC team was allowed to dig several trenches for systematic excavation on the same site, below the level of the former mound; a smaller number of artifacts and ancestral remains were more carefully removed.

The oldest known Bay Area settlement, the West Berkeley shell mound, was eighteen feet high and occupied five acres by the mouth of

Strawberry Creek. Radiocarbon measurements of charcoal and shells indicate an origin about 5,700 years ago; the top of the mound was circa 1,100–1,300 years old, suggesting disuse.[19] Merriam directed limited excavations there in 1902 and 1904; within a few decades, development had destroyed much of the mound. Its area was mostly under streets, railroad tracks, and factory buildings, but the part seen in figure 8.4 survived until 1950. In the summer of that year, when it was threatened with total destruction, what William Wallace and Donald Lathrap (1975:1) called "a large-scale excavation" was undertaken. Further salvage was permitted a few months later as the landowner destroyed the mound. More than 3,400 artifacts were recovered in all: tools, fishing and hunting implements, textiles, beads, and so on. There were also enormous quantities of food residue (especially mollusk shells), burials of a coyote and a condor, and at least ninety-five human skeletons.

Two miles up Strawberry Creek, another Berkeley site of ancestral remains was described by David Buckley et al. (2008:48–53). In 1907, workers digging a construction trench near the UC Faculty Club encountered a deposit of bones and shells. Merriam dug up an adult and a child there in addition to shells, a charmstone, and other artifacts. More objects and remains were found during Faculty Club construction projects in 1914 and 1925. Kroeber was reported to have suggested that this site at Faculty Glade had been inhabited five hundred to one thousand years earlier ("Shell Mounds" 1914).

In these and other cases, ancestral remains were deposited in the UC anthropology museum, which in 2022 still holds remains from the Faculty Club site and the Ellis Landing, Emeryville, and West Berkeley mounds. They represent more than 1,900 items in a catalog with more than twenty thousand entries identified as human remains in the United States, of which 4,043 have been deaccessioned (in most cases, repatriated).[20] Generally, Bay Area ancestral remains have not been repatriated because of a combination of technical challenges in the law, the lack of federal recognition for Bay Area tribes, and resistance from UC administrators and faculty.

Separate from repatriation concerns, Indigenous community members and activists have pressed for an end to land development on Bay Area shell mounds. The West Berkeley mound is the best-known example. In 2022, the only undeveloped land on the location of the mound or in its

Figure 8.4
General view of the remaining unleveled part of the West Berkeley shell mound in 1950 (Wallace and Lathrap 1975: Plate 1). A man standing on the mound provides scale.

Figure 8.5
"Protect Ohlone Lisjan sacred sites," 2017: activists at the remaining undeveloped area of the West Berkeley shell mound and village site. Photo by Scott Braley.

immediate vicinity is a parking lot spanning a city block between Third and Fourth Streets and (as it happens) Hearst and University Avenues.[21] The landowner has proposed to build apartments and retail stores on the lot. Local tribes, activists, and the City of Berkeley have opposed the project; Figure 8.5 shows a protest. "This land is an important cultural landscape," said Ohlone leader Corinna Gould (Dinkelspiel 2020). "We must do everything we can to stop the desecration of this sacred site." As of September 2022, efforts to block development have been unsuccessful.

At the shell mounds, both archaeological projects and cultural-heritage activism illustrate a sense of urgency during 120 years of development. The early-twentieth-century archaeologists who worked for Phoebe Hearst and UC evidently had three key assumptions that Kroeber would have shared. First, these features of built landscape had much to teach about human history and cultures. Second, urban growth was not just covering the shell mounds but removing them, as Schneider (2021:46–49) also emphasized. "The streets of Berkeley and Emeryville are paved with their contents," in the words of Daniel Elkind (2019). Third, no Indigenous communities had a stake in any shell mounds. This mistaken belief was derived from the vanishment assumption. If the Bay Area's Native people were gone (or had lost their cultural identity), it must have seemed natural to treat their archaeological past as the Egyptian or Etruscan pasts were then treated.

ARCHAEOLOGICAL EXPEDITIONS

During the first decades of the twentieth century, UC researchers engaged in several archaeological projects outside the Bay Area, including digs and recovery trips. Donations of artifacts and remains were also gratefully received. As secretary and then director of the anthropology museum, Kroeber often corresponded with researchers; in a few cases he directed them. One example occurred on 20 February 1909 near Buena Vista Lake, Kern County, where Nels Nelson collected the remains of at least four people together with associated objects, mostly small fragments of cloth, basketry, and the like. They had been exposed "by the elements" in 1908, as Kroeber told Wheeler, leading to newspaper articles and then Nelson's trip to retrieve the ancestral remains and associated objects "through the courtesy of the Miller and Lux Company" (30 June 1909,

UCOPAF Box 22:26). What was collected from this site remains in the museum.[22] In other instances, construction exposed ancestral remains. In 1910, Kroeber wrote to Wheeler's office to call attention to a news article about a railroad work project near Tulare Lake in which "a crew operating a steam shovel found human skeletons forty feet under ground," and to say that he had asked a railroad official if they could be sent to the university (27 October, UCOPAF Box 41:27).

Ancestral remains were sometimes exposed not by construction or the "elements," but by treasure hunters. In 1905, for example, Kroeber's student Samuel Barrett was doing survey work near Winters, Yolo County. Quoting Barrett's notes, Samuel Redman (2016:79) described a burial site Barrett encountered along Putah Creek:

> After examining the site, he wrote, "owing to the more recent relic hunters' visits to this site, there is at present evidently very little to be found in the way of scientific materials." . . . Nevertheless, Barrett noted, "Little or no attention has ever been paid by anyone evidently to the taking of skeletons or parts of the skeletons, although there are reported two or three skulls now in the possession of white people of the vicinity." He concluded, "Usually, however, the bones have either been cast aside on the surface or have been thrown back promiscuously into the pits as dug." Barrett . . . sent three cases of human bones to the museum at the University of California.

According to museum notes (PAHMA 12-1608), this burial was at a village site of which Barrett (1908:299–300) found "no visible signs. . . . Old residents say, however, that there were formerly a number of dance-house pits and various other evidences of an old village here." Its inhabitants might have been taken to the Sonoma mission in the early nineteenth century, driven off their land, or forced by disease or other disruptions to relocate.

Another kind of discovery took place as a by-product of other research. Northeast of Sacramento, Hawver Cave is a site notable for Pleistocene animal fossils where some human bones were also found below the surface.[23] Wallace and Lathrap (1952) mentioned finding artifacts unlike those used by contemporary people and reported that Kroeber spent a day there in 1910, "made a sketch," collected human bone samples, and took them to the university. "Entombment in limestone grottos seems to have been a widespread prehistoric practice," they wrote, concluding that the remains and artifacts were "dropped down the vertical shaft" more than four thousand years ago.

In a few cases, Kroeber or others planned excavations of sites outside the Bay Area known to contain burials. An example noted above was Lovelock Cave, Nevada, a place of historic significance to Paiute people. According to Gilbert Natches, born fewer than ten miles away, it was once inhabited by the Saiduka'a, said to be enemies of the Paiutes whom the Paiutes drove away perhaps as recently as the nineteenth century.[24]

Lovelock Cave was full of bats, whose accumulated guano was three to six feet deep. A newspaper reported that the cave might hold "several hundred tons" of guano that would sell for $40 a ton ("Relics Found" 1911). In 1911 and early 1912, a crew removed some 250 tons. This involved blasting, picks and shovels, laying track for mine cars, and the removal of objects. "The guano and assorted cave debris was dumped onto a large screen," Robert Heizer and Lewis Napton (1970:4) explained, "and the materials held by the 3/4-inch mesh, including sticks, rushes, stones, Indian artifacts, piece[s] of mummies, and bone fragments, were discarded on the hillside." Universities were notified, and news circulated; Kroeber decided to arrange a dig.[25] Much of the cave's contents was already "scattered, sold, or destroyed," he explained to Frederic Ward Putnam, but "I am hoping that a good deal may remain" (18 March 1912, RDA Box 22). He explained that in what he had seen "not a single fragment shows any trace of white man's influence," that reports indicated that the material was "of very great antiquity," and that it "will therefore be very valuable as a contribution to the little known culture history of the Nevada Indians."

Museum guard L. L. Loud was sent to do the work and spent four solitary months in Nevada in 1912. Despite little training, a disorganized research style, and an adversarial relationship with Kroeber and other professional anthropologists, he collected a large quantity of material and laid the groundwork for more careful excavation by others in later years. The awl in figure 8.6 is one of thousands of objects (including human remains) that Loud sent from Nevada in 1912.[26] Two years later, working with Kroeber, Natches shared information about Paiute geography, lifeways, and stories (Loud and Harrington 1929:152–164). As illustrated in figure 8.7, Natches also recorded the Paiute names of some objects Loud had collected.

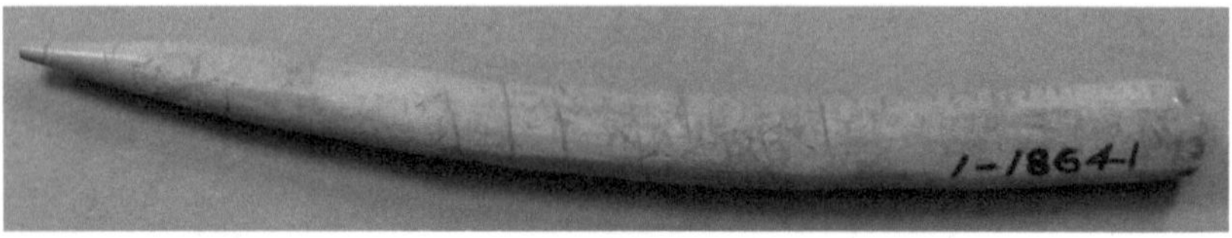

Figure 8.6
Bone awl, collected by L. L. Loud in the area of Lovelock Cave, Nevada (site NV-Ch-13, PAHMA 1-18641). This object was identified by Gilbert Natches in figure 8.7.

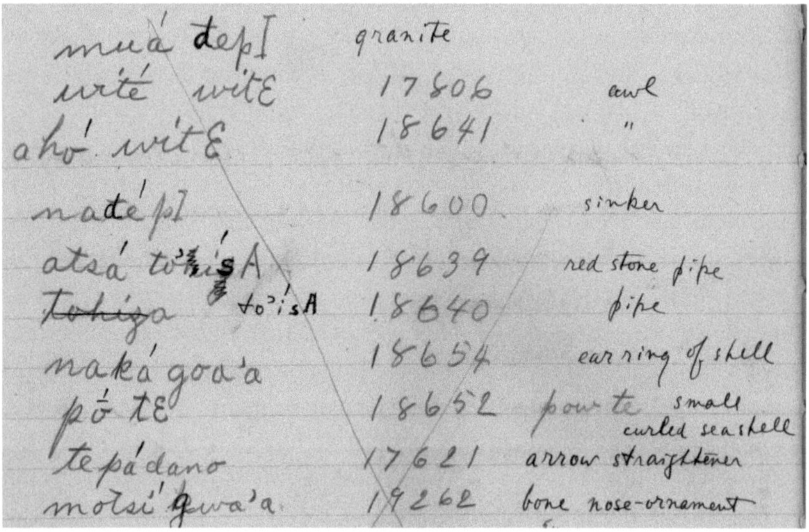

Figure 8.7
Gilbert Natches, Numu vocabulary relating to artifacts collected by L. L. Loud at and near Lovelock Cave, Nevada, ca. 1914 (CLA Marsden.015, p. 92). Items have PAHMA identifiers (e.g., 18641 *ahó witɨ* "awl"). Stress marks and English glosses were added by Kroeber.

Kroeber's interest in Lovelock Cave was, as indicated above, based on the apparent "great antiquity" of its artifacts. The miners who worked there in 1911–1912 reported that "Indian objects" only began to appear "about four feet below the surface of the guano" (Loud and Harrington 1929:168), implying that the cave had not been used for many centuries. However, the meticulous scientific examination described by Heizer and Napton (1970), based on radiocarbon, chemical, and mineral analyses, led them to a very different conclusion. The intensity of human habitation (since at least ca. 2700 BCE) was reduced because of rock falls around 700 CE, but "occupation of the outer rockshelter and infrequent use of the cave interior probably continued . . . until 1829," when the first white people reached the area (41).[27] While it is therefore true, as Kroeber hoped, that much of what was collected at Lovelock Cave is of "great antiquity," the site was not abandoned in ancient times. Instead, though Kroeber would never know, it was an integral part of Paiute land and lifeways at the time of the American invasion. More recently, artifacts and ancestral remains from Lovelock Cave are seen as part of the heritage of the Lovelock Paiute Tribe.[28]

A 1913 expedition also involved Loud, whom Kroeber sent to northwest California to do mainly geographic research near Humboldt Bay and Mad River and to make sound recordings of local Dene and Wiyot place names.[29] Their disputatious correspondence (Heizer 1970) opens a window on the interaction of two strong-willed researchers. Kroeber's instructions were precise, emphasizing geography and survey work (12 July). He made it clear that he thought Loud lacked the training for ethnographic or linguistic research, and was irritated when Loud seemed to be trying his hand at ethnography or, even further afield, historical research. Kroeber mentioned Nelson's Bay Area shell mound survey as a model for what Loud might attempt around Humboldt Bay, and asked him to dig at a mound. He seems to have thought that Humboldt Bay might be like the San Francisco Bay Area and that a mound might cast light on past lifeways. When Loud chose a mound on Tuluwat Island (chapter 5), Kroeber asked him to make sure the landowners approved and to "advise me of their names" (23 July). Kroeber expressed interest in "the general scientific features of the relation of the mounds to topography, shell contents, artefacts, and similarity and dissimilarity of conditions to those on San Francisco bay" (6 August). "It is the general lay of the land," he said, "in regard to which I want to be informed."

Loud's work led to a 1918 monograph that included not just what Kroeber had sent him to study but also an original and damning ethnohistorical account of the 1860 Tuluwat massacre. At a time when atrocities were usually ignored, it was a remarkable contribution. This case is also notable because Tony Platt (2011:89–90) has cited it as evidence of Kroeber's interest in "the collection and analysis of crania" and disinterest in documenting genocide. My reading of the Kroeber-Loud correspondence differs from Platt's.[30] Kroeber's instructions expressed no special interest in ancestral remains, though he knew they might be present wherever Loud chose to dig. Nor is there evidence that he thought Loud's "historical" work concerned the 1860 massacre.[31] Kroeber's increasingly impatient letters to Loud in 1913 echoed their Lovelock Cave correspondence in 1912 and what he wrote to others about Loud, a notoriously truculent employee.[32] What Kroeber envisioned at Humboldt Bay, as elsewhere, was a project focused on geography, toponymy, and material evidence of precolonial lifeways.

REPATRIATION AND INDIGENOUS RIGHTS

Today, many anthropologists (and most of their professional organizations) support Indigenous efforts to repatriate ancestral remains from museums; some resist, citing the loss of scientific knowledge. One can only guess how Kroeber would have positioned himself in relation to repatriation movements that emerged after he died. He had lived in Native communities, had many Indigenous friends, and advocated for Indian rights (chapter 9), but he contributed to archaeological research, including excavations of burial sites, and appreciated what it can reveal about human history. In his publications and private letters, I have not found any substantial discussion that would clarify his sense of Indigenous rights to the buried past. But three episodes seem revealing.

The first episode was early in Kroeber's career. In 1905, anticipating a substantial budget from Phoebe Hearst, he submitted to UC President Wheeler a proposal for anthropological research in the coming year (6 November 1905, UCOPAF Box 22). This added up to several thousand dollars, mostly for ethnological and linguistic documentation, but also including two archaeological projects north of San Francisco. "Excavations at Inverness and other points in Marin County" were proposed ($50), as well as excavations in Mendocino County ($100) "to obtain somatological material regarding the Pomo Indians. Not a single skeleton or skull of a Pomo Indian is to be found in any institution of learning or has ever been described." He told Hearst that the plan was to excavate "a certain Pomo burying ground" because no "Pomo skeleton or skull" was "known in any museum" (9 February 1906, GPAHP Box

43:10). From his diachronic perspective, the research goal would be to learn whether "somatological" data might illuminate the early history and relationships of Pomo people. The Pomo burial ground in question was one of two that Kroeber's student Barrett described to him, writing that the landowner was "agreeable to the excavations" as long as UC would buy hay to replace lost pasture (10 March 1906, RDA Box 9:1). Barrett also said he had "been questioning the Indians," who "estimate the number of burials at this site at from 40 to 50." He suggested that he could be present for the dig itself if it was in April, but in the end, because of the San Francisco earthquake (18 April 1906) and Barrett's other university duties, he was not involved.

To carry out the project, Kroeber enlisted three undergraduate students, including Malcolm Goddard, then finishing his final semester in the UC College of Natural Science.[33] Kroeber's letters to Goddard show that he planned a field trip for the three students that would include "excavation at Inverness, and possibly at Ukiah" in Mendocino County, to begin "on one of the days immediately following commencement" in May 1906.[34] The Inverness work was at a shell mound in what is now Tomales Bay State Park, whose mounds Schneider (2009:66) has described as "unrivaled in their state of preservation and capacity to contribute to a diachronic understanding of coastal hunter-gatherers before and after contact with Europeans." In 2022, the UC anthropology museum holds forty-six items from the Tomales Bay work, about half of which are unrepatriated human remains.

From Ukiah, Goddard sent five cases of material, including "twelve bodies," some of which "were infants and so far gone that practically none of the bones could be saved" (Kroeber to F. W. Putnam, 11 June 1906, RDA Vol. 6). But Kroeber congratulated Goddard on "five well conditioned skulls" and a "mass of beads" (12 June 1906, RDA Vol. 6). Kroeber also summarized the outcome in a note to Wheeler (13 June 1906, UCOPAF Box 22), enclosing a news release. This announced that an "expedition recently sent . . . for the purpose of obtaining remains of the Pomo Indians . . . has returned with five complete skeletons besides a number of partial remains and a large quantity of beads and other objects buried with the dead." Many California newspapers carried the story, including the *San Francisco Examiner* on 16 June ("Students Discover First Skeletons" 1906). The news release explained that "determination of the physical characteristics of the Indians will give much information as to their origin, connections and migrations that cannot be obtained by a study of their language and customs."

As it turned out, those exhumed near Ukiah had family in the Yokayo Band who became aware of the violation and hired an attorney. Local physician, ethnographer, and collector John W. Hudson wrote to warn Kroeber (30 June 1906, ALK Box 18:31, emphasis original):

> My dear doctor you should know of a condition of Indian affairs here that threatens a member possibly of your corps. *Someone* dug up some family skeletons (Indian) here a short time ago and unfortunately published the fact in the Examiner afterward. The identity of each body taken is now known among these Indians who went over their cemetery a few days after the digging and en masse have come to town breathing vengeance and have engaged the services of our best criminal lawyer.

A complaint followed from Ukiah attorney John McNab, who wrote to UC president Wheeler that a UC team had "visited a deserted Indian village here and unearthed two or three bodies that had long been buried" and that the Indians of their tribe "are exceedingly indignant" (5 July, RDA Box 14:18). Delayed by fieldwork travel, Kroeber wrote from northwestern California on 20 July (RDA Vol. 6): "If we . . . have infringed upon anyone's rights, full restitution will of course be made. I am entirely responsible in the matter." McNab wrote again on 2 August (RDA Box 14:18): "We have no doubt that the parties who unearthed these skeletons believed that they were merely getting scientific relics and did not think that they were trespassing on the rights of anyone, but this graveyard is guarded very jealously by the Indian tribe and the tribe is in a dangerous mood."

After Kroeber's return to San Francisco, he reiterated that "the entire responsibility rests with me. The specimens were obtained by three students working under my direction" (4 August, RDA Vol. 6). Two and a half weeks later, he wrote that he was shipping all the "bones and relics found in the course of excavations on Mr. Romer's ranch near Ukiah. There are twelve packages each containing the remains from apparently one burial, infant or adult" (22 August, RDA Vol. 6). These packages presumably corresponded to the twelve bodies Kroeber had mentioned to Putnam on 11 June.

Meanwhile, McNab had alerted the press. Several newspapers covered the story, but the *Ukiah Dispatch Democrat* on 24 August had the most detail ("May Arrest the Professor" 1906):

> Last June three students of the university came here and dug up the skeletons of several Indians that had been buried over a quarter of a century and took these skeletons, beads and trinkets to the university where they were to be kept in the department of anthropology. These skeletons, beads and etc., are supposed to be very valuable from the standpoint of science. . . . Prof. Kroeber desiring to have these specimens on hand sent the students here to dig up the bodies. The students went to the Romer ranch and found several deserted graves and dug up the skeletons, and the beads and trinkets are very valuable, probably worth $1000. Among the remains were the bones of Dick Ruddick's father and mother and Dick hired McNab & Hirsch to bring suit for the return of the skeletons and valuables.

Ruddick was one of the leaders of the Yokayo Band. UC president Wheeler issued a confused, defensive statement, quoted on 25 August by the *Santa Barbara Independent* ("Will Investigate" 1906):

> The purpose of the expedition was to collect facts about the tribes of Indians which are dying out. One tribe was found of which there were but four members surviving. The opportunities for adding to the science of anthropology were in[num]erable. In the course of the investigation the expedition obtained some skulls for the purpose of taking measurements for comparison with other races. No recent graves were robbed, however. The rumor of trouble is totally unfounded. The matter has all been settled.

Wheeler's reference to a tribe with "four members surviving" is inexplicable. His account of the "purpose of the expedition" was also misleading: the students had gone to Ukiah in order to excavate. Less than a week later, the *Dispatch Democrat* reported that the remains and "beads and other trinkets" had been returned and that this would "dispose of the suit" ("Indian Bodies" 1906). Finally, on 18 December 1906 (RDA Box 14:18), McNab's firm asked Kroeber for $50 for the Yokayo Tribe's expenses in "burying the remains of their Tribe which were returned by you. . . . There were portions of several bodies exhumed and it was necessary to purchase a cheap coffin." After the money was sent, McNab & Hirsch predicted on 31 January 1907 that "no further trouble will arise" (RDA 14:18).[35]

One last detail merits discussion. Among the newspapers carrying Kroeber's June 1906 news release was the *San Francisco Chronicle* ("Indian Relics" 1906), which added that the expedition was "headed by Dr. Samuel A. Barrett, museum assistant in the department of anthropology." He had indeed identified the site, but the addition was a mistake; perhaps Barrett as museum assistant had sent out the notice. Kroeber's letters to Goddard make clear that only the three undergraduates participated. For example, on 20 June 1906 (RDA Vol. 6), he asked for certain details that would help in cataloging objects: "If you remember . . . will you advise me accordingly, or if not, forward the question to Nelson or Morse if you think they may have the information?" He did not mention Barrett and would have no reason to omit his name if he had participated in the excavation. Perhaps Kroeber was disingenuous in insisting to McNab that "Mr. Barrett has had no connection to the matter, except for a personal acquaintance with Mr. Romer" (the landowner); or maybe Kroeber felt he should take full responsibility, since Barrett had neither organized nor joined the dig.[36]

The *Chronicle* addition of Barrett was picked up by the *Ukiah Republican Press* and came to the attention of Yokayo Band members. They "felt aggrieved at Mr. Barrett," according to McNab, "because they thought that he being familiar with the local conditions would know that it was the burying ground of the [I]ndians" (8 August 1906, RDA Box 14:18).[37] Their concern, understandably, was with a violation of their burial site. McNab's wording does not suggest a broader concern; the implication is that Barrett's knowledge might have led him to excavate another burial site. Kroeber, too, evidently distinguished sites connected to present-day family or living stakeholders, like the Yokayo burial ground, from "ancient" sites like Hawver or Lovelock Cave or shell mounds after centuries of desuetude. His interest, after all, was diachronic.

I draw three conclusions from this first episode. First, Kroeber believed that an excavation should be authorized by the current landowner (who in this case should have known whose cemetery it was). California landowners had acquired their property directly or indirectly through the theft of Indigenous land, but the possibility of another kind of cultural or heritage ownership seems not to have been recognized. Second, when confronted with a repatriation request, Kroeber took responsibility and returned what was sought. Finally, what angered the Yokayo Band was

Figure 8.8
Julio Tello (left) and Alfred Kroeber, at the Museo de Arqueología, Callao, Peru, 1 November 1926. Photograph by Waldo L. Schmitt (Smithsonian Institution Archives Record Unit 7231, Box 85, Folder 130, 94-12231).

that students had excavated not just *any* burials but *their* cemetery. It was another kind of case, where no family or community asserted such a relationship, that predominated during Kroeber's UC career.

A second episode is Kroeber's Peruvian field research. While he never excavated in the United States, he did dig in the 1920s in Mexico and in Peru, where he even collected human remains, eventually becoming a leading figure in Peruvian archaeology.[38] His interest in Latin America grew out of a sense that US Indigenous cultures do not exist in isolation, but are what he called "a chapter in a book" (1942:6).[39] "The north and the south of the double continent were only peripheries," he wrote, vis-à-vis the cultural centers of Mexico and Peru.

Kroeber had studied Peruvian pottery for several years before his first visit to Peru in 1925. There he collaborated with the director of the Museo de Arqueología Peruana, Julio Tello (figure 8.8), whom he later called a "human dynamo, founder of three important museums and discoverer of culture after culture" (1944b:5–6).[40] Tello's oeuvre included linguistics, ethnography, physical anthropology, and especially archaeology throughout highland and coastal Peru.[41] Today, his symbolic role in Peru is unlike that of any anthropologist or archaeologist in the United States. According to Richard Burger (2009:65), "Hundreds, perhaps even thousands of places are named for him," including streets, institutes, museums, and towns. There is even an annual "pilgrimage to his tomb" at the Museo Nacional de Arqueología, according to Gabriel Ramón Joffré (2014:16), "to commemorate his birth and celebrate 'Peruvian archeology day.' "

Kroeber and Tello became good friends.[42] The relationship would have exposed Kroeber to a different nexus of archaeology and indigeneity than he was used to. Tello was a native speaker of the Aymaran language Jaqaru, from a middle-class Indigenous family.[43] He was an accomplished physical anthropologist with medical and anthropological degrees from Harvard and the National University of San Marcos. He had collected at least ten thousand skulls and mummies by the time he completed his bachelor's thesis, which drew on archaeological, ethnological, linguistic, and osteological data to study syphillis in precolonial Peru.[44] His MA thesis was a study of trepanning (a cranial surgery) in Yauyos and Huarochirí (1912); his 1918 doctoral thesis concerned the use of artificially mummified heads in ancient Peruvian art. As Christopher Heaney (2018:363) put it, Tello's work on trepanning convinced others "to see healing and civilization where they once had seen only violence and savagery." It is ironic, he went on to say, that Tello challenged "the racial and intellectual prejudices of both Peru and North America by compiling the hemisphere's largest collection of Indigenous skulls" (365–366).

Tello's major intellectual legacy is his insistence that precolonial Peruvian civilization was autochthonous rather than a result of diffusion from the north, as maintained by northern scholars like Uhle. This was grounded in discoveries like that of Chavín de Huántar in the Andean highlands, but it had a political dimension in the context of Peruvian indigenismo.[45] In 1928, the Marxist writer José Carlos Mariátegui described indigenismo as "an assertion of the autochthonous" (2007:281), while the novelist and anthropologist José María Arguedas (1975:189) wrote that "indigenismo begins" with Tello himself. The archaeologist served in the Peruvian Congress from 1917 to 1929 and joined debates around indigenismo, social justice, and educational rights. Eugenicist social policies, then popular in the United States, were actively discussed in Peru, as Burger (2009:68) noted, including pro-European immigration laws and even "the prohibition of reproduction by Indians." In a 1917 speech in the Chamber of Deputies, Tello said that "from a national point of view, there is but one race in Peru. We are descendants of Spaniards, Indians, Japanese and even Chinese"—"a true miscellany of races," all of them "forming the Peruvian type" (Padilla Deza 2018:97).[46]

Similarly, in a book on the ancient history of Peru, Tello (1921:48, 2009a) dismissed those who sought "to shape a nationality on the Spanish or Latin base" and argued that "the knowledge and methods of Science," if used correctly, "would permit us to know our soil and our history . . . and thus secure our nationality. Our present Hispano-Peruvian civilization cannot stand except on an indigenous pedestal." Even in his will, written just before his death in 1947, Tello referred to "the creative genius of the Peruvian native" as "the basis of our nationality" (Murra 2009:61).

In the formation of a modern Peruvian national identity, Tello saw archaeological research and education as beneficial to Indigenous communities. At the 1924 inauguration of the Museo de Arqueología, he said that the Conquest and the "painful spectacle of Spanish domination" had nearly destroyed an "awareness of nationality" by its insistence that life is a "place of expiation and pain for the sake of happiness beyond this earth" (2009b:108). The population was "enslaved and destroyed" as its art was burned and its architecture "converted into masses of rubble." Healing would involve reclaiming precolonial history through scientific study, which reveals "the degree of culture reached by our predecessors" and restores "the dignity of our patrimony" (108–109):

> To convert a man semi-enslaved by the weight of the ignorance and injustices of four centuries into a man worthy and proud of his ancestry through accurate knowledge of his glorious past, is the best, if the not the only, way of asserting the foundations of future ethnic prosperity and to definitively reconsecrate our nationality.
>
> Our genealogical tree has profound and vigorous roots which, in other times, extracted from this land the sap which nourished a race of giants. Then, the stalk was cut by the European Conquest, but new and vigorous shoots of the gigantic trunk of nationality—new sprouts—begin to appear. They grow and they will grow, nourished by the indigenous sap itself at the urging of new ideas from the century in which we are living.

The contrast between Tello's view of the social mission of his archaeology museum and Phoebe Hearst's view of the mission of her anthropology museum could not be more striking. Tello's museum was an instrument of indigenismo, while Hearst's was meant to educate and elevate Euro-American San Francisco.

Tello was not the only Indigenous participant in Peruvian archaeology. His protégé and close associate Toribio Mejía Xesspe, for example, was a native speaker of Quechua whose work involved ethnography and linguistics (Mejía Xesspe 1922, 1954) as well as archaeology. It was Mejía Xesspe (1942) who discovered the ancient geoglyphs known as the Nazca Lines during work directed by Tello; he excavated with Tello at Paracas and other sites, and later edited Tello's work for posthumous publication. When Kroeber made a second field trip to Peru in 1926, he excavated at Nazca sites (Kroeber and Collier 1998). His work in that year included over a month of daily interaction with Tello, as well as UC colleague Egbert Schenck and three Indigenous people from Huarochirí: Pedro Macavilca, Pablo Pomajulcu, and Pablo Torres, the core members of the work crew.

In sum, visiting and doing field research in Peru, Kroeber encountered an archaeological field with Indigenous participants at all levels. Among its leaders were Indigenous scholars who articulated a humanistic vision he would have found congenial. Like him, they argued against eugenics and anti-Indigenous racism and saw social value in physical anthropology and archaeology. This is not to say that Kroeber was a kind of sleeper indigenista (his impulses were too conventional and pacific), but to call attention to the milieu of his Peruvian collaborations and relationships.

The third episode was in 1948, after Kroeber's retirement, when he was asked about a proposed archaeological project in Yurok country. It was to be led by Robert Heizer as part of a new Archaeological Survey of California; excavation was proposed in what is now Sue-meg State Park. Kroeber wrote to Ted McCown (13 April 1948, ALK Box 4:5) that "there are other Yurok sites, both coast and river, which are larger and richer, but there are also likely to be living descendants of people buried in them." The proposed site, he said, "has not had a settlement for a century and perhaps not for centuries, so I think there will be no objections and a dig there may get the Indians used to the idea for a follow-up elsewhere later."

There is no record of Yurok objections to the 1948 Sue-meg excavations, but Tony Platt (2011:113–116) reported that Heizer apparently broke an agreement with park officials regarding what could be taken to Berkeley. In 1949, Heizer also began exploratory archaeological work in Trinidad, a few miles to the south, at the site of the Yurok village Chuerey—a village that had been occupied by living people's grandparents. As detailed by Platt (2011:116–119), there were strenuous objections to the 1949 work. Kroeber's friend Alice Spott was one of a group of elders who lodged a complaint with the sheriff. In his letter to McCown, Kroeber had recommended not digging at a site associated with living people, but Heizer either did not see the letter or did not take its advice seriously.

Given global archaeological practices in the first half of the twentieth century and the absence of a US repatriation movement, Kroeber may never have thought carefully about the scope of Indigenous rights to burial sites. His choices may just reflect an assumption that knowledge of antiquity is a common good, with little if any experience pushing him to a different view. Over the years, as discussed elsewhere in this book, Kroeber did learn about injustices and receive requests for help from Indigenous California friends and collaborators. These concerned citizenship, education, health, cultural practices, and land rights, but not (as far as I know) the care of the dead. The record seems consistent with Kroeber having distinguished implicitly between "ancient" sites, centuries old and in disuse, and those in active use. The former he seems to have viewed as appropriate for archaeological study, with the permission of current landowners or the state, just as elsewhere in the world; the latter he seems to have judged out of bounds. This is not where most archaeologists and bioanthropologists today would draw the boundary line, but it was principled and responsive to local interests as Kroeber understood them.

ANTIQUITY, AUTOCHTHONY, AND NATIONALISM

California, Egypt, and Peru were the major sites of early-twentieth-century archaeological research organized and supported by Phoebe Hearst for the University of California—research that included excavation of graves; disinterral, unwrapping, and dismembering of bodies; and collection of objects buried with them. As the twentieth century went on, California, Egypt, and Peru also experienced avatars of nationalism that laid claim to antiquity. Claims of autochthony are often critical in nationalist projects; asssertions of authority over antiquity are a corollary.

In Peru, as discussed above, Julio Tello posited a national identity that was not "on the Spanish or Latin base" but was "nourished by indigenous sap" and informed by a "glorious" precolonial past. This inspiring or nourishing past is a recurrent theme in nationalist movements, as described by Anthony Smith (2009:96): "The golden age holds up a mirror to the 'true' lineaments of the nation, and invites emulation of its original spirit." It was not a highland or specifically Indigenous nationalism that Tello encouraged, but a "Hispano-Peruvian" identity that integrated Hispanic and Indigenous cultures. As an archaeologist, he played a role in literally uncovering the historical foundation of a reïmagined nation. Smith even saw a connection between the roles (65–66): "Just as the archaeologist seeks to relate the excavated material culture to its historic time, so the nationalist aims to place his or her nation within its own time-frame by relating it to a rediscovered past or pasts."

A rediscovered past was also an important symbol for modern Egyptian nationalists. Medieval writing, according to Michael Cook (1983:102), "displays a considerable pride in the ancient monuments of the country; but it conveys no sense whatever of identification with the people and culture which created them."[47] Pharaonic ruins were sometimes seen as proof of the fate of disbelievers, their builders "polytheistic idolaters," in Donald Reid's (1985:233) phrase.[48] In 1817, Elliott Colla (2007:72–73) reported, the scholar 'Abd al-Rahman al-Jabarti referred to ancient monuments as "curious objects" and "trivial details." A massive bust of Ramesses II, then being removed for export to Britain, was "a large idol." But in 1912, the activist and intellectual Ahmad Lutfi al-Sayyid was explicit in his identification with the ancient past (Colla 2007:149–150): "Our nation today does not exist independently from the nation of our past. The nation is a single, unbroken, unbreakable whole." One's patriotism "is not complete until he knows his nation, both its ancient past and its present." Antiquity was also prominent in the discourse of the 1919 revolution. "We are the sons of the Pharaohs," went a popular song. "Long live Egypt! Best of all nations; mother of the brave; and this has been for all time." Reid (2015:42–50) quoted these verses among a variety of pharaonizing expressions of nationalism, ranging from journalistic cartoons to Mahmoud Muktar's monumental sculpture *Nahdat*

Misr ("Egypt's Awakening," 1920–1928), featuring a sphinx and a peasant woman lifting her veil.

A naïve critic in the grip of cultural essentialism might doubt that Egypt (or Peru) could have remained an "unbroken, unbreakable whole" over millennia. The land of the pharaohs was successively under Persian, Greek, Roman, Islamic, Ottoman, and British rule for 2,500 years until its twentieth-century independence; each shift meant cultural change in a nation that was Christianized before the Islamic era and whose language is now Arabic, not Coptic. The territory of modern Peru, too, home to a heterogeneous set of changing polities culminating in the Inca Empire, was then thoroughly transformed by Spanish colonization in the sixteenth century. Such doubts are beside the point: Benedict Anderson's (1983, 1991) national "imagined communities" often include remote ancestors. Relationships with the past are constructed in the present.

In Egypt and Peru, early-twentieth-century nationalism, resistance to foreign domination and extractivism, and identification with the ancient past led to laws and policies meant to forestall the taking of antiquities for European and US museums. After Howard Carter's 1922 discovery of the tomb of Tutankhamun, the Egyptian Antiquities Service updated its practices to ensure that the tomb's contents would remain in Egypt. A long-dead pharaoh became a national symbol, with the poet Ahmad Shawqi's "Tut 'Ankh Amun" (1930) urging others to "head toward the chambers of the setting suns, Pass through their stony places, pass humbly by their funereal couches, Salute the remains of glory of our Tutankhamen" (Colla 2007:216). In the same year, Tutankhamun appeared on the one-pound note (Reid 2020:476). And in Peru, Tello himself not only defended precolonial patrimony but formulated a law that made archaeological sites the property of the state (Burger 2009:83). Though not always successful, resistance to US and European antiquities extraction was a global theme during the twentieth century (and into the twenty-first).

Native American activism led similarly to NAGPRA legislation in 1990 (federal law) and 2001 (California). This was explained as a matter of human rights. "In light of the important role that death and burial rites play in native American cultures," Senator Daniel Inouye said, "it is all the more offensive that the civil rights of America's first citizens have been so flagrantly violated" (United States 1990:35678). People have human rights as humans, independent of nationality. But Indian tribes are also sovereign nations in the United States; their territorial sovereignty has come to play an increasingly critical role as NAGPRA laws and regulations have evolved.[49]

The 2001 version of Cal NAGPRA was modeled on the federal law, providing for repatriation in certain cases where institutions hold ancestral remains or artifacts. A key test was "cultural affiliation," defined as "a relationship of shared group identity" between a present-day tribe and an earlier group from which the remains or objects originated. The terms "relationship" and "group identity" were not defined, but regulations implementing the federal law explained that the present-day tribe must "descend" from the earlier group. Archaeologists have pointed out that NAGPRA presupposes essentialist ideas of "culture" as a stable property of groups, forcing institutions and tribes to craft arguments for "cultural descent" and "identity" across millennia.[50] Indigenous people, as Chris Gosden (2001:242) put it, "have to prove that they are not creolized or hybrid cultures, but have maintained some essential identity through time and into the present." In principle, similar arguments pertain everywhere. Do Egyptians "descend culturally" from Tutankhamun's people 3,300 years ago? Is a "group identity" shared by the builders of Stonehenge and the English more than four thousand years later, or by the West Berkeley shell-mound builders five millennia ago and Ohlone people in 2022? Answers to such questions depend on identity construction and ideological formation. But as James Clifford (1988:338) wrote in an influential discussion of Mashpee Wampanoag identity, based on a legal case involving tribal recognition and continuity across many generations, "the critical elements of identity are in specific conditions replaceable: language, land, blood, leadership, religion." Identities themselves are fluid, too, as the case of Egypt makes clear. By making participants pretend they are immalleable facts, NAGPRA all but guaranteed conflicts.

One such conflict that happens to be publicly documented concerns a set of bodies that were buried in what is now La Jolla (in San Diego County) at least 5,500 years ago.[51] Excavated in 1959, the skeletonized remains were held by UCLA's Fowler Museum in 2000, when a Kumeyaay tribal coalition sought repatriation. There was no question that the excavation was on Kumeyaay traditional land, nor that Kumeyaay people have lived there for a long time. According to a Kumeyaay leader quoted in UC documentation, "We consider them our people, it's still our traditional territory, and we have a history of at least 10,000 years." UCLA undertook a thorough analysis of evidence from many sources, including Indigenous knowledge, to assess how likely it was that people in La Jolla five or six millennia ago were among the biological ancestors of Kumeyaay people today, spoke a language ancestral to Kumeyaay, or had sociocultural practices that have been continued in more recent times. It was as if archaeology, genetics, or linguistics could reveal whether the people of Ankara and Florence share "group identities" with Hittites and Etruscans. Especially striking in this context are discussions of human genetics, given the independence of biological and cultural traits that Kroeber and many others have emphasized over the last century.[52] The UCLA conclusion in 2001 was that more likely than not, despite the long time span, the La Jolla remains were "culturally affiliated" with Kumeyaay people. After other archaeologists disagreed, the UCLA NAGPRA coordinator wrote in April 2002 that "until we agree what constitutes evidence of a 'shared group identity', 'continuity', and 'discontinuity', we will go on giving different interpretations to the same sets of data ad infinitum." Even this may have been too optimistic, given the inherent problems of NAGPRA's "culture" construct.

Federal and state NAGPRA laws and regulations list sources of evidence that may contribute to showing cultural affiliation. Indigenous knowledge is as valid as evidence from other sources, according to Cal NAGPRA in 2001: "Tribal oral histories, documentations, and testimonies shall not be afforded less evidentiary weight than other relevant categories of evidence on account of being in those categories." Institutions were thus charged with balancing different kinds of evidence in assessing cultural affiliation. Almost inevitably, given this mandate and their own biases, non-Native institutions sometimes judged tribal knowledge and Indigenous histories to be outweighed by evidence generated within the academy. This was seen by many as a particular problem at Berkeley. As a result, one of several 2020 revisions to Cal NAGPRA was a stricter proviso: "If there is conflicting evidence, tribal traditional knowledge shall be provided deference." Regardless of other evidence, Indigenous knowledge was to be determinative. As noted in chapter 2, Native people throughout California tell creation stories about the places where they have lived "since time immemorial" (to use a common phrase). For this reason, virtually everything of precolonial age that comes from Indigenous land is part of local cultural heritage.

In short, the 2020 Cal NAGPRA revision turned a framework based on an old-fashioned, impractical conception of "culture" into one based on the territorial rights of sovereign tribal nations. This was reinforced by a second change. The 2001 law required that "cultural affiliation" be shown, but the 2020 revision added an alternative basis: a repatriation claim may simply indicate that ancestral remains or cultural objects come from the "aboriginal territory" of the tribe claiming them. The two changes have put California tribal nations on a footing with other nations that exercise authority over antiquities from long before the ancestors of their national languages were spoken on their land. In England, for example, it does not matter if pre-English-speaking populations were "invaded" by "Anglo-Saxons" or share a "group identity" with their successors today: their remains are part of English cultural heritage. Similarly, California tribes may now reclaim ancestors and antiquities taken from their land without having to prove "cultural affiliation" with people whose languages are unknown and whose lifeways may have been very different. It is no longer necessary to develop detailed analyses of archaeological and linguistic data to discern "shared group identity" over millennia.

In criticizing NAGPRA's presuppositions, I do not mean that Egyptian, English, Italian, Kumeyaay, Ohlone, Peruvian, or Turkish people are mistaken about their own cultural identities or their rootedness in the past. I mean that archaeology, genetics, and linguistics have nothing to say about such matters. The original NAGPRA process obliged tribes and institutions to accept the "culture" concept, shackling them to an otiose essentialism. Anthropologists had moved on, but the law was stuck in the ethnographic salvage era. For California, therefore, the shift to what amounts to national sovereignty as a basis for repatriation is a healthy legal move.

All this leaves two questions. Looking backward, how do we assess Kroeber's actions in relation to the collection of ancestral remains and objects buried with and near them? Looking forward, is there any value to the California archaeology of a century ago?

When Kroeber's colleagues Merriam and Uhle excavated in 1902 at the Emeryville shell mound, and when he himself sent Loud to Lovelock

Cave in 1912, Indigenous sovereignty was hardly recognized in American society. California Indians, lacking formal reservations, were mostly landless and often depended on government and philanthropic largesse. Throughout the United States, Native people remained in the "state of pupilage" defined in nineteenth-century Supreme Court decisions.[53] In that era, there was no hint of a later awareness, made law in the 2020 Cal NAGPRA revision, that Indigenous polities retain rights throughout their aboriginal territory.

NAGPRA's "culture" concept might have made sense to Kroeber, but the essentialist assumptions behind that concept meant that he perceived some Indigenous people and communities as having lost their essential "cultures." Sites like the Bay Area shell mounds were seen as having no cultural stakeholders. It must have seemed to researchers that excavation could proceed as in other nations, with permission of the government and landowners. In 2021, the chair of Berkeley's NAGPRA Advisory Committee decried the collection of ancestral remains "without the free, prior and informed consent" of Indigenous communities as "scientific racism."[54] In 1901, however, circumstances were murky. Lovelock Cave is on Paiute land, but its ostensibly ancient occupants were said to be Paiute "enemies." The UC Berkeley Faculty Club and the Ellis Landing, Emeryville, and West Berkeley shell mounds are on Ohlone land, but anthropologists did not understand that living people had connections to these sites. Kroeber himself had worked with two Chochenyo-speaking Ohlone people (among other Indigenous people) at the Verona rancheria, but what he knew about their histories was only that they had been associated with Mission San José in Fremont. It might not have occurred to him that some of their families could have come from what are now Berkeley, Emeryville, or Richmond.[55] His assumptions may well have blinded him to the possibility that people subjected to the mission system still felt a connection to precolonial cultural sites.

In sum, the California archaeological work that Kroeber's colleagues undertook and that he directed in a few cases is similar to what he himself did in Mexico and Peru, what Phoebe Hearst supported in Egypt and Peru, and what other researchers undertook in Europe, Latin America, Oceania, and elsewhere. They aimed to understand the human past, as they saw it; another perspective is that their extractive projects suited Euro-American elites. Nationalisms and ideologies of autochthony throughout the world transformed the social contexts and implications of archaeology during the twentieth century. In the United States, where these changes mainly followed Kroeber's time, Berkeley's distinctive moral failure lies with anthropologists and university leaders in recent decades who chose to oppose and deflect increasingly urgent requests from the state's Indigenous people.

Looking forward, while the stain of repatriation failures is indelible, a legacy of early UC archaeology is what it preserved in the face of urban development. It may be unnecessary to say that food remains, tools, and other material collected from shell mounds continue to inform interpretations of Bay Area cultural history; even sediment from prior excavations can be analyzed with new scientific methods.[56] Most importantly, research in collaboration with tribes now integrates Indigenous knowledge, the findings of new excavation, and reïnterpretations of early work. For example, in *The Archaeology of Refuge and Recourse* (2021), Tsim Schneider (Federated Indians of Graton Rancheria) tells a story of resilient Indigenous lives outside the missions and during American colonization based on his own collaborative archaeology and archival research, Coast Miwok histories and knowledge, and earlier work like Nelson's 1909 shell-mound survey. As he pointed out (e.g., 85–86), Nelson not only mapped the locations of past communities but, in parts of the Bay Area, documented the continued presence of Indigenous people living in relation to shell mounds.

In 2019, Ohlone leader Corinna Gould also offered a perspective on Nelson's work (NoiseCat et al. 2019):

> He knew that these special places were going to be destroyed, and he created this map. I really believe that our ancestor was in the ear of this guy. Because who cares, right? A bunch of Indian cemeteries are going to get destroyed? Why should he care? But he did that work so that we who are here today, alive, could find those places and re-connect to those spiritual touchstones.

According to this view, it is partly due to "salvage" archaeology that some of California's oldest built sites continue to structure its Indigenous landscape and lifeways.

KEECH KEEMCHUEN

Death is a central part of social life and a locus of significant crosscultural variation. Kroeber therefore sought to document practices associated with death, including burial, cremation, mourning, purification, and naming. In June 1903, a Mojave friend notified him of the death of an elder who in 1902 had sold a war bow and two arrows for the UC anthropology museum.[57] To witness the all-day mourning ceremony a week later, on 21 June, Kroeber made an impromptu trip to Needles, writing a detailed description (ALK Ctn 10:7, pp. 1–5; 10:30). A young man addressed elders in the ceremony: "My relatives, we have lived here. This is our country. We had much to eat. Now it is all changed. We work and it is different." His reference to work alludes to the new wage economy; his mention of abundance indexes the value of cultivation, gathering, and food preparation and the catastrophic impacts of American land and water seizures.

Lifeways of death also loomed large in Kroeber's Yurok work. He documented three versions of a Yurok-language medicine for cleansing one who has handled a body—from Mary Marshall in 1906, Dave Durban in 1907, and Skirk in 1909. At about 20 and 40 minutes, the two that were recorded are among the longest early Yurok recordings. And at least eight narratives in Kroeber's *Yurok Myths* explain the origin of death.[58] As several stories relate, the prehuman *'woogey* debated alternatives to death as they arranged the world for people. Some thought people should live long lives, never dying young, or should be reborn once. Others disagreed, saying people should die whenever it was time. Durban recorded his account on 7 June 1907. In it, referring to the human beings who are to come, the *'woogey* repeatedly exclaim *'aawokw 'o'lolekweeshol'* "alas, people" (literally "village dwellers"); *'aawokw* is an expression of sorrow used today in mentioning the departed. Durban also recounted how those who opposed death recounted their dispute with its advocates:

> *"Yaa', chyue', tue' to' kee cheetaa kegohchee keemchuenowohl.*
> [We said:] "Well then, they [human beings] should be reborn once each.
> *Tue' weeshtue' tue' kee cheetaa nue soo hoole'mehl."*
> That is how they should live."

Kem tue' nee yesee', "Peyowo'k'w, to' kee nenomey' nue 'woole'mek'.
Again they just said, "No, they should live different lengths (of time).
To' weeshtue' kee shoo nue hoole'mehl."
That is how they should live."
Peesh, wee' tue' kem tema 'negolohkeen,
So this is what we again in vain said,
"Yaa', chyue', tue' to' kee cheetaa meguuekw cheguenowohl.
"Well then, they should grow very old.
To' weeshtue' tue' kee cheetaa nue soo hoole'mehl."
That is how they should live."
Kem tue' nee yesee', "Peyowo'k'w, peyowo'k'w, to' kee nenomey' nue 'woole'mek'.
Again they just said, "No, no, they should live different lengths.
To' weeshtue' kee shoo nue hoole'mehl."
That is how they should live."

The first sentence above includes a phrase *kegohchee keemchuenowohl*, with iterative *kegohchee* "once each" and a verb *keemchuenowohl* "they are reborn." Another form of this rare verb was recorded on 20 June 1939, when Fanny Flounder told Kroeber that the idiom *keech keemchuen* "(someone is) born again" refers to an "old person at [the] birth of a (grand) child."[59] Children and grandchildren give an old person the new life that death, as arranged by the *'woogey*, will otherwise thwart.

Two years later, on 29 July 1941, Kroeber was at Stoowen (a few miles up the Klamath River) with elder James Mennow; Maggie Pilgrim (figure 8.9) interpreted and shared other linguistic and cultural information.[60] They provided the only known account of one method of getting California condor feathers: a man hid in a pit covered with brush, on which a fish was set; when a condor came for the fish, the man grabbed it, took some white underwing feathers, and released it. Condors were not killed. Their feathers are used in ceremonial regalia; the Yurok Tribe has secured the return of condor feathers from museum collections. Condors are critically endangered and were for some years extinct in the wild, but the tribe's Condor Restoration Program is a model in the field of wildlife restoration.[61]

Pilgrim's father, Pecwan Jim, himself recorded eight Yurok-language narratives with Kroeber on 12 June 1907; only translations are published.

Figure 8.9
Maggie Pilgrim with surf fish, 1951. Photograph by Thelma Moore (1999.03.1699, Boyle Collection, Cal Poly Humboldt Library).

One was the story of *pechkue 'o segep* "upriver coyote," who sought water for the people of the world.[62] He looked for it in all directions:

"Peesh tue' weetee' nee mehl hegook',
[He said:] "This is why I travel around,
'nesek' kee 'ok'w 'ue-pa'aanah."
thinking they should have water."

He found water with *mer'wermery 'ue-mey'* "daughter of the headwaters" far inland. She explained that water would come from her body:

"Hes? Kwelekw to' kee 'ok'w 'ue-pa'aanah.
[She said:] "Is it so [that they do not have water]? They should have water.
Kwelekw nekee' kee yohkuemek' keekee 'wo-'ohkwek' 'ue-pa'aanah." . . .
I will make it so that they have water." . . .
"Kwelekw nek 'ne-weskwelohl kee mer'wermeryk'.
"From my body it will flow.
Weet kee yohkue' 'ue-pa'aanah: tue' nek 'ne-weskwelohl kee mer'wermeryk'."
That is how their water will be made: from my body it will flow."

Water would flow into every inland ravine:

> *"Kee nuemeechyue 'ok'w 'ue-pa'aanah."*
> [She said:] "Each will have water."

After water was made, she and *pechkue 'o segep* made salmon and other fish:

> *"Mosee kem kee 'we-skuyenek' mocho kee mok'w 'we-nepuyonah."* . . .
> [She said:] "It will not be good if they will not have salmon." . . .
> *Weykee' kee 'we-nepuyonah.*
> It was accomplished that there would be salmon.

In Yurok creation stories, *weykee'* "it was accomplished, finished, ordained" is a verb often used to describe setting up the world.

Other creation stories say how water came into rivers, and *mer'wermery 'ue-mey'* figures in stories told by Robert Spott and Lowana Brantner, but no other Yurok story tells that the rivers first flowed from her body.[63] In "The First Water Is The Body," Mojave poet Natalie Diaz (2020:52) underscored the same link: "Will we remember from where we've come? The water." As Yurok activist, artist, and teacher Annelia Hillman has said about the Klamath River: "This river is our umbilical cord, what feeds us and what nurtures us." To reclaim the Klamath's ancestral body from the dams that have impounded its waters for a century and may now finally be demolished has been the work of activists like Hillman and groups like the Klamath Justice Coalition and Ancestral Guard.[64] With them, in the generations of Pecwan Jim's great-grandchildren and their children and grandchildren in turn, the mission of *pechkue 'o segep* is reborn.

Jim's granddaughter and Maggie Pilgrim's daughter was *'aawokw* Aileen Figueroa (figure 8.10), who contributed to Yurok linguistic and cultural documentation over a longer period than any other person. In 1927, when Aileen was thirteen, the composer Derrick Lehmer recorded her singing four brush-dance songs. At UCLA fifty years later, she joined a prominent song performance and discussion of northwest California cultural practices.[65] For the next three decades, until she died in 2008, she was active in tribal and academic linguistic projects and taught a weekly community class where scores learned Yurok. Aileen would look at each

Figure 8.10
Aileen Figueroa and Jimmie James at a Yurok language gathering, 2006. Photograph by Andrew Garrett. Figueroa and James were talented first-language speakers of Yurok who worked to pass the language on to younger people.

person in turn: "Let me hear you say it," she would say, smiling with delight to hear a new speaker.

I met Aileen and her daughter *'aawokw* Kathleen Vigil in 2001, when my colleague and friend Juliette Blevins and I visited to learn about the Yurok language and community. Aileen and Kathleen were generous hosts then and on our subsequent visits, and later when I came alone. Kathleen herself was a major figure in language revitalization, serving as a high-school Yurok teacher, in the Yurok Tribe language office, and as the founder of the Yurok Elder Wisdom Preservation Project, a grassroots effort that originated after a language gathering. Hank Sims (2006) reported that Kathleen said "a cry came out" at that gathering and that the possible future loss of the language when the elders were gone "was a great weight on Figueroa's heart." But if "the physical side of our culture has been preserved somewhat," as Yurok cultural activist Skip Lowry told Sims, he saw the "the spiritual side coming back" with language revival. Perhaps the resurgence of Indigenous languages, cultural life, and environmental rights is like the renewal of the waters that *mer'wermery 'ue-mey'* promised in the creation of the world, as Kathleen's great-grandfather told Kroeber in 1907:

"Kwelekw kee nuemee meyrkwenee wek toomek k'ee 'we-hlkelonah.
"It will be all over the world.
Tue' weetue' kee nuemeechyue mer'wermeryk'.
It will flow from everywhere.
Kee nuemeechyue 'ok'w 'ue-pa'aanah."
Everywhere will have water."

IV

INDIAN LAND

9

PUBLIC WORKS

> Anthropologists now agree that each culture must be examined in terms of its own structure and values, instead of being rated by the standard of some other civilization exalted as absolute—which in practice of course is always our own civilization. This anthropological principle leads, it is true, to a relativistic or pluralistic philosophy—a belief in many values rather than a single value system. But why not, if the facts so demand?
>
> —Alfred Kroeber, "Anthropology," 1950

Some treatments of Kroeber's work charge that Indigenous Californians were denied land and tribal recognition because of his work. This became a major theme in discussions of Kroeber Hall, with commentators even describing Kroeber as racist. Yet documentary evidence reveals his support for Indian land, cultural, and political rights throughout his career, going beyond most colleagues in the field. Neither the Proposal to Un-Name Kroeber Hall nor UC responses to it mentioned this, nor did the Proposal record his forceful advocacy against eugenic and racist ideologies. In this chapter, I describe Kroeber's record of advocacy and his support for Indigenous rights during an era when open racism was widespread.

EUGENICS AND RACISM

As noted in chapter 1, after the Proposal was submitted, the *Daily Cal* deplored Kroeber's "advocacy of racial oppression and subjugation," and many public comments called him a racist (DKH 2). One wrote that he "was a racist man and his life's work led to extreme pain, suffering, and degradation of Native American individuals." Another stated simply, "UC Berkeley should not be glorifying racists." Yet another, from

Tony Platt (2020a), suggested that Kroeber encouraged work "in the eugenics tradition."[1] These are striking criticisms of "one of the most outspoken scientific critics of eugenics in the United States in the 1910s," as John Jackson and David Depew (2017:70) described Kroeber. In that decade, wrote Carl Degler (1989:11), no social scientist rejected "race as an explanation for human social differences . . . more pointedly nor more profoundly than Alfred L. Kroeber."

Widely accepted in the 1910s and 1920s, eugenics was "a part of the Progressive ethos," in Jason Lantzer's (2011:27) words, "advocated by scientific professionals and supported in many states by a broad upper- and middle-class constituency of educated reformers."[2] Eugenicists encouraged sterilization or euthanasia of people with allegedly undesirable traits, and limits on immigration from undesirable nations. Until the Nazi program could no longer be ignored, organizations like the Eugenics Record Office (1910–1939), the Galton Society of America (1918–1939), and the American Eugenics Society (1926–) had broad institutional support. They were generously funded by the Carnegie Institution under its president, John Merriam, who had until 1920 been a UC paleontologist. Eugenics, Thomas Leonard (2016:xii) has written, "offered scientific legitimacy to established American hierarchies of race, gender, class, and intellect."

Looming in the background of eugenics was an ominous global aspect. Early in the twentieth century, in fieldwork during the Namibian genocide, the anthropologist, linguist, and zoologist Leonhard Schultze (1908:viii) dismembered "fresh corpses" and studied "the living bodies" of "captured" Nama people. He described "Bushmen" as "the last remnant of the primeval era of the human race," lacking "the prerequisite for any cultural development, the drive to create something beyond everyday needs" (1910:290). Only slightly later, according to Robert Gordon (2009:47), the anthropologist and eugenicist Eugen Fischer sought specimen body parts of Africans condemned to death; Fischer's (1913:302) book on biracial Namibians argued that "race mixture" leads to "intellectual, cultural decline." Josef Mengele studied at Fischer's institute in Berlin; Benjamin Madley (2005:455) has described Fischer as "influenc[ing] Hitler's own thinking on race and interracial mixing."

In the United States, the anti-Semitic eugenicist Madison Grant's popular *The Passing of the Great Race* (1916) called for the subjugation and

Figure 9.1
Ku Klux Klan members at the US Capitol, 1925 (Bettmann / Getty Images).

internment of "inferior races." According to Robert Sussman (2014:168), Grant was "stimulated by [his] rage over and fear of Boas's antiracist, anti-eugenics writings." Hitler praised Grant, while Boas's books were burned in Nazi Germany. The German-born Boas was Jewish, as were many of his students; Kroeber, the grandson of German immigrants, grew up in a New York German-Jewish cultural milieu. Jonathan Spiro (2009:302) described the battle between Grant (and his followers) and the Boasians as "a confrontation between the ethos of native Protestants and the zeitgeist of immigrant Jews." Anti-Boasians included Henry Fairfield Osborn, president of the American Museum of Natural History, who disparaged Boasian anthropology as the unscientific "gossip of natives" (Spiro 2009:303). At the Second International Congress of Eugenics, he also dismissed "the 'melting pot' theory" and defended the "right of the state to safeguard the character and integrity of the race or races on which its future depends." His full address was published in *Science* (Osborn 1921).

The Immigration Act of 1924 banned Asian immigration to the United States and restricted immigration from southern and eastern Europe. Supported by the Ku Klux Klan (figure 9.1) and other advocates of Nordicism, its goals were explained in 1924 by US Representative Carl Vinson (Committee on the Judiciary 1950:64). He "would have no concern" if "the immigrants now flooding our shores" had "the same traits, characteristics, and blood of our forefathers." These forebears "belonged to the same branch of the Aryan race," and Vinson's objection was not to northern Europeans. "The emigrants affected by this bill are those from Italy, Greece, Russia, Poland, Bulgaria, Armenia, Czechoslovakia, Yugoslavia, and Turkey," he said, explaining that "people from these countries do not yield their national characteristics, but retain them practically unimpaired by contact with others." Anti-Asian, anti-Black, anti-Indigenous, and anti-immigrant racist speech of this kind was normal in American public discourse.

Throughout this period, in public and privately, Kroeber criticized eugenics and racism. In 1911, after publicity about Ishi, a man in Texas wrote with a personal question about interracial marriage. Kroeber responded that "such a union is not itself objectionable or dangerous." He added that "it all depends on the man. If he is desirable and worthy . . . I can see no objection to the union" (1 December 1911, ALK Box 2:11).[3]

In a widely reported 1914 lecture, "Heredity, Instinct, and Environment," Kroeber called eugenics a "snare" and a "joke" (though it was no joke, as subsequent decades would show).[4] His remarks were quoted in the *Los Angeles Times* (via the Associated Press, "Eugenic Fad" 1914):

> Even [Francis] Galton, founder of the eugenic movement, and an eminent scientist, was deluded through overlooking the influence of civilization on man. . . . It is easier to talk of breeding improved human beings than to begin by improving oneself and training one's children better. The future of the human race can be enhanced only through character building by individuals and courageous adherence to ideals by nations.

In other words, the traits that were supposedly of concern to eugenicists are malleable and determined by social context ("civilization"), not biology. As Kroeber later declared (1915:285, emphasis his): "*The absolute equality and identity of all human races and strains as carriers of civilization must be assumed.*"

Letters of protest came from across the United States; Kroeber responded to some (ALK Box 2:16). On 11 April 1914, he told one correspondent that eugenicists who "introduce biological observations and points of view into social problems . . . are following a wrong and misleading method." He wrote on the same day to Yale economist Irving Fisher, first president of the American Eugenics Society. He had spoken strongly, he said, "in order to emphasize a fundamental distinction between the biological and social science which is very frequently forgotten at the present time. Had I spoken more temperately my lecture would have been without any effect."

In the following year, Kroeber had an exchange with the prominent eugenicist David Starr Jordan, president of Stanford University (ALK Box 19:34). It was Jordan who had hired Kroeber in 1900 for his short-term position at the Academy of Sciences; he was now finishing *War and the Breed: The Relation of War to the Downfall of Nations* (1915). In it, Jordan would more fully develop ideas about "race degeneration" that he had articulated a few years earlier (1911:86): "A degenerate race is a race which has lost its best elements." As Jordan put it in 1915, "war leads toward racial decadence by the obliteration of the most virile elements, these being thereby left unrepresented in heredity" (xv). On 6 March 1915, Jordan wrote to ask Kroeber if it would be accurate to include this statement in his book:

> The total number [of precolonial California Indians] was about 200,000, reduced by war, diseases, drink, and the like to about 20,000 at the present time, and in the wars the stronger braves were killed off more or less purposely by their enemies, leaving the weaker stock to reproduce themselves.

Kroeber wrote back on 13 March:

> You have come to the wrong man this time. The views on war and race degeneration which you express so brilliantly are my pet quarrel. I should therefore hardly be ready to subscribe unqualifiedly to your statement about the California Indians even if it had some demonstrable basis of fact; but war has clearly been so very negligible a factor in the decrease of the California Indians that to mention it at all is almost certain to be misleading. Many tribes did not resist the whites at all. Those that did suffered most from indiscriminate massacres, in which strong and weak, old and young, men and women, were sacrificed together.

Three days later, Jordan responded in a huff: "I have no doubt as to my theory of the effect of war on the race, it being thoroughly proved in theory and in practice." His ideas about "race degeneration" were discussed by a well-researched Stanford report that led to the unnaming of its former Jordan Hall.[5] Kroeber's word "brilliantly" was meant to praise his former employer's exposition (which is indeed lively), not his ideas; his point in mentioning "indiscriminate" massacres that affected "strong and weak" was to contradict the idea that war brought about the "degeneration" of Indian people.

A couple of years later, Kroeber's influential theoretical paper "The Superorganic" (1917a) was equally clear. The paper's text never used the term *superorganic*, but it was understood to index a conception of cultural traits as socially transmitted. Its position was plain (180–181): "Not a single piece of evidence has yet been produced to support the assumption that the differences which one nation shows from another—let alone the superiority of one people to another—are racially inherent, that is organically founded." As for eugenics itself, Kroeber (1917a:189) echoed his 1914 lecture in calling it "a fallacy. It is a mirage like the philosopher's stone, the elixir of life, the ring of Solomon, or the material efficacy of prayer; and to those who are led by its learned modernity to receive it earnestly, it is a destructive snare."

Kroeber's idea that cultural traits are not mainly determined by biology or psychology is still contested. The psychologist Steven Pinker (2002:23) criticized Kroeber for allegedly denying that "social behavior … could be explained by *any* properties of minds," but this is not what he argued.[6] Kroeber (1918:359) summarized his position as follows:

> The anthropologist works, then, not by denying the reality of the factors of heredity and environment but by going beyond them. … The progress which he has made … has been achieved … by explaining phenomena of civilization not in terms of the underlying organic condition or surrounding nature, but in terms of civilizational phenomena themselves; with human mentality never left out, but always regarded only as it is acted on by custom and institution and reacts on them.

Even if the human slate is blank, he wrote elsewhere, "heredity gives us the slate and the pencil" (1916b:31).

Strands of Kroeber's anti-racist writing from the 1910s were interwoven in his influential textbook, *Anthropology* (1923). The book's fourth chapter was a sustained argument, using evidence from anatomy, physiology, and psychology, against the belief that some "races" are innately superior in any cognitive, evolutionary, or intellectual way. "Most of the alleged evidence" for intrinsic racial disparities, he concluded (85), "is likely to be worthless." It is important to add that Kroeber in 1923 did not (as scientists do today) reject the biological existence of human "races." But in contrast to other writers, he did argue that anatomical and physiological differences within "races" are as great as differences between them, that they do not differ in cognitive or intellectual capacity, and that all people are capable of developing equally complex cultures.

At the end of his textbook (506), Kroeber compared global dossiers of "culture elements," the various abstract and concrete traits that (according to his understanding) accrete and ultimately define "civilizations" or cultures. As a hardly veiled critique of contemporary Nordicism, he wrote that "the Nordic branch looms insignificant." He added a further rebuke of eugenicist thinking: "Any fears of the arrest and decay of human progress if a particular race should lose in fertility or become absorbed in others, are unfounded. Such alarms may be attributed to egocentric imagination." This was an echo of his teacher Boas (1901b:289, 1911d:207): "The value which we attribute to our own civilization is due to the fact that we participate in this civilization, and that it has been controlling all our actions since the time of our birth."

INDIAN RIGHTS

Privately and in public, Kroeber supported Indigenous rights from early in his career. For example, in 1904, his Mojave friend Jack Jones asked him about citizenship and voting rights. Kroeber corresponded with C. E. Kelsey of the Northern California Indian Association and reported back to Jones (ALK Box 1:6):

> You are a citizen of the United States all right. It is not quite sure whether you can vote. Generally Indians have not been allowed to vote, but it looks as if the law allowed them to. If you want to vote you must first register, like every body else. If the clerk objects to your registering, tell him you have the

> right by Act of Congress [Kroeber cites specific statutes and a court case]. Then if they don't let you register, let me know.

This advice may have been naïve—many Native people were not legally US citizens until 1924, and roadblocks were often put in the way of their voting even after 1924—but the point is Kroeber's interest in helping.[7]

Kroeber was also aware of (and may have guided) his student Samuel Barrett's correspondence with Kelsey in 1906, after a summer when Barrett worked with Miwok people in the Sierra Nevada. Barrett wrote on 30 October to detail an instance of land seizure from Indians near Groveland: "The Indians are in a good way to sooner or later lose their home, and if something could be done now to adjust the matter it could probably be arranged without expense to the government," adding a complaint "which I found almost everywhere that I went":

> These people . . . adhere to their old ways of living, particularly in the matter of foods, using the aboriginal foods to a large extent; and everywhere I found them complaining that they had been dispossessed of their lands and were now obliged not only to live upon the land of the whites, or, in certain instances upon small pieces which they owned themselves, but they were forbidden in many cases by the whites from gathering acorns, manzanita berries, seeds, and other old time vegetable foods from the lands to which they had formerly had free access. . . . The game laws are so arranged that when it is lawful to hunt deer, particularly, the deer have nearly all migrated to the high Sierra. . . . Of this the Indians complain: that they are not allowed to hunt when the deer are in their vicinity, and that in certain parts, upon the forest reserve and the national parks, they are not permitted to carry arms in the season when they might legally hunt.

Kelsey, by then a special agent of the Office of Indian Affairs, replied on 31 October that he would try to have the seized land returned, and hoped to buy land for Indians near Groveland. Kroeber kept this correspondence in the anthropology department files (RDA Box 14).[8]

Kroeber himself, in a 1909 lecture, echoed advocacy organizations in saying what he thought Indigenous Californians "primarily" needed: "not money, not food, not advice, not even education, . . . but land" (1909b:437). In the early 1910s, he was active in the Indian Board of Cooperation, a social-welfare organization whose work included advocacy for local public school facilities for California Indian children.[9] In 1923, he was one of nine non-Indian anthropologists invited to join the

Committee of One Hundred, a US government advisory group led by prominent American Indian activists and scholars; its recommendations included educational reforms, legal reforms like letting Indians sue the United States in the Court of Claims, and improved reservation health and sanitation. And in 1933–1934, after a California ban on lower Klamath River commercial fishing, Kroeber worked with Robert Spott to help Yurok Indians find alternatives, personally organizing an outreach campaign among sport fishermen (RDA Boxes 75, 139).

A key national figure in the 1920s and 1930s was John Collier, whom Vine Deloria and Clifford Lyttle called the "the first non-Indian . . . to understand, appreciate, articulate, and fight zealously for" Native American traditions.[10] "The story of the reform movement" after 1922, they wrote, "is largely a story of [his] rise to prominence in the private organizational world that sought reform in federal Indian policy." He formed the American Indian Defense Association in 1923, lobbied against assimilationist policies, and was a reforming BIA commissioner from 1933 to 1945. In his memoir, Collier (1963:216–217) singled out Kroeber for praise. In the early twentieth century, he wrote, typical anthropologists were "apologists" for the "view of Indians and Indian cultures as inferior and dying—as fast-fading curiosities in the modern world." But when the program that became the Indian New Deal was formulated in the 1920s, Kroeber gave it "his unconditioned endorsement, and he thereafter became a board member of the American Indian Defense Association. Of all the other anthropologists, I can name only two who helped the Indians in their struggles of the 1920s."

The central plank of the Indian New Deal was the Indian Reorganization Act of 1934, which Kroeber praised in a letter to Charles Elkus (9 March 1934, RDA Box 75): "My hat is off to Collier both for his courage and his ability to see straight. He certainly strikes right at fundamentals." Kroeber was "unqualifiedly in favor on principle of everything he is now undertaking." In 1937, Kroeber wrote to Collier to recommend against restrictions on the use of peyote (4 May, RDA Box 75): "It is the basis of the religion of some tens of thousands of Indians, and prohibition of its ritual use would be equivalent to forbidding these people the practice of their religion."

A few years later, Kroeber nominated Collier for an honorary doctorate. In praising his work to UC president Gordon Sproul (4 October

1940, RDA Box 75), he clearly expressed his alignment with Collier's reformist program.

> For the last twenty years he has concerned himself with the status of the American Indian: first, as a merciless analyst and critic of governmental policies which had fallen a century behind the times but were being perpetuated by bureaucratic inertia and lack of knowledge on the part of the wider public; later, as the developer of renovating and fundamentally constructive policies which he initiated as Commissioner. Others had realized that our treatment of the Indians constituted an unfortunate page in our national history. John Collier was the first to succeed in translating feeling into successful action. He has operated throughout on the principle of habilitating the Indian as an American citizen and at the same time leaving him free to remain as much of an Indian, culturally and socially, as he wishes to be.

This also shows Kroeber's lifelong pragmatic, conflict-avoidant style. He called the treatment of Indigenous people "unfortunate" rather than mustering the anger later expressed by Theodora Kroeber and his students, one of whom, George Foster (2003:98), would call it "a stain on all of European American civilization."

Finally, in retirement in the 1950s, Kroeber made crucial contributions to a legal determination against the US government and in favor of tribal interests. This was in a case brought to the Indian Land Claims Commission by California Indians who sued to establish that they occupied and used all the land of California before Europeans invaded.[11] The US position was that compensation was warranted only for areas with permanent habitations and especially frequent land use. Seven of Kroeber's former students testified for the United States.

For the plaintiffs, Kroeber and three UC Berkeley colleagues presented memory-documentation evidence that all areas were traditionally owned by one tribal group or another. At issue was whether areas without habitation sites were exclusively owned by one community, or were shared; if the latter, case law would not require compensation. Kroeber's view was that Indigenous California had fully demarcated boundaries: "Each community owned, wholly in and by itself and by inherent right, a certain tract of land" (1962:46). In this instance, as discussed by Arthur Ray (2006), essentialist assumptions about territory dovetailed with the actual needs of Indian communities. Kroeber rather casually explained his participation in a letter to Ursula Le Guin: "I know the stuff, my Indian friends will approve, and it brings in some needed dough" (7 June 1954, UKLG Box 62:11).

In 1954, after several years of preparation as the plaintiffs' primary witness (T. Kroeber 1970:222), the seventy-eight-year-old Kroeber testified and was cross-examined before the commission for ten days, three hours a day; he also testified later in rebuttal of the government case. After his last day of testimony in 1954, according to the *Oakland Tribune* ("Papal Bulls" 1954), "many of the California Indians seated in the audience arose to shake hands with the well-known Indian authority. Many said they remembered the college professor when they were children and he would visit their parents to ask questions on early California Indian life."

Asked in court if the United States should "pay the Indian for . . . the loss of his native culture," Kroeber responded, "We ought to pay him for his native possessory rights which he felt he had and which were violated from his point of view," adding that this included spiritual and emotional rights as well as mere subsistence (Ray 2006:267–268). Testifying on the same side, Robert Heizer was cross-examined by Ralph Barney. This led to an exchange reported by Charmian Crittenden (1954):

> The government lawyer . . . was trying to pin him down to exactly what areas were permanently occupied by the Indians. Heizer said they hunted deer here, and gathered acorns there, fished at some other place, etc., and Barney was all tied up with the details of use and occupancy by the Indians. He lamented, "I wish I could get just one general statement out of you anthropologists!" Heizer smiled sweetly . . . at the two Commissioners in the judges' seats, and said, "If the Commissioners will permit, I could give Mr. Barney a generalization." The Commissioners nodded permission and Heizer said, "In early times the Indians owned practically all of California."

In their eventual (1959) decision, the commissioners accepted Heizer's and Kroeber's assessment: "The Indians have proven aboriginal Indian title to all of said lands" (Stewart 1961:190). Kroeber was quoted afterwards (Riley 1959): "If as recent[ly] as 25 years ago I had been asked what the chances would be to obtain recompense for the Indians and their heirs who lost lands to the whites, I would have said they were very slim. I'm amazed and delighted with the decision last Tuesday." Yet the eventual recompense was just "the sort of expensive-meaningless *dénouement* Kroeber had feared" (T. Kroeber 1970:223)—"forty-five cents an acre" (Ray 2006:272).

In sum, for more than fifty years, Kroeber worked to support California Indian cultural and legal rights. He was no activist, in an era when activism and scholarship were rarely integrated, and his impulses were sometimes paternalistic. He was, however, a committed ally whose actions helped Indians in their efforts to reclaim collective sovereignty and individual dignity.[12]

THE DORRINGTON MEMORANDUM

Cultural essentialism leads to the vanishment assumption, which is often expressed in statements that a cultural group is "extinct." Such statements were commonly made by popular and scholarly writers in the nineteenth and early twentieth centuries. California newspaper readers would thus have been accustomed to headlines like "Indians Almost Extinct" (in the *San Francisco Chronicle*, 1901) or "Indians Will Soon Be Extinct" (in the *Oakland Tribune*, 1910). Kroeber also wrote in this way. In 1904, he said that the "Esselen people and language" had "become extinct" (1904:49) and that he had to rely mainly on earlier documentation to describe the language. He had actually recorded a page or two of Esselen in January 1902 from Rumsen speakers Jacinta Gonzalez and Maria Viviana Soto in Monterey; Gonzalez had "learned the Esselen from a Spaniard who had learned the Esselen" (ALK Ctn 9:12, p. 29 rev.). This was not enough to change his judgment.

Twenty years later, among Patwin people northeast of the Bay Area, "no individuals were found whose ancestral home" was south of Rumsey or below Grimes on the Sacramento River, leading Kroeber (1932a:254) to say, "The southern half of the Patwin group has thus become wholly extinct." If he concluded that a language was no longer used, he called it extinct. Similarly, if he judged a system of cultural practices to be otiose, he called that extinct. "Greco-Roman civilization," for example, was "essentially dead in the West" by 500 CE (1951a:102). Anthropologists no longer speak of cultures in this way, but linguists commonly say languages are "dead" or "extinct" if, like Gaulish or Sumerian, they have no first-language speakers and no speech community (on this controversial metaphor see chapter 11).

The particular "extinction" statement critiqued in the Proposal is one of many in Kroeber's *Handbook of the Indians of California* (1925, completed in 1919). This massive book was an account of what its author had learned or could infer about languages, social practices, and material culture in precolonial California. In it, Kroeber described more than twenty tribal groups as "culturally," "ethnologically," or "for all practical purposes" "extinct" or "perished."[13]

Ohlone land is around San Francisco Bay and to the south. At Monterey and on what was then Phoebe Hearst's land at the Verona rancheria, Kroeber recorded information about two Ohlone languages, Rumsen and Chochenyo. At Monterey, this included Rumsen (and some Esselen) songs, stories, vocabulary, and cultural practices; at Verona, he recorded vocabulary from Yokuts and three Miwok languages as well as Chochenyo. Writing in his *Handbook* about Ohlone people, then called Costanoan, Kroeber offered a grim assessment (464):

> The Costanoan group is extinct so far as all practical purposes are concerned. A few scattered individuals survive, whose parents are attached to the missions of San Jose, San Juan Bautista, and San Carlos; but they are of mixed tribal ancestry and live almost lost among other Indians or obscure Mexicans. At best some knowledge of the ancestral speech remains among them. The old habits of life have long since been abandoned. The larger part of a century has passed since the missions were abolished, and nearly a century and a half since they commenced to be founded. These periods have sufficed to efface even traditional recollections of the forefathers' habits, except for occasional fragments of knowledge.

The respective languages associated with the San Jose, San Juan Bautista, and San Carlos (Carmel) missions are Chochenyo, Mutsun, and Rumsen.

Kroeber's statement exposed his essentialist assumptions. To avoid a death sentence, Indigenous groups should have pure rather than "mixed" ancestry, should live on their own land rather than "lost" among others, and should use their "ancestral speech" and "old habits of life." As discussed in chapter 2, this way of understanding cultures and languages made it impossible to appreciate the changes many California Indians had experienced. And it is naturally hurtful to read, especially from a putative expert, that the community you are part of is "extinct." Kroeber seemed to be saying, as Alan Leventhal et al. (1994:312) put it, "If descendants do not know the details [of] traditional culture or practice, then the question should be asked, 'Are they Indian?' "[14]

In 1954, while working on the Indian claims case, Kroeber walked back his terminology somewhat: if anthropologists "can no longer learn from living informants the speech and modes of life of the ancestors of these informants, they talk of that tribe or group as being extinct—when they mean merely that *knowledge* of the aboriginal language and culture has become extinct among the survivors" (Kroeber and Heizer 1970:2–3). But in his *Handbook* he never wrote in such terms, nor would this formulation have fit into his analytic framework. From the essentialist perspective, Indigenous groups *were* "extinct" if they did not exhibit what analysts deemed their "essential" traits. As Kroeber's colleague Robert Lowie (1950:84) wrote, "a culture survives so long as a considerable number of its bearers use the vernacular" language for communication, implying that it no longer survives if the language is not used. Maybe Kroeber began to see the limitations of this perspective as the field began to change, or how his wording could be hurtful; or maybe he was responding to concerns in the claims case.

Some Indigenous people also kept their linguistic and cultural knowledge to themselves. Early in the twentieth century, as Randall Milliken et al. (2009:211–216) described, responses to discrimination included "remain[ing] quiet about one's Indianness" and "passing as non-Indian." The Rumsen Ohlone artist and cultural leader Linda Yamane (2001:429) wrote similarly about the nineteenth and early twentieth centuries. "Traditions went underground" as Indigenous people experienced bigotry and discrimination. "Our families learned to blend in so well that we eventually 'disappeared' to the outside world," she wrote, "and the anthropologists declared us extinct." And presenting what they called a "perspective from the Muwekma Costanoan/Ohlone Indians," Les Field et al. (2013:415) wrote that "missionization's devastation of the ancestral Muwekma was so traumatic that it is understandable that ... Kroeber could surmise the extinction of this people with such assurance."[15]

It has also been said that Kroeber contributed to government decisions that effectively terminated Indian tribes. This was first stated by Field et al. (2013:413). Despite calling Kroeber's Ohlone "extinction" statement "understandable," they said that it "would ultimately affect the views of anthropologists, historians, educators, public agency staff and planners, elected officials, school children, and the general public." It could even have "served as a tribal death knell." Yet the vanishment and extinction tropes were prevalent before and during Kroeber's life. He did not push back, but a 995-page volume in a BIA monograph series is unlikely to have added much to public sensibilities. It was so poorly circulated that a University of Southern California colleague twenty years later could not obtain a copy "for love or money." Only after a 1953 commercial reprint was it more widely available.[16] At the same time, as Alan Leventhal et al. (2020) wrote, the extinction idea was "strongly felt for many decades" after Kroeber's book as researchers disposed of "Ohlone human remains and associated funerary objects uncovered during the post–World War II construction booms in the Bay Area."

A more specific assertion became critical in discussions of Kroeber Hall. Its seeds lie in Field's (1999:198) observation that "the published materials of academic anthropologists coincided with the disempowerment of these bands." (In early parlance, "bands" were distinct sociopolitical groups.) His point was that Kroeber's 1925 *Handbook* appeared only two years before a memorandum in which a US official declined to recommend land purchases for numerous California bands, including the Verona Band. Land was held in trust when such purchases occurred. The modern system of tribal recognition was not yet in place, but an eventual consequence of not having collective land of this kind was that recognition was easy to lose and hard to regain. For example, Bay Area tribal groups whose members are descended from members of the Verona Band have not yet (as of 2022) been successful in seeking the reaffirmation of their federal recognition.[17]

The 1927 memorandum was written by L. A. Dorrington, a government agent in Sacramento (Dorrington 1927, quoted repeatedly in the following paragraphs). As superintendent of the BIA's Sacramento Agency, he had been instructed to identify Indian bands and tribes that did not yet have land of their own.[18] Dorrington's memorandum covered forty-five California counties, listing about 220 bands and recommending land purchases for at most sixteen of them.[19] The list began with Alameda County, whose "estimated Indian population" was 125, "but all of this number, with the exception mentioned below, reside in the cities of Alameda County, where they have gone to procure employment." Dorrington described the exception: "There is one band in Alameda County commonly known as the Verona Band, which consists of about thirty individuals, located near the town of Verona; these Indians were formerly those that resided in close proximity of the Mission San Jose."[20] His recommendation followed: "It does not appear at the present time that there is need for the purchase of land for the establishment of their homes." It is this one sentence that has led to extensive criticism of Kroeber.

Field (2003:87–88) noted that Dorrington's 1927 recommendation "was matched by" Kroeber's 1925 remark that the Ohlone "group is extinct" for practical purposes, saying he had "always assumed that the relationship . . . was more than coincidental."[21] This assumed relationship was accepted without further scrutiny by other scholars and in the public sphere.[22] In 2015, for example, *Indian Country Today* reported that Verona Band recognition was "revoked in 1927 . . . due to the claim made by Alfred Kroeber" about Ohlone extinction ("California Students" 2015). The Muwekma Ohlone Tribe asserted in 2020 that Kroeber's "untruthful declaration" (which it had previously deemed "understandable") "was taken as fact" by Dorrington (Nijmeh 2020). This was also a key element of the Proposal to Un-Name Kroeber Hall, according to which the Ohlone extinction statement "had terrible consequences for these people." Details were spelled out in a sentence referring to the Muwekma Ohlone Tribe:

> Kroeber wrote erroneously in 1925 that for all practical purposes this tribe was culturally extinct, and based on Kroeber's statement the federal government removed the tribe's recognized status and forced the surviving members of the band to vacate land protected for Native Americans.

But while Dorrington was apparently unsympathetic to the needs of Native people, there is no evidence for the claim that his 1927 recommendations relied on Kroeber's "extinction" judgments. Leventhal et al. (2020) have acknowledged that "it is not possible to substantively link" the two. I contend that they are plainly independent.

One crucial point is that Dorrington's description of the Verona Band itself contradicted Kroeber's perspective. In Dorrington's usage, a "band" was an Indigenous group whose members lived in proximity and with some degree of collective organization apart from Euro-American social structures. Native people not living in "bands" were assumed to have fully joined Euro-American society and were judged ineligible for land purchases. In Alpine County, for example, Dorrington wrote that most Indian people "reside on public domain allotments" and "have never been considered as bands," so "there is no need to consider the purchase of tracts for them to establish their homes." Similarly, "in the vicinity of Averys," Calaveras County, there were many Native people, but they were "not considered as one band and they are scattered over a considerable area." Dorrington thought no land purchase was needed.

Dorrington described other groups as "bands." Some of these, like the Verona Band, were associated with Kroeber's "extinct" groups; many, in his view, did not need land. Dorrington also said land was not needed for three Salinan bands in Monterey County, including the Pleyto Band, which "have provided their own homes and are not in need of any home site." Kroeber (1925:368) called the Salinan language and group "extinct for all practical purposes," but Dorrington used the term "band" and based his decision on home ownership. In San Benito County, he offered a patronizing judgment concerning Mutsun people: "The San Juan Baptista band . . . have been well cared for by the Catholic priests and no land is required." But his point was that they did not "require" land, not that they were not a band, even though, as an Ohlone group, they fell under Kroeber's "extinct" verdict.

Because Dorrington identified the Verona Band as such and did not describe its members as "scattered," in contrast to other urbanized Indians in Alameda County, the Bureau of Indian Affairs (2001:10) has treated his memorandum as evidence that the Verona Band was "recognized as late as 1927."[23] Deplorable as it is, the US failure to recognize the Muwekma Ohlone Tribe thus stems from a dispute over "its continuous existence as a group only from 1927 to the present," in the BIA's words.[24] Rather than "revoking" recognition of the Verona Band, Dorrington affirmed it.

To be sure, Dorrington's statements that the Verona Band and dozens of other groups did not need land had destructive long-term impacts, given the later importance of such land purchases in federal recognition. But Kroeber's writing played no role, as three further arguments show.

First, Kroeber's precolonial population and language groups were only loosely correlated with twentieth-century bands. In the Bay Area, where missionization yielded nineteenth-century multicultural communities, the Verona Band included Ohlone, Miwok, and Yokuts people. It is not obvious how Dorrington would have known which chapter of Kroeber's *Handbook* to check. This situation was not rare. For example, in Siskiyou County in northern California, Dorrington's list included Salmon River bands at Butler Flat, Fork(s) of Salmon, and Black Bear. These were on the land of Konomihu and New River Shasta people, said by Kroeber (1925:889) to be "vanished . . . or on the very brink of extinction"; but were also inhabited by Karuk people, definitely not "extinct," who had fled up the Salmon River from the depredations of miners. Kroeber's essentialist categories were often not meaningful in the twentieth century; his book would not have been useful to Dorrington.

Second, if Kroeber's judgments had guided Dorrington, he would not have proposed buying land for "extinct" groups. But this was precisely what he did in two of the seven cases where he definitely recommended land purchases. At Knight's Ferry in Stanislaus County, Dorrington said, "15 or 20 acres of good land should be purchased for this band" of about twenty-five people. This was Lakisamne land, or Delta Yokuts, which Kroeber (1925:442) called "practically extinct." In Marin County, the largest band for which Dorrington recommended buying land had "approximately 150 persons . . . at a point known as Tomales Bay." Expressing uncertainty about "their best interests," Dorrington concluded "that land will probably be required for their benefit." The land by Tomales Bay is Coast Miwok territory. Kroeber (1925:272–278) made it clear that he considered Coast Miwok culture gone: "little has been recorded," he said, in a chapter largely devoted to whether Francis Drake landed in Coast Miwok land in 1579 and, if so, what his reports reveal.[25] If Dorrington had relied on Kroeber's view of cultural persistence, he would not have supported the Knight's Ferry and Tomales Bay bands. That even two of his seven definite recommendations were of this kind is striking, given that the vast majority of the 220 bands he listed were on lands whose people Kroeber did *not* deem "extinct" or "vanished."

Third, Dorrington's explanations show that anthropologists' opinions and the use of precolonial languages and cultural traditions had nothing to do with his recommendations. These recommendations were based on two factors: whether a group was a band, living as a distinct community, and whether in his opinion it "needed" land or already had it. For example, in Tuolumne County, the "Indians of Groveland band are making satisfactory progress, many of them having their own homes," so "it will not be necessary to purchase land for this band." In Butte County, most Yankee Hill Band families "own property. . . . It would therefore not appear to [be in] their best interests to purchase land on which they might establish homes." But the Yosemite Band in Mariposa County "has been somewhat nomadic," he observed, ignoring the negative impact of Yosemite National Park. He wrote that "it may be advisable to acquire a tract for homesite, as it will be in their best interests to be assigned a specific locality for their colony." Whether this was actually in their interest or merely suited park management, Dorrington's suggestions were unrelated to Kroeber's essentializing "extinction" judgments.

In sum, Dorrington's recommendations were based not on cultural status as "extinct" or not, but on home ownership and a perception of current social organization ("band" status) that sometimes contradicted Kroeber. I have belabored the details only because Dorrington's memorandum has assumed an outsized role in discussions of anthropological policy impacts and was critical in the unnaming of Kroeber Hall. Contrary to the Proposal's statement, it is false that "based on Kroeber's statement the federal government removed the tribe's recognized status," since if anything the government affirmed the status of the Verona Band in 1927. Also baffling is the Proposal's statement that "the federal government . . . forced the surviving members of the band to vacate land protected for Native Americans." The Verona rancheria had never been "protected," because land was never purchased for the band. Nor did the government force people to leave: depopulation followed a railway fire and the sale of Phoebe Hearst's land. A land purchase might well have led to modern federal recognition, to be sure, but the lack of one was not Kroeber's failure. His impacts on public policy were largely in support of Indigenous rights.

GOVERNMENT WORK

What is the role of an academic researcher under a colonial government? At the University of California, Kroeber was employed by a state responsible for what we now name genocide; people who looked like him had displaced and killed Native people and still oppressed them. In the decades of social tumult after his death, many writers within and outside the academy critiqued anthropologists' choices and reflected on their roles in colonialism.[26] For example, writing about British anthropologists in Africa, Jack Stauder (1974:43–44) commented that "few if any" opposed the colonial system "with the perspective of overthrowing it. In fact, probably most anthropologists, consciously or unconsciously, accepted unquestioned their roles and concomitant privileges in the colonial system, and their work was generally confined and directed by it." Kroeber too had a privileged position in a (settler) colonial state, though it would be anachronistic to imagine that he saw himself as part of a system of oppression. He viewed himself and others like him as liberal actors whose research benefited society and whose writing nudged public opinion toward cultural ecumenicity. In the final sentence of *Anthropology* (1923:506), he wrote that his field contributes to a "larger tolerance and balance of mind." This view of anthropology's uplifting impact was, I am sure, deeply felt by many in Kroeber's circle. Yet his "larger tolerance" was mostly for white elites, and did not necessarily benefit Indigenous people. The cultural relativism and liberal humanism that were among his core values remained compatible with a paternalistic state.

Kroeber was undoubtedly "confined" by the system around him, but it would be simplistic to treat his work as a mere implementation of US (or California) Indian policy. Whether he was complicit in Indigenous erasure is also complex. Kroeber seems never to have questioned the vanishment assumption, a key plank of memory documentation. But he was active in support of Native rights throughout his career, including interventions directed at the US government.

Though Kroeber was not disposed to reflection, a 1909 letter offered a glimpse of his view of government work. At the end of his eighth UC year, he wrote to David Barrows, superintendent of education in the US colonial government of the Philippines.[27] In this letter, the thirty-three-year-old Kroeber brought up the prospect of spending a year or two in the Philippines:

> I am becoming very desirous of doing ethnology with more practical bearings than I have heretofore had opportunity. The Indian offers a sufficiently large and deep field for purely scientific research, but he is a very small element in our population, whose new status has already been in the main determined. In the Philippines, however, as in all the Orient, conditions are the reverse, and I find the wish growing in me to do something, for a time at least, that will bear more relation to actual problems and the work of the world than mere scientific investigation does.

In June 1909, the recent reduction of Phoebe Hearst's funding and the departure of Kroeber's colleague Pliny Goddard must have created a sense of professional uncertainty. Kroeber's wife Henriette suffered from tuberculosis, with occasional stays in sanitaria; he might have thought he could improve his salary in demanding personal circumstances.

The "practical" work Kroeber proposed to Barrows was language documentation along the lines of his California research. A classification of Philippine languages "would throw some light on the movements, and possibly the origins," of its people and "in turn would have political and other practical significance." Kroeber apparently had in mind that US policies toward specific Indigenous populations might depend on their diachronic relations to other populations—on whether different groups of people were "essentially different kinds or strata of men." It is hard to credit the idea that it might have mattered for administrative or educational purposes whether two populations spoke different languages that were related or unrelated genealogically, but maybe Kroeber's opinion was that related ethnolinguistic groups would share relevant social traits or would be less likely to object to being treated the same. Yet it did not matter in the end. Though the head of the ethnology division of the Bureau of Science in Manila wrote that he agreed with "the importance of making a study of the Philippine languages" and mentioned a position that might be suitable if Kroeber could commit two years, Kroeber took no further action.[28] There is no indication, unfortunately, that he had any reservations about the American colonial project in the Philippines.

What interests me most in the letter to Barrows is what it shows, early in Kroeber's career, about his sense of the public purposes of anthropology. In California, a settler-colonial state, he accepted assimilation as the "new status" of Native people. One can see why he thought it was "determined," given the era's realities, while wishing he had tried to resist it. But because of this, in his view, California anthropology was irrelevant to "the work of the world." In 1909, Kroeber did not think his research would have public impacts beyond scholarly and scientific edification. He did not envision what some anthropologists came to see after his death, that their discipline should advocate for Indigenous people and be responsive to their needs.

Perhaps Kroeber's sense of the irrelevance of California anthropology was mitigated in the 1910s and 1920s, as he wrote more broadly about the fallacy of eugenics and the anti-racist implications of anthropology. He had maybe finally seen how his research addressed "actual problems." This

Figure 9.2
Alfred Kroeber, New York, ca. 1907–1908 (ALKFP Box 1).

was not the same as forging an anthropological practice serving the goals of the Indigenous people whose languages and cultures it scrutinized, but in the first half of the twentieth century it was a significant public contribution.

Kroeber did work directly for the US government later in his career. Between 1943 and 1945, the Army Specialized Training Program provided instruction at American universities for soldiers heading to Europe and Asia. Among its subjects were foreign languages. Prominent academic linguists were "mobilized," as Milton Cowan (1975:29) put it; institutional support came from the Linguistic Society of America.[29] The involvement of linguists who had studied unwritten languages was a key factor in structuring ASTP language teaching as intensive small classes focused on oral communication, a decision with a long-term impact on US foreign-language education. Kroeber, then a former LSA president in his late sixties, wanted to help. "What can an old man do?" he asked, according to Theodora Kroeber (1961:179). He then set up Berkeley's ASTP language classes on Chinese, Japanese, Thai (bringing

Figure 9.3
Ursula Kroeber, St. Helena, ca. 1937 (ALKFP ALB v. 4). Her book appears to have grammatical paradigms on the top of the page.

the linguist Mary Haas to Berkeley), Vietnamese, and several eastern European languages; each language program also included area-studies instruction. (Afterward, Kroeber and historian Raymond Sontag developed a new area-studies major at Berkeley on this model.[30]) Kroeber's involvement was cut short by a heart attack in September 1943, but he deemed the work successful. "I gave them a good program," he told James Rosenberg, "and made the Army come through" (26 March 1944, ALK Box 3:24). For Kroeber and other linguists, as for US universities, supporting the war effort was assumed to be a manifest good.

In a later era with different presuppositions, anthropologists and their critics reflected on colonialism and academic complicity. Ursula Le Guin's fiction also examined anthropologists' role and the problem of humanistic anthropological inquiry in a colonial or authoritarian system. An example is her *The Word for World Is Forest* (1972). Often seen as a reaction to the Vietnam War, this novella describes the colonization of a forest world by Terrans, people from Earth: loggers and a military force whose aim is resource extraction. The invaders mostly regard the indigenous

Athsheans as sub-human; they enslave and brutalize many, and kill freely. No doubt what Le Guin (1972:118) herself called a "moralistic tale" indicts US imperialism broadly; a napalm-like "fire-jelly" recalls atrocities in southeast Asia. The novella also dates from a period when Le Guin's mother wrote a biography of Alfred Kroeber and (co)authored some of the first books that addressed the California genocide.[31] The Athsheans echo California Indian experiences, as James Clifford's reading highlights (2013:176–177). The novella, he wrote, "portrays a lethal confrontation of different worlds, recalling the world Ishi was born into: a situation of invasion where genocidal extermination is considered simply part of the 'progress' brought by technologically superior outsiders."

Clifford also observed that this is one of many works in Le Guin's oeuvre that "focuses on a cross-cultural friendship" (178). The friendships between her father and his Indigenous collaborators, salient in her own formation, naturally come to mind. This is not to embrace naïve biographical criticism, but to suggest that Le Guin's values emerged from her parents' household (see figures 9.2–9.3). As she herself said, referring to intellectual curiosity and an openness to other cultures, "my father's interest and temperament set . . . a moral tone" (2012:52). From him, she learned (in her words) "curiosity about people different from one's own kind; interest in artifacts; interest in languages; delight in the idiosyncrasies of various cultures" (Phillips 2019). Through her, therefore, we can sometimes read what is opaque in his writing.

Many critics have noted the prominence of anthropologists and anthropological thinking in Le Guin's fiction.[32] One of her early stories, "The Dowry of Angyar" (1964), begins with the repatriation of indigenous cultural heritage from a museum run by the interplanetary league that she would later call the Ekumen.[33] Its curator explains to a colleague, the anthropologist Rocannon, that "these claims come up now and then" (60). Another anthropological protagonist, Genly Ai in *The Left Hand of Darkness* (1969), refers to the Ekumen as "an experiment in the superorganic" (99). As Jan Horner (1985:10–11) has written, these terms nod playfully to Kroeber's Oikoumenê and superorganic (chapters 3 and 9 in this volume).

In *The Word for World Is Forest*, anthropologist Raj Lyubov sympathizes with the Athsheans, has a collaborator and friend among them, and speaks their language. But he works for the Terran army, which uses his reports for its own exploitative purposes. Among the invaders he is something of an outsider; even his name suggests alterity in relation to the brutal officers Benton and Davidson. In any case, Le Guin highlights the colonial anthropologist's ethical dilemma when a colleague says (85), "The people you're studying are going to get plowed under, and probably wiped out. It's the way things are. It's human nature." Lyubov replies: "I don't know what 'human nature' is. Maybe leaving descriptions of what we wipe out is part of human nature." This is the voice of a scholar hoping the work he does within a destructive system has value. Unlike Kroeber, to be sure, Lyubov (through his "we") acknowledges a role in that system. The question of his moral complicity does not come up.

An early scene features a debate over cultural differences between Terrans and Athsheans. Arguing against others who (like Kroeber's opponents fifty to sixty years earlier) insist on racial explanations and see some people as less than human, Lyubov explains that Athshean practices "may have some innate basis" but are largely "socially developed and expanded, and of course learned" (61). "They have no history," he says (62–63); "like the forest they live in, they've attained a climax state." The anthropological concept of the culture climax is due to Kroeber (1939), who described it as "a florescence in the several facets of culture" (5) and "a focus of cultural intensity" (222). For him, to be sure, culture climaxes were ordinarily limited in time, not ahistorical: "Their finest flowerings are evidently brief" (223). And the end of Le Guin's novella raises the prospect that the Terran invasion, by introducing murder as a cultural practice, has permanently disrupted the Athshean equilibrium.

It is Lyubov's Athshean friend Selver who introduces murder to the Athsheans. One of his people, seeing Terrans' capacity for brutality, says they must not be human. Selver corrects her (137): "They are men, men, like us, men." This echoes Kroeber's (1910b:446) emphatic statement: "Men are men and essentially alike wherever born and however reared." As Le Guin reflected in 2008, "what I got from living in my father's household and intellectual milieu was . . . the sense that nothing and no one is irremediably foreign—alien—Other."[34] Selver's echo of this idea is ironically inverted: it is the technologically advanced invaders whose humanity is in doubt.

Lyubov is killed accidentally in an Athshean attack on the Terrans, an unintended casualty of indigenous revolution. Selver rescues his work,

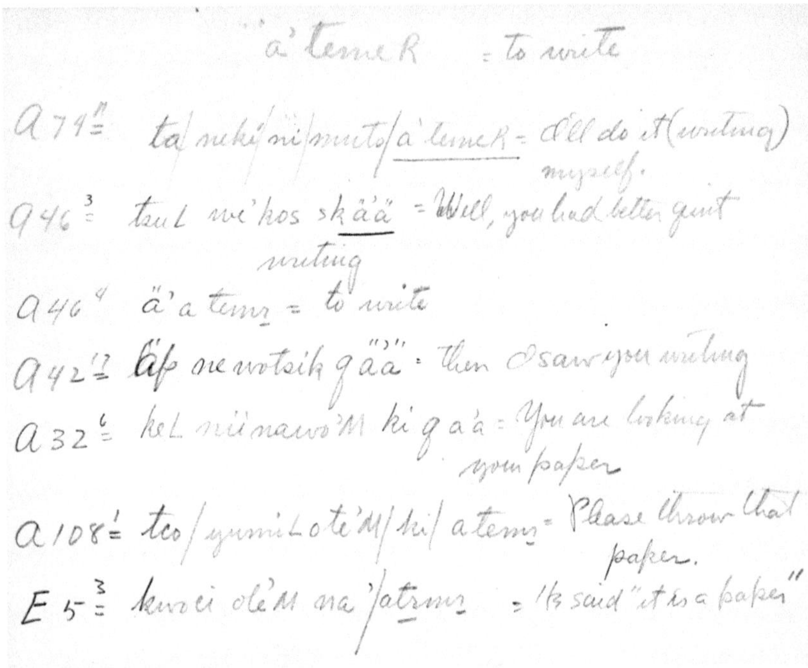

Figure 9.4
Yurok dictionary file slip for the word *'a'temeyr* "to write, paper," undated (ALK Box 38). Example sentences are drawn from texts and grammatical elicitation with Yurok people and might have been included in an eventual dictionary.

including a dictionary the two had created "in four months of exhausting but harmonious work" (86). As the Terrans prepare to leave Athshe at the novella's end, Selver gives Lyubov's documentary corpus to an observer from the interplanetary league. "He learned my language and the Men's Tongue," Selver tells the observer (115); "we wrote all that down. He understood somehow how we live and dream. The others do not. I'll give you the work, if you'll take it to the place he wished." Lyubov's understanding of the indigenous people of Athshe is embodied in a dictionary, a translation of their language.

Kroeber, too, devoted his final years to translations that were published only after his death: *More Mohave Myths* (1972), *Yurok Myths* (1976), and *Karok Myths* (1980). And the dictionaries of Luiseño, Mojave, Yokuts, and Yurok that he assembled in long work with many Indigenous collaborators remain unfinished as lexical notes in a documentary corpus.

The example in figure 9.4, featuring the word *'a'temeyr* "to write, paper" and its short form *'a'*, is one of about six thousand Yurok lexical file slips that illustrate word meanings, grammatical patterns, and cultural details.[35] This one especially interests me because it answers a question I have often been asked by Yurok teachers: Are words like *newochek'* "I saw you" also used in sentences like "I saw you writing," where the object of "see" is understood as the subject of the complement verb "writing"? Though arcane, this detail is of great practical interest in learning to speak. The fourth sentence in figure 9.4, *'Ap newochek' k'a-'a'?* "Then I saw you writing" (*k'a-'a'* "for you to write, your writing"), shows that the answer to the question is yes. After the dust settles, Kroeber (like Lyubov) will have left a legacy in language, a record of how people talked and a resource for their future.

10

INSTITUTIONAL ELISIONS

"Erasure is an art we must learn."

—Tong Ov, in Ursula K. Le Guin, *The Telling*, 2000

This chapter is about erasure and forgetting at the University of California, and how an institution chose to remember its own foundation. All memory is selective, to be sure; elision is always its shadow. In Ursula Le Guin's *The Telling*, the planet Aka is ruled by a Corporation that zealously stamps out local traditions, cultural diversity, and knowledge of the past. A linguist and folklorist from the Ekumen has been sent to find what capitalist modernity has suppressed. Her superior, Tong Ov, expresses ambivalence (Le Guin 2000:24). Some "want to hang on to everything," he says. "The Akans want to throw everything away. Maybe there's a middle way?" In moving forward, what merits elision? What are the consequences of forgetting?

In this chapter, I scrutinize the process by which Kroeber Hall was unnamed and the institutional myopia surrounding that process. I also describe aspects of UC's historical foundation and present self-construction that its leaders have chosen to ignore. Condemning Alfred Kroeber allowed a colonial institution to sidestep examination that would have been as uncomfortable as it might prove beneficial.

UNNAMING KROEBER HALL

After the comment period described in chapter 1, the Proposal to Un-Name Kroeber Hall was endorsed by the UC Berkeley Building Name Review Committee on 30 October 2020.[1] If the Proposal was like a prosecutor's indictment, to use the metaphor in one public comment, then the BNRC recommendation was more like a jury's verdict than a judicial decision that engaged with the arguments presented to it. Like a jury, the BNRC presented no assessment of the evidence or explanation of its reasoning.

In a section of its report called "Kroeber Hall Proposal," the BNRC summarized the Proposal's arguments (DKH 3):

> The proposal articulated several reasons for un-naming Kroeber Hall. First, Kroeber collected or authorized the collection of the remains of Native American ancestors from grave sites and curated a repository of these human remains for research study. This practice, labeled "Salvage Anthropology" by some scholars, is now illegal. The proposal argues that although this practice was not illegal when Kroeber engaged in it, it was immoral and unethical, even for the time. Second, Kroeber and colleagues took custody of a Native American man called "Ishi," who they allowed to live in the Museum of Anthropology; Ishi was given a janitorial position at the museum and used as "a living exhibit" for museum visitors. He was also taught racial slurs that were used to refer to Asian and African Americans. Third, Kroeber's claim that the Ohlone people were culturally extinct contributed to the decision by the Federal Government to delist the Ohlone from the national register of Native peoples, leading to the Muwekma Ohlone tribe having no land and no political power. Fourth, given this history, Kroeber is a public symbol of the discrimination against and disdain for Native Americans. A building named in his honor is an ongoing affront to Native Americans generally, an emblem of hostility to Native American members of the UC Berkeley community, and is not in keeping with Regent's policy 4400 listed above.

BNRC chair Paul Fine confirmed to me that "[in] the beginning of our statement we were summarizing the Proposal" (27 January 2021 email). In other words, the summary above is not an expression of the BNRC's views, but a synopsis of the Proposal's arguments.[2] It is immediately followed by a section called "Our Committee's Outreach and Deliberations."

The "Outreach and Deliberations" section focused on outreach, or the call for public comments. "Some of the claims made in the proposal were supported by some and contested by others," the BNRC noted; some comments were "quite detailed, substantively sourced, and rigorously argued." Others were brief, Twitter-style. Campus policy permits research: "if the cases submitted by the initiator and the commenters differ on basic facts," the BNRC may arrange "an independent analysis of the historical record concerning the naming of the building and the history of the relevant person(s)." This did not happen with Kroeber Hall. Instead, the BNRC simply summarized public comments on both sides of the matter and quoted a few selections from them.

The BNRC's verdict was presented in a "Conclusion," whose first sentence contained the totality of its independent assessment of Kroeber:

> After weighing the multiple viewpoints, all of the voting members of the Committee agreed that Kroeber's name should be removed, with weight being given to the negative impact of the name on the Native American members of our communities on campus, in the Bay Area, and beyond. The Committee also noted that simply changing the name is not sufficient and that work will need to be done to communicate the complexities and nuances reflected in the comments and to allow for engagement by all the groups that are stakeholders. To that end, we recommend authorizing and providing a budget for a working group to develop an appropriate restorative approach to reckon with the legacy of Alfred Kroeber, particularly in regards to indigenous communities in California.

The BNRC's mention of the "negative impact" of the Kroeber name could be taken as an endorsement of the fourth point in the BNRC summary: "Kroeber is a public symbol of the discrimination against and disdain for Native Americans." It was the one point that did not refer to what Kroeber did, said, or believed; whether or not a person is a symbol cannot be tested with evidence from that person's actions, writing, or views. The BNRC report made no comment on the more specific charges (beyond summarizing them and others' comments on them), nor did it assess Kroeber's work or activities, or mention the title of more than one of his publications—which was one of the two mentioned in the Proposal.

On 30 November 2020, UC Berkeley chancellor Carol Christ wrote to UC president Michael Drake with a recommendation that Kroeber Hall be unnamed (DKH 4). Her letter to Drake inaccurately described the BNRC's conclusions:

> According to the BNRC and the un-naming proposal, Alfred Kroeber engaged in activities that negatively impacted the Native American members of our communities on campus, the Bay Area, and beyond. The BNRC cites the following key reasons for un-naming Kroeber Hall:

- Kroeber collected or authorized the collection of the remains of Native American ancestors from grave sites and curated a repository of these human remains for research study. This practice, labeled "Salvage Anthropology" by some scholars, is now illegal. The proposal argues that although this practice was not illegal when Kroeber engaged in it, it was immoral and unethical, even for the time.
- Kroeber and colleagues took custody of a Native American man called "Ishi," who they allowed to live in the Museum of Anthropology; Ishi was given a janitorial position at the museum and used as "a living exhibit" for museum visitors. He was also taught racial slurs that were used to refer to Asian and African Americans.
- Kroeber's claim that the Ohlone people were culturally extinct contributed to the decision by the Federal Government to delist the Ohlone from the national register of Native peoples, leading to the Muwekma Ohlone tribe having no land and no political power.
- Given this history, Kroeber is a public symbol of the discrimination against Native Americans. A building named in his honor is an ongoing affront to Native Americans generally, an emblem of hostility to Native American members of the UC Berkeley community, and is not in keeping with Regent's policy 4400 listed above.

Kroeber's views and writings clearly stand in opposition to our university's values of inclusion and our belief in promoting diversity and excellence.

Christ's bullet points were copied from the BNRC "Summary" of the Proposal, but framed differently.[3] The BNRC wrote, "The proposal articulated several reasons for un-naming Kroeber Hall." Christ wrote, "The BNRC cites the following key reasons for un-naming Kroeber Hall." Her framing erroneously implied BNRC endorsement. BNRC chair Fine confirmed that "we did not EXPLICITLY support or reject the charges in the proposal in our letter" (27 January 2021 email, emphasis original).

Factual errors and unsupported claims in the Proposal, summarized without evaluation by the BNRC, were thus transmitted to the UC president as if an assessment process had validated them. But the last statement quoted above from Christ's letter—that "Kroeber's views and writings" are "clearly" opposed to "our university's values"—was not part of the BNRC report. Such a statement was needed, given campus policy (chapter 1): "The legacy of a building's namesake should be in alignment with the values and mission of the university." Yet Christ did not specify then or later which of Kroeber's views or writings were opposed to inclusion, diversity, or excellence.[4] This was a conspicuous failing, as the BNRC did not discuss or give evidence of having read any of Kroeber's writings, nor did Christ herself seem to rectify its omission. A university leader publicly disparaged a long-dead faculty member's values based on what was at best hasty reading of a committee report and at worst indifference to evidence.

Drake's decision to approve the unnaming of Kroeber Hall was made public on 26 January 2021. In announcing the decision to the Berkeley campus (DKH 5), Christ again reiterated the Proposal's three main charges:

> Kroeber's scholarly record is important and impressive, but so, too, is it marred by what the review community [sic; presumably a typo for "committee"] described as his "immoral and unethical" activities. Today, Kroeber is harshly judged for the role he played in the collection of the remains of Native American ancestors for storage in a repository on the Berkeley campus so they could be studied. In 1911 Kroeber and colleagues also took custody of a Native American man, who he named Ishi, and used as a "living exhibit" for museum guests. Additionally, it was Kroeber's pronouncement that the Ohlone people were culturally extinct that contributed to the federal government's decision to exclude the Ohlone from the national register of Native peoples, stripping them of recognition, land and influence.

But whatever its individual members may have thought, the BNRC did not describe Kroeber's activities as "immoral and unethical." And the reference to the "federal government's decision" was a garbled mischaracterization (see chapter 9; see chapters 7–8 for discussion of the other charges).

From this point the errors were quickly propagated. They were part of a Berkeley campus news story (Kell 2021, emphasis added):

> Among the key reasons highlighted . . . in **the review committee's recommendation** . . . was that Kroeber collected or authorized the collection of the remains of Native American ancestors and curated a repository of them for study. While the research practice was not illegal then, **the review committee wrote**, "it was immoral and unethical, even for the time." . . . Additionally, Kroeber's pronouncement that the Ohlone people were culturally extinct contributed to the federal government not recognizing the Ohlone and "leading to the Muwekma Ohlone Tribe having no land and no political power," **according to the committee**.

The story also quoted Christ's statement that "Kroeber's views and writings clearly stand in opposition to our university's values of inclusion and our belief in promoting diversity and excellence."

The campus news story was then paraphrased by the *Los Angeles Times* (Gomez 2021): "Kroeber also declared the Ohlone people . . . to be culturally extinct, which led to the federal government not recognizing the tribe and leaving the present-day Muwekma Ohlone Tribe politically powerless and without land, the committee said." Similarly, according to the *New York Times* (Fuller 2021), "A committee that made the decision noted that although Alfred Kroeber was considered one of the most influential American anthropologists in the first half of the twentieth century, his research methods were 'immoral and unethical, even for the time.'" Whether or not the charges against Kroeber are accurate, these statements about the Berkeley decision were false. The only conclusion that the BNRC expressed about Kroeber was to register the "negative impact" of his name.

As the unnaming was announced, the letters of the building's former name were removed (see figure 10.1). The worker excising Kroeber's name wore a hoodie distributed by a company that sells apparel with messages like "Share a round with ISIS" and "Weapons are part of my religion." This hoodie featured nationalist slogans ("Don't tread on me," "Land of the free") and an image from the Gadsden flag, a right-wing favorite (Walker 2016). UC Berkeley distributed photos cropped to exclude these unsavory details.

According to Lumbee scholar David Shane Lowry (2021), "the de-nailing of K,R,O,E,B,E, and R . . . is perhaps the first substantial crack in the façade of American anthropology's imprisonment of Native America." A peppering of social-media posts variously condemned the unnaming of Kroeber Hall (as "cancel-culture" presentism) and celebrated it (as a progressive first step). Mostly the reaction was celebratory, and then died down in a year when all were focused on the COVID-19 pandemic. A few months later, campus attention had turned to final exams, graduation, and the prospect of a 2021–2022 academic year with in-person classes.

Meanwhile, Berkeley campus leaders' unreflecting censure of Kroeber had become conventional wisdom: a UC Berkeley campus news piece identified him as a "Berkeley professor known for his white supremacist views" (Natividad 2022), while the Proposal's charges were repeated as

Figure 10.1
Dismantling colonialism? UC Berkeley facilities staff removing signage at the former Kroeber Hall, 26 January 2021. Photograph by Irene Yi.

fact in the *New York Times* and *San Francisco Chronicle* (Imbler 2022, Kadvany 2022). Another *New York Times* article (Brown 2022) that reiterated the same charges even contrasted "Auntie Phoebe" Hearst as providing "a modicum of stability" to Ohlone people living on her land, without mentioning that she was also the architect and funder of Berkeley's program of colonial dispossession and worldwide burial excavation.

THE FALL GUY

In 2020, the year before the unnaming of Kroeber Hall, three buildings at UC Berkeley were unnamed. Their former eponyms are like many whose memorials have been removed or renamed elsewhere: defenders of racism or slavery, advocates (or purported advocates) of racial hierarchy. The first was John Boalt (1837–1901), the eponym of a law school building; he had no personal UC connection, but was honored because of his widow's philanthropy. His 1877 pamphlet *The Chinese Question* argued that while a Scandinavian immigrant "readily accepts . . . our ways of life," the "Mongolian race" would never assimilate; "the Chinaman has . . . planted within our border all the vicious practices and evil tendencies of his home." Reichmann (2018:7) has contended that Boalt "was instrumental in legitimizing anti-Chinese racism and catalyzing support in California for what became the Chinese Exclusion Act of 1882."

The second and third were Joseph LeConte (1823–1901) and David Barrows (1873–1954). LeConte, eponym of a physics building, was an eminent scientist and president of the American Association for the Advancement of Science. Having grown up on a plantation with more than two hundred "orderly, contented, and happy" enslaved people, he asserted in *The Race Problem in the South* (1892) that "the possession and use of inherited slaves is consistent with, and may even be conducive to, the highest morality." In the "contact of races," he argued, "the higher race must control and determine the policy of the community." If a "lower race" is "plastic, docile, imitative, some form of subordination will be the result; if . . . it be highly specialized and rigid, extermination is unavoidable. The Negro is probably the best type of the former and the American Indian of the latter."[5]

Barrows, a president of the University of California (1919–1923), was the eponym of a social sciences building. From 1900 to 1909, he worked for the US Philippine colonial administration (chapter 9). His *A History of the Philippines* (1905), "written for the young men and young women of the Philippines," contains condescending, racialized descriptions of Indigenous people, and offers an evolutionary view of populations. "Malays and Hindus," he said, are "of a higher plane of intelligence than any who had preceded them in the occupation of the islands." Ron Hendel (2020) has argued that the proposal to unname Barrows Hall was based on an uninformed interpretation of the historical record, though Upton Sinclair (1923:137–141) long ago called Barrows "the Dean of Imperialism."[6]

A key question here has been how Alfred Kroeber, who advocated for Indigenous societies and Native rights and opposed the eugenicist and racist views associated with Boalt, LeConte, and Barrows, ended up as the fourth member of their undesirable club.[7] If the specific charges in the Proposal are erroneous, how do we explain this history?

Highly relevant, as I have indicated, are recent decades of resistance to repatriation. Considerable push-back came from faculty with research stakes in human remains. According to Karen Biestman (2003:150), UC faculty "lobbied heavily and successfully" around 1990 against a proposed state law favoring repatriation, and Berkeley anthropologists F. Clark Howell and Vincent Sarich were among the authors of a 1989 request to colleagues for support to keep a "jeopardized" collection of ancestral remains under university control.[8] Tim White, a paleoanthropologist who moved from Berkeley's anthropology department to its integrative biology department in 1995, was in the news a few years later for a dispute with the anthropology museum (Curtius 1998). He had refused to return Indigenous remains that he had borrowed for teaching purposes, saying that "my students are robbed of an ability to learn" if the remains are unavailable. "Perhaps I understand the value of these remains in a way that nobody else does." But Native people may think they understand the value of ancestral remains in a way that scientists do not, and may perceive an earlier robbery. Perhaps because White's work had support from Getty family members who were major donors to UC Berkeley, campus leaders chose not to take a stand.[9]

White also coauthored a letter to *Science* that asserted that UC San Diego, in proposing repatriation of certain ancestral remains, "favors the ideology . . . of a local American Indian group over the legitimacy of science" (Schoeninger et al. 2011). With colleagues, he even filed a federal lawsuit in 2012 to prevent the repatriation of certain "culturally unaffiliated" remains. As the prominent paleoanthropologist Richard Klein (2013) said, "if you're a scientist involved in studying human remains, you obviously don't want to see these things sequestered somewhere where you can't get at them. Or worse yet, reburied." Indigenous requests for repatriation, he suggested, were "more a matter of the politics than of any deep-seated feelings about treating human remains one way or another." A theme throughout this period was the insistence that repatriation is a product of ideologies and politics, but science is not.

Researchers were not the only obstacle. As director of Berkeley's anthropology museum from 1994 to 1999, anthropologist Rosemary Joyce was committed to repatriation but encountered not just "professors who had curated the museum as though it were their private club," as a news report put it (Curtius 1998), but a campus administration that saw itself as merely "caught between two impassioned academics" rather than offering decisive leadership. An assistant vice chancellor referred to professorial pushback against repatriation as "fight[ing] for these collections."

In another conflict ten years later, it was reported that Berkeley chancellor Robert Birgeneau refused to meet with tribal leaders and that campus officials overseeing NAGPRA refused to give tribal representatives a role in reviewing repatriation processes (Paddock 2008). Vice Chancellor for Research Beth Burnside wrote in an email that it might be "better to stonewall altogether," while Associate Vice Chancellor for Research Robert Price said that "Native American tribes would have had no knowledge or expertise to bring to the table." It is understandable that some Indigenous people by 2020 might feel they had been dismissed and gaslighted for decades. Even today, Berkeley's repatriation processes are not working well. As I was completing this manuscript in summer 2022, an Indigenous California cultural leader who was seeking to reclaim ceremonial objects held at Berkeley told me about a meeting with campus officials (not affiliated with the anthropology museum) that felt like one of the most demeaning interactions my interlocutor had ever experienced.

In the 2020 campus conversation about Kroeber Hall, some powerful voices spoke not about Kroeber's early-twentieth-century actions but about Indigenous experiences of UC. Responding to a defense of Kroeber by UC Berkeley anthropologist Nancy Scheper-Hughes (2020), four Native students articulated their sense of campus culture (Cesspooch et al. 2020):

> The violence perpetrated against the Indigenous peoples of what is today California should not be discounted or minimized by UC Berkeley faculty members in order to preserve the fictionalized benevolence of their disciplines. These defenses fit into a long-standing culture on campus that normalizes white fragility and pressures students, staff and faculty who are Black, Indigenous or people of color to remain silent about institutionalized racism and their own experiences. Whether or not current professors acknowledge our concerns, UC Berkeley harmed Indigenous communities before, during and after Alfred Kroeber's tenure.

The chair of the campus NAGPRA committee, bioanthropologist Sabrina Agarwal, also emphasized the lived experiences of Indigenous people. She wrote that the Proposal "was not intended to be a balanced or even-handed discussion of the historical legacy of Kroeber. It was intended to give us an understanding of what the alternative historical experience and truth is for Native American peoples" (2020). She added an exhortation: "Supporting the proposal, in its intended format, is to actually listen. To listen without adding a 'but' or crafting a counter argument." I cannot believe that she meant to assert that the Proposal's historical assertions should be immune from debate in a university. I think she meant instead that the more important question was not about the early twentieth century.

Discussion of Kroeber Hall thus evoked two rather different discursive frames. One, mandated by university policies governing building names, entailed discussion of Kroeber himself—what he actually did and meant to do, in what sociohistorical context, and why. This is what the campus unnaming process was set up to accomplish. Another frame, grounded in the ongoing lives of Native Californians, necessitated change in order to ameliorate their experiences and shake the university out of a destructive cycle of patronizing lip service and failures of action.

The disconnect was especially striking in the statement of Berkeley's anthropology department. Its faculty could speak with authority in assessing and contextualizing work in their field. Two who had previously published about Kroeber wrote public comments opposed to unnaming; two others also submitted public comments, one on each side of the question. The faculty as a whole approved a statement in favor of unnaming.[10] It included no specific criticism of Kroeber, instead expressing support for Indigenous people, emphasizing repatriation, and acknowledging "a long history of violence toward Native Americans in which UC Berkeley and the anthropology department are implicated." It also distanced itself from the anthropology museum, though all museum directors up to 2002 were department faculty members, as were half of the faculty curators in 2020, and despite the fact that some vocal repatriation opponents over the years were anthropologists (as were some repatriation advocates). Throughout the unnaming process, a point that came up again and again was Berkeley's failure to repatriate ancestral remains and cultural materials in the decades after Kroeber's death.

Comments by campus leaders underscored the disconnect between the frames. NAGPRA committee chair Agarwal offered a historical précis (Smith 2022): "We kill them, and then we take their dead, and keep them in a museum. And then we don't give them back when they ask." She continued: "This is all equated with Kroeber," implying that his role was at least partly symbolic. BNRC chair Fine said that unnaming Kroeber Hall "was less about passing judgment on Alfred Kroeber and more about the university forging better relationships with Native Americans" (Kell 2021). Berkeley's vice chancellor for research called it "part of a broader initiative," including new administrative personnel and a "reorientation toward restorative justice" (Katz 2021) His deputy said the unnaming helped remove the "edifice of racialized understanding of human beings" (Rugg 2021). This suggests that Kroeber was held to account even for ambient ideologies that he resisted. He had become a scapegoat.

Chancellor Christ echoed the BNRC chair: "I agree with those who see this move as being less about condemning Kroeber and much more about creating a truly inclusive campus that provides a true sense of belonging for one and all" (DKH 5). These nuances escaped the news media, understandably, since campus communications had simply reproduced the Proposal's specific charges and stated that Kroeber's views and writings are opposed to Berkeley values. The *New York Times* noted no complexity; the *Los Angeles Times* headline was "UC Berkeley Removes Kroeber Hall Name, Citing Namesake's 'Immoral' Work with Native Americans."

In a thoughtful commentary after Kroeber Hall was unnamed, former anthropology museum director Joyce (2021) wrote that the "pain felt by members of the campus community was harm done in the present by the building name" and asked "what it means to name a building after anyone." Negative impacts are part of such meanings, she answered, concluding that "those experiencing the harm have told us. We needed to listen. My campus did, and acted appropriately." I agree that the outcome was appropriate given those present experiences, but Joyce elided a critical point when she wrote that the accuracy of criticisms of Kroeber was "decidedly beside the point." On the contrary, the validity of such criticisms was at the heart of the process that UC Berkeley set up to evaluate unnaming proposals. What Joyce exposed was thus precisely the disconnect underlying campus leaders' evident discomfort. When they said a decision was "less about" what their own process required it to be about (the past), and "much more about" something else (the future), they revealed that their process was hollow and that the unnaming of Kroeber Hall was not about Alfred Kroeber.

I interpret the unnaming of Kroeber Hall as follows. A set of claims had circulated—that Kroeber did "immoral and unethical" work, for example, and that his writing led to anti-Indigenous government decisions. These passed from their understandable place in the Proposal's advocacy through the voice of Berkeley's chancellor to major US newspapers, without being examined critically or receiving analytic or historical support from the campus body charged with studying the evidence. In announcing the outcome, campus leaders emphasized that a decision that Kroeber's work is opposed to contemporary values is "less about condemning" him than creating an inclusive campus. The need to remove a name that had come to evoke feelings of exclusion and damaged relations with Indigenous communities outweighed the "scholarly judgment" that Yale had recommended in such cases (chapter 1). Accuracy was beside the point, and a bygone colleague was the campus fall guy.

This is not to say that Kroeber is entitled to have a building named after him (nobody is), or that he was more than just a person, formed in a certain sociohistorical era. I have tried not to neglect his blind spots and weaknesses. One is that the assumption of cultural essentialism led him to accept the inevitability of Indigenous decline: the "myth of the 'vanishing Indian' " (DKH 1). He thus undervalued evidence of linguistic and cultural hybridity, renewal, and self-assertion among Native Californians, attaching labels like "extinct" to cultures that had simply changed. His precolonial research focus was meant to inculcate respect for cultural diversity, but did not promote awareness of the circumstances facing living Native people. The logic of memory documentation mirrored a rift between California's public university and its Indigenous population, which later actions exacerbated and UC now seeks to mend.

Another problem is the relentlessly Euro-American positionality of academic discourse of the time. Middle-class white audiences could feel at home in a lecture or reading a book by Kroeber or his peers: they were the Oikoumenê, included in every "we." Native people were the Other: civilized, admirable, and fascinating in their own right, but objects of study all the same. This goes together with condescending language and an extractivist research stance, features that seem inescapable in the era's anthropological and linguistic writing. Despite Kroeber's support of research and writing by Indigenous people, it would have been hard for most to feel they belonged in the academy, and challenging for the few who did enter it.

In their relations with their state's university, Indigenous Californians have experienced true injuries. I do not presume to enumerate all of them, but they include UC Berkeley's long omission of Native people in its construction of California identity; its inability to create a campus where Indigenous students, staff, and faculty feel welcome; and its failure in recent decades to repatriate ancestral remains (and cultural patrimony) with due speed and respect. Where there is injury, it is understandable that someone has to take the blame.

It is understandable that campus leaders prefer not to blame their immediate, still living predecessors, who are responsible for much of the injury; or earlier predecessors like Phoebe Hearst, who set up the program of collecting Indigenous cultural artifacts and ancestral remains. The Hearst name looms large at Berkeley (figure 10.3). It is also understandable that university leaders would not wish to draw attention to how UC capital was created by the displacement of Indigenous people and the despoiling and theft of their land. Yet that is what sits at the foundation of building after building at Berkeley.

BUILDERS OF BERKELEY

The Proposal to Un-Name Kroeber Hall was submitted with a letter of endorsement signed by influential faculty, staff, and administrative leaders, including Berkeley's second-highest official, Executive Vice-Chancellor and Provost Paul Alivisatos (now president of the University of Chicago). They wrote that "Kroeber's name does not represent the values of UC Berkeley and the campus is working to overcome its involvement in the disastrous legacy that Kroeber's name has come to symbolize." This referred partly to efforts to rectify Berkeley's long-term failure to repatriate ancestral remains, a failure from decades after Kroeber's retirement. By accepting the premise that Kroeber's name symbolized a disaster he did not live to witness, campus leaders immunized their predecessors.

They also "affirm[ed] that Kroeber did not act alone," suggesting that he had mere allies or help in his work. But UC leaders planned that work, hired him (a PhD student) to do it, and almost fired him when he was insufficiently loyal to their plan. The ringleader was UC regent and benefactor Phoebe Hearst, architect and funder of UC archaeological and Indigenous research programs, who made key operational and financial decisions from her Pleasanton hacienda (figure 10.2). She was also a generous philanthropist, having inherited her husband's mining wealth when he died in 1891.

While the fruits of George Hearst's labor enriched Berkeley, his own life did not reflect its eventual twenty-first-century values.[11] As a young man in Missouri he possessed two enslaved people whom he sold for $700 to pay debts. At the onset of the Paiute War in 1860, his Ophir Mine stake in Nevada was threatened by Paiute resistance to killings, rapes, and kidnappings by miners and settlers, so he sought military action against the Paiutes. "This Indian war was playing the very Dickens with us," he wrote in 1890. "It cost me a good deal and I had to sell some of my ground" (Hearst 1972:18). As a California State Assembly member in 1865, Hearst voted against ratifying the Thirteenth Amendment to the US Constitution, which abolished slavery. When he unsuccessfully sought the Democratic nomination for California governor, Hearst (1882) supported the Chinese Exclusion Act. Later, as a US senator, he was a "national joke," according to Matthew Bernstein (2021:171). He voted against women's suffrage and a bill protecting California rivers, and enthusiastically endorsed child labor as a solution to the "Chinese problem" (Hearst 1972:32–33, 38–39):

> The great objection I have to the Chinese is, they work so cheap, and do a great deal of work that might be done by our children. If there were no Chinamen in California, a great deal of the fruit there would necessarily have to be gathered by the children, and this would make them industrious. I believe the time will come in California, when there will be tens of thousands of children working on the fruit farms, and they could easily make a dollar a day; that would put us so far ahead. But if you give it to the Chinese, it goes out of the country. I think that all of our children should work at least four or five months in each year, and there would be ample time outside of that to go to school. . . .
>
> If you were to sweep all the Chinamen out of the country at once, it would ruin all the great fruit growers, but if you let them go away gradually, their place could be taken by degrees by our children, and I certainly believe in putting the little fellows to work.

By 1891, he had made a fortune from the displacement of Native people in California and Nevada and the destruction of their land; from similar activities in other western states; and from copper and silver mines in Cerro de Pasco, Peru, that relied on coerced Indigenous labor.[12] These

Figure 10.2
Phoebe Hearst's Hacienda del Pozo de Verona, 1915 Christmas card (Julia Morgan Papers, MS 010, 010-3-b-31-09-01, California Polytechnic State University, San Luis Obispo).

are not obscure facts; Hearst is well enough known to have been made into an exaggeratedly murderous character on the HBO television series *Deadwood*, though the precise extent of his actual crimes is uncertain.[13]

UC Berkeley has three buildings named for Phoebe and George Hearst, including the one in figure 10.3, and another named for their son. In its self-presentation George and especially Phoebe loom large, with no hint that he made his fortune from Indigenous dispossession and worse, or that she spent it digging up ancestral remains from California and around the world and accumulating Indigenous cultural heritage. Instead, campus web pages tell Phoebe Hearst's life story and praise the generosity of "the matriarch of Access and Excellence," as Chancellor Robert Birgeneau dubbed her at a 2011 exhibit in her honor.[14] The *Daily Cal* has published articles on Hearst philanthropy and marveled at its ubiquity: "It seems like every corner of the UC Berkeley campus is branded with their name."[15] My point is not that Berkeley should (or should not) remove the Hearst name from its buildings, but that when

Figure 10.3
Hearst Memorial Mining Building, UC Berkeley, designed by John Galen Howard. Construction was funded by Phoebe Hearst in memory of George Hearst, and completed in 1907. Photograph from Berkeley Material Sciences & Engineering (https://mse.berkeley.edu).

a university aims its disapprobation at faculty like Kroeber and calls its symbolic work done, then it chooses not to see the foundational nature of what it purports to deplore.

The University of California's early history, like that of other American universities, is connected to crimes one can understand wanting to ignore.[16] California is a settler-colonial state. It was founded by the seizure of Native land for grazing, agriculture, timber, and minerals like gold; and by the state-sponsored killing and removal of the Indigenous people who owned the land. Its public university was also a settler-colonial project, as was made clear by Benjamin Ide Wheeler, who oversaw its transformation into a great research university. In his 1899 presidential inaugural address, he said that the university sits "on the soil which Spain took as its portion of the New World" and that Spain's "heritage has, in large measure, fallen to us" (Wheeler 1926:32). He did not mention who Alta California was taken from, or what had befallen their heritage; much was in Phoebe Hearst's anthropology museum. In 1910, he called the UC founders “idealists” who “left the trodden fields of life as it was and plunged into the open fields of imagination” (Wheeler 1926:317). Representations that highlight the western “frontier” and cast the land beyond as “wilderness” efface Indigenous histories, lives, and societies.

UC still advertises itself as a settler-colonial project. A 2019 webpage honoring the “Builders of Berkeley” proclaimed, “With the same daring and high hopes that brought adventurers, farmers, miners, and merchants to the American West, the University of California’s earliest benefactors set out to create a great public university on the frontier.”[17] Another webpage celebrates “the audacious idea that California should have a great public university—one that would serve equally the children of immigrants and settlers, landowners and industrial barons” (UC News 2018). Not served, it seems, are the children of those whose land was taken.

Like many peers, UC was a beneficiary of the Morrill land-grant acts of 1862 and 1890. According to its self-presentation, these “called for donating land left over from the building of the Transcontinental Railroad to provide states with the funding to create institutions that would educate people from all walks of life . . . so that everyone could benefit” (UC News 2018). But not everyone did benefit, and the land was not just “left over.” The United States had taken it from Native people, paying “little or nothing,” in the words of Tristan Ahtone and Robert Lee (2020), and turned it “into endowments for fledgling universities,” eventually distributing “nearly 11 million acres, which is almost the size of Denmark.” The University of California got 148,636 acres.[18]

Individuals also gave generously. Many donors and philanthropic families gained their wealth from the gold rush—from land theft and the killing and displacement of Indigenous people. Benefactors who were not themselves miners outfitted miners and other participants in the gold rush. In the Levi Strauss & Co. Archives, the “earliest retailer invoice” shows a large sale to a dealer in Benton, California. This mining town on Paiute land was near a series of massacres of Native people, in the 1860s, by miners and a California volunteer cavalry. Strauss supplied miners; he and his family became major UC benefactors. These connections appear unironically on a webpage that celebrates Berkeley’s history, encourages philanthropy, and displays an 1882 photograph of miners wearing Levi Strauss jeans at a Placer County mine. This was on Nisenan land, which had seen multiple massacres of Indigenous people to make space for mining and all that came with it.[19]

In other instances, the Hearst pattern was replicated when a profiteer's family members laundered gold rush wealth through UC philanthropy. One such person was Cora Jane Flood, founder of UC's business school in 1898, whose wealth came from her father James Flood, a UC regent with a fortune from Nevada's Comstock Lode. Her history and that of Strauss's family are celebrated by the business school ("Our History" n.d.), which "owes its existence to visionaries, teachers, and gold rush pioneers."

Another pattern is illustrated by the paleontologist and philanthropist Annie Montague Alexander, founder of Berkeley's Museum of Vertebrate Zoology and a lifelong benefactor of paleontological and zoological research. She inherited her wealth from her father Samuel Alexander, one of the founders of the California and Hawaiian Sugar Company (and other enterprises) and therefore a key actor in the US colonial conquest of Hawai'i. She may also be the only "builder of Berkeley" who personally excavated ancestral remains. In 1901, noting Phoebe Hearst's interest in archaeology, Alexander wrote in a letter that she and UC paleontologist John Merriam could also participate in excavating ancestral remains. "Mrs. Hearst has given quite a sum of money towards investigations for ancient human remains," she said, "and Dr. Merriam is put at the head of it. Now there are some caves in Shasta Co. that deserve attention from this point of view" (Stein 2001:114). In 1925, Alexander donated the remains of six people she excavated on Maui to Honolulu's Bishop Museum.[20] As the disturbing image in figure 10.4 shows, she also shot game animals for fun, including even elephants. On the Berkeley campus, where banners extoll her philanthropy and scientific interests, Alexander is celebrated without reservation.[21]

Alexander's mentor, the paleontologist Merriam, led major UC excavations of Indigenous burial sites in California. In the Berkeley anthropology museum catalog, his name is associated (as "collector") with 198 items identified as "human remains," mainly from the Emeryville shell mound but also from other sites in Alameda and Shasta Counties; and he supervised Nels Nelson's doctoral work on Bay Area shell mounds. Merriam is especially well known for his properly paleontological work, such as describing the sabre-toothed cat, *Smilodon californicus*, at the La Brea

Figure 10.4
Left to right: Samuel Alexander, Annie Montague Alexander, and their guide, 4 August 1904, on an elephant they had killed (MVZ 6018, Bancroft Library, UC Berkeley).

Tar Pits. He left Berkeley in 1920 to become president of the Carnegie Institution, where he was a supporter of eugenics and important funder of eugenics research.[22] Merriam stated his views clearly at a 1929 anthropological meeting. Anthropologists, he said, in what could be a rebuke of his former colleague Kroeber, "do not take their responsibilities seriously enough." These included the improvement of humankind—"the development of life to higher and higher levels." Eugenics is "the idea that we have the right to be well-born" and indeed "to be better and better born through the ages." It is a "great" subject that "will help us to make man so much better that nothing he builds will ever overpower him."[23] Kroeber called eugenics a "fallacy" and a "mirage" (chapter 9), while Berkeley websites praise Merriam's foundational role, ignore his work excavating ancestral remains, and express sympathy for an "evolutionary worldview" (Waggoner and Smith 2006) that in his case slid directly into eugenics.

All the people I have just discussed are major figures in the origin story UC Berkeley proudly tells about itself. Most made significant contributions to education or knowledge and were liberal, even progressive figures in the context of their era. For this they deserve praise. At the same time, they dug up Indigenous ancestral remains, promoted eugenics, and gained wealth from genocide. This, too, is the UC origin story: beginning in 1848, Americans swarmed to California to use its natural resources in mining, ranching, logging, and agriculture. They did not ask permission from the Indigenous owners, and killed or incarcerated them if they made trouble. The invaders made a lot of money; with it, as Gray Brechin (2006) has detailed, they built civic institutions. One of these is a great university that still celebrates its settler, gold-rush origins. Today, Berkeley leaders rightly want to repair their relationship with Indigenous people. But in a foray into UC origins, rather than scrutinizing the builders of Berkeley, they chose to censure the builders' employee, a faculty member whose views, they say vaguely and without evidence, are in opposition to contemporary values. Having done so, they promise to turn their eyes forward to an improved future.

A final example epitomizes the contradictions of the era in which the University of California was built. One of UC's great philanthropists was Jane Krom Sather, whose gifts include two professorships, Sather Gate at the south campus entrance, and Sather Tower overlooking the campus and city. She inherited her wealth from her husband Peder Sather, a Norwegian immigrant who came to New York in 1832 and California in 1851.[24] Rising from modest origins to cofound a major San Francisco bank, and thereby indirectly accumulating gold-rush wealth, he had become one of California's richest men by 1860. After his first wife Sarah (Thompson) died in 1881, Sather married Jane (Krom Read) in 1882, himself living only a few more years until 1886.

Sather was locally active in civic affairs and a prominent figure in an organization supporting formerly enslaved people after the Civil War. For some years he lived in San Francisco, but after his wife and family joined him in California in 1858, they took up residence in Alameda, a small island city by the east shore of San Francisco Bay. There, Sather became the largest landowner after buying two tracts of land in 1854 and 1864. The eventual sale of his land enriched a significant UC Berkeley philanthropist.

On Sather's Alameda land was a conspicuous shell mound. "For some reason or other," a newspaper reported in 1893, he "thought it would be desirable to build a residence upon this Indian cemetery. All Alameda was quite certain that it had been an Indian burial place."[25] At various times

Figure 10.5
Dedication by the Daughters of the American Revolution of a historical marker indicating the Alameda (a.k.a. Sather) Mound, 18 June 1914. Standing behind the marker are Ishi and T. T. Waterman (both in light-colored suits). Photograph in Alameda Museum (Historical Marker Database, https://www.hmdb.org/m.asp?m=79861).

over the years, ancestral remains were found (or deliberately excavated) on this land. In 1887, part of "the skeleton of an Indian child" was dug up by sewer workers. It was "lying beneath a bed of mussel shells . . . in the Sather estate, in a large mound which is supposed to have once been an Indian burial-ground." In September 1892, the Sather Trust even allowed a newspaper to organize its own excavation. The *San Francisco Call* dug up "skeletons and relics" and wrote that "the California Academy of Sciences and the University of California at Berkeley have been enriched by the discoveries." The curator of the UC museum, John J. Rivers, "went over the mound" and "accumulated an armful of valuable relics, which will soon find their way into the university museum." Eventually, according to Imelda Merlin (1977:20), the remaining "contents of this mound of shells and cement-like bones [were] hauled away in 1908 to nearby Bay Farm Island where they made admirable though grisly paving and filling material."

Figure 10.6
Maria de los Angeles (Ángela) Colós, Verona rancheria, 1921. Photograph by John Peabody Harrington (NAA 91-30289).

Several threads examined in this book are woven together in Alameda. In a 1914 event covered by the *Evening Times-Star and Alameda Daily Argus*, the local Daughters of the American Revolution chapter set up a bronze plaque commemorating the Alameda shell mound (figure 10.5). "There being no battlefields or graves or revolutionary sites in this part of the land," a DAR representative said in memorializing this Indigenous grave site, "the preservation of the memory of the first inhabitants of this island was considered of great historical importance." The original plaque (later replaced) read, "One thousand feet due west was a prehistoric mound, 400 feet long, 150 feet wide, and 14 feet high. The remains of 450 Indians with stone implements and shell ornaments were found when the mound was removed in 1908."

Ishi and T. T. Waterman were featured guests at a ceremony with music and speeches. The shell mound "was the site of an Indian community while the Children of Israel were still in bondage," Waterman said in his speech. "For the history of humanity as a whole," he continued, "the remains of Indian mounds in Alameda are just as important as Athens or Nineveh." The ceremonial high point was described by the *Argus* in language redolent of the era's assumptions: "Ishi, the only survivor of his tribe, . . . removed the American flag which hid the monument, inscribed with the tribute to the prehistoric people who inhabited this island many centuries ago." Then "two little grandsons" of DAR members "placed the floral decorations in the national colors at the base of the monument."[26]

But it was not only "many centuries ago" that "prehistoric" Indigenous people had lived in Alameda. Twenty miles to the southeast, at the Verona rancheria on Phoebe Hearst's land (chapter 3), lived Ohlone elder Ángela Colós (figure 10.6), who in the 1920s would tell linguist J. P. Harrington how Alameda "used to be very rich in animal life." As a child a few years before Sather began buying land there, Colós gathered quail eggs in Alameda and watched men catch quail in nets. The "leading quail flew in," she recalled; "the rest followed."[27]

As for the Alameda (or Sather) Mound memorial, some will react with understandable anger to yet another declaration that Indigenous people had vanished, save for a "survivor" compelled to unveil a monument that is readily interpreted as a symbol of the Americanization of Indian land. My personal response is sadness at the misguided choices of well-intentioned actors. Civic elites imagined they honored Native people while consigning them to the past; Waterman spoke passionately about the value of bygone Indian cultures; and his friend Ishi played the part assigned to him. None of them could have imagined a future when Indigenous people would serve not as sources of wealth for a new state university and knowledge for the global Oikoumenê, but as partners in those enterprises, with full control of their own lives, lands, communities, languages, and stories.

11

LAST WORDS

Neekeechyue 'ok'w 'wewolek'.
Everything has a name.
—Domingo, 1907

"*All* things have a name."
—Ogion, in Ursula K. Le Guin, *A Wizard of Earthsea*, 1968

When Domingo told Kroeber that every place on Yurok land has a name (chapter 5), he meant it as an assertion of Native sovereignty. White people imagined that the land was "wild," but one of many proofs of Indigenous ownership was that Yurok people had named the landscape, including its creeks, springs, fishing places, rocks, and mountains, not to mention their villages. Ursula Le Guin was unaware of Domingo's words (which Kroeber never published) when she had Ogion, her young protagonist Ged's first teacher in *A Wizard of Earthsea*, tell Ged that even the shadow he has summoned has a name (1968:145). Only by learning its name can Ged conquer it. Names give power.

In 2023, the former Kroeber Hall is called the Anthropology and Art Practice Building. In time, after committees and stakeholders weigh in, maybe it will get a new name. Some public comments on the Proposal to Un-Name Kroeber Hall favored Ishi Hall; others said Indigenous people should decide on an Indigenous name. The Muwekma Ohlone Tribe, whose families are from the Verona Band and of the people whose land UC Berkeley occupies, suggested Muwekma Ohlone Hall. The Yana word anglicized as Ishi means "man" (that is, "male person"). The Chochenyo word *muwekma* "people" was first recorded by Kroeber with Ángela Colós (figure 10.6) at the Verona rancheria in 1904 (see figure 11.1). An Ishi or Muwekma Hall—a People's Hall, as it were—would

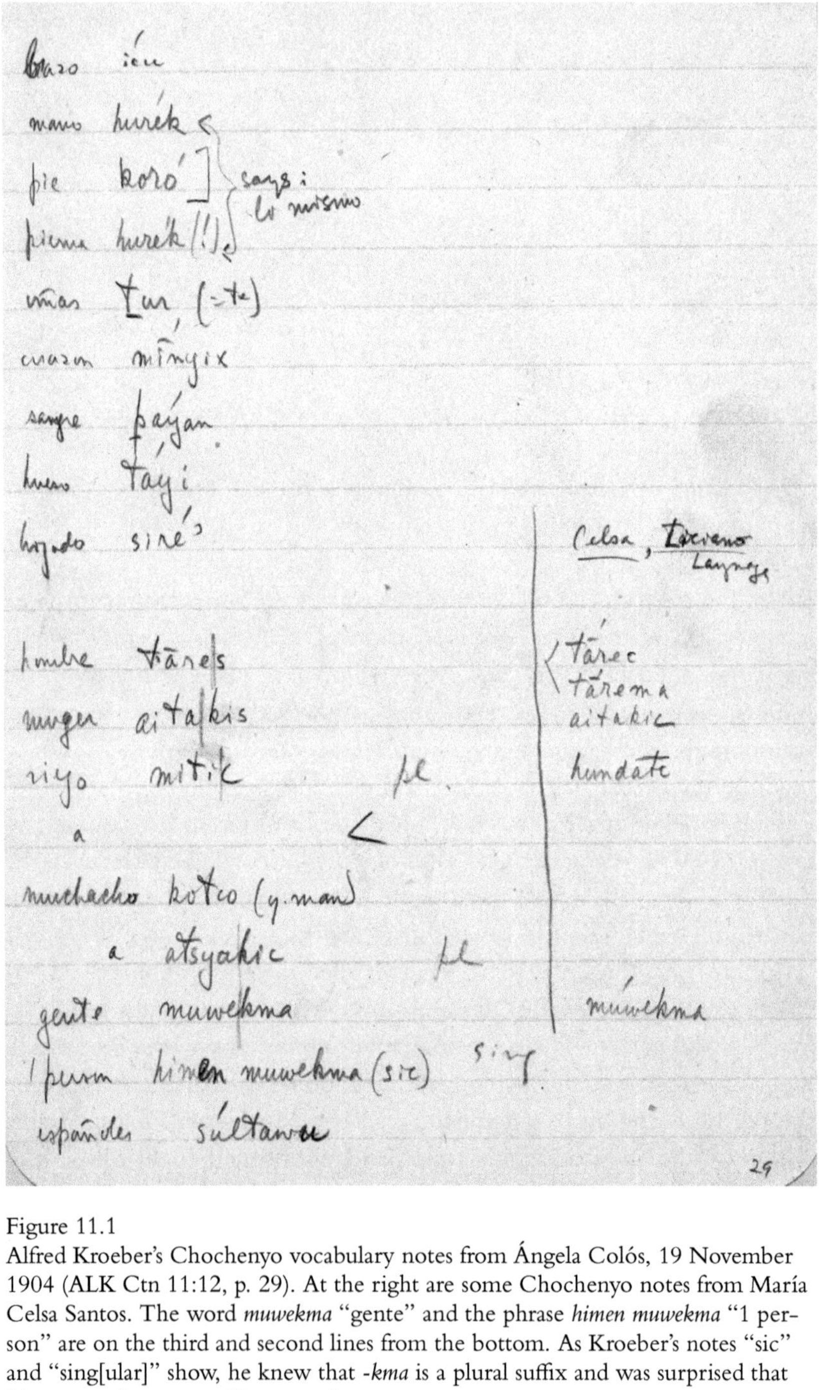

brazo icu
mano hurék
pie koró } says: lo mismo
pierna hurék (!)
uñas ṯur, (-ṯe)
corazon mĩnyix
sangre payan.
hueso tayi
hojado siré
hombre tārec
muger aitakis
niño mitik pl.
a
muchacho kotco (y. man)
a atsyakic pl
gente muwekma
1 person himen muwekma (sic) sing.
españoles súltawa

Celsa, Ercano, Language
tārec
tārema
aitakic
hundate
muwekma

29

Figure 11.1
Alfred Kroeber's Chochenyo vocabulary notes from Ángela Colós, 19 November 1904 (ALK Ctn 11:12, p. 29). At the right are some Chochenyo notes from María Celsa Santos. The word *muwekma* "gente" and the phrase *himen muwekma* "1 person" are on the third and second lines from the bottom. As Kroeber's notes "sic" and "sing[ular]" show, he knew that *-kma* is a plural suffix and was surprised that *himen muwekma* means "1 person."

bear an Indigenous name "salvaged" by colonial anthropologists, perhaps a more fitting memorial to their accomplishments.

"THE LONG TASK"

After a volume of previously published essays and a book on the "culture" concept (Kroeber 1952, Kroeber and Kluckhohn 1952), Kroeber's work in the last decade of his life returned to the linguistic and textual material he had collected early in the twentieth century. He was able to publish shorter pieces during that decade, and a Luiseño grammar in the year he died, but the most substantial of these projects were posthumously published Karuk, Mojave, and Yurok text collections.

One of them was a 1972 collection of Mojave narratives in English translation that Kroeber transcribed from dictation by a variety of Mojave elders in the years between 1902 and 1910 and then, after a long hiatus, in 1953 and 1954. In a 1967 preface to that volume, Theodora Kroeber described its Prologue as her husband's last scholarly writing, finished just a few days before they left for the overseas trip on which he would die in October 1960. "When he wrote *finis*," she said (vi), "there must have been some at-the-back-of-the-mind sense that this might well be the last field report he would be making. And thus it was he wrote a few pages of summing-up, an almost intimate statement of how he felt toward the long task now done." Her phrase "almost intimate" is striking in light of her insistence just three years later that her biography of him was "not intimate" precisely because of his wish for privacy (chapter 1). Here, I take it, we glimpse something that mattered deeply to Kroeber.

More Mohave Myths contains texts in translation; historical, linguistic, and sociocultural details; meticulous descriptions of the narratives' sacred landscapes; and other geographical knowledge shared with Kroeber in 1953 and 1954. Theodora's term "field report" implied that this was a less significant genre. Alfred called it "scholarship in the old-fashioned sense" (1972:xii) and justified it as follows:

> I have often pondered to whom we owe the saving of human religious and aesthetic achievements such as are recorded here. It is probably not to the group that produced them. Why should we preserve Mohave values when they themselves cannot preserve them, and their descendants will likely be

> indifferent? It is the future of our own world culture that preservation of these values can enrich, and our ultimate understandings grow wider as well as deeper thereby.

It disturbs me to read this. I know that Kroeber's casual remark that Native people "cannot preserve" and "will likely be indifferent" to their heritage reflects his specific experiences with traumatized communities whose young people suffered from colonial alienation; and I was not there to judge his experiences. Yet his words seem disdainful. I wish he had seen how his work would be used by Indigenous people. They are now far from indifferent to the records of languages, stories, and cultural practices that he and others assembled with "close to . . . an obsessive addiction" (Kroeber 1972:xii).

That even Alfred and Theodora Kroeber could downplay the value of texts shows how priorities had shifted. Already in 1932, the British anthropologist A. R. Radcliffe-Brown asked, about a Navajo text collection, "What are such texts as these for?" If they "are to be treasured merely because they are disappearing, and because they are accurately transcribed," he said dismissively about what Alfred Kroeber might call "old-fashioned" scholarship, "their publication would then be supported by mere antiquarian sentiment."[1] The shift has had an impact. Among anthropologists, Kroeber is associated with cultural essentialism, trait assemblages, and "salvage" methods. Rosemary Joyce (2021:475) has described teaching his work at Berkeley: "We explore the flaws in his model of 'culture' and explain how his methodologies are no longer those practiced by contemporary anthropologists." Language and text documentation has migrated to linguistics, folklore, and specialized areas of anthropology, which as a whole no longer sees what mattered most in Kroeber's career.

Kroeber himself identified translation as a defining goal late in his life. Having begun his career transcribing and translating Inuktun texts (figure 1.3), he ended it translating Karuk, Mojave, and Yurok texts. In describing this as preserving Indigenous "values" and "religious and aesthetic achievements" for "our own world culture," he expressed an unawareness of Indigenous cultural persistence and a corresponding naïve acceptance of appropriation by global elites. At the same time, he articulated an ecumenical openness to cultural diversity. In translation, he wrote in *More*

Mohave Myths (1972:xi), new values enter the "bone marrow" of other cultures. Evidently, for him, this was an aspect of the anthropological goal of promoting a "larger tolerance and balance of mind" (chapter 9).

Kroeber's daughter Ursula Le Guin and the Mojave poet Natalie Diaz have also reflected on translating Indigenous speech into the language of colonizers. Diaz's "The First Water Is the Body" (2020:46–52) meditates on the relation between the Colorado River and the bodies of Mojave people. In her words, the creator "built" the river "into our living bodies." Written in English, Diaz's poem questions her translation from Mojave and imagines a traditional funeral for her language if it cannot flow freely:

> But who is this translation for? And will they come to my language's four-night funeral to grieve what has been lost in my efforts at translation? When they have drunk dry my river will they join the mourning procession across our bleached desert?

To adapt her metaphor, this book's central question is whether Kroeber's legacy gives sustenance today, or is like the aqueducts and dams that divert and impound Indigenous water. This is the question of whether and how to value the humanistic mission of his life.

Writing about her father, Le Guin (2004b:29) emphasized that translation both humanizes and alienates:

> [A] white immigrant's son learning Indian cultures and languages in the first half of the twentieth century, he tried to save meaning. To learn and tell the stories that might otherwise be lost. The only means he had to do so was by translating, recording in his foreign language: the language of science, the language of the conqueror. An act of imperialism. An act of human solidarity.

"To learn and tell the stories that might otherwise be lost" is also the work of several of Le Guin's fictional protagonists, like Orrec Caspro (chapter 1).

More broadly, Le Guin's fiction often articulates the Boasian sense that language and discursive practice are central for the anthropological project. In *The Telling*, the Ekumen has sent a linguist and folklorist to report on customs banned by the government of Aka. "Everything's kept secret now," yet "in plain sight," an old man tells her (Le Guin 2000:97):

> "But to so many they aren't words, only old scratches. . . . In my mother's time, all children could read. They could begin to read the story. The telling never stopped. In the forests and the mountains, in the villages and the cities, they were telling the story, telling it aloud, reading it aloud."

When she reaches the greatest center of traditional culture, high in the mountains, what she finds is a hidden library (197):

> She read the texts of blessings, the protocols of ceremonies, recipes, prescriptions for curing cold sores and for living to a great age, stories, legends, annals, lives of famous maz [cultural leaders], lives of obscure merchants, testimonies of people who lived thousands of years ago and a few years ago, tales of travel, meditations of mystics, treatises of philosophy and of mathematics, herbals, bestiaries, anatomies, geometries both real and metaphysical, maps of Aka, maps of imaginary worlds, histories of ancient lands, poems. All the poems in the world were here.

This is a "world made of words" (127), rich in visual art, music, dance, and other forms of expression. "But first and last there were the words." That, I argue, is also true of Kroeber's legacy.[2]

In a perceptive, wide-ranging book on Yurok spirituality and history, Thomas Buckley (2002) noted a striking distinction. "Contemporary native northwestern Californians," he wrote, "say that Kroeber 'got his facts right' (for which they are grateful), but that he didn't know what anything meant" (15–16). This resonates with what I argue. Kroeber's interpretations of cultures have come to seem stale, for many reasons (including some elucidated by Buckley). Maybe they were always stale. But what he recorded, including details of languages, texts, and cultural practices, is even more valuable now than it was a century ago.

Kroeber did not "save" Native languages or cultures. That is a patronizing fantasy. He had his own scholarly or even "ecumenical" purposes, sometimes but not always aligned with the interests of Indigenous people. But it is they who have always done the hard work of maintaining and reclaiming their languages and cultures. Still, Kroeber played a critical role. He looked for what many in California could or would not see, what even his own employers sometimes disdained, and found spaces for Native people to tell their stories in their own words. On paper and wax cylinders, in dozens of languages, Kroeber and his protégés recorded creation stories, biographies, songs, oratory, travel narratives, conversations, laws, and family histories. They wrote down the names of people, animals, birds, foods, houses, colors, diseases and healing plants, mountains, fishes, waterways, winds, tides, and constellations, mapping the worlds of many Indigenous nations. Had they not done so, much of that cultural heritage would be forgotten. If Kroeber had not come to California, or had left when he was almost fired in 1902, Juan Dolores and Gilbert Natches would not have learned to write O'odham and Numu and would not have created the first bodies of written literature in their languages. The stories Robert Spott studied with elders in his community would mostly be gone; Ishi's *maumaiyauna* would not have endured. A scholar who did not challenge his era's vanishment assumption nevertheless played a crucial role in ensuring that Indigenous stories did not vanish; indeed, I think their tellers wanted them to live on.

IMPLICATIONS OF ESSENTIALISM

As a scholar and writer, Alfred Kroeber shared some of his era's blind spots. Several flowed from the essentialism that was baked into romantic nationalism. This oriented him toward reconstructing precolonial linguistic and sociocultural patterns—his word was "scheme" (chapter 2)—rather than Native experiences since colonization. But individuals may not fit comfortably in structural systems, and Indigenous scholars have criticized his representations of Indian identity. William Bauer (2014a:49) wrote that Kroeber's essentialist categories "denied . . . native people's modernity." Julian Lang (1991:xx) made a similar point: "While Kroeber collected myths, material artifacts, and ethnographies, he never introduced us to the living people, focusing instead on the past." At times this led him to elide what he could have studied. For example, Carolyn Smith (2016:83–91) has contrasted Kroeber's (1905a) analysis of Karuk basket weaving with the work of Lila O'Neale (1932). O'Neale documented the social and artistic meanings of baskets for contemporary weavers, including baskets made for trade or with Euro-American design elements, and so learned more than Kroeber, who neglected non-"traditional" styles and current attitudes.[3]

Kroeber's essentialism sometimes led to a misleading linguistic purism. As discussed in chapter 5, Yurok uses terms like "upriver" and "uphill" rather than cardinal directions like "north" and "east." The narratives in

Yurok Myths (Kroeber 1976) regularly use the riverine terms. Some narratives were transcribed from the speech of interpreters who rendered elders' Yurok in English; others were told in English. Among the latter is the first text in *Yurok Myths*, told by Lame Billy on 3 June 1902.[4] Its protagonist is from a coastal village by the town of Trinidad. Early in the story, he creates the promontory now called Trinidad Head. Sitting on its peak, he then does what Kroeber transcribed telegraphically: "On N. side white rock. On W. side black rock, on E red one, on S side, right here, he looked." But the published text uses different terms: "Downstream from it he set a white rock, across a black rock, above a red rock. Upstream was the side to which he looked." Later, the protagonist was at the mouth of the Klamath River. There, as Kroeber transcribed the story, people said, "Don't go up North," but the published text again differed: "Do not go downstream." On the coast, north is called *puelekw* "downstream" (the ocean current generally flows north), and Billy would have used terms like *puelekw* in Yurok, but he was speaking English. Kroeber replaced Billy's English terms with translations of the Yurok terms.[5] Kroeber's decision to use terms that would suggest the Yurok system was surely motivated by a wish to convey an "authentic" Yurok way of speaking—a well-intentioned attempt to highlight cultural diversity. But it obscured Billy's actual speech practice, which included Yurok-based and English-based patterns. Essentialism does not easily accommodate cultural or linguistic hybridization.

A related critique is that Kroeber chose not to write about Indigenous experiences of the California genocide, including survival and persistence. "Despite fascination with tribal warfare," William Willis (1972:143) observed trenchantly, "anthropologists neglect brutal conquests by white people and desperate resistance by colored peoples." Buckley (1989:439) even claimed that Kroeber "in effect . . . denied . . . all that had happened between 1849 and 1910." Maybe he thought it was pointless to speak out, or was pursuing "the ideal of objective science" that Le Guin (2004b:12) said he was "consistently loyal" to. What he did say was that studying the American invasion was the task of history, not anthropology—a convenient distinction, to be sure, if it meant he did not have to critique his own society. He has also been quoted as saying he "could not stand all the tears" in memories of suffering.[6] I do not know if the elders he worked with would have preferred that he document their experiences of genocide and its aftermath, or were pleased that he was interested in the old days.

Kroeber did contribute to documenting Native experiences of colonization. In chapter 5, I described an oral-history project he designed and supervised. Its thousands of manuscript pages are a critical source for historians studying nineteenth- and early-twentieth-century Indigenous experiences in central and northern California, including experiences of brutality and genocide. In chapter 6, I showed how Kroeber's Indigenous collaborators themselves guided their work. For Juan Dolores, this involved writing a memoir that did not avoid describing the brutality of a US Indian school; for Robert Spott, it included narratives of recent times. And Kroeber himself published papers on specific "historical" topics, both on his own and in collaboration with a historian, his son Clifton.[7] These included accounts of conflict between Indian and white people. But it is true that he did not in his own writing confront the California genocide or focus on the twentieth-century lives of Indigenous people. His choice to do neither was at best a kind of blind spot. If he had taken up a different area of study, though, he and his students would not have engaged in the language documentation that created resources for Native communities and scholars alike today. I wish more such work had been done, not less.

Finally, essentialism was linked to the idea of Indigenous vanishment. Kroeber's acceptance of this pervasive idea explains how he framed the goals of his documentary project. Such work enriches "the future of our own world culture," just as anthropology promotes "tolerance and balance of mind." But these were benefits for outsiders; to use a twenty-first-century term, Kroeber's research was extractive. I regret that he and so many others in his lifetime and later did not see how documentation would benefit Native communities, but treating this as a moral failure seems like presentism. The openness to other perspectives and values that Kroeber often emphasized is as desirable today as it ever was.

THE PRACTICE OF LINGUISTICS

As described in chapters 1 and 2, US linguistics emerged a century ago from two scholarly traditions: a European tradition of research on language history, philology, and relationships; and an American tradition of documenting mostly unwritten languages. The latter was thought to be urgent: "These tribes are on the verge of extinction," Franz Boas wrote in 1901 (chapter 2); in "a very few years . . . their languages, and with them their traditions and the records of their customs, will have disappeared." But if the vanishment assumption was misguided, Boas, Kroeber, and others were not mistaken in observing that Indigenous languages were being used less and less for a multitude of reasons (including suppression and violence) and were known by fewer and fewer people.

Despite having partly been founded on what was said to be an urgent mission, after a few decades American linguistics lost sight of the urgency. Beginning in the late 1950s, the field was profoundly transformed by Noam Chomsky and his students and grew to include new kinds of research and a self-definition as one of the cognitive sciences. Language documentation was sometimes derided as "taxonomic" specimen collection; those who practiced it could feel defensive or marginalized. "It was pretty terrible there for a while," Berkeley linguist Mary Haas recalled in 1978 (Murray 1997:709). Earlier, "students had been eager to do fieldwork," she said, but now they "were stung by this attitude and felt they would have to do something else."

It took several decades for the erstwhile Boasian documentation project to start reasserting itself, for example with a 1991 symposium organized by the linguist Ken Hale and a collection of programmatic papers published in the following year. Hale (1992:1) himself wrote that "language loss" (as he put it) was an aspect of "a much larger process of loss of cultural and intellectual diversity in which politically dominant languages and cultures simply overwhelm indigenous local languages and cultures." Michael Krauss (1992:10) got the attention of many readers when he asked, "To what extent are endangered languages a priority in modern linguistics? . . . Are graduate students encouraged to document moribund or endangered languages for their dissertations?" The implied answers were negative. "Obviously we must do some serious rethinking of our priorities," he concluded, "lest linguistics go down in history as the only science that presided obliviously over the disappearance of 90% of the very field to which it is dedicated." Krauss (1998:11) later wrote that "the only Native North American language that might be considered 'safe' is Greenlandic Inuit, no doubt related to the fact that it is administratively not in North America." He referred to a "major American tragedy" (15).

Hale, Krauss, and a few other linguists like Nora England and Margaret Langdon were leading figures in a move to change the culture of the field. Despite a "Western idea that knowledge in and of itself is valuable for society," England (1992:30) explained that linguistic research "can have negative or positive consequences for the group where that research is carried out." To serve communities, Hale (1976:37) wrote, "scholarship should be put to *use*" (emphasis his). In that spirit, he spent decades supporting Indigenous language education and reclamation, including collaborations with Jessie Little Doe Baird on Wampanoag language revival and with Ulwa language activists in Nicaragua.[8] England herself trained scores of Mayan linguists, cofounding both Oxlajuuj Keej Maya' Ajtz'iib' (in Guatemala) and the Center for Indigenous Languages of Latin America (at the University of Texas at Austin) to support documentation, teaching, training, and infrastructure development.[9] Krauss founded the Alaska Native Language Center, a key resource for recording and teaching that state's languages for fifty years. Yet in his advocacy, it is striking that he chose to stress the value of endangered languages for linguistic science rather than Indigenous people's human and linguistic rights.

While much has changed in linguistics in the thirty years since 1992, there is more to be done. The field still privileges some of the research practices and assumptions that led to the unnaming of Kroeber Hall, whose story therefore has broad implications. This is surely true in other fields, such as anthropology, but I am a linguist and will not tell anthropologists how to fix their house. Linguistics has more than enough rebuilding to do.

Delimiting "linguistics" raises one challenge. In a recent critique, Anne Charity Hudley, Christine Mallinson, and Mary Bucholtz (2020:e223) have pointed to "overt or covert ideologies about the boundaries of . . . linguistic scholarship" as obstacles, especially to students of color. Boundary maintenance goes back to the founding of the Linguistic Society of America and its quasi-official justification, Leonard Bloomfield's (1925b) "Why a Linguistic Society?" He did not mention social uses of language or the interests of language communities, describing language users just as sources of data to be analyzed and of unscientific beliefs about language to be corrected. Some linguists had other interests, like Edward

Sapir, who called language "the symbolic guide to culture" (1929:210), but decontextualized analyses of grammatical patterns have dominated the discipline for a century. Those who contributed to community language work, like the anthropologist and linguist Gladys Reichard, were professionally marginalized in the first half of the twentieth century; similar work today may be deprecated as "applied" or "service."[10] The rhetorical apogee of decontextualized analysis came with Chomsky's (1965:2) statement that linguistic theorizing concerns "an ideal speaker-listener, in a completely homogeneous speech-community, who knows its language perfectly and is unaffected by such grammatically irrelevant conditions as memory limitations, distractions, shifts of attention and interest, and errors." In opposition to positions like this that some saw as absurd, two new fields emerged, sociolinguistics and the ethnography of communication, but it would take years for the culture of linguistics as a whole to see change.[11]

As noted in chapter 2, Roman Jakobson saw a link between linguistic structuralism and Boasian essentialism. From this perspective, Kroeber's goal of elucidating the dehistoricized "scheme" of cultures and languages anticipated the decontextualized abstraction of later American linguistics. Yet it was Kroeber's idealization, or what Joyce (2021) called "normative ... abstractions from behavior," that led to the critique that he neglected living people. A similar critique has now also been directed at linguistics. Chickasaw linguist and anthropologist Jenny Davis (2017:40) condemned "linguistic extraction," such as analyzing languages and people "separately from the complex socio-historical, political, and deeply personal contexts in which they actually occur." Hannah McElgunn (2021) framed this as "intertextual erasure," in which language is "severed" from people. Tobique First Nation scholar Bernard Perley asserted that linguistic analysis "*dismembers* language in two ways; first, it breaks the language apart into formal analytical categories and second, it *dismembers* the language from the community of speakers" (2013:244; emphasis his). It should go without saying that such assertions are figurative: a linguist's analysis dismembers language no more than an earth scientist dismantles an actual planet. But the vivid wording shows that the organic metaphor that pervaded Boasian essentialism is inescapable and that "scientific" research may evoke strong feelings of injury.

A second challenge is specific to work with Indigenous and minoritized languages. Since 1992, the Boasian documentary imperative has been revived in a new concern with "language loss" (Hale's term). Books and articles on "language death" and "endangerment" and on "endangered languages" are numerous and visible.[12] It is surely better to be concerned with these phenomena than to ignore them (as my graduate training did in the 1980s). But as critics have emphasized, framings as "endangerment," "loss," and "death" reinforce the vanishment idea (that Indigenous people and their languages are disappearing), a deficit perspective (on the capacity of those who use languages), and an evasive accounting (since "loss" is actually the result of genocide and ethnocide, and "death" is from murder). Jane Hill (2002:128) pointed out that calling a language endangered "may be heard as dismissive and insulting by members of younger generations in the community who make claims of speakerhood in some form." In language advocacy, Perley argued, "we must shift our metaphorical conceptualization away from the death and extinction metaphors toward a conceptualization that provides the conditions for language life." He suggested instead centering "possible futures for indigenous language, culture, and identity," and emphasized what he called "emergent vitalities" (2013:248).[13]

Two decades ago, describing a project centered on the Ulwa language and people, Hale (2001:100) wrote that its success "will be measured by the extent to which work on the language is integrated in a meaningful way into the life of the community of people who speak it." If this standard is applied to linguistics as a whole, a generous assessment might find that the field "shows improvement"—or it might be judged a failure. Referring to the program initiated by Hale, Krauss, and others, Gerald Roche (2020:166) has written that "endangerment linguistics has had little to no impact on global language endangerment." Despite funding and many resources, as Frank Seifart et al. (2018:e336) put it, "little has changed." We need to do more.

A third challenge is related to the first two. Essentialism implies that some linguistic phenomena are "natural" and others are not. Studying what is "natural" is a goal in many areas of linguistics; "unnatural" phenomena are deëmphasized. For example, an influential paper by Nikolaus Himmelmann (1998:168) stressed the importance of documenting "communicative events [that are] as natural as possible." Less "natural" events involve observers or researchers; these include elicitations of vocabulary and grammar, which are often "a new type of communicative event for the members of the speech community," as well as "staged communicative events" like elicited narratives (186). In some settings, however, as Stefan Schnell (2018) has observed, narrated descriptions of cultural practices are not traditional communicative events but can be invaluable resources. And in some communities experiencing language shift, Claire Bowern (2018b) pointed out, language classes and documentation sessions themselves are the main contexts of language use. Researchers who bring the assumption that some contexts are less "natural" than others may unwittingly impose their own language ideologies, replicate a central mistake of Boasian research, and run the risk of classifying individuals as "not fluent" and languages as "extinct"—just as Kroeber did. Critics have often pointed out the problematic consequences of assuming that some individuals or speech types are more "authentic" than others.[14]

Essentialism is likewise associated with the assumption that some kinds of change are "natural" and others can be set aside. This sits near the center of an ongoing debate over creole exceptionalism, the genealogical status of creole languages, and the interpretation of language mixing. According to Pieter Muysken and Norval Smith (1995:4), creoles show "a break in the natural development of the language, the natural transmission of the language from generation to generation." The implication that some languages came about "unnaturally" and may themselves therefore be "unnatural" is understandably objectionable to many. In turn, the terms used to describe the origins of creole languages matters for classification. For example, do creoles whose vocabulary is mostly from English (like Tok Pisin or Gullah) "count" as Germanic languages (like English or Danish)? If debates over these questions sometimes involve as much heat as light, the questions remain deeply important.[15]

The foregoing are three ways that linguists today may unwittingly be following problematic models from Kroeber's era. Aspects of his legacy also suggest some positive actions linguists can take, among those suggested by Alice Gaby and Lesley Woods (2020), Wesley Leonard (2020), and others.

Linguists can see their work not simply as answering current research questions but also as creating documentary corpora like those that resulted from Kroeber's work. These will be available for linguistic research answering currently unimagined questions; for research involving history, geography, verbal art, music, and other areas; and for Indigenous reclamation of linguistic and cultural knowledge. A corpus assembled in collaboration with a community may be a linguist's single most enduring legacy—more significant in the long run than any analytic research.

Linguists can also follow the example of Kroeber and others whose Indigenous collaborators were sometimes credited as authors (chapter 6). This is unusual even today, even if a single person provided all the information in a publication. Representative is the long history of *Language*, the field's flagship journal (including its monograph series). Mark Watkins credited fellow University of Chicago student Kamuzu Banda with "all the information" in his 1937 grammar of the Chichewa language, calling him "a very excellent informant . . . without [whose] cooperation this study would contain many more defects than it does." Einar Haugen's 1938 analysis of loan phonology in American Norwegian was based on the speech of a single University of Wisconsin student, Odin Anderson, who "spent many weary hours preparing a tentatively complete list of the words employed in his Norwegian dialect." And in a 1942 study of Ilokano syntax, Leonard Bloomfield wrote that "our data were obtained from Mr. Severino Monta[n]o of Laoag, Ilocos Norte, a student in the Yale School of Drama." Despite Anderson's list of 5,500 words and the crucial contributions of Banda and Montano, none was a coauthor.[16]

The pattern remains common. Not until 2020, after ninety-five years, did *Language* publish a paper whose authors included native-speaker collaborators who were not also researchers.[17] In other major journals, this has never happened. But those who participate in documentation commit time and effort to make critical intellectual contributions; acknowledging these is more than just a gesture of respect. In addition to crediting work done, as emphasized by Gaby and Woods (2020:e271–e272), this practice encourages collaborative research choices, promotes community engagement and skills training, and registers Indigenous intellectual property rights.

Finally, linguists can emphasize the repatriation of intangible cultural and linguistic heritage from academic archives, museums, and offices back to communities. Programs like Berkeley's Breath of Life Archival Institute (chapter 4) exist at several institutions and can be set up at others. Students, language activists and teachers, librarians, and professors often find a common purpose in such work. Linguists can also emphasize Indigenous training, including along the lines Kroeber followed in his own collaborations (chapter 6) and in directing Abraham Halpern's Quechan work (chapter 5). Indigenous literacy training is valuable in some places. In their own training, linguists acquire technical skills in a range of areas, including phonetics and sound processing, videography, transcription and linguistic database management, and lexicography and dictionary making. These and other skills are useful in language communities. And linguists can find ways to support Indigenous students in academia, whether their long-term career goals are academic or otherwise.

Opening up archives through forms of repatriation makes it possible for documentary collections to help heal colonial alienation. Yet an archive evokes many reactions. In a graduate class not long ago, I was introducing the California Language Archive and Berkeley's collections of Indigenous language documentation. For historical reasons, these are distributed among campus repositories whose structures and processes are confusingly different.[18] The class had a mix of linguists and non-linguists, and Indigenous and non-Indigenous students. I explained how visitors can find archival materials and read or listen to digitized materials online, or request access if it is restricted because of cultural sensitivity. After class, a student expressed anger at the obstacles that keep Indigenous people from their own cultural heritage—knowledge taken years ago from their communities. I have heard this understandable, appropriate reaction before. What struck me on this occasion was a dissonance between that reaction and my own feeling, in the same moment, that it is a marvel that so much knowledge and so many stories have been recorded with so many people over the last twelve decades. These two impulses, each as valid as it is incomplete, index the paradox of humanistic scholarship in a colonial regime, like that of California early in the twentieth century, and of collaborations within such a regime among well-intentioned actors whose choices were constrained by their inability to imagine or pursue alternative futures.

ENVOI

Erasure pervades this story. Kroeber's name was literally erased from a UC Berkeley building; he elided evidence of linguistic, discursive, and cultural adaptation and persistence in Native communities; activists objecting to his name ignored his contributions to Indigenous knowledge, his

Figure 11.2
'Aha 'Avulypo, in El Dorado Canyon on the west side of the Colorado River, 2019 (hpbfotos/Alamy Stock Photo). Several erosion pinnacles are visible along the canyon.

advocacy for Indian rights, and his work against eugenics and racism; in scapegoating him, the University of California effaced the violent history of its own colonial foundation; and for decades, Indigenous people were vanished as living Californians and members of an academic community.

As a non-Indigenous linguist, I have surely also privileged certain facets of the story and paid insufficient attention to others. So I want to reiterate that I believe it was right to unname Kroeber Hall—not because Kroeber is guilty of what his critics alleged, but because the passionate debate over a university building name was actually not about the person it was named for, but about how to memorialize a university's relationship with Native people. Kroeber was a convenient symbol of the failures in that relationship over 150 years. It did not matter that some of the most egregious failures followed his death, that he was not guilty of what was charged, or that he was an opponent of racism who helped Indigenous people tell their stories throughout California. For the university itself to escape scrutiny, his name had to go. And as Raymond Chandler wrote in *The Long Goodbye* (1954:59), "A dead man is the best fall guy in the world."

Alfred Kroeber's primary legacy for the twenty-first century lies in the collections he facilitated with scores of Indigenous people from dozens of communities: the stories, songs, and words he wrote down and recorded with them; what they themselves wrote down and recorded using tools he gave them; and the names and places he and his collaborators mapped together. These records are the creation of those whose knowledge and artistry they preserve, but Kroeber's lifelong labor was essential. Almost sixty years passed from his first day of language documentation on 12 October 1897, with the Inuktun language in New York, to his last day on 9 February 1954, transcribing Mojave near Parker, Arizona. Almost seventy years later, the collections Kroeber helped create are used every day in Indigenous communities, and are the basis for publications that benefit both the academy and those whose ancestors shared their knowledge.

On his first day of documentation in 1897, Kroeber recorded Inuktun sentences, pronouns, and words for body parts, animals, clothing, tools, and landscape features. These words reveal a linguistic stage before twentieth-century changes—when *siirquq* "knee," for example, had not yet become *hiiqquq*.[19] On Kroeber's last two days of documentation in 1954, working with Robert Martin (figure 5.3), Agnes Savilla, and Emmett Van Fleet, he transcribed Mojave names of mountain peaks, sicknesses, parts of houses, games, and pottery designs. On the last day, he was also told the location of 'Aha 'Avulypo, whose name means "housepost water." This is where Mataviily built his house at the center of the world, where he later died, and where Mojave song cycles begin (chapter 5). The site of 'Aha 'Avulypo (figure 11.2) is where there are several erosion pinnacles "in Eldorado Canyon betw[een] 2 [and] 3 miles up from" the Colorado River (ALK Ctn 10:24, p. 39); the pinnacles "are the houseposts that remained after the first house was burned and washed out" (Kroeber 1972: Plate 1e). Here, Kroeber told a colleague, is "where the world took shape."[20]

NOTES

NOTES FOR CHAPTER 1

1. Later in the twentieth century, public universities in Alaska, Arizona, Hawai'i, Washington, and other US states were very involved with the Indigenous people of their states.

2. On the early history of American linguistics see Andresen 1990 and Falk 1994; for the LSA call see Barret et al. 1925.

3. The others were Franz Boas, Edward Sapir, and Dell Hymes; the most recent of the twelve presidencies was in 1982. Wheeler received his PhD in 1885 at Heidelberg, where his dissertation adviser was the Indo-Europeanist Hermann Osthoff; his historical linguistics publications include Wheeler 1885, 1887, and Strong et al. 1891.

4. Smith (2022) suggested that the Proposal was initiated from within the executive vice chancellor's office.

5. See Moss 2018 and "UC Berkeley Needs to Be Efficient" 2018. See Foster 2003 on the anthropology statement, Bergman 2011 on the conference, and Glazer 2012 and Cole 2015 on the play.

6. See Platt 2020b and Scheper-Hughes 2020.

7. For the current policy and its original formulation, see Building Name Review Committee n.d. and Nasir et al. 2017:10, respectively.

8. See Nasir et al. 2017:10–11. Douglass said in 1879 that Black people are "too fond of civilizing influences" to "die out like the Indians," explaining as follows: "An Indian is contented with a blanket, while a negro's ambition is a swallow-tailed coat; the Indians don't like churches and steeples, while the negro thinks the higher the steeple the nearer they are to heaven" (Blight 2018:600).

9. See Witt et al. 2016.

10. This episode featured deplorable actions by Peary, Boas, and leaders of the American Museum of Natural History (Harper 2000). Kroeber must have known what they did.

11. See Kroeber 1899 for the English translations. Kroeber (1955–1956) later recalled that he did not publish the Inuktun texts because "the phonetics was not reliable" and "the syntax suffered from omissions resulting from the informants'

impatience at my writing not being able to keep up with their natural speech rate."

12. Henriette Rothschild was born in Württemberg, Germany, in 1876 and came to the United States in the following year with her parents, who settled in San Francisco. She met Kroeber at a local meeting of the American Folklore Society (T. Kroeber 1970:77)

13. Theodora Kracaw was born in 1897 in Denver. She received BA and MA degrees from the University of California in 1919 and 1920, married Clifton Brown in July 1921, and with him had two children. After he died in October 1923, she returned to UC as an anthropology graduate student; there she met Kroeber. On her life, see Buzaljko 1988.

14. Overviews of Kroeber's life and career include Hymes 1961; Rowe 1962; Steward 1962; Steward 1973; T. Kroeber 1970; Wolf 2001; Rolston 2011; and Lewis 2022.

15. Du Bois's memories were shared with Seymour (1988:73, 2015:77).

16. See Le Guin 1989:76–77. As she recounted, when she became pregnant as a college student in 1950 and chose to terminate the pregnancy, her parents borrowed $1,000—"a year's tuition, room, and board" (Phillips 2022:128)—and arranged an (illegal) abortion. Her father said that what she called "evading the consequences of her own actions" was "a lesser sin than the crass irresponsibility of sacrificing your training, your talent, and the children you will want to have, in order to have one nobody wants to have."

17. For the advice, see de Angulo 1995:297; cf. Steward 1973:18. The epithet was in a letter to Berna Pinner. Freeland "is struggling a little," Kroeber added, "but it will be a long time before she breaks his hold: two to five years until she finally is rid of him, I would guess" (11 July 1924, ALK Box 3:7). In another letter, Kroeber called de Angulo a "pitiable psychopath" (16 November 1924, ALK Box 3:7).

18. See Leeds-Hurwitz 2004:61. To Boas, Kroeber wrote that Freeland's "ability is unusual" (4 May 1927, ALK Box 3:10).

19. O'Neale did teach courses in anthropology, and regularly acted as director of the anthropology museum when Kroeber was away for a summer or year. On O'Neale's career, see Harrison 1948 and Schevill 1986, 1988, 1992.

20. In fact, as Buzaljko (n.d.a) pointed out, the first UC graduate degree in anthropology was an MA awarded in 1904 to Louisa McDermott, who wrote a thesis on Montana Salish ethnography and folklore.

21. Hanks's recollections appear among her notes on Kroeber (Hanks 1951–2002). Studies that Kroeber coauthored with women students examined masks and moieties (Kroeber and Holt 1920), Peruvian pottery (Gayton and Kroeber

1927) and textiles (O'Neale and Kroeber 1930), Wiyot towns (Nomland and Kroeber 1936), and change in fashion (Richardson and Kroeber 1940).

22. These comments were made to Buzaljko (n.d.a); later Thompson (1991:38–39) wrote in a different vein that Kroeber was "disgusted" when women joined the graduate program but "known for his fairness" to them. Isabel Kelly thought Kroeber was not supportive (Knobloch 1988:177).

23. Kroeber brought Haas to Berkeley in 1943 to teach Thai as part of the US Army Specialized Training Program (chapter 9). On efforts to make her position permanent, see his letters to J. M. Cowan and Mortimer Graves at the American Council of Learned Societies (29 July and 9 August 1944, ALK Box 3:24). On Haas, see Emeneau 1997, Golla et al. 1997, and Pike 1999.

24. Du Bois was offered the position, accepted the offer, and would have been the first woman faculty member in Berkeley's anthropology department, but she refused to sign the anti-Communist loyalty oath then required of all faculty. For discussion see Seymour 2015:239–246. Kroeber's comments on Du Bois were made in letters to Ted McCown (5 November 1948, Seymour 2015:239) and William Dennes (22 January 1949, ALK Box 4:7).

25. Yowlumne is a Yokuts language that was classically described by Kroeber 1907d and Newman 1944, 1946. On recent changes, see Weigel 2005.

26. For his paper, see Kroeber 1955; for her 29 August 1955 letter, see KFP Box 1:13.

27. The book Le Guin read was edited by Lee (1949). I quote her from what appears to be an undated draft on Emory University letterhead, ca. 1955–1956 (UKLG Box 62, emphasis original). Kroeber's response to what she did write was undated (UKLG Box 62:14).

28. See Le Guin 1980:198 and Le Guin and Attebery 2007:374.

29. These 1956 letters were dated 27 May (KFP Box 1:15, emphasis original) and 2 June (UKLG Box 62:14).

30. This point has been emphasized for language by many writers, such as Hinton et al. (2018:xxiv): "Language revitalization is and must be an effort of the speech community. Nevertheless, researchers from outside of the community often play a big role."

31. My title alludes to John McPhee's *Assembling California* (1993).

NOTES FOR CHAPTER 2

1. Wayland's story (ED 154.5) was discussed in part, with other stories, by Bauer (2016:10–27); two creation stories told by Wayland were published by Curtis (1907–1930:15.123–129).

2. See Golla 2011 and Hinton 2022 for overviews of California languages, and Lightfoot and Parrish 2009 for an introduction to California's Indigenous cultural diversity.

3. See Flores Santis 2014:114–122. On impacts of the Spanish invasion see also Cook 1976, Sandos 2004, Hackel 2005, Milliken et al. 2009, Haas 2014, Panich and Schneider 2014, Rizzo 2016, and Akins and Bauer 2021:64–85.

4. See T. Kroeber 1961:40–100, G. Garrett 1969, Cook 1976, Heizer 1993, Norton 1979, Trafzer and Hyer 1999, Platt 2011, Lindsay 2012, Madley 2016, and Akins and Bauer 2021:126–156, among others.

5. All Native Americans became US citizens through the Indian Citizenship Act of 1924. Previously, only certain Native Americans had been granted US citizenship, such as those who accepted land grants under the Dawes Act (1887) and World War I veterans (1919).

6. For discussion see Buckley 1996:279–282.

7. On Native American boarding school experiences, see Child 1998, Lomawaima and McCarty 2006, Woolford 2015, and Lomawaima et al. 2018, among others.

8. For these memories, see Sherer 1965:42 and Penfield 2005:93.

9. See Berry 1960 and Dippie 1982. At the end of the nineteenth century, as Treuer (2019:9–10) showed, even some prominent Native Americans seemed to accept the inevitability of assimilation and disappearance.

10. See Gidley 1998, Egan 2006, and Vizenor 2009:191–206 on the contexts, representational choices, and sociopolitical associations of Curtis's photographs.

11. For Indigenous advocacy during this period, see Hoxie 2001.

12. See Cohodas 1997, Smith-Ferri 1998, Smith 2016, Roberts 2018, and Chavez 2019 on weaving practices and the California basket trade.

13. See Hantman and Dunham 1993:46. Wallace (1999:20) described Jefferson's scholarly work as serving "a public relations function: to convince Europeans that America was already a civilized nation, whose white citizens were capable of a parting salute to a red race doomed to cultural, if not physical, extinction."

14. See also Bieder 1992, Thomas 2000:52–63, Platt 2011, and Lindquist 2014.

15. Hearst changed her name's spelling from Phebe to Phoebe around 1902 (Nickliss 2018:xxx).

16. Recent contributions to the extensive literature on Boas include Darnell et al. 2015, Darnell 2018, Blackhawk and Wilner 2018, King 2019, Baker 2020, Ocasio 2020, and Zumwalt 2019, 2022. On language description see Boas 1889, 1911c, 1917; for the *Handbook* see Boas 1911b, 1922.

17. See Boas 1894, 1901a, 1911a; Boas and Hunt 1902, 1906; Boas and Deloria 1941; and Boas et al. 1947.

18. See Thoresen 1973. On Boas and texts, see, for example, Bunzl 1996, Briggs and Bauman 1999, Darnell 2001, Silverstein 2015, and Epps et al. 2017.

19. These quotations are from a 24 July 1905 letter to W. H. Holmes (Stocking 1974:122–23). Briggs and Bauman (1999) centered Boas's phrase "the foundation of all future researches" in their critique of his practice.

20. The term "salvage" in this context is due to Gruber (1970); for a recent assessment, see Redman 2021. On memory documentation in California, see Lightfoot 2005:30–48. A striking twist on the vanishment assumption appeared in an obituary of Kroeber by Lévi-Strauss (1960), who called him "the last of the ethnologists who, in the United States, knew . . . the Indians who had themselves lived a traditional existence in their youth. With him, in a sense, it is thus the Indian of the past who disappears."

21. For the kinds of language change mentioned, see, for example, Fishman 1965, Selinker 1972, and Meakins 2018. The Boasians were "highly sensitive to cultural hybridities," according to Bashkow (2004:444); in a section of his *Anthropology* textbook added to the second edition, Kroeber (1948a:259) himself wrote that "cultures can blend to almost any degree and not only thrive but perpetuate themselves." But this statement was absent in the first, 1923, edition; and hybridity was in practice often downplayed in his search for authentic exemplars of traditional culture.

22. See also Lewis 2014:125–129, 2018:31–34.

23. On this difference, see Fabian (1983). Kroeber might have known (but did not cite) Ratzel's 1904 paper on "history, ethnology, and historical perspective," in which the term Ökumene was used to refer to the global "human community," as Fabian (1983:20) put it. In the form *ecumene*, and probably independently from Kroeber (and Ratzel), the term was popularized by McNeill (1963) and later writers; see also Hewes 1961.

24. The American exceptionality claim was reiterated by Meillet and Cohen (1924:9) and explicitly critiqued by Bloomfield (1925a); see Goddard 1996, Campbell 1997, and Mithun 1999 on relationships among Native American languages, and Golla 2011 on California. Claims of Australian exceptionality by Dixon (1997, 2002) have been effectively rebutted by many scholars (e.g., Bowern and Koch 2004, Bowern et al. 2011, McConvell and Bowern 2011). Common to both claims was an assertion that sociohistorical language dynamics in more recently colonized areas of the world are fundamentally different from those in Africa and Eurasia.

25. See Du Bois 1970:21; on her perspective, see Castaneda 2020:191. See ALK Box 8:22 for Barrett's letter (13 September 1908).

26. On the evolution of what eventually became Kroeber's *Handbook*, beginning with its early antecedents, see Long 1998:187–217.

NOTES FOR CHAPTER 3

1. See also Field et al. 2013; Field 1999, 2003; Milliken 2008; Milliken et al. 2009; Laverty 2010; and Panich 2020 on the history of this community.

2. For these details, see Older 1936:107.

3. Kroeber's disparaging description ("hovels") is contradicted by documentation of a roundhouse and long-lasting houses (Cambra et al. 2017:60).

4. The examples to follow are listed by Putnam 1905.

5. For these examples, see Putnam 1905.

6. On this contrast, see Fabian 1983.

7. I have found biographical information in DeWitt-Warr 1913:140, Dickey 2008, the 1900 and 1910 census, the *Indian Advance* (1 September 1899), the *Indian Leader* (12 June 1903, 11 November 1904, 14 March 1913, 19 November 1915), and Stewart records ("Register of Pupils" 1892–1899). According to the 1900 census, Washington's mother was Washoe and her father was white; Stewart records identify Daisy as "Town Washoe" from a former mining town (Franktown, Nevada) and the 1900 census (at Haskell) records her father's birthplace as "Un[known]."

8. Stewart records identify this simply as the Williams family of Empire, Nevada, but 1900 census records show only one family by that name living in Empire.

9. See Nickliss 2018:329–365.

10. See chapter 10 for more discussion. On the exploitation of Washoe land for mining and its destructive direct and indirect consequences, see Makley 2018: 46–75.

11. The year is not quite legible, but 1918 seems likely given Washington's death in 1919. The date of this letter was 20 June (GPAHP Box 67:28).

12. See Thoreson 1975, Darnell 2000b:148–155, Jacknis 2000, Nickliss 2018:271–284, and especially Long 1998. For details about the 1903–1904 academic year, see University of California 1904:158–159.

13. Some details are in UCOPAF Boxes 7:74, 10:97, and 17:145–146. See also Long 1998:231–233.

14. See also Bennett et al. 2017:131–173.

15. See Nickliss 2018:281. This episode was also discussed with additional details by Buzaljko (n.d.b:18–19).

16. See Golla 1984:28, 36; Long 1998:114–118; and Rolston 2011:49–54.

17. Kroeber's parents "had expected to send their sons to Harvard and their daughters to Bryn Mawr" (T. Kroeber 1970:34), but financial realities did not permit this.

18. In a scathing critique of American higher education, Sinclair (1923:134) wrote that Wheeler "called himself a liberal, but never enough to offend Mrs. Hearst, who gave the university a Greek theater, with her son's name carved across the front of the stage."

NOTES FOR CHAPTER 4

1. See Kroeber 1910c, 1911b, and, in the modern era, Mithun 1984, Baker 1988, Evans 1996, and Caballero et al. 2008. For an appreciation of Kroeber's linguistic work, see Stanlaw 2022.

2. For the original proposals, see Dixon and Kroeber 1903, 1913, 1919. For dif ferent perspectives on Hokan and Penutian see Kaufman 1988, Campbell 1997, DeLancey and Golla 1997, and Mithun 1999.

3. See, for example, Bowern 2018a, Goldstein 2020, and Michael and Chousou-Polydouri 2020.

4. For statistical studies of culture change, see Kroeber 1919a, Driver and Kroeber 1932, and Richardson and Kroeber 1940. On language, see Kroeber and Chrétien 1937 and Kroeber 1955, 1960a.

5. See, for example, Keeling 1982.

6. I owe my awareness of their formulation to Darnell (2001:6).

7. See also Himmelmann 1998, 2012; Bird and Simons 2003; Woodbury 2003; Gippert et al. 2006; McDonnell et al. 2018; and Seifart et al. 2018.

8. See Kroeber 1904, 1907c,d, 1910a, 1911d for the overviews and sketches; Kroeber 1916a, 1959, 1963 on dialectology; Kroeber 1911e,f, and Kroeber and Harrington 1914 on phonetics; and Kroeber 1916c on learning Zuni.

9. In a short research summary prepared as a press release (11 September 1909, UCOPAF Box 22:26), Kroeber made no specific reference to Yurok: "All the [ninety-two California] Indian languages examined have been found to be much more developed than is commonly supposed. They all possess a vocabulary of at least 5000 words and many show a complex grammar, rivaling or surpassing that of Greek or Latin in intricacy."

10. See Keeling 1991. The California languages are Atsugewi, Esselen, Huchnom, Karuk, Maidu, Mattole, Modoc, Mojave, Nomlaki, Numu, Purisimeño, Rumsen, Shoshone, Sierra Miwok, Tachi Yokuts, Tolowa, Wailaki, Whilkut, Wiyot, Yana, Yawdanchi Yokuts, Yowlumne Yokuts, Yuki, and Yurok. The others include Chinook Wawa, Chukchi, Hopi, Marshallese, Nlaka'pamux (Thompson River Salish), and Sioux.

11. As far as I know, the only recordings of Indigenous languages in this collection that were not made by Indigenous people are three Nlaka'pamux and six Chinook Wawa recordings, all translations of Catholic texts spoken by a white cleric visiting San Francisco.

12. On this optical scanning and digitization project, implemented with funding from the National Endowment for the Humanities and the National Science Foundation, see Hoban 2018, Ding 2019, and Berkeley Library n.d. All these recordings (including those made by Kroeber) are held in UC Berkeley's anthropology museum.

13. On Karuk see Bright 1957, Lang 1994 and Garrett et al. 2023. Strictly speaking, Karuk belongs to the putative Hokan group, whose genealogical reality is in doubt.

14. On this process see Bright 1957:17–18. Apparently Kroeber did not notice the lengthening in the same word in the previous line.

15. More precisely, the change was absent in Bennett's speech. Conathan (2006:225–227) showed that some Karuk contemporaries of Bennett did have [θ].

16. Freeland's work was published as de Angulo and Freeland 1931; for the Karuk dictionary, see Bright and Gehr 2005.

17. For instance, a story dictated in 1931–1932 by Margaret Harrie to Hans Jørgen Uldall (a visiting researcher under Kroeber's supervision) has been published in a community-oriented volume edited and translated by Karuk artist, scholar, and language teacher Julian Lang (1994:64–95).

18. The Karuk story was dictated on 15 October 1901 (ALK Ctn 10:48, pp. 35–37); an English translation was published by Kroeber and Gifford (1980:86).

19. Tac's Luiseño sketch was first published in 1926 as a short monograph in Italy, and his dictionary in 1930; see Haas 2011.

20. For these quotations see Kroeber and Grace 1960:2 and Malécot 1963:89.

21. For Sparkman's work and later publications derived from his work, see Sparkman 1908, Kroeber and Grace 1960, and Bright 1968. It is uncertain who killed Sparkman; see Mallios 2020:91–92.

22. For Kroeber's notes, see ALK Ctn 9:19, pp. 1–64.

23. Major grammars of Takic languages other than Luiseño include J. Hill 1966, 2005; K. Hill 1967; Seiler 1977; and Anderton 1988.

24. The photocopy is at the American Philosophical Society (Pitkin 1884–1980: Series IIA-3, Notebook 29); the published edition is by Balodis (2016:521–624).

25. The date of this photo is fixed by a label on a similar photo with Theodora Kroeber and the Kroeber children (ALKFP ALB v. 4).

26. This memory was in a letter to Alice H. Woodcock, 20 January 1921 (RDA Box 182).

27. In English-language usage, Yurok people born in precolonial times or in the first few decades after 1850 often had a single name, like Frank or Spott (which usually became their children's family name), preceded by a place name (e.g., Weitchpec) or other moniker (e.g., Captain).

28. Alfred's name was reported by Orick Bob to J. P. Harrington (National Anthropological Archives, NMNH Harrington_mf2_r2_0311); see T. Kroeber 1970:158 for Theodora's name.

29. For Johnson's work with Kroeber, see ALK Ctn 12:27, p. 32, and 12:33 (e.g., p. 17 for the winds).

30. On Yurok numeral classification see Haas 1967, Conathan 2004, and O'Neill 2008.

31. For the relative homogeneity of Yurok along the Klamath, see Quinby 2003.

32. Kroeber himself made three recordings (with Stone and with Susie Crane) in 1902, seven in 1906, and forty-four in 1907. Recordings were also made at his behest by Weitchpec Frank in 1907 and T. T. Waterman in 1909. Thirty-three of the recordings are translated in Kroeber 1976; a full inventory of the corpus is in Keeling 1991.

33. The texts are transcribed in ALK Ctn 12:20, pp. 1–42a; the fish-dam text was published in rudimentary form by Waterman and Kroeber (1938:75–77).

34. On this parallelism, see Conathan 2006:216.

35. This recording (CLA 24-1034) is partially transcribed in ALK Ctn 12:30, pp. 2–16. Kroeber's other notes from work with her are in ALK Ctn 12:25, pp. 26–44.

36. For this memory of Kroeber, see Fryer 1995:165 (emphasis original).

37. On Yurok language pedagogy and revitalization, see Garrett 2009, 2011, 2014 and Gellman 2022, 2023; for analytic research, see Garrett 2001 and Conathan 2004, 2006.

38. On the distribution of this pattern, see Blevins and Garrett 2007.

39. His friendship with Parsons began in 1915, and became emotionally intimate and fraught by 1918 (Deacon 1997:201–213).

40. Unlike some other anthropologists, however, Kroeber did not write about Zuni ceremonialism or ritual.

41. See Parsons 1917:249; Dennis Tedlock was also called *kamme* (Tedlock 1992:291), the familiar form of *kaka* "mother's brother" (Schneider and Roberts 1965:13). See Johnson 2018a:139–141 on the roles of William and Margaret Lewis in Zuni anthropological work. Outsiders like Bunzel (1952:xv) described

what was called an "intense factionalism" in which a Zuni faction "favorable to Americans and friendly to anthropologists," including Kroeber's hosts, was later discredited. See Pandey 1967 for detailed discussion.

42. I have normalized the spelling and punctuation of this letter (ALK Ctn 32:39).

43. For this work see Bunzel 1933, 1933–1938. For Kroeber's anthropological and archaeological work at Zuni, see Kroeber 1916d and Kroeber 1917c.

44. In three major publications on Zuni, Newman (1958, 1965, 1996) did not mention its existence; nor did Tedlock (1971) in an overview of texts published by the "army" of Boasian researchers at Zuni. Newman (1965:10) did comment on aspects of Kroeber's (1916c) language-acquisition paper, praising his "perceptive observations" but criticizing "faulty and inaccurate" transcriptions.

45. The two stories just mentioned were transcribed in a single notebook (ALK Ctn 13:37, pp. 3–5, 18–24). For English translations and discussion of "Salt-Lady Story," see Bunzel 1932:1032–1035, Benedict 1935:1.43–49 and Zuni People 1972:205–206.

46. See LaDuke 2002 and Valtin 2003 on this project and resistance to it.

47. Kroeber gave this story the title "Zuni Girl Captured by Navajos" (ALK Ctn 13:37, pp. 25–32).

48. In a later era, even Tedlock's "On Praying, Exclaiming, and Saying Hello in Zuni" (1983:178–193) focuses mainly on speech that "is not ordinary" (in the words of a Zuni man whom Tedlock quotes).

49. See ALK Ctn 13:33, p. 28. Note that Kroeber wrote *kw* for /kw/, *L* for /ɬ/, and *c* for /ʃ/. Zuni toponyms are given as Kroeber spelled them.

50. Many of the toponyms recorded by Kroeber are not among the names in Ferguson and Hart 1985:125–134. On geographical knowledge in Zuni cultural reclamation, see Iralu 2021; compare the discussion of Mojave and Yurok geography in chapter 5.

51. On Parry see, for example, Parry 1971, Lord 2000, and Kanigel 2021.

52. For these facts, see Kanigel 2021:135, 236.

53. This was sponsored by the American Council of Learned Societies with a grant from the Carnegie Corporation; see Leeds-Hurwitz 1985 and Darnell 2000a:260–261.

54. For example, Kroeber's notes typically included precise records of how much each consultant was paid per day.

55. See Heaton 2013, Maxwell 2013, and Patricia Anderson 2020.

56. This was shown by Woodbury's (1998) study of affective expressions in Cup'ik narratives and English translations by their narrators.

57. On the Breath of Life model as developed at Berkeley and applied elsewhere, see Hinton 2001, Gehr 2013, Baldwin et al. 2018, Lang and Begay 2020, Linn 2021, and Hinton 2022:240–243, 262–277, 288–289. On new uses of early documentation, see also Warren and Barnes 2018.

NOTES FOR CHAPTER 5

1. Jones also made sound recordings of parts of the narrative (CLA 24-585 and ALK Ctn 10:14; also CLA Kroeber.002). The English was mainly rewritten by Kroeber (1948b:56); what he transcribed was fragmentary (ALK Ctn 10:12, p. 12).

2. Also in 1935, working with some of the same people in Owens Valley, the anthropologist Julian Steward paid consultants $2 a day (Kerns 2010:41).

3. For correspondence and documents relating to this work see RDA Boxes 54, 74, and 134.

4. For these letters (one undated, one on 5 July 1935) from W. J. Sterrett, and Kroeber's justification in a 16 July 1935 submission to the Works Progress Administration, see RDA Box 134.

5. See Halpern 1984, 1997, and Halpern and Miller 2014. The 1935 notebooks are archived at Berkeley (ED 122); see also Halpern 1946a,b, 1947.

6. See Walton 1993:17–45, Bauer 2003, 2009, 2012, 2016, and Steenland 2015.

7. Autobiographies by Sam Newland and Jack Stewart in 1927–1928 (Steward 1934) are similar to those in this corpus.

8. The twenty-nine elders were John Alston (ED 151), George Brierly (154.2, 213.5), Mattie Bulpitt (154.3, 154.5, 154.7, 207.4), Susie Butcher (152.2, 205.1), Jennie Cashbaugh (154.1), Tina Charley (149), Mary Cornwell (155, 213.2), Edith Dewey (154.1, 154.2), Maggie Earl (153.3), Willie Goodale (210.5), George Gregory (212.11), Mamie Gregory (212.11), Mary Harry (152.1, 152.4, 205.1), Jim Jones (150.2, 211.1–4), Dee Lacey (212.7–8), Jennie Newlan (206.4, 213.1), James Reynolds (208.9), George Robinson (153.3, 208.8, 209.3), John Shaw (154.4), John T. Shepard (212.2–3), Susie Shepard (212.6), Bridgeport Tom (150.1), George Turner (154.6), Ben Tibbits (152.3), Tom Watterson (154.5, 154.7), Mose Wayland (154.5), Susie Westerville (153.1, 208.2, 209.1), Charlie Wrinkle (212.9–10), and Dave Yandell (154.6). In quoting from these notebooks, I tacitly adjust punctuation and spelling; I name the community interviewer-transcribers if identified.

9. On this practice see Fowler and Walter 1985.

10. Compare Rumsey's (1999) perceptive discussion of Indigenous imputations of cannibalism to Europeans in Highland New Guinea.

11. For details of the California genocide in Owens Valley, see Madley 2016:309–316, 328–330.

12. See Walton 1993:21–22, Madley 2016:315, and especially Bauer 2016:98–103.

13. Bauer (2016:101) wrote that Harry and her mother were on the march and escaped, but that was Harry's story about "a woman and her young daughter" (ED 205.1), not about herself.

14. The classic examples are Steward 1933, 1938.

15. Harrington's (1926–1942) notes are in the National Anthropological Archives; Kroeber's and Waterman's are at Berkeley (ALK, ED 99).

16. Toponyms are cited by ALK carton number. The following individuals shared these place names: Weitchpec Frank (WF), Muerekw Jack (MJ), Trinidad Jim (TJ), Juanita of Weitchpec (JW), George Mahatch (GM), Captain Spott (CS), and Robert Spott (RS).

17. Burenhult and Levinson (2008:145) dismissed such explanations as often "highly likely to be folk etymologies having little to do with historical reality. Such folk etymologies can represent conventions upheld by the whole speech community." This is beside the point. If the goal is to characterize conventional understandings, then it is irrelevant whether these are diachronically "genuine" or based on folk etymology.

18. On linguistic and cognitive aspects of spatial reference, see, for example, Pederson et al. 1998; Levinson 1996, 2003; O'Meara and Báez 2011; and Palmer et al. 2017.

19. See Kroeber 1902, 1911e, and Kroeber 1925:755–769.

20. I use the spelling Mojave as per the Fort Mojave Indian Tribe; Kroeber usually wrote Mohave. Kroeber's Mojave transcriptions are phonetically unreliable, so I spell words from manuscripts as per Munro et al. (1992) if possible. I have not changed spellings used in published work. For a sketch of the Mojave sound system see also Wares 1968:31–34. For Mojave texts and historical studies see Kroeber 1948b, 1951b,c, 1972, and A. Kroeber and C. Kroeber 1973.

21. Martin served as an interpreter in 1953 and was actively involved in language documentation in later years, working with linguists Judith Crawford (Brown et al. 1967–1972, Martin et al. 1967–1972) and Pamela Munro (Munro 1976, Munro et al. 1992).

22. This quotation (ALK Ctn 10:11, p. 5) was somewhat freely adapted in print by Kroeber (1948b:37). In his publications, Kroeber also described the narrative and songs as Raven Songs, translating *'aqaaq* as "raven." Munro et al. (1992:31) glossed it as "crow," as did Jack Jones in 1900 (ALK 10:6, pp. 5, 17), Tokwatha in 1903 (ALK 10:7, p. 26), and Robert Martin in 1967 (Crawford 1967:24).

23. The story was transcribed by Crawford (1968a:35–124, 1968b:1–43) from the sound recording in CLA LA 248.015 (Martin et al. 1967–1972). The translation is adapted from her notes; line breaks follow my sense of Martin's prosody.

24. See Cultural Systems Research 1987:126–127.

25. On Salt Song revival see also Trafzer 2015:4–6, 237–240 and Stringfellow 2020. Nuwuvi people speak the closely related Chemehuevi, Southern Paiute, and Ute dialects or languages, sometimes collectively called Colorado River Numic.

26. See Weinberg and Penfield 2000, Penfield et al. 2008, Penfield and Tucker 2011, and Davis 2013.

27. The manuscript has *tsakiŭ̄́ut, tsakiŭ̄́uwit* (ALK Ctn 12:19, p. W16). Kroeber (n.d.) included the toponym (as *tsakiuuwit*) in an unpublished report on Wiyot geography, from which it was published by Loud (1918:296). For the Tsakiyuwit rally see https://www.yournec.org/tsakiyuwit-rally/.

28. On Sue-meg State Park see Kamisher (2021).

29. The recording was made on 3 June 1907 on three wax cylinders (CLA 24-987); Kroeber made a rough transcript with the help of Weitchpec Frank (ALK Ctn 12:26, pp. 2–13). Part of this text was published by Conathan (2006:213).

30. The form *megetohl* has no ending, or it can be inflected with verbal endings, which I omit in the translation.

31. This was the title of a 1969 film by Michael Kanentakeron Mitchell and a widely publicized graffito at Alcatraz (Johnson 1995). See Nevins 2017 on Indigenous "political voice" in early texts; Domingo's speech is a clear example.

NOTES FOR CHAPTER 6

1. I have mentioned the examples of Karuk speaker Jeannette Horne (chapter 4) and Yuma literacy training (chapter 5.) Kroeber's interest in Indigenous writing was not original or unique to him; important precursors and counterparts include the Meskwaki anthropologist William Jones (also a PhD student of Boas) and the Meskwaki writer Alfred Kiyana, among others.

2. Again, Kroeber's practice was not unique. Boas is also known for his Indigenous co-authors, Ella Deloria and George Hunt, though neither was a simple collaboration; on Boas and Hunt, see, for example, Berman 1994, Wilner 2015, and Bruchac 2018:20–47.

3. For a discussion of Dolores's life and work, adapted and expanded from parts of this chapter, see Garrett 2023.

4. On Dolores's life, see Kroeber 1949 and Mathiot 1991.

5. Documents concerning his UC career are in RDA Boxes 11, 21, and 49. I have normalized the punctuation and spelling of Dolores's letters quoted in the text.

6. An important example is Mathiot's 84-page edition of his memoir, "The reminiscences of Juan Dolores, an early O'odham linguist" (1991). Note that Saxton and Saxton's (1973:361–366) inventory of Dolores's corpus is based on sets of copies of the originals and is not easy to use; it is also probably incomplete. In Berkeley, material from Dolores's O'odham corpus is in the Bancroft Library (ED 134) and the anthropology museum (https://cla.berkeley.edu/list.php?pplid=11122); in Philadelphia, it is in Mason's papers at the American Philosophical Society (Mason 1911–1967); and in Tucson, it is in the Arizona State Museum Library (TLKP).

7. See Dolores 1913, 1923, 1936, and O'Neale and Dolores 1943. Some traditional narratives drawn from work with Dolores were published in English translation by Henriette Kroeber (1909c, 1912b).

8. Dolores was also the interpreter of a migration narrative told to Mason by Abraham Pablo in January 1919, though not named in Mason's (1921) publication of the story; a partial adapted version of the O'odham text was published by Saxton and Saxton (1973:349–357).

9. Mason (1950) wrote *p, t, tc, k* and *b, d, ḍ, dj, g*. The sounds written *(t)c* and *(d)j* were described by Mason (1950:8) as affricates, similar to those in English *church* and *judge* (cf. Zepeda 1983:4), but by Hale (1965:296) as lamino-alveolar stops (cf. Dart 1993). Alternative terms for the two stop series are fortis or tense (for the sharp series) and lenis or lax (for the mellow series).

10. The sibilants *s* and *ṣ* are also sometimes preaspirated, but do not have "mellow" counterparts. According to Hale (1959:13–14), *ḍ* is also preaspirated in some contexts (between unstressed vowels and immediately before fricatives). Saxton (1963:30–31) likewise described a voiceless allophone of *ḍ* preceded by preaspiration ("voiceless [vowel] offglides").

11. In this analysis he anticipated Clayton (2010:182–183), who has shown that O'odham preaspiration has a longer duration after long vowels than after short vowels (unlike preaspiration in some languages) and suggested for this reason that preaspiration "is phonologically associated with the vowel nucleus" (but with the following consonant in some languages).

12. The latter are preglottalized in some contexts; Dolores sometimes wrote *'p, 't, 'ṭ, 'tc, 'k*.

13. Later writers whose analysis was similar to Mason include Hale (1959), Saxton (1963), and Alvarez and Hale (1970).

14. In initial position, the O'odham sharp stops have "a narrow (or piercing) burst" (Alvarez and Hale 1970:95). This probably means they are postaspirated,

which was described by Kroeber (1913:243) and implied by Hill and Zepeda (1992). In this position, while Kroeber observed that the series are phonetically distinct, he and Dolores wrote them identically as *p, t, ṭ, tc, k*. This can be seen in spellings like Dolores's ***k****i'ihk* "four" (ED 134.1.1, p. 36, now written ***g****i'ik*) and ***k****oi* "sleep" (ED 134.1.4, pp. 40–41, for ***k****oi*).

15. See also Alvarez and Hale 1970, Saxton and Saxton 1973, and Zepeda 1983.

16. Both Mason (here) and Dolores referred to the O'odham language in English as Papago, a term that is now regarded as a slur.

17. Compare *'aM-hihi'* "they went there" with deictic *'am* and *ma-'tE-p-o-dju'* "if it rains" with subordinating *m* (Mason 1950:42, 44). Capitalized *M, K, TC, LI* indicate Dolores's perception that these sounds were devoiced in final position. Note that he regularly and unexpectedly omitted preaspiration in some words, including the word for "rain" (despite its *k*). On the final vowel in "wind" see Mason (1950:11–12). Finally, note that while Dolores wrote *K tcukI* "the rain" as two words, he regularly wrote the definite article as part of the following noun if it began with *h* or *'*, as in *kohks* "the old woman" (ED 134.1.1, pp. 33, 36) and *kihkiviTC* "the woodpecker" (ED 134.1.3, p. 82).

18. Cf. Mason's (1950:50) *na-'p-eḍ-se-main-t-a't-kaM* "are you a mapmaker?"

19. Dolores changed his orthographic practice late in life: he stopped indicating preaspiration and wrote the mellow and sharp stops identically, just as he already wrote short and long vowels the same. Speakers of O'odham, he said, would have no difficulty reading this. This reflects a tension in orthography design between writing systems for fluent speakers and those meant to help learners who do not know a language well. Examples of the former include the Latin system, which did not indicate vowel length, and the Hebrew and Arabic systems, which do not ordinarily write vowels. By contrast, in a system meant for language learners, it is helpful if a word's pronunciation is predictable from its spelling.

20. Kroeber was a witness at their city hall marriage ceremony on 19 November 1935, according to a front-page article in the *Oakland Tribune* ("U.C. Co-ed" 1935).

21. The word *nɨmɨ* means "(Numu) people," so strictly speaking *nɨmɨ yadua* designates the language. It is spelled using different orthographic systems in different places; I have chosen a linguistically oriented system similar to Gilbert Natches's.

22. See Heizer et al. 1972 for an overview of the Marsden corpus and translations of many of its texts.

23. Kroeber organized Numana's visit in correspondence with Jeanne Elizabeth Weir (RDA Box 180); for Numana's language materials see CLA 24-2517 and ED 37.1–4.

24. See "Local and Personals" 1901. On Natches's life, see Bandurraga 1990.

25. See "Scion of Indian Aristocracy" 1914. Some information about Natches's 1914 visit is from letters between Kroeber and Kendall Severance (RDA Box 134).

26. In the bulleted list of Natches's texts, references like "24-2306" are short for "CLA 24-2306" and references like "15.65–66" are short for "CLA Marsden.015, pp. 65–66." Publications are abbreviated as H (Heizer et al. 1972) and N (Natches 1923). Titles in quotation marks were given by Natches himself. Thornes (2020:S147) mistakenly wrote that "Owl" is "the only [Natches] story that has an accompanying audio recording." Note that the first text in the list ("Bird story") was recorded on a cylinder that was broken and discarded in 1958 (Keeling 1991:310).

27. See Merrill 2018 on the cross-linguistic typology of consonant mutation.

28. This phenomenon was first described, famously, by Sapir (1933). Note that the mutated *g* is actually phonetically a fricative [ɣ], which is even more distinct than *g* from the voiceless stop *k*.

29. The uncompounded *akwammu*, *atɨna*, and *apitakwa* refer generally to rhizomes, roots, and stalks or trunks, respectively, not necessarily of cattails. The suffix *-bɨ* (omitted in compounds) is referred to as "absolutive" in Uto-Aztecanist parlance. Note that Natches and Kroeber wrote *e* for the sound now usually written *ɨ* (a high central vowel).

30. For Numu cattail vocabulary, see Fowler's (1990) monograph on Paiute marsh technology as well as relevant entries in Liljeblad et al. 2012.

31. The song and explanation were recorded by Natches (CLA 24-2300) and transcribed by Natches and Kroeber (CLA Marsden.010, p. 18, CLA Marsden.015, pp. 66–67). Natches's father was Natches Overton, brother of the famous Sarah Winnemucca and himself also an important figure in Paiute history; see Zanjani 2001.

32. Natches wrote *tabé*, meaning *tabɨ*. For some reason Kroeber corrected this to *kabé*, which is not a Numu word. I take *tabɨ* as Natches's reduced form of *tabɨa* "it looks like" (Liljeblad et al. 2012:478–479).

33. The lyrics of both songs feature "an Indian maid." The recordings mentioned are at CLA 24-2278, 24-2281, 24-2321, and 24-2324.

34. These quotations are from letters to Dr. Henry E. Goodrich (9 February 1915, RDA Box 64) and Mrs. C. E. Severance (9 February 1915, RDA Box 134).

35. These letters were dated 24 January 1916 and 21 September 1917 (ALK Box 24:5).

36. On Natches's death, see Earl 1990.

37. For the notebook and a typed transcript, together with Riesenberg's 1 October 1969 account of their origin, see Natches and Riesenberg 1940.

38. For this information, I thank Heidi Barlese and Nicholas Cortez, writing for the Pyramid Lake Cultural/Language Program (email 4 August 2022).

39. See Lowry 2007:18 (Croix de Guerre) and Putnam 1917 (advocacy).

40. Buckley (2002:64–65) wrote with some justification that "Kroeber virtually ignores Spott's (often very subtle and always very Yurok) commentaries on the traditional narratives that he himself performed, overriding them and capping each chapter with his own ethnological commentaries," but what matters most is that Spott's commentaries remain. For additional discussion see Buckley 1987.

41. See T. Kroeber 1976:xv. This story was famously retold in Theodora Kroeber's collection *The Inland Whale* (1963b).

42. See Spott and Kroeber 1942:226. According to Robert Spott (ALK Ctn 12:39, p. 73), the *kaamuueks* status can be acquired in other ways than by birth.

43. Harry Roberts (2011:54) recalled Spott saying that there were things he never told to white people, "because I worry that I won't be understood." When "old people . . . realized that the anthropologists and psychologists couldn't understand them, they stopped speaking of personal things or developed things and only gave them what they could understand." It is hard to judge the reliability of Roberts' memories of Spott's words. A contradictory statement, reportedly made by Spott to Roberts (Buckley 2002:106), was that Spott "tried and tried to teach Kroeber, but he just couldn't learn." Whether Kroeber understood or not, it is my sense that Spott did try to articulate his cultural values to him.

44. Harry Roberts (see note 43) was another outsider whom Spott taught much about Yurok culture.

45. The setting of the photograph in figure 6.9 is uncertain. The catalog of Berkeley's anthropology museum suggests that it was Requa ("Hupa Reservation"), but Le Guin (2004b:19) thought that it was the Kroeber summer place in St. Helena.

46. See Fryer 1995:169. Researchers who worked with Spott included the anthropologists E. W. Gifford and T. T. Waterman, the psychologist Erik Erikson, the linguist R. H. Robins, and a number of Kroeber's students. No doubt they sometimes made him feel like a specimen. On Spott's relationship with the Kroeber family, see also T. Kroeber 1970:158–160.

47. These three narratives, respectively, are transcribed in ED 134.1.6, pp. 5, 7, 9, 11; ED 134.1.7, pp. 1–9; and ED 134.1.8, pp. 101–107.

48. These speeches were recorded from Antonio Lopez (CLA 24-2459, ED 134.1.7, pp. 10–17) and Ba·im:u·TE·kam (CLA 24-2460, ED 134.1.7, pp. 19–22).

49. See Spott and Kroeber 1942:222 (drawn from ALK Ctn 12:33, p. 29); I modernize the Yurok spelling. The word *'er'gerp* is derived from the verb *'erperk'* "I tell."

50. For the linguistic pattern, compare *'ahspeyuer'* "soup," which is something drunk; its root is *'ahsp-*, as in *'ahspek'* "I drink."

51. See Spott and Kroeber 1942:250–251 (drawn from ALK Ctn 12:37, pp. 12–13).

NOTES FOR CHAPTER 7

The chapter epigraph is quoted from Waterman 1917:537.

1. Akins and Bauer (2021:193) called the word Ishi a "bastardization." They may have misunderstood what they transcribed as *i'citi*, phonetically [ihṣiti], whose final *-ti* is the quotative clitic and not part of the word. It is hard to see how better to render [ihṣi] in English, which lacks coda [h] and retroflex [ṣ]. Note that the information that "Ishi is te·ˊt'mawi" (ED 68.1, p. 1, Sapir) was misinterpreted as meaning that this was Ishi's name (Sapir and Swadesh 1960:173); in fact it was a term for Yahi people (Kroeber 1925:345).

2. "Having lost my residence," Kroeber wrote Hearst on 23 April 1906 (Buzaljko n.d.b), "I shall for the present live at the Museum."

3. For these terms see Waterman 1918:68 and Buzaljko 2003:54.

4. Published sources relating to Ishi include Kroeber 1912a; Waterman 1918; Pope 1920; T. Kroeber 1961; Kessler 1973; Heizer and T. Kroeber 1979; C. Kroeber and K. Kroeber 2002; Scheper-Hughes 2002:355–364; K. Kroeber and C. Kroeber 2003; Starn 2004; Sackman 2010; Clifford 2013:91–191; and Burrill 2001, 2004, 2011. I have also had access to four recorded oral histories of Ishi (Swartzlow 1971, Pope 1972, Davis 1973, Strange 1976). Burrill's books are the fullest source of information about Ishi's time in Oroville; Sackman's book is the fullest modern source for his San Francisco life. The Proposal to Un-Name Kroeber Hall referred only to Starn 2004.

5. See https://hearstmuseum.berkeley.edu/ishi/.

6. As evidence of Kroeber's allegedly racist actions, the Proposal asserted that Ishi's "white benefactors ... taught [him] racial slurs as a way to refer to Black and Chinese people" (DKH 1); the BNRC made a point of citing the charge (DKH 3). There is no evidence for this assertion. Ishi knew many people, and it was "from his many hours of conversation with [small boys] and with Museum visitors [that] he learned much of his English" (Pope 1920:188).

7. On these events see Madley 2016:318–321 and Curtin 1898:519, respectively.

8. For this letter, see C. Kroeber and K. Kroeber 2002:362-365

9. For Waterman's statement see "First Train Ride" 1911.

10. For Ishi's dislike of Sam Batwi, see Waterman 1918:65.

11. The following quotations are successively from C. Kroeber and K. Kroeber 2002:370, Kroeber 1911c, Kroeber 1912a:306, C. Kroeber and K. Kroeber 2002:378, Waterman 1918:68, and Pope 1920:193.

12. On Berkeley's racially exclusionary zoning history, see Weiss 1986.

13. As Hearst's adverb *fully* shows, she meant *exploit* in the sense "make full use of," not "take unfair or unethical advantage of." Her classist disdain of "the show business" was also manifest in disapproval of her son's relationships with showgirls and actresses (Nickliss 2018:110–111).

14. For this correspondence, see RDA Box 22.

15. See T. Kroeber 1961:147–178.

16. Ray Clar described Ishi's coat in a letter to Anne Rothkopf (November 1973, C. Raymond Clar papers, BANC MSS 75/66 c, Box 2, Bancroft Library, UC Berkeley). For Ishi's cats, see "Ishi Wants" 1911.

17. A written version of his oral remarks also survives (Kuhn 1967–78).

18. See also T. Kroeber 1970:80–92 and Le Guin 2004b:13.

19. This quotation (emphasis original) is from a 6 February 1961 letter to Jane Richardson Hanks, included among other material collected in Hanks 1951–2002. Starn (2004:160–161) wrote that Theodora Kroeber "exaggerated" her husband's grief over Ishi, but his professional correspondence likewise exhibited almost no emotional reaction to the death of his first wife Henriette. For example, just over a week after she died, he wrote this short note to Phoebe Hearst (6 December 1913, ALK Box 2:15): "Dear Mrs. Hearst, Mrs. Kroeber's death has prevented me from answering your inquiry regarding the Cheyenne dictionary. Mr. Petter's work is excellent, and in view of the smallness of the edition, the book would be a valuable addition to the University Library."

20. Kroeber's choice and its consequences decades later were at the center of Orin Starn's book *Ishi's Brain* (2004).

21. See Jacknis 2003 on Ishi's sound recordings.

22. The booklet was informally bound as if finished for Ishi's use, but the project seems incomplete: only a few of Yana's many syllable types are included. If the booklet were actually "reading lessons" meant to help Ishi read English, *si* would have been spelled SEE or SEA, not SI.

23. See https://cla.berkeley.edu/list.php?pplid=304 for these sound recordings, made with Kroeber, Waterman, and San Francisco composer William F. Kretschmer. For transcriptions and discussion see ALK Vol. 9 and Nettl 1965.

24. For these notes see ED 35.1–5, 36.1–5 (Waterman); ED 68.1, pp. 1–45 (Sapir); ED 199 (Gifford and Kroeber); and ALK Ctn 17:30–32 (Kroeber).

25. For Sapir's translations of these terms, see Sapir and Swadesh 1960:158. I have generally modernized Kroeber's manuscript spellings to accord with Golla's (2011:102) phonological analysis. Note that *c* and *j* are postalveolar affricates; I use an apostrophe (') for the glottal stop.

26. The meaning of *-k'al* is unknown; *-la* and *-si*, respectively, are the nominal absolute and the verbal past-present suffixes (Sapir and Swadesh 1960). In the verb forms cited here, *-si* causes lengthening of the vowel in the previous syllable.

27. Linguistically, Kroeber's transcriptions clarify a Yahi phonetic process in which *h* and *'* are inserted between short vowels and certain consonants. Sapir (1923:288) expressed doubt about *w* as a trigger, but *ju**h**wajuusi* (= *ju* + *-waju* + *-si*) is a clear example. Laryngeal incrementation of this kind is a feature of multiple Indigenous languages of the area (Gensler 1986, Buckley 1992, Golla 2011:102). Its distribution will cast light on language contact, phonetics, and phonology in northern California.

28. The same conclusion is supported by numerous mini-paradigms elicited in Sapir's work with Ishi, such as the following: *hahduwilgamsi* "she comes back from N," *hahduwiltkiisi* "from E," *hahduwilwajuusi* "from S," *hahduwilxaujuusi* "from W" (ED 68.1, p. 42).

29. The example is from Sam Batwi's story "Bluejay's Journey" (Sapir 1910:57). The verb contains the root *da-* "look," the directional suffixes *-ri* "down" and *-gam* "from the north," and the first-person singular future suffix *-sit'oo'*.

30. For some of Vizenor's other discussions of Ishi, see Vizenor 1995, 2003, 2008.

31. For her scholarly work see Deloria 1932, 1944, and Boas and Deloria 1941; for her literary work see Deloria 1988 and Rice 1992.

32. A visit to the Ishi Wilderness frames Smith's (2022) discussion of Ishi and Kroeber.

33. An undated letter from Theodora Kroeber to Ursula Le Guin (ULKG Box 65) indicates that Le Guin, her husband Charles, and her brother Theodore expressed their dislike of the book's subtitle even before its publication.

34. Nearly complete inventories based on their notes have been published by Baumhoff (1957:49–54) and Burrill (2011:210–233).

35. See Sapir and Swadesh 1960:124 for the verb *mauma* "teach, tell." The suffix *-yauna* derives nouns from verbs. The derived word *maumaiyauna* is known in this form only from Ishi (ED 36.1, p. 1, with Waterman; ED 68.5, pp. 23–24, with Sapir). Sapir (1910:6) transcribed it with *ô* in the first syllable as *mô'maiyauna* in the first line of Sam Batwi's narrative "Flint Boy." The Yana *maumaiyauna* is the same kind of story as the Yurok *chpeyuer'* (chapter 6) or the Karuk *pikvah*

(Lang 1994). For English translations of Ishi's stories, see Ishi et al. 2002; Luthin and Hinton 2003a,b; and Perry 2003.

36. For these sentences in Sapir's manuscript, see ED 68.5, pp. 23–24. The verbs are *bai-* "hunt deer," *juwa'c'i-* "hunt small game," and *galaahi-* "fish, trout" (only a nominal form in Sapir and Swadesh 1960), with the suffixes *-ru* "go to do (something)," *-'andi*, and *-'* (narrative infinitive).

37. For the beginning of the Story of Lizard, see Ishi et al. 2002:159, edited from Sapir's manuscript (ED 68.5, p. 25).

38. Edith and Frances were seven and six, respectively, when Ishi came to San Francisco.

39. In the quoted sentence, the noun stems are *jau-* "grasshopper" and *juri-* "snow," combined with *-'a* (causative), *-ti* (clitic quotative), and *-k'u* (absolute). The translation by Perry (2003:292) is based on Sapir's manuscript (ED 68.5, p. 24).

40. The text and translation are from Sapir's manuscript (ED 68.5, p. 24); cf. Perry 2003:292. The second sentence ends with the quotative clitic *-ti*; the third sentence has the verb *gi't'ab'-* "tell, teach" with the indirect-object suffix *-pau*, the present-tense suffix *-si*, and the third-person passive suffix *-wa*. Apparently *gi't'ab'-* and *mauma* were near-synonyms in Ishi's usage: Sapir elicited a pair *maumaasiwaaji* "you teach me" and *gi't'ap'pausiwaa'ma* "I teach you" (ED 68.1, p. 29).

NOTES FOR CHAPTER 8

1. Kroeber's manuscript (ALK Ctn 12:19, p. 95j, quoted in the epigraph of this chapter) was much reorganized in the published version (Kroeber 1976: 443–444).

2. The global scope of UC "somatological collections" at the start of the twentieth century was described by Putnam (1905:33) as including "unique and abundant material" from Egypt; "a large series of mummies and skulls" from Peru; "skulls from ancient Etruria; from China; and skulls and skeletons from New Mexico, Utah, Colorado, several of the Plains tribes, the Chinook and other Indians of the Columbia River region, from Alaska, and from Mexico." From California, there was "an extensive collection of skulls from Santa Rosa Island and a considerable number of both skulls and skeletons from other localities, especially the San Francisco Bay region."

3. See Fine-Dare 2002, 2007, and Colwell 2017:74–88 on the Indigenous advocacy that helped lead to NAGPRA. Foundational Native scholarship includes Nason 1971.

4. See Rosen 1980:15.

5. See Alexander 2020 and Koseff 2020.

6. In North America, wrote Rowe (1962:408), "there was effectively no time depth in archaeology at all. Archaeological research consisted of classifying and describing the monuments, usually with a view to tracing regional differences. This kind of activity naturally had no attractions to someone who was interested in 'history' in Kroeber's sense." See also Steward 1973:38–43 and Baumhoff 1980:843.

7. For these projects, see Johnson 2018b,c (Palenque); Agarwal et al. 2015 and Trombley et al. 2018 (Villamagna); Kvapil and Shelton 2019 (Aidonia); Cradic 2017, 2018 (Tel Megiddo); and Anwar 2021 (Egypt).

8. On the collaboration, see Bader et al. 2021.

9. See Meloche et al. 2021 and Raff 2022 for discussion of such collaborative research.

10. See Fleming 2010, 2021 on Germanic settlers and Romano-British indigenes.

11. On selected aspects of second-millennium Crete, see Duhoux and Morpurgo Davies 2007–14 (Linear B writing), Shelmerdine 2008 and Schoep 2018 (artistic traditions), and Younger and Rehak 2008 and Girella 2020 (mortuary evidence).

12. See Haak et al. 2015 and Papac et al. 2021.

13. On the chronology of Indo-European language spread, see Anthony and Ringe 2015 and Chang et al. 2015.

14. On Boas's (1912) study of cranial plasticity among immigrants, intended to undermine racial typologies, see Sparks and Jantz 2002, 2003 and Gravlee et al. 2003a,b.

15. See Kroeber and Strong 1924:128.

16. See Hunt and Smyly 1933:3–12 and Carden 1974:57–71 on this papyrus fragment.

17. On discoveries like these, see also Schneider 2021:50–51.

18. The cases mentioned in this paragraph were reported in "Unearthed Indian Skeletons" 1908, "Found Twenty" 1909, "Indian Skeletons" 1916, and "Twenty-Two Skeletons" 1908.

19. See Ingram 1998.

20. The museum's public catalog identifies 398 items as human remains from the Ellis Landing mound (CA-CCo-295), 927 from the Emeryville mound (CA-Ala-309), 565 from the West Berkeley mound (CA-Ala-307), and 13 from the Faculty Club (CA-Ala-308).

21. For details, see Dinkelspiel 2020, 2021 and LaPena and LeBeau 2021.

22. An exception is a remarkable eagle skull with an abalone pendant (PAHMA 12-1738), which is now apparently lost. Some of the objects from this collection were not continuously kept by the museum. For example, according to the museum's online catalog (PAHMA 12-1731), parts of at least one ancestral body from the same site (including part of a face that had been pierced by an arrow) were among thousands of human bones or bone fragments on loan from the museum to faculty curator Tim White for up to fifteen years (or sometimes longer), until November 2020.

23. See Merriam 1909 and Stock 1918 on Hawver Cave.

24. See Loud and Harrington 1929:1–2; for other accounts of the Saiduka'a, see Bengston 2002:A15–18.

25. For representative news, see "University Professor Inspects Guano Cave" 1911.

26. Heizer and Napton (1970:5) wrote that Loud "collected approximately 10,000 archaeological specimens," not all of which came to UC. The UC anthropology museum catalog lists 2,569 entries from Loud in Nevada; 135 are human remains.

27. Tuohy and Napton (1986) used newer instrumental methods to date two of Lovelock Cave's famous duck decoys to circa 2,080 and circa 2,250 years ago.

28. See Bengston 2002:E67, quoting McGuckian 1996.

29. Loud's recordings of Dandy Bill and John Stephens speaking place names in Wiyot and in the Whilkut dialect of Hupa, respectively, are indexed through the California Language Archive (http://cla.berkeley.edu/collection/11054).

30. Platt (2011:90) wrote that "Kroeber wanted Loud to devote all his time on Indian Island [Tuluwat] to purely archaeological matters" and "implied" that Kroeber wanted Loud not to document the 1860 Tuluwat massacre. In fact Kroeber had told Loud to do "exploration of at least one mound" (12 July) or to "excavate one or two of the most promising mounds" (30 August) anywhere along Humboldt Bay. He was responding to Loud's 24 August report that he was "getting something of value from the [white] pioneers" when he wrote on 30 August that "I know of no reason why you should be operating as far away from Humboldt Bay as Little river, nor why you should be planning to work up a historical paper, or any kind of a paper, except along the lines of work specified in your instructions."

31. For example, Kroeber wrote on 16 September that "I have not yet been able to get from your letters a clear idea of what you have been doing, or even of what you have been trying to do."

32. On the Kroeber-Loud correspondence while Loud was at Lovelock Cave in 1912, see Heizer 1970:1.

33. The others were Nels Nelson and David Morse (Long 1998:104). Kroeber's letters to Goddard are dated 26 April, 2 May, 11 May, 12 June, and 8 August 1906 (RDA Vol. 6).

34. Goddard had tried to do part of the work earlier, but because of the earthquake, he reported, Inverness "is in complete ruins and contains no accom[m]odation whatever," so that it would be necessary to return with camping gear (2 May 1906, RDA Box 12:3).

35. Several years later came a puzzling footnote. In 1910, BIA officials in Washington asked California special agent C. E. Kelsey for "a report in the Ukiah skeleton case," as he put it to Kroeber on 23 July. He told Kroeber in January 1911 that Ruddick said each burial had included valuables for which UC should make payment. The Band wanted $50 each "for the four captains of the band" and $60 for another casket. There was also a suggestion that the wrong remains had been returned, though Kroeber's 1906 correspondence makes that seem unlikely. Differences between the parties' accounts, Kelsey wrote, "might indicate that the proper bones had not been returned or that the bones [the Yokayo Indians] talk of had never been taken." He suggested that Kroeber and Ruddick should meet to resolve the matter. For the Kelsey-Kroeber correspondence, see RDA Box 14:2 (23 July 1910; 18, 19, and 22 or 23 January 1911).

36. An otherwise perspicacious account by Platt (2012/13) erroneously stated that Barrett "supervised the excavation," the students "help[ed]" him, and Kroeber "lied" in saying otherwise. I should note that I have not had access to a later report by Kelsey that Platt mentioned.

37. Barrett's familiarity with local conditions is illustrated by the meticulously detailed description of rancheria, village, and camp sites south of Ukiah in his dissertation (Barrett 1908:168–182). For the *Republican Press* piece see "Indian Skull" 1906.

38. For his publications in this area see, for example, Kroeber 1926, 1926–37, 1944b. For a study of Peruvian human remains he collected, see Williams et al. 2001.

39. The English-language manuscript from which Kroeber 1942 was translated is in ALK Ctn 4:38.

40. Kroeber and Tello may have met as early as 1915, when they both gave presentations at the Second Pan American Scientific Congress in Washington (Kroeber 1917b, Tello 1917).

41. See Tello 1913, 1923a (linguistics), Tello 1923b (ethnography), and, for example, Tello 1917 and Tello and Mejía Xesspe 1959–79 (archaeology).

42. A friendship is not evident in Kroeber's letters, but was reported by Peruvian archaeologist John Rowe (1962:503).

43. See Heaney 2018:355–356 and Padilla Deza 2018:45–47, 242, 254.

44. See Tello 1909 and Mesía-Montenegro 2018.

45. For Chavín de Huántar, see Tello 1943, 1960. I have benefited from discussions of broader historical, social, and intellectual contexts by de la Cadena (2000), Molinié (2004), Mesía-Montenegro (2006), Castillo (2009), Ramón Joffré (2014, especially pp. 55–72), Tantaleán (2014:44–55), and Padilla Deza (2018:35–43).

46. This was not a pluralistic view, as shown by his assessment of Indigenous languages in the same legislative debate: "The language of the Indians is a dead language, a historical monument, similar to one of those monoliths that our ancestors have left us, worthy of admiration and study, only for its historical significance." The chamber is said to have applauded (Padilla Deza 2018:97). As Mesía-Montenegro (2006:147) pointed out, Tello (1923b:2) also referred to Indigenous people of the Peruvian Amazon as "people of a lower degree of civilization."

47. For further discussion see Haarmann 1991, Smith 2007, and Stephan 2017.

48. This negative ideology continued in the twentieth century. Wood (1998:186) observed that Anwar Sadat's assassins "were still able to identify him as a non-Islamic tyrant, crying out at their trial: 'We have killed Pharaoh!' "

49. See https://www.nps.gov/subjects/nagpra/law-and-policy.htm for the federal law, legislative history, and regulations. Cal NAGPRA (AB 978, 2001) was amended in 2018 and again in 2020 (AB-275); see http://nahc.ca.gov/calnagpra/.

50. See Bray 1996, Gosden 2001, and Liebmann 2008. Liebmann argued that the phrase "relationship of shared group identity," which replaced "continuity of group identity" as NAGPRA was being drafted, "makes space for a slightly more fluid, flexible, and socially constructed notion of identity" (82). I hope his interpretation is right and that those who implement the law accept it, but this is not what I have observed. The evidence noted by Gerstenblith (2002:192–193) suggests that the shift from "continuity" to "relationship" was motivated by the understanding that there are often temporal gaps in the historical and archaeological records and that such gaps should not preclude a successful NAGPRA claim.

51. Information about this example (site CA-SDI-525) is drawn from UC documents made available by Ross Frank (https://pages.ucsd.edu/~rfrank/NAGPRAdocs.html). On repatriation from the Fowler Museum see Padilla 2019 and Teeter et al. 2021.

52. Biological evidence has sometimes been determinative. A well-known controversy involving ancestral remains concerned the Ancient One ("Kennewick Man"), who died more than eight thousand years ago and whose skeletonized

body was found in 1996 by the Columbia River in Washington State (Thomas 2000, Burke et al. 2008, Owsley and Jantz 2014, Colwell 2017:243–247). The conflict ended when DNA analysis by Rasmussen et al. (2015) showed a biological relationship to members of the nearby Confederated Tribes of the Colville Reservation.

53. See *Cherokee Nation v. Georgia*, 30 U.S. 1 (1831), and *Elk v. Wilkins*, 112 U.S. 94 (1884).

54. This comment was made at an online meeting I attended.

55. Kroeber (1910a:239) wrote, "Nothing has been published regarding the dialects of northern Alameda or Contra Costa counties." This may imply that he was uncertain about the precolonial inhabitants of Berkeley and adjoining places.

56. See, for example, Luby et al. 2006 and Lightfoot 2018, respectively.

57. See Kroeber 1972:79. The bow is made of willow and horse sinew, the arrows of arrowweed (PAHMA 1–1716a); to buy them, Kroeber used $1 from Hearst funds (ALK Ctn 10:9, p. 53).

58. These texts are from Lame Billy (Kroeber 1976:47–54, A6), Mack of Weitchpec (289–291, F4), Dave Durban (305–307, H2), Saints' Rest Jack (329–331, K3), Muerekw Jack (364–365, P4), Captain Spott (420–422, X1; 426–427, X8), and Johnny Shortman (443–444, Z3, quoted at the beginning of this chapter). The quotation is from the final record of CLA 24-1001 (#14-542, partly transcribed in ALK Ctn 12:31, pp. 12–13); unclear is the force of *cheetaa*, in later usage a negative-polarity intensifier "(not) at all."

59. This expression has the perfect(ive) preverb *keech* and the noninflected form *keemchuen* (ALK Ctn 12:37, p. 19).

60. Kroeber's notes (ALK Ctn 12:41, pp. 34–39) do not always clearly show which information is from Mennow (whom he called Menol') and which is from Pilgrim.

61. On Yurok condor restoration, see "Yurok Tribe Celebrates" 2010, Smith 2020, and Li et al. 2022.

62. This text was recorded on five cylinders (CLA 24-1015) and transcribed by Kroeber with Weitchpec Frank (ALK Ctn 12:26, pp. 35–50) and by Waterman with Catherine Goodwin (in part: ED 99.4.11, pp. 25–32; ED 99.4.12, pp. 5–9). See Kroeber 1976:387–406 for translations of Jim's narratives. Jim was living with the Pilgrim family at the time of the 1920 census and was identified as Maggie Pilgrim's father.

63. Both the noun *mer'wermery* "headwaters" and the verb *mer'wermeryk'* "it flows from (a source)" are derived from the root *me'wom-* "come from" and the suffix *-ery(k)-* "stream" (Proulx 1985:356). See Spott and Kroeber 1942:250–251

and Robins 1958:162–163 for Spott's and Brantner's stories about *mer'wermery 'ue-mey'*. Other Yurok stories about the origin of waters have been told by Lame Billy (Kroeber 1976:134–145, A18), Pechuesloo (Kroeber 1976:412–414, V1), and Ann of 'Espew (Kroeber 1976:460–465, BB3). In Pechuesloo's story, ocean water was made from urine and river water was made from saliva (Kroeber 1976:413n10); and in some Karuk creation stories (Kroeber and Gifford 1980:48–49, 275–276, 278–279), water comes into the streams from the tears of one of the prehuman inhabitants of the world.

64. See Leslie 2021 (Klamath Justice Coalition) and Shane Anderson 2020 (Hillman).

65. Figueroa's recordings from 1927 are at CLA 24-2733 through 24-2736. A recording of the UCLA event is accessible online (Bommelyn et al. 1977).

NOTES FOR CHAPTER 9

This chapter's epigraph is quoted from Kroeber 1950:98.

1. Platt, who has also called Kroeber "extraordinarily racist" (Scheer 2021), wrote that Kroeber encouraged his colleague E. W. Gifford's physical anthropology work and that this led to "essentialist scientific quackery to justify the civilizational superiority of white Europeans and innate inferiority of Native peoples." Racist pseudoscience is legion, but Platt identified no examples drawing on Gifford's work. Platt has also mistakenly cast Gifford as a eugenicist, asserting that his "search for the biological basis of social differences was consistent with the ideas and assumptions of the racist eugenics movement" (2009, 2011:96). But the work Platt cited (Gifford 1926b) never mentioned any social traits of California populations or differences among them, let alone hinting at a biological basis for such traits or differences. In fact, Gifford shared Kroeber's opposition to eugenics. In one scholarly publication he stressed the "fundamental distinctness" of cultural and physical traits (Gifford 1926a:58); his studies of California and other cultural groups (e.g., Gifford 1929b, 1936, 1939) ignored physical traits entirely. "Humanity stands on a vast foundation of common characters [i.e., traits]," he wrote in a magazine article (Gifford 1929a:72), "beside which the differentiating characters of race are dwarfed into insignificance." Gifford even mentioned linguistic evidence against racism: the complex grammatical structures and multilingualism found in "primitive" societies prove "equality in innate mental endowment" (73). These details matter because state officials have adopted Platt's mistake. According to California's Native American Heritage Commission (2021), citing Platt, "Gifford followed up on Prof. Kroeber's work by testing Native American skulls to validate his eugenic theories." Whether "his" refers to Gifford or Kroeber, this statement is false.

2. For careful documentation of the California eugenics program, see Stern 2015.

3. This letter was written to H. D. Snapp of Wichita Falls, Texas. Snapp's letter to Kroeber, which seems not to survive, was apparently about a marriage within his family to a Native person.

4. The title of Kroeber's 26 February 1914 lecture is noted in ALK Box 2:16 (9 April 1914). Articles about it were published by newspapers in Atlanta, Baltimore, Chattanooga, Chicago, Decatur, Indianapolis, Lincoln (Nebraska), Los Angeles, Minneapolis, Oakland, Pittsburgh, San Francisco, Sioux City, Tacoma, Topeka, Wichita, and elsewhere.

5. For the Stanford report see Chappelle et al. 2020; see also Rutherford 2021.

6. See Jackson and Depew 2017:59–92. They concluded (219–220) that Pinker may not have read any of Kroeber's work. Pinker (2002:23) also stated that Boas "considered European civilization superior to tribal cultures"—a perspective that would fit comfortably with his own Enlightenment "humanism" (Pinker 2011, 2018). In fact Boas (1920b:312) wrote that the "evolutionary" hypothesis that all cultures evolve in a general, uniform direction "implies the thought that our modern Western European civilization represents the highest cultural development towards which all other more primitive cultural types tend, and that, therefore, retrospectively, we construct an orthogenetic development towards our own modern civilization. It is clear that if we admit that there may be different ultimate and co-existing types of civilization, the hypothesis of one single general line of development cannot be maintained." It is the idea of "different ultimate and co-existing types of civilization" that Boas and Kroeber defended. See Micale 2018 on Pinker's understanding of "tribal cultures" and the impacts of European colonialism and imperialism.

7. On roadblocks, see Rollings 2004. In the case at hand, unfortunately, Jones missed the registration deadline (17 November 1904, ALK Box 19:32).

8. Sackman (2010:84) mistakenly interpreted Barrett's letters as having been written by Kroeber. They survive as unsigned carbon copies, but Kelsey addressed Barrett by name.

9. For this work by the Indian Board of Cooperation, see Hendrick 1976:177.

10. See Deloria and Lyttle 1984:41. A less positive assessment was that of Akins and Bauer (2021:246–251), who criticized "the one-dimensionality and heavy-handed nature" of Collier's vision.

11. On Indian Land Claims Commission cases, see Stewart 1961, 1978; Heizer and Kroeber 1976; and Ray 2006.

12. My perspective thus differs from that of Sowry (2020:289), who wrote, "Although occasionally sympathetic towards the suffering and marginalization of contemporary Native Americans, Alfred L. Kroeber was hardly an advocate for their causes or rights."

13. These include Chimariko (109); Lile'ek Wappo (221); Southern Yana and Yahi (339); Salinan (368); Ohlone (Costanoan, 464); Esselen (544); Toloim (610); Tataviam (611); Vanyume (614); Alakwisa (797); Delta, Tuholi, Toltichi, Koyeti, Apiachi, and Fresno Valley Yokuts (442, 478, 481–482, 484, 489); New River Shasta, Konomihu, and Okwanuchu (889); and Gabrielino (910); as well as "the societies of southwestern Oregon" (4).

14. Kroeber's Ohlone statement was mischaracterized by Akins and Bauer (2021:302), according to whom he "declared the Verona Band extinct." In fact he wrote about the "Costanoan group." Kroeber had visited Verona, documented multiple languages there, and called Plains Miwok its "prevailing language" (chapter 3). He could not have judged the Verona Band "extinct," but he probably did believe, in line with the presuppositions of cultural essentialism, that it was "mixed" and thus not culturally or linguistically Ohlone "as far as all practical purposes are concerned."

15. For many details and valuable discussion see Field et al. 2013; Leventhal et al. 1994; Field 1999, 2003; Lightfoot 2005:229–233; Milliken et al. 2009; Laverty 2010; Field et al. 2013; and Cambra et al. 2017; see also Bureau of Indian Affairs 2001. See Barron 2022 for an insightful analysis of Kroeber's work in relation to the Dorrington memorandum and other government policy questions.

16. Leventhal et al. (1994:312–314) quoted two later academic books that drew on Kroeber's Ohlone statement before adding that popular authors "probably did not read Kroeber." The USC colleague was Richard Slobodin (letter to Kroeber, 28 April 1948, ALK Box 4:5).

17. Since the Verona Band was a recognized tribal entity, what the Muwekma Ohlone Tribe seeks is not recognition de novo but reaffirmation of a previously recognized status. I am indebted to Les Field for clarifying this point to me.

18. See Cambra et al. 2017:65. Predecessors had produced lists with suggested land purchases in 1906, 1914, and 1923 (Bureau of Indian Affairs 2001:5–7, Field 2003:86–87).

19. In seven cases he wrote that "provision should be made to secure land," in seven less clear cases "it is probable that it will be necessary to purchase land," and in two final cases "additional purchases will be necessary" for bands that already had government land.

20. There was a Verona Station (figure 3.4), but there was no "town of Verona," as Cambra et al. (2017:52) remarked, so Dorrington may not have worked very diligently.

21. See also Field et al. 2013:301.

22. For scholarly mention see, for example, Laverty 2010:353–354, Soza War Soldier 2013:228–229, Becks 2018:109–110, and Panich 2020:159.

23. See also Maddox 1995 and Field 1999.

24. See Bureau of Indian Affairs 2001:10.

25. Kroeber's emphasis suggests, as Coast Miwok archaeologist Peter Nelson (2021:469–470) commented, "that the most salient point about our history is our 'discovery' by an Englishman rather than a Spaniard." Kelly (1978:415) wrote that Coast Miwok "people and culture have disappeared," but recent scholarship has shown how Coast Miwok communities instead persisted at Tomales Bay and elsewhere, continuing and transforming their lifeways throughout the nineteenth and twentieth centuries (Schneider and Panich 2019, Schneider 2021, Panich et al. 2021).

26. See Lévi-Strauss 1966, Gough 1968, Deloria 1969, Césaire 1972, Willis 1972, Asad 1973, Lewis 1973, and Stauder 1974.

27. This letter is from 25 June 1909 (ALK Box 2:4). Barrows later became UC president; UC Berkeley's Barrows Hall was unnamed in 2020 (chapter 10).

28. The head of the ethnology division was an American anthropologist, Merton Miller, whose letter to Kroeber was dated 7 August 1909 (ALK Box 30:47). Some of the analytic work that Kroeber envisaged was found in his later monograph on Philippine peoples (Kroeber 1919b), but with no hint of "political and other practical significance." There he commented only that the Americans had brought Philippine peoples closer to "participation in contemporaneous Western civilization" (213).

29. See Keefer 1988 on the ASTP; see Cowan 1975 and Velleman 2008 on linguists' role (and a precursor, the Intensive Language Program). Theodora Kroeber's (1970:179–185) discussion is also worth reading, but gave too much credit to Kroeber as an innovator of pedagogical methods that in fact predated his involvement.

30. A committee headed by Kroeber and Sontag (who had worked with Kroeber on ASTP) proposed an "undergraduate regional group major" to UC President Robert Sproul (10 August 1944, RDA Box 149).

31. See T. Kroeber 1961, T. Kroeber and Heizer 1968, and Heizer and T. Kroeber 1979.

32. See Horner 1985, Senior 1996, Darnell 2001:251–257, 2021, Baker-Cristales 2012, Clifford 2013:175–189, Phillips 2019, and Pandian 2019:97–103.

33. "The Dowry of Angyar" (later called "Semley's Necklace") became the prologue to Le Guin's first novel, *Rocannon's World* (1966).

34. See Baker-Cristales 2012:23–24.

35. These Yurok file slips are in ALK Boxes 36–38; Kroeber's Mojave lexical notes are on some four thousand file slips (ALK Box 35; Ctn 14, File box 1).

Many individual slips, like the one in Figure 9.4, were completed under Kroeber's direction rather than in his own hand.

NOTES FOR CHAPTER 10

1. UCB documents relating to the unnaming of Kroeber Hall are reproduced in DKH (Garrett 2021).

2. The BNRC was mistaken in its assertion that "the collection of the remains of Native American ancestors" is "labeled 'Salvage Anthropology' by some scholars." Salvage anthropology (memory documentation) was not the collection of ancestral remains but a style of ethnographic fieldwork; see chapter 2.

3. The cut-and-paste work left telltale traces: the phrase "listed above" was retained even though policy 4400 was not listed in Christ's letter; and the BNRC's expression "discrimination against and disdain for Native Americans" was simplified by replacing "and disdain for" with an apparent tab character (visible as a long horizontal space).

4. The only view or writing mentioned was Kroeber's view that the Ohlone group was "extinct as far as all practical purposes are concerned," surely a naïve judgment rather than a view that is opposed to Berkeley values. As noted in chapter 9, even the Muwekma Ohlone Indians in 1992 regarded Kroeber's assessment as "understandable."

5. See Warma 2018 on LeConte.

6. I am grateful to Adam Benkato for calling my attention to Sinclair's critique.

7. A fifth is the historian and political scientist Bernard Moses; in February 2023, UC Berkeley's Moses Hall was unnamed.

8. Sarich notoriously also taught an introductory anthropology class in which students learned that "homosexuals 'choose' their sexual orientation" and that complex social behaviors, like "crime, college performance, gender roles, athletic ability, even career choice, can be understood in terms of our genetic makeup" (Selvin 1991).

9. See Hudetz and Brewer 2023 on White's use of Native remains at Berkeley.

10. See Hirschkind 2020a,b. A Berkeley anthropologist later wrote that "the Department of Anthropology and Chancellor Christ decided to accept an anti-intellectual, populist attack on Kroeber" (Scheper-Hughes 2022).

11. For the following details see Gregory 1965:78; Robinson 1991:34–36, 43, 81, 392; and Bernstein 2021:13.

12. On Cerro de Pasco, see Brass 1990, Deustua 1994, Bedoya Garland 1997, and Brechin 2006:240–241.

13. According to Smith (2003), Hearst's Deadwood employees in the late 1870s manipulated an election, beat up a newspaper editor, and "killed a man who refused to sell his property. But witnesses disappeared . . . and the trial ended in acquital." Fielder (1970:63–66) was skeptical (Hearst "was not a man addicted to murder") and Bernstein (2021:127–131) was uncertain (Hearst's guilt "went unconfirmed"). Hearst mining investments continued in the twentieth century; George and Phoebe's son William Randolph Hearst, after whom UC Berkeley's Hearst Theater is named, tolerated coercive and unsafe practices in Cerro de Pasco and in Deadwood, South Dakota, and the murder of workers (Lundberg 1936:176–193)—to say nothing of his infamous work as a propagandist.

14. See Finacom 2011, "A Master Plan" 2019, "Our Founder" n.d., and Epstein n.d.

15. See Ram 2014 and Salah 2019.

16. On the early entanglements of American universities and slavery, see Wilder 2013, Harris et al. 2019, and Brown-Nagin et al. 2022.

17. The webpage featuring this statement was accessible in 2022 (as part of https://builders.berkeley.edu/), but had been removed by March 2023.

18. See Lee et al. 2020; cf. Nash 2019. Commenting in an article about the Morrill acts (Royster 2022), UC Berkeley chancellor Christ wrote that "we, as a university, must take immediate action to acknowledge past wrongs, build trusting and respectful relationships, and accelerate change and justice for our Native Nations and Tribal communities." But despite good intensions, the examples discussed in this chapter show that colonial assumptions are baked in.

19. For the points in this paragraph, see Downey 2007:18 (Levi Strauss invoice), Key 1979 (massacres near Benton), "150 Years" 2018 (miners in jeans), and Madley 2016:85–99, 178–185 (massacres on Nisenan land).

20. See Gregory 1926:31 and Stein 2001:352n9.

21. See Lindberg and Waggoner 1996 and "150 Years" 2018.

22. See Allen 2013:42n11. For *Smilodon*, see Merriam and Stock 1932.

23. See "Meetings" 1930:196–198.

24. On Peder Sather, including the following details, see Sveen 2014. On Berkeley's Sather professorships, see Dow 1965.

25. The news articles quoted in this and the following paragraphs are "A Mossy Mansion" 1893, "Alameda" 1887, "Alameda Antiquities" 1892, and "Indian Monument" 1914. See Pellegatti 2020 for discussion of the 1892 *San Francisco Call* excavation, objects from it in the UC anthropology museum, and the 1914 Alameda shell mound memorial event.

26. William Hansen, the boy on the left in figure 10.5, went on to be a Stanford physicist and was among the founders of microwave electronics (Bloch 1952); at the age of thirty-nine he died of berylliosis, from inhaling beryllium dust in wartime research (Amaldi 2015:217). The other boy, Edwin Otis, died in 1930 at the age of twenty.

27. See Colós et al. 1921:302. Colós was born in 1839 or 1840 and lived as a child south of Alameda, around what are now San Leandro and San Lorenzo (Panich 2020:135).

NOTES FOR CHAPTER 11

1. See Darnell 1990:138.

2. The metaphor is imprecise, because Le Guin's hidden library on Aka is an indigenous creation, not maintained by the Ekumen or by a colonial government in the manner of Kroeber's documentary archive.

3. Another form of cultural expression that Kroeber's research mainly ignored is music (Alarcón-Jiménez et al. 2021), even though he documented music extensively and it was of immense importance in the communities where he worked (Keeling 1992). I am grateful to Elisabeth Le Guin for calling my attention to this point.

4. See Kroeber 1976:18–28; the manuscript is in Kroeber's Yurok notebook 39 (ALK Ctn 12:14, pp. 33–50). I have substituted the spelling Chuerey for Kroeber's Tsuräu.

5. Kroeber's translations are also mistaken, for what it is worth, not indicative of what Billy would have said in Yurok. At the end of his transcript, Kroeber wrote down what can only be interpreted as a garbled set of associations: the white rock was placed "to *hehlkeek* (N.)," the red one "to *perwerh* (E)," the black one "to *puelew* (W)," and the remaining direction is "to *peeshkaahl* (S)." But these translations are wrong: *hehlkeek* means "inland" (i.e., east on the coast); *perwerh* means "south along the coast"; *puelekw* means "downriver" (i.e., north on the coast); and *peeshkaahl* means "ocean" (i.e., west). Something went wrong in Kroeber's interpretation of Billy's words. It may be relevant that Billy told the story in Weitchpec, an inland village where the same directional terms have different English translations.

6. Buckley (1989:440) quoted this comment from Arnold Pilling. Platt (2011:52, 2020b) went so far as to call Kroeber's choice "moral cowardice" without presenting evidence for this charge, that is, evidence that Kroeber knew he should document experiences of genocide and was afraid to do it.

7. See Kroeber 1951b,c and A. Kroeber and C. Kroeber 1962, 1973.

8. See Hale 1972, Hale and Alvarez 1972, Fermino 2000, Feldman 2001, Hale 2001, and Hinton and Hale 2001.

9. On this work see Woodbury and England 2006.

10. Or minimized, as in a thirty-page biographical memoir of Ken Hale by close colleagues who chose to describe his analytic contributions in detail while devoting only two vague paragraphs to his decades of work supporting language reclamation (Halle and Richards 2007:4–5). On the marginalization of community-based language reclamation, see also Leonard 2020. On the treatment of Reichard by Sapir and others, see Mattina 2019.

11. I am not suggesting that Chomskyan or generative linguistics was the dominant approach in the field during the 1960s or 1970s—it was not (Newmeyer 2020)—but it was defining in the sense that those who did not accept it felt the need to distinguish themselves or react in some way. This is illustrated by the comments of Mary Haas quoted in the text. For early work in sociolinguistics and the ethnography of communication, see Hymes 1962, Labov 1963, Gumperz and Hymes 1964, and Bright 1966.

12. See, for example, Crystal 2000, Harrison 2007, and Evans 2010.

13. See also Perley 2011, 2012.

14. See, for example, Wong 1999, Leonard and Haynes 2010, Thieberger 2013, and Sallabank 2017. A classic linguistic example was Bloomfield's (1927:437) description of a person who, he said (naming him), "speaks less English than Menomini, and that is a strong indictment, for his Menomini is atrocious. His vocabulary is small, his inflections are often barbarous; he constructs sentences on a few threadbare models. He may be said to speak no language tolerably." This individual was relegated to the linguistic margins by the assumption that fluency means replicating an ancestral code without code-switching or interlanguage.

15. For discussion see, for example, Thomason 2002, 2003 and Mufwene 2003.

16. See Watkins 1937:7 (based on a 1933 dissertation), Haugen 1938:7, and Bloomfield 1942:193. Banda was later the autocratic president of Malawi, and Anderson was an eminent medical sociologist. Montano became a celebrated playwright and director in the Philippines.

17. See Davis et al. 2020.

18. For an overview of Berkeley's Indigenous language and cultural heritage collections, see Garrett et al. 2019.

19. I quote the form *hiiqquq* from Fortescue 1991:49. Kroeber transcribed *ssierqók* (ALK Ctn 9:24, p. 1); in writing *ii* and *u* as *ie* and *o*, Kroeber was accurately rendering the vowel lowering caused by adjacent uvular consonants in Inuit languages. On Inuktun phonological changes, see Holtved 1952 and Fortescue 1991:2–4.

20. This statement was made in a letter to J. P. Harrington (19 February 1954, ALK Box 5:6).

REFERENCES

"150 Years of Light." 2018. Light the Way: The Campaign for Berkeley. https://light.berkeley.edu/p/promise-may-2018/150-years-light/.

Agarwal, Sabrina. 2020. On Anti-racism, Fostering Diversity and the Un-naming of Kroeber Hall. https://www.sabrinaagarwal.com/post/on-anti-racism-fostering-diversity-and-the-un-naming-of-kroeber-hall.

Agarwal, Sabrina C., Patrick Beauchesne, Katherine Kinkopf, and Trent Trombley. 2015. A Bioarchaeological Study of Growth, Aging, and Lifestyle in Medieval Rural Italy. Stahl Field Report 2015, Archaeological Research Facility, UC Berkeley. https://escholarship.org/content/qt12h8b3zf/qt12h8b3zf.pdf.

Ahtone, Tristan, and Robert Lee. 2020. "Ask Who Paid for America's Universities." *New York Times*, 20 May 2020.

Akins, Damon B., and William J. Bauer Jr. 2021. *We Are the Land: A History of Native California*. Oakland: University of California Press.

Alameda. 1887. *San Francisco Examiner*, 28 December 1887, 4.

Alameda Antiquities. 1892. *San Francisco Call*, 17 September 1892, 8.

Alarcón-Jiménez, Ana-María, Raquel Jiménez Pasalodos, and Margarita Díaz-Andreu. 2021. "A Glimpse Behind Closed Doors: Alfred L. Kroeber and the Representation of Native Californian Music." *History and Anthropology*, 2021, 1–19. https://doi.org/10.1080/02757206.2021.1983561.

Alexander, Sage. 2020. "Grave Robbing at UC Berkeley: A History of Failed Repatriation." *Daily Cal*, 5 December 2020.

Allen, Garland E. 2013. "'Culling the Herd': Eugenics and the Conservation Movement in the United States, 1900–1940." *Journal of the History of Biology* 46:31–72.

Alvarez, Albert, and Kenneth Hale. 1970. "Toward a Manual of Papago Grammar: Some Phonological Terms." *International Journal of American Linguistics* 36:83–97.

Amaldi, Ugo. 2015. *Particle Accelerators: From Big Bang Physics to Hadron Therapy*. Translated by Geoffrey Hall. Cham: Springer.

"A Mossy Mansion: The Old Sather Homestead in Alameda." 1893. *San Francisco Chronicle*, 21 May 1893, 12.

"An Indian Who Gave Our College Professors Pointers." 1902. *San Francisco Call*, 16 March 1902, 7.

Anderson, Benedict. 1983. *Imagined Communities: Reflections on the Origin and Spread of Nationalism*. London: Verso.

Anderson, Benedict. 1991. *Imagined Communities: Reflections on the Origin and Spread of Nationalism*. Rev. ed. London: Verso.

Anderson, Patricia M. 2020. *Revitalization Lexicography: The Making of the New Tunica Dictionary.* Tucson: University of Arizona Press.

Anderson, Shane. 2020. "Guardians of the River." American Rivers and Swiftwater Films. https://www.youtube.com/watch?v=e5lcP_9ateE.

Anderton, Alice. 1988. "The Language of the Kitanemuks of California." PhD dissertation, UCLA. https://linguistics.ucla.edu/images/stories/Anderton.1988.pdf.

Andresen, Julie Tetel. 1990. *Linguistics in America 1769–1924: A Critical History.* London: Routledge.

Anthony, David W., and Don Ringe. 2015. "The Indo-European Homeland from Linguistic and Archaeological Perspectives." *Annual Review of Linguistics* 1:13.1–13.21.

Anwar, Yasmin. 2021. A Tomb with a View: Egyptologist Recreates After-Death Experience. *Berkeley News*, 8 March 2021. https://news.berkeley.edu/2021/03/08/a-tomb-with-a-view-egyptologist-recreates-after-death-experience/.

Appiah, Kwame Anthony. 2020. The Defender of Differences: Franz Boas and His Critics. *New York Review of Books*, 28 May 2020. https://www.nybooks.com/articles/2020/05/28/franz-boas-anthropologist-defender-differences/.

Arguedas, José María. 1975. "Razón de ser del indigenismo en el Perú." In *Formación de una cultura nacional indoamericana*, 189–197. Mexico City: Siglo Veintiuno.

Asad, Talal, ed. 1973. *Anthropology and the Colonial Encounter.* London: Ithaca Press.

Babel, Molly, Andrew Garrett, Michael Houser, and Maziar Toosarvandani. 2013. "Descent and Diffusion in Language Diversification: A Study of Western Numic Dialectology." *International Journal of American Linguistics* 79:445–489.

Bader, Alyssa C., Aimée E. Carbaugh, Jessica Bardill, Ripan S. Malhi, Barbara Petzelt, and Joycelynn Mitchell. 2021. "Building Relationships to Shift Accountability: Doing Paleogenomic Research with Indigenous Nations and Ancestors." In *Working with and for Ancestors: Collaboration in the Care and Study of Ancestral Remains*, 166–177. London: Routledge.

Baker, Lee D. 2020. "The Racist Anti-racism of American Anthropology." *Transforming Anthropology* 290:127–142.

Baker, Mark. 1988. *Incorporation: A Theory of Grammatical Function Changing.* Chicago: University of Chicago Press.

Baker-Cristales, Beth. 2012. "Poiesis of Possibility: The Ethnographic Sensibilities of Ursula K. Le Guin." *Anthropology and Humanism* 37:15–26.

Baldwin, Daryl, Leanne Hinton, and Gabriela Pérez-Báez. 2018. "The Breath of Life Workshops and Institutes." In *The Routledge Handbook of Language Revitalization*, edited by Leanne Hinton, Leena Huss, and Gerald Roche, 188–196. New York: Routledge.

Balodis, Uldis. 2016. *Yuki Grammar with Sketches of Huchnom and Coast Yuki.* Berkeley: University of California Press.

Bandurraga, Peter L. 1990. "Gilbert Natches." *Nevada Historical Society Quarterly* 33 (2). http://www.onlinenevada.org/articles/gilbert-natches.

Barret, Leroy C., Harold L. Bender, Leonard Bloomfield, Maurice Bloomfield, Franz Boas, George M. Bolling, Carl D. Buck, et al. 1925. "The Call for the Organization Meeting." *Language* 1:6–7.

Barrett, S. A. 1908. "The Ethno-geography of the Pomo and Neighboring Indians." *University of California Publications in American Archaeology and Ethnology* 6:1–322.

Barron, Nicholas. 2022. Alfred Kroeber's *Handbook* and Land Claims: Anthros, Agents, and Federal (Un)acknowledgment in Native California. *BEROSE International Encyclopaedia of the Histories of Anthropology.* https://www.berose.fr/article2551.html.

Barrows, David P. 1905. *A History of the Philippines.* New York: American Book Company.

Barsh, Russel Lawrence. 1993. "An American Heart of Darkness: The 1913 Expedition for American Indian Citizenship." *Great Plains Quarterly* 13:91–115.

Bashkow, Ira. 2004. "A Neo-Boasian Conception of Cultural Boundaries." *American Anthropologist* 106:443–458.

Bassett, Aidan. 2020. "Rename Buildings to Rectify Racial Injustice." *Daily Cal*, 16 July 2020.

Basso, Keith H. 1988. " 'Speaking with Names': Language and Landscape among the Western Apache." *Cultural Anthropology* 3:99–130.

Bauer, William J., Jr. 2003. "Agricultural Labor, Race, and Indian Policy on the Round Valley Reservation, 1850–1941." PhD dissertation, University of Oklahoma. https://shareok.org/handle/11244/613.

Bauer, William J., Jr. 2009. *We Were All Like Migrant Workers Here: Work, Community, and Memory on California's Round Valley Reservation, 1850–1941*. Chapel Hill: University of North Carolina Press.

Bauer, William J., Jr. 2012. "The Giant and the Waterbaby: Paiute Oral Traditions and the Owens Valley Water Wars." *Boom: A Journal of California* 2:104–117.

Bauer, William J., Jr. 2014a. "Native Californians in the Nineteenth Century." In *A Companion to California History*, edited by William Deverrell and David Igler, 192–214. Malden, MA: Wiley Blackwell.

Bauer, William J., Jr. 2014b. "Stop Hunting Ishi." *Boom: A Journal of California* 4:46–50.

Bauer, William J., Jr. 2016. *California through Native Eyes: Reclaiming History*. Seattle: University of Washington Press.

Bauman, Richard, and Charles L. Briggs. 1990. "Poetics and Performances as Critical Perspectives on Language and Social Life." *Annual Review of Anthropology* 19:59–88.

Baumhoff, M. A. 1957. *An Introduction to Yana Archaeology*. Berkeley: University of California Archaeological Survey, Department of Anthropology, University of California. https://digitalassets.lib.berkeley.edu/anthpubs/ucb/text/ucas040-001.pdf.

Baumhoff, M. A. 1980. "Robert Fleming Heizer 1915–1979." *American Anthropologist* 82:843–847.

Becks, Fanya Sandili. 2018. "Articulations of the Ineffable: Narratives, Engagement, and Historical Anthropology with the Muwekma Tribe of the San Francisco Bay Area." Unpublished PhD dissertation, Stanford University.

Bedoya Garland, Eduardo. 1997. "Bonded Labor, Coercion and Capitalist Development in Perú." *Quaderns de l'Institut Català d'Antropologia* 10:9–38.

Beers, Keiko. 2020. "Exploring Language Endangerment and Language Change in Tohono O'odham." Unpublished PhD dissertation, University of New Mexico. https://digitalrepository.unm.edu/ling_etds/72/.

Benedict, Ruth. 1935. *Zuni Mythology*. New York: Columbia University Press.

Bengston, Ginny. 2002. "Northern Paiute and Western Shoshone Land Use in Northern Nevada: A Class I Ethnographic/Ethnohistoric Overview." US Department of the Interior, Bureau of Land Management, Cultural Resource Series, 12. SWCA Cultural Resources Report No. 02-551. https://www.blm.gov/sites/blm.gov/files/documents/files/Library_Nevada_CulturalResourceSeries12.pdf.

Bennett, Tony, Fiona Cameron, Nélia Dias, Ben Dibley, Rodney Harrison, Ira Jacknis, and Conal McCarthy. 2017. *Collecting, Ordering, Governing: Anthropology, Museums, and Liberal Government*. Durham, NC: Duke University Press.

Bergman, Barry. 2011. "A Century Later, Ishi Still Has Lessons to Teach." *Berkeley News*, 12 September 2011. https://news.berkeley.edu/2011/09/12/century-of-ishi/.

Berkeley Library. n.d. Project IRENE: Using Optical Scanning to Digitize Ethnographic Field Recordings on Wax Cylinders. https://exhibits.lib.berkeley.edu/spotlight/project-irene.

Berman, Howard. 2001. "Yurok Texts." In *Northwest California Linguistics,* edited by Victor Golla and Sean O'Neill, vol. 14 of *The Collected Works of Edward Sapir,* 1015–1038. Berlin: Mouton de Gruyter.

Berman, Judith. 1994. "George Hunt and the Kwak'wala Texts." *Anthropological Linguistics* 36:483–514.

Bernstein, Matthew. 2021. *George Hearst: Silver King of the Gilded Age.* Norman: University of Oklahoma Press.

Berry, Brewton. 1960. "The Myth of the Vanishing Indian." *Phylon* 21:51–57.

Bieder, Robert E. 1992. "The Collecting of Bones for Anthropological Narratives." *American Indian Culture and Research Journal* 16:21–35.

Biestman, Karen. 2003. "Ishi and the University." In *Ishi in Three Centuries,* edited by Karl Kroeber and Clifton Kroeber, 146–154. Berkeley: University of California Press.

Bird, Steven, and Gary Simons. 2003. "Seven Dimensions of Portability for Language Documentation and Description." *Language* 79:557–582.

Blackhawk, Ned, and Isaiah Wilner, eds. 2018. *Indigenous Visions: Rediscovering the World of Franz Boas.* New Haven, CT: Yale University Press.

Blevins, Juliette, and Andrew Garrett. 2007. "The Rise and Fall of *l*-Sandhi in California Algic." *International Journal of American Linguistics* 73:72–93.

Blight, David W. 2018. *Frederick Douglass: Prophet of Freedom.* New York: Simon and Schuster.

Bloch, Felix. 1952. *William Webster Hansen, 1909–1949: A Biographical Memoir.* Washington, DC: National Academy of Sciences.

Bloomfield, Leonard. 1925a. "On the Sound System of Central Algonquian." *Language* 1:130–156.

Bloomfield, Leonard. 1925b. "Why a Linguistic Society?" *Language* 1:1–5.

Bloomfield, Leonard. 1927. "Literate and Illiterate Speech." *American Speech* 2:432–439.

Bloomfield, Leonard. 1942. "Outline of Ilocano Syntax." *Language* 18:193–200.

Boas, Franz. 1887. "The Occurrence of Similar Inventions in Areas Widely Apart." *Science* 9:485–486.

Boas, Franz. 1889. On Alternating Sounds. *American Anthropologist* 2:47–53.

Boas, Franz. 1894. *Chinook Texts.* Washington, DC: US Government Printing Office.

Boas, Franz. 1896. The Limitations of the Comparative Method of Anthropology. *Science* 4:901–908.

Boas, Franz. 1901a. *Kathlamet Texts.* Smithsonian Institution, Bureau of American Ethnology, Bulletin 26, Washington, DC: Government Printing Office.

Boas, Franz. 1901b. "The Mind of Primitive Man." *Science* 13:281–289.

Boas, Franz. 1911a. "Chinook." In *Handbook of American Indian Languages,* edited by Franz Boas, vol. 40 of *Bulletin of the Bureau of American Ethnology,* 559–677. Washington, DC: Government Printing Office.

Boas, Franz, ed. 1911b. *Handbook of American Indian Languages.* Washington, DC: Government Printing Office.

Boas, Franz. 1911c. "Introduction." In *Handbook of American Indian languages,* edited by Franz Boas, vol. 40 of *Bulletin of the Bureau of American Ethnology,* 5–83. Washington, DC: Government Printing Office.

Boas, Franz. 1911d. *The Mind of Primitive Man.* New York: Macmillan.

Boas, Franz. 1912. "Changes in Bodily Form of Descendants of Immigrants." *American Anthropologist* 14:530–562.

Boas, Franz. 1917. "Introductory." *International Journal of American Linguistics* 1: 1–8.

Boas, Franz. 1920a. "The Classification of American Languages." *American Anthropologist* 22:367–376.

Boas, Franz. 1920b. "The Methods of Ethnology." *American Anthropologist* 22:311–321.

Boas, Franz, ed. 1922. *Handbook of American Indian Languages, Part 2.* Washington, DC: Government Printing Office.

Boas, Franz. 1929. "Classification of American Indian Languages." *Language* 5: 1–7.

Boas, Franz. 1934. *Geographical Names of the Kwakiutl Indians.* New York: Columbia University Press.

Boas, Franz. 1936. "History and Science in Anthropology: A Reply." *American Anthropologist* 38:137–141.

Boas, Franz, and Ella Deloria. 1941. *A Dakota Grammar,* vol. 23 of *Memoirs of the National Academy of Science.* Washington, DC: Government Printing Office.

Boas, Franz, and George Hunt. 1902. *Kwakiutl Texts,* vol. 5 of *Memoirs of the American Museum of Natural History.* New York: American Museum of Natural History.

Boas, Franz, and George Hunt. 1906. *Kwakiutl Texts: Second Series,* vol. 14, pt. 1 of *Memoirs of the American Museum of Natural History.* New York: G. E. Stechert.

Boas, Franz, Helene Boas Yampolsky, and Zellig S. Harris. 1947. "Kwakiutl Grammar with a Glossary of the Suffixes." *Transactions of the American Philosophical Society* 37:203–377.

Bommelyn, Loren, Aileen Figueroa, Joy Sundberg, and Charlotte Heth. 1977. Songs and Stories from Native Northwest California. Traditional Music of Native Northwest California: Brush Dance, Feather Dance, and Gambling Songs. Discussion and performances by Loren Bommelyn (Tolowa), Aileen Figueroa (Yurok), Joy Sundberg (Yurok) and Charlotte Heth (Cherokee). Recorded at the UCLA Media Engineering Center on 23 May 1977, during the class session of UCLA Music 153C, Sociology of American Indian music. https://californiarevealed.org/islandora/object/cavpp:17774.

Bowern, Claire. 2018a. "Computational Phylogenetics." *Annual Review of Linguistics* 4:12.1–12.16.

Bowern, Claire. 2018b. "Reflections on Linguistic Fieldwork." In *Reflections on Language Documentation 20 Years after Himmelmann 1998,* edited by Bradley McDonnell, Andrea L. Berez-Kroeker, and Gary Holton, 202–209. Honolulu: University of Hawai'i Press.

Bowern, Claire, and Harold Koch, eds. 2004. *Australian Languages: Classification and the Comparative Method.* Amsterdam: Benjamins.

Bowern, Claire, Patience Epps, Russell Gray, Jane Hill, Keith Hunley, Patrick McConvell, and Jason Zentz. 2011. "Does Lateral Transmission Obscure Inheritance in Hunter-Gatherer Languages?" *PLoS One* 6(9):e25195.

Brass, Tom. 1990. "The Latin American *Enganche* System: Some Revisionist Reinterpretations Revisited." *Slavery and Abolition* 11:74–103.

Bray, Tamara L. 1996. "Repatriation, Power Relations and the Politics of the Past." *Antiquity* 70:440–444.

Brechin, Gray. 2006. *Imperial San Francisco: Urban Power, Earthly Ruin.* Berkeley: University of California Press.

Briggs, Charles L., and Richard Bauman. 1999. " 'The Foundation of All Future Researches': Franz Boas, Native American Texts, and the Construction of Modernity." *American Quarterly* 51:479–528.

Bright, William. 1957. *The Karok Language.* Berkeley: University of California Press.

Bright, William, ed. 1966. *Sociolinguistics: Proceedings of the UCLA Sociolinguistics Conference, 1964.* The Hague: Mouton.

Bright, William. 1968. *A Luiseño Dictionary.* University of California Publications in Linguistics. Berkeley: University of California Press.

Bright, William, and Susan Gehr. 2005. *Karuk Dictionary.* Happy Camp, CA: Karuk Tribe of California.

Brinton, Daniel G. 1895. "The Aims of Anthropology." *Science* 2:241–252.

Broughton, Jack M. 1999. *Resource Depression and Intensification during the Late Holocene, San Francisco Bay: Evidence from the Emeryville Shellmound Vertebrate Fauna.* Berkeley: University of California Press.

Brown, Nellie, Duane Drennon, Elmer Gates, Robert Martin, Rose Martin, Flora Sands, Emmett Van Fleet, and Judith G. Crawford. 1967–1972. Judy Gray Crawford Papers on the Mojave Language. CrawfordJu, Survey of California and Other Indian Languages, University of California, Berkeley. http://dx.doi.org/doi:10.7297/X21N7Z2J.

Brown, Patricia Leigh. 2022. "Indigenous Founders of a Museum Café Put Repatriation on the Menu." *New York Times*, 11 December 2022. https://www.nytimes.com/2022/12/11/arts/design/hearst-museum-ohlone-cafe-repatriate-medina.html.

Brown-Nagin, Tomiko, Sven Beckert, Annette Gordon-Reed, Stephen Gray, Evelynn M. Hammonds, Nancy F. Koehn, Meira Levinson, et al. 2022. *Harvard and the Legacy of Slavery.* Cambridge, MA: Harvard University. https://legacyofslavery.harvard.edu/report.

Bruchac, Margaret M. 2018. *Savage Kin: Indigenous Informants and American Anthropologists.* Tucson: University of Arizona Press.

Buckley, David, Angela Cook, Allen Estes, Paul Farnsworth, and Nazih Fino. 2008. *Geoarchaeological Testing Report for the University of California, Berkeley Student Athlete High Performance Center, Alameda County, California.* Orinda: William Self Associates. https://www.berkeley.edu/news/media/releases/2009/01/stadium-archreport.pdf.

Buckley, Eugene. 1992. "Kashaya Laryngeal Increments, Contour Segments, and the Moraic Tier." *Linguistic Inquiry* 23:487–496.

Buckley, Thomas. 1987. "Dialogue and Shared Authority: Informants as Critics." *Central Issues in Anthropology* 7:13–23.

Buckley, Thomas. 1989. "Suffering in the Cultural Construction of Others: Robert Spott and A. L. Kroeber." *American Indian Quarterly* 13:437–445.

Buckley, Thomas. 1996. " 'The Little History of Pitiful Events': The Epistemological and Moral Contexts of Kroeber's Californian Ethnology." In *Volksgeist as Method and Ethic: Essays on Boasian Ethnography and the German Anthropological*

Tradition, edited by George W. Stocking Jr. and George W. Stocking, 257–297. Madison: University of Wisconsin Press.

Buckley, Thomas. 2002. *Standing Ground: Yurok Indian Spirituality, 1850–1990.* Berkeley: University of California Press.

Building Name Review Committee. n.d. Building Name Review Committee Principles. Office of the Chancellor, University of California, Berkeley, https://chancellor.berkeley.edu/building-name-review-committee/principles.

Bunzel, Ruth. 1932. "Zuñi Katcinas: An Analytical Study." In *Forty-Seventh Annual Report of the Bureau of American Ethnology,* edited by M. W. Stirling. Washington, DC: US Government Printing Office.

Bunzel, Ruth L. 1933. *Zuni Texts.* New York: G. E. Stechert.

Bunzel, Ruth L. 1933–1938. "Zuni." In *Handbook of American Indian Languages, Part 3,* edited by Franz Boas, 385–515. Glückstadt: J. J. Augustin.

Bunzel, Ruth L. 1952. *Chichicastenango.* New York: J. J. Augustin.

Bunzl, Matti. 1996. "Franz Boas and the Humboldtian Tradition: From *Volksgeist* and *Nationalcharakter* to an Anthropological Concept of Culture." In *Volksgeist as Method and Ethic: Essays on Boasian Ethnography and the German Anthropological Tradition,* edited by George W. Stocking Jr. and George W. Stocking. Madison: University of Wisconsin Press.

Bunzl, Matti. 2004. "Boas, Foucault, and the 'Native Anthropologist': Notes Toward a Neo-Boasian Anthropology." *American Anthropologist* 106:435–442.

Bureau of Indian Affairs. 2001. Summary under the Criteria for the Proposed Finding on the Ohlone/Costanoan Muwekma Tribe. https://www.bia.gov/sites/bia.gov/files/assets/as-ia/ofa/petition/111_muwekm_CA/111_pf.pdf.

Burenhult, Niclas, and Stephen C. Levinson. 2008. "Language and Landscape: A Cross-Linguistic Perspective." *Language Sciences* 30:135–150.

Burger, Richard L. 2009. "The Intellectual Legacy of Julio C. Tello." In *The Life and Writings of Julio C. Tello: America's First Indigenous Archaeologist,* edited by Richard L. Burger, 65–88. Iowa City: University of Iowa Press.

Burke, Heather, Claire Smith, Dorothy Lippert, Joe Watkins, and Larry Zimmerman, eds. 2008. *Kennewick Man: Perspectives on the Ancient One.* Walnut Creek, CA: Left Coast Press.

Burrill, Richard. 2001. *Ishi Rediscovered.* Sacramento, CA: Anthro Company.

Burrill, Richard. 2004. *Ishi in His Second World: The Untold Story of Ishi in Oroville.* Susanville, CA: Anthro Company.

Burrill, Richard. 2011. *Ishi's Untold Story in His First World: A Biography of the Last of His Band of Yahi Indians in North America, Parts I and II.* Red Bluff, CA: Anthro Company.

Buzaljko, Grace Wilson. 1988. "Theodora Kracaw Kroeber (1897–1979)." In *Women Anthropologists: A Biographical Dictionary,* edited by Ute Gacs, Aisha Khan, Jerrie McIntyre, and Ruth Weinberg, 188–193. New York: Greenwood Press.

Buzaljko, Grace Wilson. 2003. "Kroeber, Pope, and Ishi." In *Ishi in Three Centuries,* edited by Karl Kroeber and Clifton Kroeber, 48–64. Lincoln: University of Nebraska Press.

Buzaljko, Grace Wilson. n.d. *A. L. Kroeber as Mentor to Women.* Unpublished manuscript. Grace Buzaljko papers, 1945–2009. BANC MSS 2010/246, Bancroft Library, University of California, Berkeley.

Buzaljko, Grace Wilson. n.d. *The Berkeley Anthropologists, 1901–1991.* Unpublished manuscript ("third draft"). Grace Buzaljko papers, 1945–2009. BANC MSS 2010/246, Bancroft Library, University of California, Berkeley.

Caballero, Gabriela, Michael J. Houser, Nicole Marcus, Teresa McFarland, Anne Pycha, Maziar Toosarvandani, and Johanna Nichols. 2008. "Nonsyntactic Ordering Effects in Noun Incorporation." *Linguistic Typology* 12:383–421.

"California Indian Tongue Most Perfect in World." 1909. *San Francisco Examiner,* 8 August 1909.

"California Students Research Federal Recognition and Water Rights." 2015. *Indian Country Today*, 5 March 2015. https://indiancountrytoday.com/archive/california-students-research-federal-recognition-and-water-rights.

Cambra, Rosemary, Alan Leventhal, Monica V. Arellano, Sheila Guzman Schmidt, Gloria E. Arellano Gomez, and Arnold Sanchez. 2017. "An Ethnohistory of Santa Clara Valley and Adjacent Regions: Historic Ties of the Muwekma Ohlone Tribe of the San Francisco Bay Area and Tribal Stewardship Over the *Cashrishmini 'Awweš̓ 'Írek 'Innutka* (Yellow Salt [Alum] Rock Road) Site." In *Report on the Burial and Archaeological Data Recovery Program, Analysis and AMS Dating of Ancestral Muwekma Ohlone Human Remains Recovered from the Cashrishmini 'Awweš̓ 'Írek 'Innutka (Yellow Salt [Alum] Rock Road) Site, CA-SCL-950),* chap. 6, 1–147. San Jose: Report prepared for Santa Clara Valley Transportation Authority. https://works.bepress.com/alan_leventhal/105/.

Campbell, Lyle. 1997. *American Indian Languages: The Historical Linguistics of Native America.* Oxford: Oxford University Press.

Canter, Adam. 2020. "Kin to the Earth: Cheryl Seidner." Northcoast Environmental Center, 30 January 2020. https://www.yournec.org/kin-to-the-earth-cheryl-seidner/.

Carden, Richard. 1974. *The Papyrus Fragments of Sophocles: An Edition with Prolegomena and Commentary.* Berlin: Walter de Gruyter.

Castaneda, Terri A. 2020. *Marie Mason Potts: The Lettered Life of a California Indian Activist.* Norman: University of Oklahoma Press.

Castillo, Victoria A. 2009. "Indigenous 'Messengers' Petitioning for Justice: Citizenship and Indigenous Rights in Peru, 1900–1945." Unpublished PhD dissertation, University of Michigan.

Cesspooch, Ataya, Alyssa Kewenvoyouma, Paloma Sanchez, and Valentin Sierra. 2020. "Native Student Organizations Want to Un-name Kroeber Hall, Are Frustrated with Faculty Pushback." *Daily Cal,* 25 August 2020.

Chandler, Raymond. 1954. *The Long Goodbye.* Boston: Houghton Mifflin.

Chang, Will, Chundra Cathcart, David Hall, and Andrew Garrett. 2015. "Ancestry-Constrained Phylogenetic Analysis Supports the Indo-European Steppe Hypothesis." *Language* 91:194–244.

Chappelle, Marc, Peter Chen, Diane T. Chin, Ari Y. Kelman, Bernadette Meyler, Ato Quayson, Anna Toledano, Josh Tycko, Vaughn C. Williams, and Matthew Tiews. 2020. Reports of the Advisory Committee on Renaming Jordan Hall and Removing the Statue of Louis Agassiz. Stanford University. https://campusnames.stanford.edu/wp-content/uploads/sites/14/2020/10/Jordan-report.pdf.

Charity Hudley, Anne H., Christine Mallinson, and Mary Bucholtz. 2020. "Toward Racial Justice in Linguistics: Interdisciplinary Insights into Theorizing Race in the Discipline and Diversifying the Profession." *Language* 96:e200–e235.

Chavez, Yve. 2019. "Basket Weaving in Coastal Southern California: A Social History of Survivance." *Arts* 8:94. http://dx.doi.org/10.3390/arts8030094.

Child, Brenda J. 1998. *Boarding School Seasons: American Indian Families, 1900–1940.* Lincoln: University of Nebraska Press.

Chomsky, Noam. 1965. *Aspects of the Theory of Syntax.* Cambridge, MA: MIT Press.

Chung, Sandra. 1974. "Remarks on Pablo Tac's *La Lingua degli Indi Luiseños.*" *International Journal of American Linguistics* 40:292–307.

Clayton, Ian D. 2010. "On the Natural History of Preaspirated Stops." Unpublished PhD dissertation, University of North Carolina at Chapel Hill.

Clifford, James. 1986. "On Ethnographic Allegory." In *Writing Culture: The Poetics and Politics of Ethnography,* edited by James Clifford and George E. Marcus, 98–121. Berkeley: University of California Press.

Clifford, James. 1988. *The Predicament of Culture: Twentieth-Century Ethnography, Literature, and Art.* Cambridge, MA: Harvard University Press.

Clifford, James. 2013. *Returns: Becoming Indigenous in the Twenty-First Century.* Cambridge, MA: Harvard University Press.

Cohodas, Marvin. 1979. *Degikup: Washoe Fancy Basketry, 1895–1935.* Vancouver: University of British Columbia, Fine Arts Gallery.

Cohodas, Marvin. 1997. *Basket Weavers for the California Curio Trade: Elizabeth and Louise Hickox.* Tucson: University of Arizona Press.

Cole, Catherine M. 2015. "Representing Genocide at Home: Ishi, Again." In *Theatre and Human Rights after 1945: Things Unspeakable,* edited by Mary Luckhurst and Emilie Morin, 128–150. Basingstoke: Palgrave Macmillan.

Colla, Elliott. 2007. *Conflicted Antiquities: Egyptology, Egyptomania, Egyptian Modernity.* Durham, NC: Duke University Press.

Collier, John. 1963. *From Every Zenith: A Memoir.* Denver: Sage Books.

Colwell, Chip. 2017. *Plundered Skulls and Stolen Spirits: Inside the Fight to Reclaim Native America's Culture.* Chicago: University of Chicago Press.

Colós, María de los Ángeles, José Guzmán, and John Peabody Harrington. 1921. [Chochenyo field notes]. Manuscript, Harrington.010.001, Survey of California and Other Indian Languages, University of California, Berkeley. http://dx.doi.org/doi:10.7297/X2M61H6G.

Committee on the Judiciary, US Senate. 1950. *The Immigration and Naturalization Systems of the United States.* Washington, DC: US Government Printing Office.

Conathan, Lisa. 2004. "Classifiers in Wiyot, Yurok and Algonquian." In *Proceedings of the Thirtieth Annual Meeting of the Berkeley Linguistics Society: Special Session on the Morphology of American Indian Languages,* edited by Marc Ettlinger, Nicholas Fleisher, and Mischa Park-Doob, 22–33. Berkeley: Berkeley Linguistics Society.

Conathan, Lisa. 2006. "Recovering Sociolinguistic Context from Early Sources: The Case of Northwestern California." *Anthropological Linguistics* 48:209–232.

Cook, Michael. 1983. "Pharaonic History in Medieval Egypt." *Studia Islamica* 57:67–103.

Cook, Sherburne F. 1976. *The Conflict between the California Indian and White Civilization.* Berkeley: University of California Press.

Cooper, James Fennimore. 1826. *The Last of the Mohicans: A Narrative of 1757.* Philadelphia: H. C. Carey and I. Lea.

Cowan, J. Milton. 1975. "Golden Reminiscences: Peace and War." *LSA Bulletin* 64:28–34.

Cowell, Andrew, and Alonzo Moss Sr. 2003. "Arapaho Place Names in Colorado: Form and Function, Language and Culture." *Anthropological Linguistics* 45:349–389.

Cradic, Melissa S. 2017. "Transformations in Death: The Archaeology of Funerary Practices and Personhood in the Bronze Age Levant." Unpublished PhD dissertation, University of California, Berkeley. https://escholarship.org/uc/item/8mk978jc.

Cradic, Melissa S. 2018. "Residential Burial and Social Memory in the Middle Bronze Age Levant." *Near Eastern Archaeology* 81:191–201.

Cragen, Dorothy Clora. 1975. *The Boys in the Sky-Blue Pants: The Men and Events at Camp Independence and Forts of Eastern California, Nevada and Utah, 1862–1877.* Independence, CA: Pioneer.

Crawford, Judith. 1967. Mohave I. Field Notebook. CrawfordJu.001.002, California Language Archive, UC Berkeley. https://doi.org/10.7297/X2QC01DN.

Crawford, Judith. 1968a. Mohave Texts II. Field Notebook. CrawfordJu.001.008, California Language Archive, UC Berkeley. https://doi.org/10.7297/X2XW4GQM.

Crawford, Judith. 1968b. Mohave Texts III. Field Notebook. CrawfordJu.001.009, California Language Archive, UC Berkeley. http://dx.doi.org/doi:10.7297/X2T43R0M.

Crawford, Judith. 1972. Texts 6. Field Notebook. CrawfordJu.001.012, California Language Archive, UC Berkeley. http://dx.doi.org/doi:10.7297/X2DZ067J.

Crittenden, Charmian. 1954. The Tracer. Newsletter, Department of Anthropology, University of California, Berkeley, 22 June 1954. A. L. Kroeber Papers, Carton 19:34, Bancroft Library, University of California, Berkeley.

Crystal, David. 2000. *Language Death.* Cambridge, UK: Cambridge University Press.

Cultural Systems Research. 1987. California Low-Level Radioactive Waste Disposal Project Cultural Resources Surveying: Ethnographic Resources Candidate Site Selection Phase. http://hdl.handle.net/10150/271232.

Curtin, Jeremiah. 1889. Pulikla Vocabulary, Klamath River, California. Manuscript no. 1459. Washington, DC: Smithsonian Institution, National Anthropological Archives.

Curtin, Jeremiah. 1898. *Creation Myths of Primitive America.* Boston: Little, Brown.

Curtis, Edward S. 1907–1930. *The North American Indian.* Seattle: E. S. Curtis.

Curtius, Mary. 1998. Indian Remains Are Bones of Contention at Berkeley. *Los Angeles Times*, 27 April 1998. https://www.latimes.com/archives/la-xpm-1998-apr-27-mn-43487-story.html.

Cushing, Frank Hamilton. 1901. *Zuñi Folk Tales.* New York: G. P. Putnam's Sons.

Césaire, Aimé. 1972. *Discourse on Colonialism.* New York: Monthly Review Press.

Darnell, Regna. 1990. Franz Boas, Edward Sapir, and the Americanist Text Tradition. *Historiographia Linguistica* 17:129–144.

Darnell, Regna. 2000a. *And Along Came Boas: Continuity and Revolution in American Anthropology.* Amsterdam: John Benjamins.

Darnell, Regna. 2000b. Reenvisioning Boas and Boasian Anthropology. *American Anthropologist* 102:896–899.

Darnell, Regna. 2001. *Invisible Genealogies: A History of Americanist Anthropology.* Lincoln: University of Nebraska Press.

Darnell, Regna. 2018. "Franz Boas's Legacy of 'Useful Knowledge': The APS Archives and the Future of Americanist Anthropology." *Proceedings of the American Philosophical Society* 162:1–14.

Darnell, Regna. 2021. "Genres of Memory: Reading Anthropology's History through Ursula K. Le Guin's Science Fiction and Contemporary Native American Oral Tradition." In *Centering the Margins of Anthropology's History,* edited by Regna Darnell and Frederic W. Gleach, 201–217. Lincoln: University of Nebraska Press.

Darnell, Regna, Michelle Hamilton, Robert L. A. Hancock, and Joshua Smith, eds. 2015. *The Franz Boas Papers, Volume 1: Franz Boas as Public Intellectual—Theory, Ethnography, Activism.* Lincoln: University of Nebraska Press.

Dart, Sarah N. 1993. "Phonetic Properties of O'odham Stop and Fricative Contrasts." *International Journal of American Linguistics* 59:16–37.

Davis, Charron (Sonny), Vina Smith, Nancy Super (née Jerry), Peter Super Jr., Charlie Thom Sr., and Line Mikkelsen. 2020. "Forms and Functions of Backward Resumption: The Case of Karuk." *Language* 96:841–873.

Davis, Elizabeth. 1973. Interview with Mrs. John Parks Davis by Marshall H. Kuhn Concerning Mrs. Davis's Reminiscences of Ishi. #24-449, Phoebe A. Hearst Museum of Anthropology, University of California, Berkeley. http://cla.berkeley.edu/item/11891.

Davis, Jenny L. 2017. "Resisting Rhetorics of Language Endangerment: Reclamation through Indigenous Language Survivance." *Language Documentation and Description* 14:37–58.

Davis, Judi. 2013. "Both Beautiful and Brutal: Natalie Diaz and the Mojave Language Recovery Project." *Tribal College: Journal of American Indian Higher Education*, 6 May 2013. https://tribalcollegejournal.org/both-beautiful-and-brutal-natalie-diaz-and-the-mojave-language-recovery-project/.

Day, Mark R. 2016. "'Still Exploiting Him': Remembering Ishi, the 'Last Wild Indian in California.'" *Indian Country Today*, 25 March 2016. https://indiancountrytoday.com/archive/still-exploiting-him-remembering-ishi-the-last-wild-indian-in-california.

Dayley, Jon P. 1989. *Tümpisa (Panamint) Shoshone Dictionary.* Berkeley: University of California Press.

de Angulo, Gui. 1995. *The Old Coyote of Big Sur: The Life of Jaime de Angulo.* Berkeley: Stonegarden Press.

de Angulo, Jaime, and Lucy S. Freeland. 1931. "Karok Texts." *International Journal of American Linguistics* 6:194–226.

de la Cadena, Marisol. 2000. *Indigenous Mestizos: The Politics of Race and Culture in Cuzco, Peru, 1919–1991.* Durham, NC: Duke University Press.

Deacon, Desley. 1997. *Elsie Clews Parsons: Inventing Modern Life.* Chicago: University of Chicago Press.

Degler, Carl N. 1989. *Culture versus Biology in the Thought of Franz Boas and Alfred L. Kroeber.* New York: Berg.

DeLancey, Scott, and Victor Golla. 1997. "The Penutian Hypothesis: Retrospect and Prospect." *International Journal of American Linguistics* 63:171–202.

Deloria, Ella. 1932. *Dakota Texts.* Publications of the American Ethnological Society. New York: G. E. Stechert.

Deloria, Ella. 1944. *Speaking of Indians.* New York: Friendship Press.

Deloria, Ella. 1988. *Waterlily.* Lincoln: University of Nebraska Press.

Deloria, Vine, Jr. 1969. *Custer Died for Your Sins: An Indian Manifesto.* New York: Macmillan.

Deloria, Vine, Jr. 1997. "Anthros, Indians, and Planetary Reality." In *Indians and Anthropologists: Vine Deloria, Jr., and the Critique of Anthropology*, edited by Thomas Biolsi and Larry J. Zimmerman, 209–221. Tucson: University of Arizona Press.

Deloria, Vine, Jr., and Clifford M. Lyttle. 1984. *The Nations Within: The Past and Future of American Indian Sovereignty.* New York: Pantheon.

Deustua, Jose. 1994. "Mining Markets, Peasants, and Power in Nineteenth-century Peru." *Latin American Research Review* 29:29–54.

DeWitt-Warr, Vernille. 1913. "Destitute Nevada Indians." In *The History of Nevada,* vol. 1, edited by Sam P. Davis, 132–147. Reno: The Elms Publishing.

Diaz, Natalie. 2020. *Postcolonial Love Poem.* Minneapolis, MN: Graywolf Press.

Dickey, Elizabeth. 2008. Daisy Washington. Find a Grave Memorial. https://www.findagrave.com/memorial/24181071/daisy-washington.

"Digs Up Ancient Grave at Piute." 1918. *Bakersfield Morning Echo*, 12 December 1918, 8.

Ding, Xiaxun. 2019. "Finding the Words: New Technology and New Thinking Are Helping Native American Communities Revitalize Their Languages." *Humanities* 40. https://www.neh.gov/article/finding-words.

Dinkelspiel, Frances. 2020. "West Berkeley Shellmound Is Now Considered One of the U.S.'s 11 Most Endangered Historic Places." *Berkeleyside*, 25 September 2020. https://www.berkeleyside.org/2020/09/25/west-berkeley-ca-shellmound-most-endangered-historic-places-national-trust-historic-preservation.

Dinkelspiel, Frances. 2021. "Spenger's Development Can Proceed on Site of Ohlone Shellmound, Court Rules." *Berkeleyside*, 29 July 2021. https://www.berkeleyside.org/2021/07/29/development-spengers-parking-lot-can-proceed-ohlone-shellmound-ruling.

Dippie, Brian W. 1982. *The Vanishing American: White Attitudes and U.S. Indian Policy.* Middletown, CT: Wesleyan University Press.

Dirks, Nicholas B. 1992. "Introduction: Colonialism and Culture." In *Colonialism and Culture,* edited by Nicholas B. Dirks, 1–25. Ann Arbor: University of Michigan Press.

Dixon, Joseph K. 1913. *The Vanishing Race: The Last Great Indian Council.* Garden City, NY: Doubleday, Page.

Dixon, R. M. W. 1997. *The Rise and Fall of Languages.* Cambridge: Cambridge University Press.

Dixon, R. M. W. 2002. *Australian Languages: Their Nature and Development.* New York: Cambridge University Press.

Dixon, Roland B., and A. L. Kroeber. 1913. "New Linguistic Families in California." *American Anthropologist* 15:647–655.

Dixon, Roland B., and A. L. Kroeber. 1919. "Linguistic Families of California." *University of California Publications in American Archaeology and Ethnology* 16:47–118.

Dixon, Roland B., and Alfred L. Kroeber. 1903. "The Native Languages of California." *American Anthropologist* 5:1–26.

Dolores, Juan [John Lolorias]. 1901a. "Address." *Proceedings of the Nineteenth Annual Meeting of the Mohonk Conference of Friends of the Indian*, edited by Isabel C. Barrows, 76–77. New York: Lake Mohonk Conference.

Dolores, Juan [J. M. Lolorias]. 1901b. "The Last Great War." *Indian Advance* 2/8, 1 April 1901, 4.

Dolores, Juan [John Miguel Lolorias]. 1902. "As an Indian Sees It." *Southern Workman* 31:476–480.

Dolores, Juan. 1913. "Papago Verb Stems." *University of California Publications in American Archaeology and Ethnology* 10:241–263.

Dolores, Juan. 1923. "Papago Nominal Stems." *University of California Publications in American Archaeology and Ethnology* 20:19–31.

Dolores, Juan. 1936. "Papago Nicknames." In *Essays in Anthropology in Honor of A. L. Kroeber in Celebration of His Sixtieth Birthday, June 11, 1936,* edited by Robert H. Lowie, 45–47. Berkeley: University of California Press.

Dorrington, Lafayette A. 1927. Letter to the Commissioner of Indian Affairs, Washington, D.C., June 23, 1927. L-A 1668-27, United States Department of the Interior, Indian Field Service. Miscellaneous Documents and Reports, Digital

Commons, California State University, Monterey Bay. https://digitalcommons.csumb.edu/hornbeck_usa_3_d/56.

Dorsey, George A., and Alfred L. Kroeber. 1903. *Traditions of the Arapaho.* Chicago: Field Columbian Museum.

Dow, Sterling. 1965. *Fifty Years of Sathers: The Sather Professorship of Classical Literature in the University of California, Berkeley, 1913/4–1963/4.* Berkeley: University of California Press.

Downey, Lynn. 2007. *Images of America: Levi Strauss & Co.* Charleston, SC: Arcadia.

Driver, H. E., and A. L. Kroeber. 1932. "Quantitative Expression of Cultural Relationships." *University of California Publications in American Archaeology and Ethnology* 31:211–256.

Du Bois, Cora. 1970. "Studies in an Indian Town." In *Women in the Field: Anthropological Experiences,* edited by Peggy Golde, 219–236. Chicago: Aldine.

Duhoux, Yves, and Anna Morpurgo Davies, eds. 2007–2014. *A Companion to Linear B: Mycenaean Greek Texts and Their World.* 3 vols. Louvain-la-Neuve: Peeters.

Earl, Phillip L. 1990. "Paiute Artist's Life Had a Tragic End." *Reno Gazette-Journal*, 25 November 1990.

Egan, Shannon. 2006. " 'Yet in a Primitive Condition': Edward S. Curtis's North American Indian." *American Art* 20:58–83.

Elkind, Daniel. 2019. "Excavating Memory: Shellmounds of the Bay Area." SFMOMA's *Open Space.* https://openspace.sfmoma.org/2019/05/excavating-memory-shellmounds-of-the-bay-area/.

Elliott, Eric Bryant. 1999. "Dictionary of Rincón Luiseño." Unpublished PhD dissertation, University of California, San Diego.

Emeneau, Murray B. 1997. "Mary R. Haas and 'Berkeley Linguistics.'" *Anthropological Linguistics* 39:617–619.

England, Nora C. 1992. "Doing Mayan Linguistics in Guatemala." *Language* 68:29–35.

Epps, Patience L., Anthony K. Webster, and Anthony C. Woodbury. 2017. "A Holistic Humanities of Speaking: Franz Boas and the Continuing Centrality of Texts." *International Journal of American Linguistics* 83:41–78.

Epstein, Sandra P. n.d. "Women Who Built the Berkeley Campus: A Virtual Tour." 150 Years of Women at Berkeley, UC Berkeley. https://150w.berkeley.edu/women-who-built-berkeley-campus-virtual-tour.

Erikson, Erik Homburger. 1943. "Observations on the Yurok: Childhood and World Image." *University of California Publications in American Archaeology and Ethnology* 35:257–302.

"Eugenic Fad Called Joke." 1914. *Los Angeles Times*, 27 February 1914, 21.

Evanoff, Karen E., ed. 2010. *Dena'ina Ełnena: A Celebration*. Research/Resource Management Report NPS/AR/CCR/2010-75, Lake Clark National Park and Preserve: National Park Service.

Evans, Nicholas. 1996. "The Syntax and Semantics of Body-Part Incorporation in Mayali." In *The Grammar of Inalienability: A Typological Perspective on Body Part Terms and the Part-Whole Relation,* edited by Hilary Chappell and William McGregory, 65–109. Berlin: Walter de Gruyter.

Evans, Nicholas. 2010. *Dying Words: Endangered Languages and What They Have to Tell Us.* Chichester: Wiley-Blackwell.

Fabian, Ann. 2010. *The Skull Collectors: Race, Science, and America's Unburied Dead.* Chicago: University of Chicago Press.

Fabian, Johannes. 1983. *Time and the Other: How Anthropology Makes Its Object.* New York: Columbia University Press.

Falk, Julia S. 1994. "The Women Foundation Members of the Linguistic Society of America." *Language* 70:455–490.

Farrell, David, and Kathleen L. Hull. 2001. Foundations of Anthropology at the University of California. Bancroft Library, University of California, Berkeley. https://web.archive.org/web/20150907133101/http://bancroft.berkeley.edu/Exhibits/anthro/index.html.

Feldman, Orna. 2001. "Inspired by a Dream." Spring 2001. https://spectrum.mit.edu/spring-2001/inspired-by-a-dream/.

Ferguson, T. J., and E. Richard Hart. 1985. *A Zuni Atlas.* Norman: University of Oklahoma Press.

Fermino, Jessie Little Doe. 2000. "An Introduction to Wampanoag Grammar." Master's thesis, Massachusetts Institute of Technology. http://dspace.mit.edu/handle/1721.1/8740.

Field, Les, Alan Leventhal, and Rosemary Cambra. 2013. "Mapping Erasure: The Power of Nominative Cartography in the Past and Present of the Muwekma Ohlones of the San Francisco Bay Area." In *Recognition, Sovereignty Struggles, and Indigenous Rights in the United States: A Sourcebook,* edited by Amy E. Den Ouden and Jean M. O'Brien, 287–309. Chapel Hill: University of North Carolina Press.

Field, Les, Alan Leventhal, Dolores Sanchez, and Rosemary Cambra. 1992. "A Contemporary Ohlone Tribal Revitalization Movement: A Perspective from the Muwekma Ohlone Indians of the San Francisco Bay Area." *California History* 71:412–431.

Field, Les W. 1999. "Complicities and Collaborations: Anthropologists and the 'Unacknowledged Tribes' of California." *Current Anthropology* 40:193–209.

Field, Les W. 2003. "Unacknowledged Tribes, Dangerous Knowledge: The Muwekma Ohlone and How Indian Identities Are 'Known.'" With the Muwekma Ohlone Tribe. *Wicazo Sa Review* 18:79–94.

Field, Les W. 2005. "Who Is This Really About Anyway? Ishi, Kroeber, and the Intertwining of California Indian and Anthropological Histories." *Journal of Anthropological Research* 61:81–93.

Fielder, Mildred. 1970. *The Treasure of Homestake Gold.* Aberdeen, SD: North Plains Press.

Finacom, Steven. 2011. "Phoebe Hearst Remembered as Premier UC Benefactor." *Berkeley Daily Planet*, 20 April 2011. https://www.berkeleydailyplanet.com/issue/2011-04-20/article/37716.

"Find Relics of Early Oaklanders." 1896. *San Francisco Chronicle*, 25 August 1896, 10.

Fine-Dare, Kathleen S. 2002. *Grave Injustice: The American Indian Repatriation Movement and NAGPRA.* Lincoln: University of Nebraska Press.

Fine-Dare, Kathleen S. 2007. "Histories of the Repatriation Movement." In *Opening Archaeology: Repatriation's Impact on Contemporary Research & Practice,* edited by Thomas W. Killion, 29–55. Santa Fe, NM: School for Advanced Research Press.

"First Train Ride for Nogi Indian." 1911. *San Francisco Chronicle*, 5 September 1911, 3.

Fischer, Eugen. 1913. *Die Rehobother Bastards und das Bastardierungsproblem beim Menschen: Anthropologische und ethnographische Studien am Rehobother Bastardvolk in Deutsch-Südwest-Afrika.* Jena: Gustav Fischer.

Fishman, Joshua A. 1965. "Who Speaks What Language to Whom and When?" *La Linguistique* 1:67–88.

Fleming, Robin. 2010. *Britain after Rome: The Fall and Rise, 400–1070.* London: Penguin.

Fleming, Robin. 2021. *The Material Fall of Roman Britain, 300–525 CE.* Philadelphia: University of Pennsylvania Press.

Flores Santis, Gustavo Adolfo. 2014. "Native American Response and Resistance to Spanish Conquest in the San Francisco Bay Area, 1769–1846." Master's thesis, San José State University, https://www.sjsu.edu/anthropology/docs/projectfolder/Flores-Gustavo-thesis.pdf.

Fortescue, Michael. 1991. *Inuktun: An Introduction to the Language of Qaanaaq, Thule.* Institut for Eskimologi, 15. København: Københavens Universitet.

Foster, George M. 2000. An Anthropologist's Life in the Twentieth Century: Theory and Practice at UC Berkeley, the Smithsonian, in Mexico, and with the World

Health Organization. Interviews conducted by Suzanne Riess in 1998–1999. http://texts.cdlib.org/view?docId=kt7s2005ng&query=&brand=calisphere.

Foster, George M. 2003. "Assuming Responsibility for Ishi: An Alternative Interpretation." In *Ishi in Three Centuries,* edited by Karl Kroeber and Clifton Kroeber, 89–98. Lincoln: University of Nebraska Press.

"Found Twenty Indian Skeletons in Sand Hill." 1909. *Bakersfield Californian*, 1 January 1909, 4.

Fowler, Catherine S. 1990. *Tule Technology: Northern Paiute Uses of Marsh Resources in Western Nevada.* Smithsonian Folklife Studies 6. Washington, DC: Smithsonian Institution Press.

Fowler, Catherine S. 2009. "Reconstructing Southern Paiute-Chemehuevi Trails in the Mojave Desert of Southern Nevada and California: Ethnographic Perspectives from the 1930s." In *Landscapes of Movement,* edited by James Snead, Clark Erickson, and Andrew Darling, 84–105. Philadelphia: University of Pennsylvania Press.

Fowler, Catherine S., and Nancy Peterson Walter. 1985. "Harvesting Pandora Moth Larvae with the Owens Valley Paiute." *Journal of California and Great Basin Anthropology* 7:155–165.

Fryer, Francesca. 1995. *Sandspit: A Redwood Northcoast Notebook.* Eureka, CA: Eureka Printing.

Fuller, Thomas. 2021. "It's Liberals vs. Liberals in San Francisco after Schools Erase Contested Names." *New York Times,* 28 January 2021.

Fusco, Coco. 1994. "The Other History of Intercultural Performance." *Drama Review* 38:143–167.

Gaby, Alice, and Lesley Woods. 2020. "Toward Linguistic Justice for Indigenous People: A Response to Charity Hudley, Mallinson, and Bucholtz." *Language* 96:e268–e280.

García, John F. 2001. "Milman Parry and A. L. Kroeber: American Anthropology and the Oral Homer." *Oral Tradition* 16:58–84.

Garrett, Andrew. 2001. "Reduplication and Infixation in Yurok: Morphology, Semantics, and Diachrony." *International Journal of American Linguistics* 67:264–312.

Garrett, Andrew. 2009. Integrating Archives and New Documentation: The Berkeley Yurok Language Project. 1st International Conference on Language Documentation. https://scholarspace.manoa.hawaii.edu/items/4eb4040c-ea1e-4481-bfa4-af13c22feea8.

Garrett, Andrew. 2011. "An Online Dictionary with Texts and Pedagogical Tools: The Yurok Language Project at Berkeley." *International Journal of Lexicography* 24:405–419.

Garrett, Andrew. 2014. *Basic Yurok.* Berkeley: Survey of California and Other Indian Languages, Department of Linguistics, UC Berkeley. https://escholarship.org/uc/item/2vw609w4.

Garrett, Andrew. 2021. Documents Relating to the Unnaming of Kroeber Hall. https://escholarship.org/uc/item/9tv6788z.

Garrett, Andrew. 2023. " 'The Correct Way of Writing the Indian Language': Juan Dolores at the University of California." *Boom California*, 27 February 2023. https://boomcalifornia.org/2023/02/27/the-correct-way-of-writing-the-indian-language-juan-dolores-at-the-university-of-california/.

Garrett, Andrew, Susan Gehr, Erik Hans Maier, Line Mikkelsen, Crystal Richardson, and Clare S. Sandy. 2023. "Karuk." In *The Languages and Linguistics of Indigenous North America: A Comprehensive Guide*, edited by Carmen Dagostino, Marianne Mithun, and Keren Rice, 1153–1184. Berlin: de Gruyter Mouton.

Garrett, Andrew, Melissa Stoner, Susan Edwards, Jeffrey MacKie-Mason, Nicole Myers-Lim, Benjamin W. Porter, Elaine C. Tennant, and Verna Bowie. 2019. *Native American Collections in Archives, Libraries, and Museums at the University of California, Berkeley.* Berkeley: Office of the Vice Chancellor for Research, University of California. https://escholarship.org/uc/item/5zh1j3hx.

Garrett, Gary E. 1969. "The Destruction of the Indian in Mendocino County, 1856–1860." Master's thesis, Sacramento State College. https://csu-csus.esploro.exlibrisgroup.com/esploro/outputs/graduate/The-destruction-of-the-Indian-in/99257831233801671.

Gayton, A. H., and A. L. Kroeber. 1927. "The Uhle Pottery Collections from Nazca." *University of California Publications in American Archaeology and Ethnology* 24:1–46.

Gehr, Susan. 2013. "Breath of Life: Revitalizing California's Native Languages through Archives." MLIS thesis, San José State University. https://doi.org/10.31979/etd.yfva-e77q.

Gellman, Mneesha. 2022. "Unsettling Settler Colonialism in Words and Land: A Case Study of Far Northern California." *International Journal of Critical Indigenous Studies* 15:22–40.

Gellman, Mneesha. 2023. *Indigenous Language Politics in the Schoolroom: Cultural Survival in Mexico and the United States.* Philadelphia: University of Pennsylvania Press.

Gensler, Orin. 1986. "Laryngeal Increments in Yurok Revisited." Unpublished handout cataloged as Gensler.002, California Language Archive, Survey of California and Other Indian Languages, University of California, Berkeley. https://cla.berkeley.edu/item/?bndlid=440.

Gerstenblith, Patty. 2002. "Cultural Significance and the Kennewick Skeleton: Some Thoughts on the Resolution of Cultural Heritage Disputes." In *Naming the Bones: Cultural Property and the Negotiation of National and Ethnic Identity,* edited by Elazar Barkan and Ronald Bush, 162–197. Los Angeles: Getty Research Institute.

Gidley, Mick. 1998. *Edward S. Curtis and the North American Indian, Incorporated.* Cambridge, UK: Cambridge University Press.

Gifford, Edward Winslow. 1926a. "California Indian Types." *Natural History* 26:50–60.

Gifford, Edward Winslow. 1926b. "California Anthropometry." *University of California Publications in American Archaeology and Ethnology* 22:217–390.

Gifford, Edward Winslow. 1929a. "Race Mixture." *University of California Chronicle* 31:72–78.

Gifford, Edward Winslow. 1929b. *Tongan Society.* Bernice P. Bishop Museum Bulletin, 61. Honolulu: Bernice P. Bishop Museum.

Gifford, Edward Winslow. 1936. "Northeastern and Western Yavapai." *University of California Publications in American Archaeology and Ethnology* 34:247–354.

Gifford, Edward Winslow. 1939. "The Coast Yuki." *Anthropos* 34:292–375.

Gippert, Jost, Nikolaus P. Himmelmann, and Ulrike Mosel, eds. 2006. *Essentials of Language Documentation.* Berlin: Walter de Gruyter.

Girella, Luca. 2020. "Middle Minoan III–Late Minoan IIIB Tombs and Funerary Practices in South-Central Crete." In *Death in Late Bronze Age Greece,* edited by Joanne M. A. Murphy, 248–281. Oxford: Oxford University Press.

Glaser, Edward F. 1926. "Health Conditions among the Indians of California." *Transactions of the Commonwealth Club of California* 21:126–130.

Glazer, Peter. 2012. "Theater Department Apologizes for 'Ishi' Production." *Daily Cal,* 13 March 2012.

Goddard, Ives, ed. 1996. *Languages,* vol. 17 of *Handbook of North American Indians.* Washington, DC: Smithsonian Institute.

Goddard, Pliny Earle. 1904. "Hupa Texts." *University of California Publications in American Archaeology and Ethnology* 1:89–368.

Goddard, Pliny Earle. 1905a. "Mechanical Aids to the Study and Recording of Language." *American Anthropologist* 7:613–619.

Goddard, Pliny Earle. 1905b. "Morphology of the Hupa Language." *University of California Publications in American Archaeology and Ethnology* 3:1–344.

Goddard, Pliny Earle. 1907. "The Phonology of the Hupa Language: Part I—The Individual Sounds." *University of California Publications in American Archaeology and Ethnology* 5:1–20.

Goldstein, David. 2020. "Indo-European Phylogenetics with R." *Indo-European Linguistics* 8:1–71.

Golla, Victor, ed. 1984. *The Sapir-Kroeber Correspondence: Letters between Edward Sapir and A. L. Kroeber 1905–1925.* Publications of the Survey of California and Other Indian Languages. Berkeley: University of California, Department of Linguistics.

Golla, Victor. 2003. "Ishi's Language." In *Ishi in Three Centuries,* edited by Karl Kroeber and Clifton Kroeber, 208–225. Lincoln: University of Nebraska Press.

Golla, Victor. 2011. *California Indian Languages.* Berkeley: University of California Press.

Golla, Victor, James A. Matisoff, and Pamela Munro. 1997. "Mary R. Haas." *Language* 73:826–837.

Gomez, Melissa. 2021. "UC Berkeley Removes Kroeber Hall Name, Citing Namesake's 'Immoral' Work with Native Americans." *Los Angeles Times,* 27 January 2021.

Gordon, Robert J. 2009. "Hiding in Full View: The 'Forgotten' Bushman Genocides of Namibia." *Genocide Studies and Prevention: An International Journal* 4 (1): Art. 4. https://scholarcommons.usf.edu/gsp/vol4/iss1/4.

Gosden, Chris. 2001. "Postcolonial Archaeology: Issues of Culture, Identity, and Knowledge." In *Archaeological Theory Today*, edited by Ian Hodder, 241–261. Cambridge, UK: Polity.

Gough, Kathleen. 1968. "New Proposals for Anthropologists." *Current Anthropology* 9:403–435.

Grant, Madison. 1916. *The Passing of the Great Race, or, The Racial Basis of European History.* New York: Charles Scribner's Sons.

Gravlee, Clarence C., H. Russell Bernard, and William R. Leonard. 2003a. "Boas's *Changes in Bodily Form*: The Immigrant Study, Cranial Plasticity, and Boas's Physical Anthropology." *American Anthropologist* 105:326–332.

Gravlee, Clarence C., H. Russell Bernard, and William R. Leonard. 2003b. "Heredity, Environment, and Cranial Form: A Re-analysis of Boas's Immigrant Data." *American Anthropologist* 105:123–136.

Gregory, Herbert E. 1926. *Report of the Director for 1925.* Bernice P. Bishop Museum Bulletin. Honolulu: Bernice P. Bishop Museum.

Gregory, Ralph. 1965. "George Hearst in Missouri." *Bulletin of the Missouri Historical Society* 21:75–86.

Gruber, Jacob W. 1970. "Ethnographic Salvage and the Shaping of Anthropology." *American Anthropologist* 72:1289–1299.

Gumperz, John J., and Dell Hymes, eds. 1964. *The Ethnography of Communication.* American Anthropologist Special Publication. Menasha: George Banta.

Haak, Wolfgang, Iosif Lazaridis, Nick Patterson, Nadin Rohland, Swapan Mallick, Bastien Llamas, Guido Brandt, et al. 2015. "Massive Migration from the Steppe Was a Source for Indo-European Languages in Europe." *Nature* 522:207–211.

Haarmann, Ulrich. 1991. "In Quest of the Spectacular: Noble and Learned Visitors to the Pyramids around 1200 A.D." In *Islamic Studies Presented to Charles J. Adams,* edited by Wael B. Hallaq, 57–67. Leiden: Brill.

Haas, Lisbeth. 2011. *Pablo Tac, Indigenous Scholar Writing on Luiseño Language and Colonial History, c. 1840.* Berkeley: University of California Press.

Haas, Lisbeth. 2014. *Saints and Citizens: Indigenous Histories of Colonial Missions and Mexican California.* Berkeley: University of California Press.

Haas, Mary R. 1967. "Language and Taxonomy in Northwestern California." *American Anthropologist* 69:358–362.

"Hacienda Camp Breaks Up To-day." 1912. *San Francisco Examiner*, 27 May 1912, 5.

Hackel, Steven W. 2005. *Children of Coyote, Missionaries of Saint Francis: Indian-Spanish Relations in Colonial California.* Chapel Hill: University of North Carolina Press.

Hale, Ken. 1992. "On Endangered Languages and the Safeguarding of Diversity." *Language* 68:1–3.

Hale, Ken. 2001. "Ulwa (Southern Sumu): The Beginnings of a Language Research Project." In *Linguistic Fieldwork,* edited by Paul Newman and Martha Ratliff, 76–101. Cambridge, UK: Cambridge University Press.

Hale, Kenneth. 1959. "A Papago Grammar." Unpublished PhD dissertation, Indiana University, Bloomington.

Hale, Kenneth. 1965. "Some Preliminary Observations on Papago Morphophonemics." *International Journal of American Linguistics* 31:295–305.

Hale, Kenneth. 1972. "Some Questions about Anthropological Linguistics: The Role of Native Knowledge." In *Reinventing Anthropology,* edited by Dell Hymes, 382–397. New York: Pantheon.

Hale, Kenneth. 1976. "Theoretical Linguistics in Relation to American Indian Communities." In *American Indian Languages and American Linguistics,* edited by Wallace L. Chafe, 35–50. Lisse: Peter de Ridder.

Hale, Kenneth, and Albert Alvarez. 1972. "A New Perspective on American Indian Linguistics." In *New Perspectives on the Pueblos,* edited by Alfonso Ortiz, 87–133. Albuquerque: University of New Mexico Press.

Halle, Morris, and Norvin Richards. 2007. *Kenneth Locke Hale, 1934–2001: A Biographical Memoir.* Washington, DC: National Academy of Sciences.

Halpern, Abraham M. 1946a. "Yuma." In *Linguistic Structures of Native America*, edited by Cornelius Osgood, 249–288. New York: Viking Fund.

Halpern, Abraham M. 1946b. "Yuma I–III." *International Journal of American Linguistics* 12:25–33, 147–151, 204–212.

Halpern, Abraham M. 1947. "Yuma IV–VI." *International Journal of American Linguistics* 13:18–30, 92–107, 147–166.

Halpern, Abraham M. 1984. "Quechan Literature." In *Spirit Mountain: An Anthology of Yuman Story and Song,* edited by Leanne Hinton and Lucille J. Watahomigie, 291–344. Tucson: University of Arizona Press.

Halpern, Abraham M. 1997. *Karʔúk: Native Accounts of the Quechan Mourning Ceremony*, edited by Amy Miller and Margaret Langdon. Berkeley: University of California Press.

Halpern, Abraham M., and Amy Miller, eds. 2014. *Stories from Quechan Oral Literature.* Cambridge, UK: Open Book Publishers.

Hanks, Jane Richardson. 1951–2002. Jane Richardson Hanks Collection on Alfred Kroeber. BANC MSS 2008/79, Bancroft Library, UC Berkeley.

Hantman, Jeffrey L., and Gary Dunham. 1993. "The Enlightened Archaeologist." *Archaeology* 46:44–49.

Harper, Kenn. 2000. *Give Me My Father's Body: The Life of Minik, the New York Eskimo.* South Royalton, VT: Steerforth Press.

Harrington, John Peabody. 1926–1942. Northern and Central California: Wiyot/Yurok/Mattole. John Peabody Harrington Papers, National Anthropological Archives. Washington, DC: Smithsonian Institution.

Harris, David Jason, and Gary Holton. 2018. "Place Naming Strategies in Lower Tanana." In *Language and Toponymy in Alaska and Beyond: Papers in Honor of James Kari,* Language Documentation and Conservation Special Publication 17, edited by Gary Holton and Thomas F. Thornton, 121–138. Honolulu: University of Hawai'i Press.

Harris, Leslie M., James T. Campbell, and Alfred L. Brophy, eds. 2019. *Slavery and the University: Histories and Legacies.* Athens: University of Georgia Press.

Harris, Marvin. 1968. *The Rise of Anthropological Theory: A History of Theories of Culture.* New York: Thomas Y. Crowell.

Harrison, K. David. 2007. *When Languages Die: The Extinction of the World's Languages and the Erosion of Human Knowledge.* Oxford: Oxford University Press.

Harrison, Margaret W. 1948. "Lila Morris O'Neale: 1886–1948." *American Anthropologist* 50:657–665.

Hatto, Arthur T. 1999. *The Mohave Heroic Epic of Inyo-kutavêre.* Folklore Fellows Communications 269. Helsinki: Academia Scientiarum Fennica.

Haugen, Einar. 1938. "Phonological Shifting in American Norwegian." *Language* 14:112–120.

Heaney, Christopher. 2018. "Seeing Like an Inca: Julio C. Tello, Indigenous Archaeology, and Pre-Columbian Trepanation in Peru." In *Indigenous Visions: Rediscovering the World of Franz Boas,* edited by Ned Blackhawk and Isaiah Lorado Wilner, 344–376. New Haven, CT: Yale University Press.

Hearst, George. 1882. "Hearst in the Field: A Card from Him Announcing His Candidature for Governor." *San Francisco Examiner,* 17 May 1882, 2.

Hearst, George. 1972 [1890]. *The Way It Was.* New York: Hearst Corporation.

Hearst, George, and Phoebe Apperson Hearst. 1849–1926. George and Phoebe Apperson Hearst Papers. BANC MSS 72/204c, Bancroft Library, University of California, Berkeley.

Heaton, Raina. 2013. The Tunica Language Revitalization Project: Methods, Challenges, and Data Conflict in Language Recreation. 3rd International Conference on Language Documentation and Conservation (ICLDC), Honolulu. http://hdl.handle.net/10125/26118.

Heizer, Robert F., ed. 1970. *An Anthropological Expedition of 1913, or Get It Through Your Head, or Yours for the Revolution: Correspondence between A. L. Kroeber and L. L. Loud, July 12, 1913–October 31, 1913.* Publications of the University of California Archaeological Research Facility. Berkeley: University of California, Archaeological Research Facility, Department of Anthropology.

Heizer, Robert F., ed. 1973. *Notes on the McCloud River Wintu and Selected Excerpts from Alexander S. Taylor's "Indianology of California."* Publications of the University of California Archaeological Research Facility. Berkeley: University of California, Archaeological Research Facility, Department of Anthropology.

Heizer, Robert F. 1975. "[Review of] A. L. Kroeber and C. B. Kroeber, *A Mohave War Reminiscence, 1854–1880.*" *Pacific Historical Review* 44:119–120.

Heizer, Robert F., ed. 1979. *Federal Concern about Conditions of California Indians 1853 to 1913: Eight Documents.* Socorro, NM: Ballena.

Heizer, Robert F., ed. 1993 [1974]. *The Destruction of California Indians: A Collection of Documents from the Period 1847–1865.* Lincoln: University of Nebraska Press.

Heizer, Robert F., Thomas R. Hester, and Michael P. Nichols, eds. 1972. *Notes on Northern Paiute Ethnography: Kroeber and Marsden Records.* Publications of the University of California Archaeological Research Facility 4. Berkeley:University of California, Archaeological Research Facility, Department of Anthropology.

Heizer, Robert F., and Alfred L. Kroeber. 1976. "For Sale: California at 47 Cents per Acre." *Journal of California Anthropology* 3:38–65.

Heizer, Robert F., and Theodora Kroeber, eds. 1979. *Ishi the Last Yahi: A Documentary History.* Berkeley: University of California Press.

Heizer, Robert F., and Lewis K. Napton. 1970. *Archaeology and the Prehistoric Great Basin Lacustrine Subsistence Regime as Seen from Lovelock Cave, Nevada.* Contributions of the University of California Archaeological Research Facility 10. Berkeley: University of California, Department of Anthropology.

Helvarg, David. 2020. "Island of Resilience: The Wiyot Reclaim Their Land and Culture from a Dark Past." *American Indian* 21 (1). https://www.americanindianmagazine.org/story/wiyot.

Hendel, Ron. 2020. "On Un-naming Barrows Hall." *Berkeley Blog*, 29 July 2020. https://blogs.berkeley.edu/2020/07/29/on-un-naming-barrows-hall/.

Hendrick, Irving G. 1976. "Federal Policy Affecting the Education of Indians in California, 1849–1934." *History of Education Quarterly* 16:163–185.

Hewes, Gordon W. 1961. "The Ecumene as a Civilizational Multiplier System." *Kroeber Anthropological Society Papers* 25:73–108.

Hill, Jane H. 1966. "A Grammar of the Cupeño Language." Unpublished PhD dissertation, University of California, Los Angeles.

Hill, Jane H. 2002. " 'Expert Rhetorics' in Advocacy for Endangered Languages: Who Is Listening, and What Do They Hear?" *Journal of Linguistic Anthropology* 12:119–133.

Hill, Jane H. 2005. *A Grammar of Cupeño.* Berkeley: University of California Press.

Hill, Jane H., and Ofelia Zepeda. 1992. "Derived Words in Tohono O'odham." *International Journal of American Linguistics* 58:355–404.

Hill, Kenneth Cushman. 1967. "A Grammar of the Serrano Language." Unpublished PhD dissertation, UCLA.

Himmelmann, Nikolaus P. 1998. "Documentary and Descriptive Linguistics." *Linguistics* 36:161–195.

Himmelmann, Nikolaus P. 2012. "Linguistic Data Types and the Interface between Language Documentation and Description." *Language Documentation and Conservation* 6:187–207.

Hinton, Leanne. 2001. "The Use of Linguistic Archives in Language Revitalization: The Native California Language Restoration Workshop." In *The Green Book of Language Revitalization in Practice,* edited by Leanne Hinton and Ken Hale, 419–424. San Diego: Academic Press.

Hinton, Leanne. 2018. "Approaches to and Strategies for Language Revitalization." In *The Oxford Handbook of Endangered Languages,* edited by Kenneth L. Rehg and Lyle Campbell, 443–465. Oxford: Oxford University Press.

Hinton, Leanne. 2022. *Flutes of Fire: An Introduction to Native California Languages.* Rev. ed. Berkeley, CA: Heyday.

Hinton, Leanne, and Ken Hale, eds. 2001. *The Green Book of Language Revitalization in Practice.* San Diego: Academic Press.

Hinton, Leanne, Leena Huss, and Gerald Roche. 2018. "Introduction: Language Revitalization as a Growing Field of Study and Practice." In *The Routledge Handbook of Language Revitalization*, edited by Leanne Hinton, Leena Huss, and Gerald Roche, xxi–xxx. New York: Routledge.

Hinton, Leanne, and Lucille Watahomigie. 1984. *Spirit Mountain: An Anthology of Yuman Story and Song.* Tucson: University of Arizona Press.

Hirschkind, Charles. 2020a. Letter from the Chair. Department of Anthropology, UC Berkeley. https://anthropology.berkeley.edu/news/letter-chair.

Hirschkind, Charles. 2020b. "UC Berkeley Anthropology Department Supports Un-naming of Kroeber Hall." *Daily Cal*, 1 September 2020.

"Historic Splendor of Ancient Egypt Revives for Dr. George A. Reisner." 1902. *San Francisco Examiner*, 19 September 1902, 8–9.

Hoban, Virgie. 2018. "Project IRENE: Lawrence Berkeley National Laboratory, Library Unite to Save Native American Voices." *Berkeley Library News*, 19 June 2018. https://goo.gl/FauJZo.

Holder, Kathleen. 2021. " 'A Monumental Step' in Reclaiming a California Indigenous Language." *News*, UC Davis College of Letters and Science, 18 June 2021. https://lettersandscience.ucdavis.edu/news/monumental-step-reclaiming-california-language.

Holtved, Erik. 1952. "Remarks on the Polar Eskimo Dialect." *International Journal of American Linguistics* 18:20–24.

"Honoring Berkeley's Greatest Benefactors." 2019. Builders of Berkeley, UC Berkeley. https://builders.berkeley.edu/.

Horner, Jan C. 1985. "Anthropology and Myth in the Works of Ursula K. Le Guin." Master's thesis, University of Manitoba. http://hdl.handle.net/1993/32699.

Howle, Elaine M. 2020. "Native American Graves Protection and Repatriation Act: The University of California Is Not Adequately Overseeing Its Return of Native American Remains and Artifacts." http://auditor.ca.gov/pdfs/reports/2019-047.pdf.

Hoxie, Frederick E., ed. 2001. *Talking Back to Civilization: Indian Voices from the Progressive Era.* Boston: Bedford/St. Martins.

Hudetz, Mary, and Graham Lee Brewer. 2023. "A Top UC Berkeley Professor Taught With Remains That May Include Dozens of Native Americans." *ProPublica*, 5 March 2023. https://www.propublica.org/article/berkeley-professor-taught-suspected-native-american-remains-repatriation.

Hunn, Eugene S. 1990. *Nch'i-Wána, "the Big River": Mid-Columbia Indians and Their Land.* Seattle: University of Washington Press.

Hunn, Eugene S. 1996. "Columbia Plateau Indian Place Names: What Can They Teach Us?" *Journal of Linguistic Anthropology* 6:3–26.

Hunt, Arthur S., and J. Gilbart Smyly. 1933. *The Tebtunis Papyri, Volume III, Part I.* University of California Publications in Graeco-Roman Archaeology 3. London: Humphrey Milford.

Hyde, Villiana. 1971. *An Introduction to the Luiseño Language.* Morongo Indian Reservation. Banning, CA: Malki Museum Press.

Hyde, Villiana Calac, and Eric Elliott. 1994. *Yumáyk yumáyk: Long Ago.* University of California Publications in Linguistics 125. Berkeley: University of California Press.

Hymes, Dell. 1961. "Alfred Louis Kroeber." *Language* 37:1–28.

Hymes, Dell. 1962. "The Ethnography of Speaking." In *Anthropology and Human Behavior,* edited by Thomas Gladwin and William C. Sturtevant, 13–53. Washington, DC: Anthropological Society of Washington.

Hymes, Dell. 2000. "A Native American Epic." *Folklore Fellows' Network* 20: 16–21. https://www.folklorefellows.fi/a-native-american-epic/.

Imbler, Sabrina. 2022. "New DNA Analysis Supports an Unrecognized Tribe's Ancient Roots in California." *New York Times*, 12 April 2022. https://www.nytimes.com/2022/04/12/science/muwekma-ohlone-tribe-california-dna.html.

"Indian Bodies Returned." 1906. *Ukiah Dispatch Democrat*, 31 August 1906, 1.

"Indian Lore at the University: Mrs. Hearst Founds New Chair to Study Aboriginal Remains." 1901. *San Francisco Chronicle*, 25 August 1901, 9.

"Indian Monument Is Presented to Alameda." 1914. *Alameda Evening Times-Star and Argus*, 18 June 1914, 1, 7.

"Indian Relics for University." 1906. *San Francisco Chronicle*, 16 June 1906, 2.

"Indian Skeleton Found in Street." 1907. *Los Angeles Evening Post-Record,* 28 February 1907, 1.

"Indian Skeletons Are Found in Canal Bed." 1916. *Long Beach Daily Telegram*, 2 March 1916, 12.

"Indian Skeletons Found." 1897. *San Francisco Chronicle*, 10 November 1897, 7.

"Indian Skull for University." 1906. *Ukiah Republican Press*, 22 June 1906, 1.

"Indians Almost Extinct." 1901. *San Francisco Chronicle*, 22 April 1901, 4.

"Indians Will Soon Be Extinct." 1910. *Oakland Tribune*, 16 May 1910, 6.

Ingram, B. Lynn. 1998. "Differences in Radiocarbon Age between Shell and Charcoal from a Holocene Shellmound in Northern California." *Quaternary Research* 49:102–110.

Iralu, Elspeth. 2021. "Putting Indian Country on the Map: Indigenous Practices of Spatial Justice." *Antipode: A Radical Journal of Geography* 53:1485–1502.

Ishi, Edward Sapir, Herbert W. Luthin, and Leanne Hinton. 2002. "A Story of Lizard." In *Surviving through the Days: Translations of Native California Stories and Songs,* edited by Herbert W. Luthin, 152–177. Berkeley: University of California Press.

"Ishi Is Second Nurse." 1912. *San Francisco Examiner*, 11 March 1912, 3.

"Ishi Wants to Live and Die in San Francisco." 1911. *Chico Enterprise*, 25 September 1911, 4.

Jacknis, Ira. 1988. "Franz Boas and Exhibits: On the Limitations of the Museum Method of Anthropology." In *Objects and Others: Essays on Museums and Material Culture,* edited by George W. Stocking, 75–111. Madison: University of Wisconsin Press.

Jacknis, Ira. 2000. "A Museum Prehistory: Phoebe Hearst and the Founding of the Museum of Anthropology, 1891–1901." *Chronicle of the University of California* 4:47–77.

Jacknis, Ira. 2002. "The First Boasian: Alfred Kroeber and Franz Boas, 1896–1905." *American Anthropologist* 104:520–532.

Jacknis, Ira. 2003. "Yahi Culture in the Wax Museum: Ishi's Sound Recordings." In *Ishi in Three Centuries,* edited by Karl Kroeber and Clifton B. Kroeber, 235–274. Lincoln: University of Nebraska Press.

Jackson, Helen Hunt. 1881. *A Century of Dishonor: A Sketch of the United States Government's Dealings with Some of the Indian Tribes.* New York: Harper and Brothers.

Jackson, Helen Hunt. 1884. *Ramona: A Story.* Boston: Roberts Brothers.

Jackson, John P., Jr., and David J. Depew. 2017. *Darwinism, Democracy, and Race: American Anthropology and Evolutionary Biology in the Twentieth Century.* London: Routledge.

Jakobson, Roman. 1944. "Franz Boas' Approach to Language." *International Journal of American Linguistics* 10:188–195.

Jefferson, Thomas. 1787. *Notes on the State of Virginia.* London: John Stockdale. First published anonymously in Paris, 1785.

Johnson, Adam Fulton. 2018a. "Secretsharers: Intersecting Systems of Knowledge and the Politics of Documentation in Southwesternist Anthropology, 1880–1930." Unpublished PhD dissertation, University of Michigan.

Johnson, Lisa M. 2018b. "Siguiendo los rastros de los depósitos rituales: Esbozo de un marco arqueológico para el estudio de las prácticas rituales en Palenque." *Estudios de Cultura Maya* 52:51–76.

Johnson, Lisa M. 2018c. "Tracing the Ritual 'Event' at the Classic Maya City of Palenque, Mexico." Unpublished PhD dissertation, University of California, Berkeley. https://escholarship.org/uc/item/4q00v44g.

Johnson, Troy R., ed. 1995. *You Are on Indian Land! Alcatraz Island, 1969–1971.* Los Angeles: University of California American Indian Studies Center.

Jones, Philip Mills. 1923. "Mound Excavations Near Stockton." *University of California Publications in American Archaeology and Ethnology* 20:111–122.

Jones, Philip Mills. 1956. *Archaeological Investigations on Santa Rosa Island in 1901*, edited by R. F. Heizer and A. B. Elsasser. University of California Anthropological Records 17/2. Berkeley: University of California Press.

Jordan, David Starr. 1911. *The Heredity of Richard Roe: A Discussion of the Principles of Eugenics.* Boston: Beacon Press.

Jordan, David Starr. 1915. *War and the Breed: The Relation of War to the Downfall of Nations.* Boston: Beacon Press.

Joyce, Rosemary A. 2015. "Grave Responsibilities: Encountering Human Remains." In *Disturbing Bodies: Perspectives on Forensic Anthropology,* edited by Zoë Crossland and Rosemary A. Joyce, 169–184. Santa Fe, NM: School for Advanced Research Press.

Joyce, Rosemary A. 2021. "Unnaming Buildings: On (Not) Honoring Ancestors and Losing Our Memory." *American Anthropologist* 123:474–475.

Kadvany, Elena. 2022. "The World's First Ohlone Restaurant Is Opening Soon at UC Berkeley." *San Francisco Chronicle*, 22 April 2022. https://www.sfchronicle.com/food/article/uc-berkeley-cafe-ohlone-17117764.php.

Kamisher, Eliyahu. 2021. "Yurok People See Victory in Decades-Long Effort to Revive Language." *The Guardian*, 10 October 2021. https://www.theguardian.com/world/2021/oct/10/yurok-indigenous-sue-meg-state-park-name.

Kanigel, Robert. 2021. *Hearing Homer's Song: The Brief Life and Big Idea of Milman Parry.* New York: Alfred A. Knopf.

Karuk Tribe Department of Natural Resources. 2020. Kúkuum yáv nukyâati peethîvthaaneen: We Make the World Good Again. Story map. https://storymaps.arcgis.com/stories/bebd5ff6a9f748968790c31448f03a2e.

Katz, Randy. 2021. "UC and Native Californians." *Los Angeles Times*, 10 February 2021, A10.

Kaufman, Terence. 1988. "A Research Program for Reconstructing Proto-Hokan: First Gropings." In *Papers from the 1988 Hokan-Penutian Languages*

Workshop, edited by Scott DeLancey, 50–168. Eugene: Department of Linguistics, University of Oregon.

Keefer, Louis E. 1988. *Scholars in Foxholes: The Story of the Army Specialized Training Program in World War II.* Jefferson, NC: McFarland and Company.

Keeling, Richard. 1982. "Kroeber's *Yurok Myths*: A Comparative Re-evaluation." *American Indian Culture and Research Journal* 6:71–81.

Keeling, Richard. 1991. *A Guide to Early Field Recordings (1900–1949) at the Robert H. Lowie Museum of Anthropology.* Berkeley: University of California Press.

Keliiaa, Caitlin. 2012. "*Washiw Wagayay Mangal*: Reweaving the Washoe Language." Master's thesis, UCLA. https://escholarship.org/uc/item/4zd060kz.

Kell, Gretchen. 2021. "Kroeber Hall, Honoring Anthropologist Who Symbolizes Exclusion, Is Unnamed." *Berkeley News,* 26 January 2021.

Kelly, Isabel. 1978. "Coast Miwok." In *California*, edited by Robert F. Heizer, 414–435. Handbook of North American Indians 8. Washington, DC: Smithsonian Institution.

Kerns, Virginia. 2010. *Journeys West: Jane and Julian Steward and Their Guides.* Lincoln: University of Nebraska Press.

Kessler, Adolph. 1973. Finding of Ishi: Oral History. Interviewed by Stephen C. Morehouse. Transcript shelved as Phonotape 828 C notes. BANC CD 534, Bancroft Library, UC Berkeley.

Key, John W. 1979. The Owens Valley Indian War, 1861–1865. Fort Leavenworth, Kansas: Faculty of U.S. Army Command and General Staff College. http://www.militarymuseum.org/OwensValley.html.

King, Charles. 2019. *Gods of the Upper Air: How a Circle of Renegade Anthropologists Reinvented Race, Sex, and Gender in the Twentieth Century.* New York: Doubleday.

Klasky, Philip M. 2000. "Song of the Land." *Yes!*, 1 October 2000, https://www.yesmagazine.org/issue/close-prisons/2000/10/01/song-of-the-land.

Klein, Richard. 2013. F. Clark Howell and the Modernization of Paleoanthropology in the United States at Michigan, Chicago, Berkeley, and Stanford. Interview conducted by Samuel J. Redman, 2012, Regional Oral History Office, The Bancroft Library, University of California, Berkeley. https://digitalassets.lib.berkeley.edu/roho/ucb/text/klein_richard_2013.pdf.

Knobloch, Patricia J. 1988. "Isabel Truesdell Kelly (1906–1983)." In *Women Anthropologists: A Biographical Dictionary,* edited by Ute Gacs, Aisha Khan, Jerrie McIntyre, and Ruth Weinberg, 175–180. New York: Greenwood Press.

Koseff, Alexei. 2020. "Boost for Tribes on Return of Remains." *San Francisco Chronicle*, 30 November 2020.

Krauss, Michael. 1992. "The World's Languages in Crisis." *Language* 68:4–10.

Krauss, Michael. 1998. "The Condition of Native North American Languages: The Need for Realistic Assessment and Action." *International Journal of the Sociology of Language* 132:9–21.

Kroeber, A. L. 1869–1972. A. L. Kroeber papers. BANC MSS C-B 925, Bancroft Library, University of California, Berkeley.

Kroeber, A. L. 1899. "Tales of the Smith Sound Eskimo." *Journal of American Folk-Lore* 12:166–182.

Kroeber, A. L. 1900. "Cheyenne Tales." *Journal of American Folk-Lore* 13: 161–190.

Kroeber, A. L. 1901a. "Decorative Symbolism of the Arapaho." *American Anthropologist* 3:308–336.

Kroeber, A. L. 1901b. "Ute Tales." *Journal of American Folk-Lore* 14:252–285.

Kroeber, A. L. 1902. "Preliminary Sketch of the Mohave Indians." *American Anthropologist* 4:276–285.

Kroeber, A. L. 1904. "The Languages of the Coast of California South of San Francisco." *University of California Publications in American Archaeology and Ethnology* 2:29–80.

Kroeber, A. L. 1905a. "Basket Designs of the Indians of Northwestern California." *University of California Publications in American Archaeology and Ethnology* 2:105–164.

Kroeber, A. L. 1905b. "Wishosk Myths." *Journal of American Folk-Lore* 18:85–107.

Kroeber, A. L. 1907a. "Gros Ventre Myths and Tales." *Anthropological Papers of the American Museum of Natural History* 1:55–139.

Kroeber, A. L. 1907b. "Shoshonean Dialects of California." *University of California Publications in American Archaeology and Ethnology* 4:65–165.

Kroeber, A. L. 1907c. "The Washo Language of East Central California and Nevada." *University of California Publications in American Archaeology and Ethnology* 4:251–317.

Kroeber, A. L. 1907d. "The Yokuts Language of South Central California." *University of California Publications in American Archaeology and Ethnology* 2:165–377.

Kroeber, A. L. 1909a. "The Bannock and Shoshoni Languages." *American Anthropologist* 11:266–277.

Kroeber, A. L. 1909b. "The Indians of California." *Transactions of the Commonwealth Club of California* 4:430–437.

Kroeber, A. L. 1910a. "The Chumash and Costanoan Languages." *University of California Publications in American Archaeology and Ethnology* 9:237–271.

Kroeber, A. L. 1910b. "The Morals of Uncivilized People." *American Anthropologist* 12:437–447.

Kroeber, A. L. 1910c. "Noun Incorporation in American Languages." In *Verhandlungen des XVI. Internationalen Amerikanisten-Kongresses, Wien, 9. bis 14. September 1908,* edited by Franz Heger, 569–576. Vienna: A. Hartleben.

Kroeber, A. L. 1911a. "The Elusive Mill Creeks: A Band of Wild Indians Roaming in Northern California To-day—Hidden for More Than Forty Years, They Still Elude the White Man." *Travel* 17:511–550.

Kroeber, A. L. 1911b. "Incorporation as a Linguistic Process." *American Anthropologist* 13:577–584.

Kroeber, A. L. 1911c. "It's All Too Much for Ishi, Says the Scientist." *San Francisco Call,* 8 October 1911, 5.

Kroeber, A. L. 1911d. "The Languages of California North of San Francisco." *University of California Publication in American Archaeology and Ethnology* 9:273–435.

Kroeber, A. L. 1911e. "Phonetic Elements of the Mohave Language." *University of California Publications in American Archaeology and Ethnology* 10:15–96.

Kroeber, A. L. 1911f. "Phonetics of the Micronesian Language of the Marshall Islands." *American Anthropologist* 13:380–393.

Kroeber, A. L. 1912a. "Ishi, the Last Aborigine." *World's Work* 24:304–308.

Kroeber, A. L. 1913. "Explanatory Note [in Juan Dolores, 'Papago Verb Stems']." *University of California Publications in American Archaeology and Ethnology* 10: 241–243.

Kroeber, A. L. 1915. "Eighteen Professions." *American Anthropologist* 17:283–288.

Kroeber, A. L. 1916a. "Arapaho Dialects." *University of California Publications in American Archaeology and Ethnology* 12:71–138.

Kroeber, A. L. 1916b. "Inheritance by Magic." *American Anthropologist* 18:19–40.

Kroeber, A. L. 1916c. "The Speech of a Zuñi Child." *American Anthropologist* 18:529–534.

Kroeber, A. L. 1916d. *Zuñi Potsherds.* Anthropological Papers of the American Museum of Natural History. New York: American Museum of Natural History.

Kroeber, A. L. 1917a. "The Superorganic." *American Anthropologist* 19:163–213.

Kroeber, A. L. 1917b. "Tribes of the Pacific Coast of North America." In *Proceedings of the Second Pan American Scientific Congress: Section I, Anthropology,* 22–37. Washington, DC: US Government Printing Office.

Kroeber, A. L. 1917c. *Zuñi Kin and Clan.* Anthropological Papers of the American Museum of Natural History. New York: American Museum of Natural History.

Kroeber, A. L. 1918. "Heredity, Environment, and Civilization." *American Museum Journal* 18:351–359.

Kroeber, A. L. 1919a. "On the Principle of Order in Civilization as Exemplified by Changes of Fashion." *American Anthropologist* 21:235–263.

Kroeber, A. L. 1919b. *Peoples of the Philippines.* New York: American Museum Press.

Kroeber, A. L. 1923. *Anthropology.* New York: Harcourt, Brace.

Kroeber, A. L. 1925. *Handbook of the Indians of California.* Bureau of American Ethnology, Bulletin 78. Washington, DC: Smithsonian Institution.

Kroeber, A. L. 1926. "Culture Stratifications in Peru." *American Anthropologist* 28:331–351.

Kroeber, A. L. 1926–1937. *Archaeological Explorations in Peru.* Field Museum of Natural History, Anthropology Memoirs 2/1, 2/2, 2/4. Chicago: Field Museum Press.

Kroeber, A. L. 1932a. "The Patwin and Their Neighbors." *University of California Publications in Archaeology and Ethnology* 29:253–423.

Kroeber, A. L. 1932b. "Yuki Myths." *Anthropos* 27:905–939.

Kroeber, A. L. 1939. "Cultural and Natural Areas of Native North America." *University of California Publications in American Archaeology and Ethnology* 38:1–242.

Kroeber, A. L. 1942. "Los métodos de la arqueología peruana." *Letras: Organo de la Facultad de Letras y Pedagogia* 22:205–226.

Kroeber, A. L. 1943. "Classification of the Yuman Languages." *University of California Publications in Linguistics* 1(3):21–40.

Kroeber, A. L. 1944a. *Configurations of Culture Growth.* Berkeley: University of California Press.

Kroeber, A. L. 1944b. *Peruvian Archaeology in 1942.* New York: Viking Fund.

Kroeber, A. L. 1945. "The Ancient *Oikoumenê* as an Historic Culture Aggregate." *Journal of the Royal Anthropological Institute of Great Britain and Ireland* 75:9–20.

Kroeber, A. L. 1948a. *Anthropology.* New ed. New York: Harcourt, Brace.

Kroeber, A. L. 1948b. "Seven Mohave Myths." *Anthropological Records* 11:i–viii, 1–70.

Kroeber, A. L. 1949. "Juan Dolores, 1880–1948." *American Anthropologist* 51: 96–97.

Kroeber, A. L. 1950. "Anthropology." *Scientific American* 183 (3):87–96.

Kroeber, A. L. 1951a. "Is Western Civilization Disintegrating or Reconstituting?" *Proceedings of the American Philosophical Society* 95:100–104.

Kroeber, A. L. 1951b. "A Mohave Historical Epic." *Anthropological Records* 11: i–vi, 71–176.

Kroeber, A. L. 1951c. "Olive Oatman's Return." *Kroeber Anthropological Society Papers* 4:1–18.

Kroeber, A. L. 1952. *The Nature of Culture.* Chicago: University of Chicago Press.

Kroeber, A. L. 1955. "Linguistic Time Depth Results So Far and Their Meaning." *International Journal of American Linguistics* 21:91–104.

Kroeber, A. L. 1955–1956. Reminiscences. A. L. Kroeber Papers, Ctn 21:39, BANC MSS C-B 925, Bancroft Library. Berkeley: University of California.

Kroeber, A. L. 1957. *Style and Civilizations.* Ithaca, NY: Cornell University Press.

Kroeber, A. L. 1958a. Early Years of Anthropology at the University of California. Carton 3:12, A. L. Kroeber Papers, BANC MSS C-B 925, Bancroft Library. Berkeley: University of California.

Kroeber, A. L. 1958b. History of the Recording of Yuki. Harvey Pitkin Papers, Mss.Ms.Coll.78, Series IIC-7, American Philosophical Society Library. Published in Uldis Balodis [2016], *Yuki Grammar with Sketches of Huchnom and Coast Yuki*, 456–459. Berkeley: University of California Press.

Kroeber, A. L. 1959. "Northern Yokuts." *Anthropological Linguistics* 1:1–19.

Kroeber, A. L. 1960a. "Statistics, Indo-European, and Taxonomy." *Language* 36:1–21.

Kroeber, A. L. 1960b. "Yurok Speech Usages." In *Culture in History: Essays in Honor of Paul Radin,* edited by Stanley Diamond, 993–999. New York: Columbia University Press.

Kroeber, A. L. 1962. "The Nature of Land-holding Groups in Aboriginal California." *University of California Archaeological Survey* 56:19–58.

Kroeber, A. L. 1963. "Yokuts Dialect Survey." *University of California Anthropological Records* 11:177–251.

Kroeber, A. L. 1972. *More Mohave Myths.* Anthropological Records 27. Berkeley: University of California Press.

Kroeber, A. L. 1976. *Yurok Myths.* Berkeley: University of California Press.

Kroeber, A. L. n.d. Geography of the Wiyot. Carton 3:32, A. L. Kroeber Papers, MSS C-B 925, Bancroft Library. Berkeley: University of California.

Kroeber, A. L., and C. D. Chrétien. 1937. "Quantitative Classification of Indo-European Languages." *Language* 13:83–103.

Kroeber, A. L., and Donald Collier. 1998. *The Archaeology and Pottery of Nazca, Peru: Alfred L. Kroeber's 1926 expedition.* Walnut Creek, CA: AltaMira.

Kroeber, A. L., and E. W. Gifford. 1949. *World Renewal: A Cult System of Native Northwest California,* vol. 13, part 1 of *University of California Anthropological Records.* Berkeley: University of California Press.

Kroeber, A. L., and E. W. Gifford. 1980. *Karok Myths.* Berkeley: University of California Press.

Kroeber, A. L., and George William Grace. 1960. *The Sparkman Grammar of Luiseño.* University of California Publications in Linguistics 16. Berkeley: University of California Press.

Kroeber, A. L., and J. P. Harrington. 1914. "Phonetic Elements of the Diegueño Language." *University of California Publications in American Archaeology and Ethnology* 11:177–188.

Kroeber, A. L., and Robert F. Heizer. 1970. "Continuity of Indian Population in California from 1770/1848 to 1955." In *Papers on California Ethnology,* 1–22. Contributions of the University of California Archaeological Research Facility 9. Berkeley: University of California Archaeological Research Facility.

Kroeber, A. L., and Catharine Holt. 1920. "Masks and Moieties as a Culture Complex." *Journal of the Royal Anthropological Institute of Great Britain and Ireland* 50:452–460.

Kroeber, A. L., and Clyde Kluckhohn. 1952. *Culture: A Critical Review of Concepts and Definitions.* New York: Vintage.

Kroeber, A. L., and Clifton B. Kroeber. 1962. "Olive Oatman's First Account of Her Captivity among the Mohave." *California Historical Society Quarterly* 41: 309–317.

Kroeber, A. L., and Clifton B. Kroeber. 1973. *A Mohave War Reminiscence, 1854–1880.* University of California Publications in Anthropology. Berkeley: University of California Press.

Kroeber, A. L., and William Duncan Strong. 1924. "The Uhle Pottery Collections from Ica." *University of California Publications in American Archaeology and Ethnology* 21:95–133.

Kroeber, Clifton, and Karl Kroeber. 2002. "Ishi: Wowonupo to Parnassus Heights, 1908–1911." *Journal of the Southwest* 44:357–381.

Kroeber, Henriette Rothschild. 1909c. "Papago Coyote Tales." *Journal of American Folklore* 22:339–342.

Kroeber, Henriette Rothschild. 1912b. "Traditions of the Papago Indians." *Journal of American Folklore* 25:95–105.

Kroeber, Karl. 2003a. "Curious Profession: Alfred Kroeber and Anthropological History." *boundary 2* 30:141–155.

Kroeber, Karl. 2003b. "The Humanity of Ishi." In *Ishi in Three Centuries,* 132–145. Lincoln: University of Nebraska Press.

Kroeber, Karl, and Clifton Kroeber, eds. 2003. *Ishi in Three Centuries.* Lincoln: University of Nebraska Press.

Kroeber, Theodora. 1961. *Ishi in Two Worlds: A Biography of the Last Wild Indian in North America.* Reprinted in 2002 with a new foreword by Karl Kroeber. Berkeley: University of California Press.

Kroeber, Theodora. 1963a. "About History." *Pacific Historical Review* 32:1–6.

Kroeber, Theodora. 1963b. *The Inland Whale.* Berkeley: University of California Press.

Kroeber, Theodora. 1970. *Alfred Kroeber: A Personal Configuration.* Berkeley: University of California Press.

Kroeber, Theodora. 1976. "Foreword." In *Yurok Myths*, by A. L. Kroeber, xiii–xvii. Berkeley: University of California Press.

Kroeber, Theodora, and Robert F. Heizer. 1968. *Almost Ancestors: The First Californians.* San Francisco: Sierra Club.

Kuhn, Marshall H. 1967–1978. Marshall H. Kuhn papers. BANC MSS 84/115 c, Bancroft Library, UC Berkeley.

Kurath, William. 1945. *A Brief Introduction to Papago: A Native Language of Arizona.* Tucson: University of Arizona Press.

Kvapil, Lynne A., and Kim Shelton. 2019. "Among the Ancestors at Aidonia." In *MNHMH / MNEME, Past and Memory in the Aegean Bronze Age: Proceedings of the 17th International Aegean Conference, University of Udine, Department of Humanities and Cultural Heritage, Ca' Foscari University of Venice, Department of Humanities, 17–21 April 2018,* edited by Elisabetta Borgna, Ilaria Caloi, Filippo Maria Carinci, and Robert Laffineur, 293–299. Leuven: Peeters.

Labov, William. 1963. "The Social Motivation of a Sound Change." *Word* 19:273–309.

LaDuke, Winona. 2002. "The Salt Woman and the Coal Mine." *Sierra Magazine*, November 2002. https://vault.sierraclub.org/sierra/200211/winona_printable.asp.

Lang, Julian. 1991. "Introduction." In *To the American Indian,* edited by Lucy Thompson, xv–xxvi. Berkeley, CA: Heyday.

Lang, Julian. 1994. *Ararapíkva: Creation Stories of the Peoples.* Berkeley, CA: Heyday.

Lang, Julian, and Kayla Begay. 2020. "Creating New Speakers in a New Decade." *News from Native California* 33 (3):10–14.

Lantzer, Jason S. 2011. "The Indiana Way of Eugenics: Sterilization Laws, 1907–74." In *A Century of Eugenics in America: From the Indiana Experiment to the Human Genome Era,* edited by Paul A. Lombardo, 26–41. Bloomington: Indiana University Press.

LaPena, Michelle, and Viola LeBeau. 2021. "The West Berkeley Shellmound: A Legal Battle That Has Inspired a Generation." *News from Native California* 34 (4):26–30.

Laverty, Philip. 2010. "Recognizing Indians: Place, Identity, History, and the Federal Acknowledgement of the Ohlone/Costanoan-Esselen Nation." PhD dissertation, University of New Mexico. https://digitalrepository.unm.edu/anth_etds/41/.

Lawton, Harry W., Philip J. Wilke, Mary DeDecker, and William M. Mason. 1976. "Agriculture among the Paiute of Owens Valley." *Journal of California Anthropology* 3:13–50.

Lawyer, Lewis C. 2021. *A Grammar of Patwin*. Lincoln: University of Nebraska Press.

Le Conte, Joseph. 1892. *The Race Problem in the South*. New York: Appleton.

Le Guin, Ursula. 1980. "It Was a Dark and Stormy Night; or, Why Are We Huddling about the Campfire?" *Critical Inquiry* 7:191–199.

Le Guin, Ursula K. 1964. "The Dowry of Angyar." *Amazing Stories: Fact and Science Fiction* 38 (9):46–63.

Le Guin, Ursula K. 1966. *Rocannon's World*. New York: Ace Books.

Le Guin, Ursula K. 1968. *A Wizard of Earthsea*. Berkeley, CA: Parnassus.

Le Guin, Ursula K. 1969. *The Left Hand of Darkness*. New York: Walker.

Le Guin, Ursula K. 1972. "The Word for World Is Forest." In *Again, Dangerous Visions,* edited by Harlan Ellison, 32–118. Garden City, NY: Doubleday.

Le Guin, Ursula K. 1985. *Always Coming Home*. New York: Harper and Row.

Le Guin, Ursula K. 1989. *Dancing at the Edge of the World: Thoughts on Words, Women, Places*. New York: Grove Press.

Le Guin, Ursula K. 1991. "Poem Written in 1991: When the Soviet Union was Disintegrating." https://www.ursulakleguin.com/blog/130-poem-written-in-1991.

Le Guin, Ursula K. 2000. *The Telling*. New York: Harcourt.

Le Guin, Ursula K. 2004a. *Gifts*. Orlando, FL: Harcourt.

Le Guin, Ursula K. 2004b. *The Wave in the Mind: Talks and Essays on the Writer, the Reader, and the Imagination*. Boston: Shambhala.

Le Guin, Ursula K. 2006. *Voices*. Orlando, FL: Harcourt.

Le Guin, Ursula K. 2012. "The Art of Fiction No. 221." *Paris Review* 206:48–78. https://www.theparisreview.org/interviews/6253/the-art-of-fiction-no-221-ursula-k-le-guin.

Le Guin, Ursula K. 2018. *The Books of Earthsea*. London: Saga Press.

Le Guin, Ursula K. 2019. *Always Coming Home.* Author's expanded edition. New York: Library of America.

Le Guin, Ursula K., and Brian Attebery. 2007. "A Conversation about Fantasy." *Journal of the Fantastic in the Arts* 17:371–382.

"Lectures on American Indian." 1911. *Fowler Ensign*, 25 February 1911, 1.

Lee, Irving J., ed. 1949. *The Language of Wisdom and Folly: Background Readings in Semantics.* New York: Harper.

Lee, Robert, Tristan Ahtone, Margaret Pearce, Kalen Goodluck, Geoff McGhee, Cody Leff, Katherine Lanpher, and Taryn Salinas. 2020. Land-Grab Universities: A *High Country News* Investigation. https://www.landgrabu.org/.

Leeds-Hurwitz, Wendy. 1985. "The Committee on Research in Native American Languages." *Proceedings of the American Philosophical Society* 129:129–160.

Leeds-Hurwitz, Wendy. 2004. *Rolling in Ditches with Shamans: Jaime de Angulo and the Professionalization of American Anthropology.* Lincoln: University of Nebraska Press.

Leonard, Thomas C. 2016. *Illiberal Reformers: Race, Eugenics, and American Economics in the Progressive Era.* Princeton, NJ: Princeton University Press.

Leonard, Wesley Y. 2020. "Insights from Native American Studies for Theorizing Race and Racism in Linguistics (Response to Charity Hudley, Mallinson, and Bucholtz)." *Language* 96:e281–e291.

Leonard, Wesley Y., and Erin Haynes. 2010. "Making 'Collaboration' Collaborative: An Examination of Perspectives That Frame Linguistic Field Research." *Language Documentation and Conservation* 4:268–293.

Leslie, Jacques. 2021. "On the Klamath, Dam Removal May Come Too Late to Save the Salmon." *Yale Environment 360*, 28 September 2021. https://e360.yale.edu/features/on-the-klamath-dam-removal-may-come-too-late-to-save-the-salmon.

Leventhal, Alan, Les Field, Hank Alvarez, and Rosemary Cambra. 1994. "The Ohlone: Back from Extinction." In *The Ohlone Past and Present: Native Americans of the San Francisco Bay Region,* edited by Lowell J. Bean, 297–336. Menlo Park, CA: Ballena.

Leventhal, Alan, Les W. Field, and Orin Starn. 2020. Renaming Kroeber Hall at UC Berkeley. Public comment on the Proposal to Un-Name Kroeber Hall, 19 July 2020. Included among the public comments in "Documents relating to the unnaming of Kroeber Hall," edited by Andrew Garrett. https://escholarship.org/uc/item/9tv6788z.

Lévi-Strauss, Claude. 1960. "Alfred Louis Kroeber." *Journal de la Société des américanistes* 49:115–116.

Lévi-Strauss, Claude. 1966. "Anthropology: Its Achievements and Future." *Current Anthropology* 7:124–127.

Levinson, Stephen C. 1996. "Language and Space." *Annual Review of Anthropology* 25:353–382.

Levinson, Stephen C. 2003. *Space in Language and Cognition: Explorations in Cognitive Diversity.* Cambridge, UK: Cambridge University Press.

Lewis, Diane. 1973. "Anthropology and Colonialism." *Current Anthropology* 14:581–602.

Lewis, Herbert S. 2014. *In Defense of Anthropology: An Investigation of the Critique of Anthropology.* New Brunswick, NJ: Transaction Publishers.

Lewis, Herbert S. 2018. "Franz Boas and Friends? Not Really." *Reviews in Anthropology* 47:21–38.

Lewis, Herbert S. 2022. "Alfred L. Kroeber's Career and Contributions to California's Indigenous Peoples." *BEROSE International Encyclopaedia of the Histories of Anthropology.* https://www.berose.fr/article2536.html.

Li, Alice, Kasha Patel, and Melina Mara. 2022. "Flight of the Condors." *Washington Post* interactive feature, 15 September 2022. https://www.washingtonpost.com/climate-solutions/interactive/2022/california-condors-yurok-program-extinction/.

Liebmann, Matthew. 2008. "Postcolonial Cultural Affiliation: Essentialism, Hybridity, and NAGPRA." In *Archaeology and the Postcolonial Critique,* edited by Matthew Liebmann and Uzma Z. Rizvi, 73–90. Lanham, MD: Altamira.

Lightfoot, Kent G. 1997. "Cultural Constructions of Coastal Landscapes: A Middle Holocene Perspective from the San Francisco Bay." In *Archaeology of the California Coast during the Middle Holocene,* edited by Jon M. Erlandson and Michael A. Glassow, 129–141. Perspectives in California Archaeology 4. Los Angeles: University of California Institute of Archaeology.

Lightfoot, Kent G. 2005. *Indians, Missionaries, and Merchants: The Legacy of Colonial Encounters on the California Frontiers.* Berkeley: University of California Press.

Lightfoot, Kent G. 2018. Study of Bulk Sediment Samples from West Berkeley Shell Mound. Archaeological Research Facility, University of California, Berkeley. https://arf.berkeley.edu/publications/study-bulk-sediment-samples-west-berkeley-shell-mound.

Lightfoot, Kent G., Edward M. Luby, and Lisa Pesnichak. 2011. "Evolutionary Typologies and Hunter-Gatherer Research: Rethinking the Mounded Landscapes of Central California." In *Hunter-Gatherer Archaeology as Historical Process,* edited by Kenneth E. Sassaman and Donald H. Holly, Jr. 55–78. Tucson: University of Arizona Press.

Lightfoot, Kent G., and Otis Parrish. 2009. *California Indians and Their Environment: An Introduction.* Berkeley: University of California Press.

Liljeblad, Sven, Catherine S. Fowler, and Glenda Powell. 2012. *Northern Paiute-Bannock Dictionary.* Salt Lake City: University of Utah Press.

Lindberg, David R., and Ben M. Waggoner. 1996. Annie Montague Alexander (1867–1950): Benefactress of UCMP. UC Museum of Paleontology. https://ucmp.berkeley.edu/about-ucmp/history-of-ucmp/annie-alexander/.

Lindo, John, Emilia Huerta-Sánchez, Shigeki Nakagome, Morten Rasmussen, Barbara Petzelt, Joycelynn Mitchell, Jerome S. Cybulski, Eske Willerslev, Michael De-Giorgio, and Ripan S. Malhi. 2016. "A Time Transect of Exomes from a Native American Population before and after European Contact." *Nature Communications* 7:13175.

Lindquist, Wendi A. 2014. "Stealing from the Dead: Scientists, Settlers, and Indian Burial Sites in Early-Nineteenth-Century Oregon." *Oregon Historical Quarterly* 115:324–343.

Lindsay, Brendan C. 2012. *Murder State: California's Native American Genocide, 1846–1873.* Lincoln: University of Nebraska Press.

Linn, Mary S. 2021. "Conclusion: The Power of Words, Relationships, and Archives." In *Indigenous Languages and the Promise of Archives,* edited by Adrianna Link, Abigail Shelton, and Patrick Spiro, 479–489. Lincoln: University of Nebraska Press and American Philosophical Society.

Local and Personals. 1901. *The Indian Advance* 2, no. 8 (April 1): 3; Carson Indian School, Carson City, Nevada.

Lolorias, John Miguel. *See* Dolores, Juan.

Lomawaima, K. Tsianina, Bryan McKinley Jones Brayboy, and Teresa L. McCarty, eds. 2018. *Native American Boarding School Stories.* Minneapolis: University of Minnesota Press. Special issue of *Journal of American Indian Education* 57.

Lomawaima, K. Tsianina, and Teresa L. McCarty. 2006. *"To Remain an Indian": Lessons in Democracy from a Century of Native American Education.* New York: Teachers College Press.

Long, Frederick Alexander. 1998. " 'The Kingdom Must Come Soon': The Role of A. L. Kroeber and the Hearst Survey in Shaping California Anthropology, 1901–1920." MA thesis, Simon Fraser University.

Lord, Albert B. 2000. Edited by Stephen Mitchell and Gregory Nagy. 2nd. ed. *The Singer of Tales.* Cambridge, MA: Harvard University Press.

Loud, Llewellyn L. 1918. "Ethnography and Archaeology of the Wiyot Territory." *University of California Publications in American Archaeology and Ethnology* 14:221–436.

Loud, Llewellyn L., and M. R. Harrington. 1929. "Lovelock Cave." *University of California Publications in American Archaeology and Ethnology* 25:1–183.

Lowie, Robert H. 1940. "Native Languages as Ethnographic Tools." *American Anthropologist* 42:81–89.

Lowry, Chag. 2007. *The Original Patriots: Northern California Indian Veterans of World War Two.* Eureka, CA: Chag Lowry.

Lowry, David Shane. 2021. "An Obituary for Alfred Kroeber (or ... Can American Indians Speak?)." *Anthrodendum,* 5 February 2021. https://anthrodendum.org/2021/02/05/an-obituary-for-alfred-kroeber-or-can-american-indians-speak/.

Luby, Edward M., Clayton D. Drescher, and Kent G. Lightfoot. 2006. "Shell Mounds and Mounded Landscapes in the San Francisco Bay Area: An Integrated Approach." *Journal of Island andCoastal Archaeology* 1:191–214.

Lummis, Charles F. 1901. "A New Indian Policy." *Land of Sunshine: A Southern California Magazine* 15:457–464.

Lummis, Charles F. 1904. "The Greatest California Patio House." *Country Life in America* 6:533–540.

Lundberg, Ferdinand. 1936. *Imperial Hearst: A Social Biography.* New York: Equinox.

Luomala, Katharine. 1986. "Some Berkeley Daze at the University of California." *Hawaiian Anthropological Association Newsletter* 11 (4). Also folder 1:13 in the Katharine Luomala Papers, 1923–1984, BANC MSS 89/122 cz, Bancroft Library, UC Berkeley.

Luthin, Herbert, and Leanne Hinton. 2003a. "The Days of a Life: What Ishi's Stories Can Tell Us about Ishi." In *Ishi in Three Centuries,* edited by Karl Kroeber and Clifton Kroeber, 318–354. Lincoln: University of Nebraska Press.

Luthin, Herbert, and Leanne Hinton. 2003b. "The Story of Lizard." In *Ishi in Three Centuries,* edited by Karl Kroeber and Clifton Kroeber, 293–317. Lincoln: University of Nebraska Press.

Luthin, Herbert W., ed. 2002. *Surviving through the Days: Translations of Native California Stories and Songs.* Berkeley: University of California Press.

Maddox, Deborah J. 1995. Letter from the Director of the Office of Tribal Services to Rosemary Cambra, Muwekma Indian Tribe, 10 October 1995. United States Department of the Interior, Office of Federal Acknowledgement, Muw V001 D006. https://www.indianz.com/adc20/Muw/V001/D006.PDF.

Madley, Benjamin. 2005. "From Africa to Auschwitz: How German South West Africa Incubated Ideas and Methods Adopted and Developed by the Nazis in Eastern Europe." *European History Quarterly* 35:429–464.

Madley, Benjamin. 2016. *An American Genocide: The United States and the California Indian Catastrophe, 1846–1873.* New Haven, CT: Yale University Press.

Madley, Benjamin. 2019. "California's First Mass Incarceration System: Franciscan Missions, California Indians, and Penal Servitude, 1769–1836." *Pacific Historical Review* 88:14–47.

Makley, Matthew S. 2018. *The Small Shall Be Strong: A History of Lake Tahoe's Washoe Indians.* Amherst: University of Massachusetts Press.

Mallios, Seth. 2020. *Born a Slave, Died a Pioneer: Nathan Harrison and the Historical Archaeology of Legend.* New York: Berghahn.

Malécot, André. 1963. "Luiseño: A Structural Analysis, I–II." *International Journal of American Linguistics* 29:89–95, 196–210.

Malécot, André. 1964. "Luiseño: A Structural Analysis, III–IV." *International Journal of American Linguistics* 30:14–31, 243–250.

Mannheim, Bruce, and Dennis Tedlock. 1995. "Introduction." In *The Dialogic Emergence of Culture,* edited by Dennis Tedlock and Bruce Mannheim, 1–32. Urbana: University of Illinois Press.

Manriquez, L. Frank. 2013. "Shadow of the Whale." *News from Native California* 26 (3):37.

Mariátegui, José Carlos. 2007. *7 ensayos de interpretación de la realidad peruana.* Caracas: Biblioteca Ayacucho. Originally published in 1928. Primera edición Biblioteca Ayacucho 1979; tercera edición con correcciones y adiciones de nuevos textos.

Mark, Joan. 1988. *A Stranger in Her Native Land: Alice Fletcher and the American Indians.* Lincoln: University of Nebraska Press.

Markel, Norman, and Mary Haas. 1984. Mary Haas interview. Visual Dialogues in Anthropology, Department of Anthropology, University of Florida. https://www.youtube.com/watch?v=hwab3RfDaWw.

Martin, Robert. 1972. Creation Story. LA 248.033, The Judy Hummell Crawford Collection of Mohave Sound Recordings, Survey of California and Other Indian Languages, University of California, Berkeley, http://cla.berkeley.edu/item/21119.

Martin, Robert, Emmett Van Fleet, and Judith G. Crawford. 1967–1972. Judy Hummell Crawford collection of Mohave sound recordings. LA248, Survey of California and Other Indian Languages, University of California, Berkeley. http://cla.berkeley.edu/collection/10207.

Mason, J. Alden. 1911–1967. John Alden Mason papers. Mss.B.M384, American Philosophical Society.

Mason, J. Alden. 1917. "Tepecano, a Piman Language of Western Mexico." *Annals of the New York Academy of Sciences* 25:309–416.

Mason, J. Alden. 1918. "The Language of the Salinan Indians." *University of California Publications in American Archaeology and Ethnology* 14:1–154.

Mason, J. Alden. 1921. "The Papago Migration Legend." *Journal of American Folklore* 34:254–268.

Mason, J. Alden. 1950. *The Language of the Papago of Arizona.* Philadelphia: University of Pennsylvania, University Museum.

"Masque Presented at Pleasanton." 1912. *San Francisco Chronicle*, 24 May 1912, 16.

Mathiot, Madeline. 1991. "The Reminiscences of Juan Dolores, an Early O'odham Linguist." *Anthropological Linguistics* 33:232–315.

Mattina, Nancy. 2019. *Uncommon Anthropologist: Gladys Reichard and Western Native American Culture.* Norman: University of Oklahoma Press.

Maxwell, Judith. 2013. Lapuhch: Tunica Language Awakening, a New Methodology? 3rd International Conference on Language Documentation and Conservation (ICLDC), Honolulu. http://hdl.handle.net/10125/26117.

"May Arrest the Professor: Grave Robbers May Have to Answer for Crime." 1906. *Ukiah Dispatch Democrat,* 24 August 1906, 1.

McConvell, Patrick, and Claire Bowern. 2011. "The Prehistory and Internal Relationships of Australian Languages." *Language and Linguistics Compass* 5:19–32.

McDonnell, Bradley, Andrea L. Berez-Kroeker, and Gary Holton, eds. 2018. *Reflections on Language Documentation 20 Years after Himmelmann 1998,* vol. 15 of *Language Documentation and Conservation, Special Publications.* Honolulu: University of Hawai'i Press.

McElgunn, Hannah. 2021. "Intertextual Politics: Presence, Erasure, and the Hopi Language." *American Ethnologist* 48:432–445.

McGuckian, Margaret Ann. 1996. "Management Uses of Contemporary Ethnography and the Lovelock Paiute." Master's thesis, University of Nevada, Reno.

McNeill, William H. 1963. *The Rise of the West: A History of the Human Community.* Chicago: University of Chicago Press.

McPhee, John. 1993. *Assembling California.* New York: Farrar, Straus and Giroux.

Meakins, Felicity. 2018. "Mixed Languages." In *Oxford Research Encyclopedias: Literature,* edited by Mark Aronoff. Oxford: Oxford University Press. https://doi.org/10.1093/acrefore/9780199384655.013.151.

Medina, Vincent. 2014. "Breath of Life / Silent No More." *News from Native California,* 1 July 2014. https://newsfromnativecalifornia.com/breath-of-life-silent-no-more/.

Meetings. 1930. "The Semi-Centennial of the Anthropological Society of Washington." *American Anthropologist* 32:189–203.

Meillet, Antoine, and Marcel Cohen. 1924. *Les langues du monde.* Paris: É. Champion.

Mejía Xesspe, M. Toribio. 1922. *Algunas costumbres y creencias de los indígenas (distrito del Toro, provincia de La Unión, departamento de Arequipa).* Lima: Talleres graficos del Asilo "Víctor Larco Herrera."

Mejía Xesspe, M. Toribio. 1942. "Acueductos y caminos antiguos de la hoya del Río Grande de Nasca." In *Adas y trabajos cientificos del XXVII Congreso International de Americanistas,* vol. 1, 559–569. Lima: Librería e Imprenta Gil.

Mejía Xesspe, M. Toribio. 1954. "Lingüística del Norte Andino." *Letras* (*Lima*) 20(50–53):204–229.

Meloche, Chelsea H., Laure Spake, and Katherine L. Nichols, eds. 2021. *Working with and for Ancestors: Collaboration in the Care and Study of Ancestral Remains.* London: Routledge.

Merlin, Imelda. 1977. *Alameda: A Geographical History.* Alameda: Friends of the Alameda Free Library. https://alamedamuseum.org/wp-content/uploads/2019/11/Imelda_smallpics_4printing.pdf.

Merriam, John C. 1909. "Note on the Occurrence of Human Remains in Californian Caves." *Science* 30:531–532.

Merriam, John C., and Chester Stock. 1932. *The Felidæ of Rancho La Brea.* Washington, DC: Carnegie Institution of Washington.

Merrill, John T. M. 2018. "The Historical Origin of Consonant Mutation in the Atlantic Languages." Unpublished PhD dissertation, University of California, Berkeley. https://escholarship.org/uc/item/1qn4m0bh.

Mesía-Montenegro, Christian. 2006. "Julio C. Tello: Teoria y practica en la arqueologia Andina." *Arqueología y Sociedad* 17:141–158.

Mesía-Montenegro, Christian. 2018. "Julio Tello as a Medical Anthropologist: Assessing the Antiquity of Syphilis in Ancient Peru." *História, Ciências, Saúde-Manguinhos* 25:541–552.

Micale, Mark S. 2018. "What Pinker Leaves Out." *Historical Reflections* 44: 128–139.

Michael, Lev, and Natalia Chousou-Polydouri. 2020. "Computational Phylogenetics and the Classification of South American Languages." *Language and Linguistics Compass* 13:e12358.

Miller, Amy. 2018. "Phonological Developments in Delta-California Yuman." *International Journal of American Linguistics* 84:383–433.

Miller, Larisa K. 2013a. "Primary Sources on C. E. Kelsey and the Northern California Indian Association." *Journal of Western Archives* 4 (1): Art. 8. https://digitalcommons.usu.edu/westernarchives/vol4/iss1/8?

Miller, Larisa K. 2013b. "The Secret Treaties with California's Indians." *Prologue* 45(3–4):38–45.

Milliken, Randall. 2008. *Native Americans at Mission San Jose.* Banning, CA: Malki-Ballena Press.

Milliken, Randall, Laurence H. Shoup, and Beverly R. Ortiz. 2009. *Ohlone/Costanoan Indians of the San Francisco Peninsula and Their Neighbors, Yesterday and Today.* Oakland, CA: Archaeological and Historical Consultants. https://digitalcommons.csumb.edu/hornbeck_ind_1/6.

Mithun, Marianne. 1984. "The Evolution of Noun Incorporation." *Language* 60:847–894.

Mithun, Marianne. 1999. *The Languages of Native North America.* Cambridge, MA: Cambridge University Press.

Molinié, Antoinette. 2004. "The Resurrection of the Inca: The Role of Indian Representations in the Invention of the Peruvian Nation." *History and Anthropology* 15:233–250.

Moss, Arianna. 2018. "How the 'Home of Free Speech' Veils a Dark, Violent Past." *Daily Cal,* 25 March 2018.

Mufwene, Salikoko S. 2003. "Genetic Linguistics and Genetic Creolistics: A Response to Sarah G. Thomason's 'Creoles and Genetic Relationships.'" *Journal of Pidgin and Creole Languages* 18:273–288.

Munro, Pamela. 1976. *Mojave Syntax.* New York: Garland.

Munro, Pamela, Nellie Brown, and Judith G. Crawford. 1992. *A Mojave Dictionary.* UCLA Occasional Papers in Linguistics 10. Los Angeles: University of California Department of Linguistics.

Murra, John V. 2009. "The International Relevance of Julio C. Tello." In *The Life and Writings of Julio C. Tello: American's First Indigenous Archaeologist,* edited by Richard L. Burger, 55–64. Iowa City: University of Iowa Press.

Murray, Stephen O. 1997. "A 1978 Interview with Mary R. Haas." *Anthropological Linguistics* 39:695–722.

Musser-Lopez, Ruth Arlene, and Steve Miller. 2010. "Archaeological Trails and Ethnographic Trails: Can They Meet?" *Proceedings of the Society for California Archaeology* 24. https://scahome.org/publications/proceedings/Proceedings.24Musser-Lopez1.pdf.

Muysken, Pieter, and Norval Smith. 1995. "The Study of Pidgin and Creole Languages." In *Pidgins and Creoles: An Introduction,* edited by Jacques Arends, Pieter Muysken, and Norval Smith, 3–24. Amsterdam: John Benjamins.

Nash, Margaret A. 2019. "Entangled Pasts: Land-grant Colleges and American Indian Dispossession." *History of Education Quarterly* 59:437–467.

Nasir, Na'ilah, Holly Doremus, Jenny Kwon, Therese Leone, Jovan Lewis, Rachel Lim, Nancy McKinney, Fred Nichols, and Cheyenne Overall. 2017. Building Naming Project Task Force: Summary Report and Recommendations. Berkeley: University of California. https://diversity.berkeley.edu/sites/default/files/building_naming_project_task_force_report_final_4-3-2017.pdf.

Nason, James D. 1971. "Museums and American Indians: An Inquiry into Relationships." *Western Museums Quarterly* 8(1):13–17.

Natches, Gilbert. 1923. "Northern Paiute Verbs." *University of California Publications in American Archaeology and Ethnology* 20:243–259.

Natches, Gilbert, and Saul H. Riesenberg. 1940. Northern Paiute Myths Related to Saul Riesenberg by Gilbert Natches. MS 4878, National Anthropological Archives. https://sova.si.edu/record/NAA.MS4878.

Native American Heritage Commission, State of California. 2021. Letter from Commission Chair Laura Miranda to UC President Michael Drake, 3 June 2021. Native American Heritage Commission's Review of the University of California's Final Draft Native American Cultural Affiliation and Repatriation Policy. http://nahc.ca.gov/wp-content/uploads/2021/08/NAHC-Response-to-UC-Repatriation-Policy_June-3-2021.pdf.

Natividad, Ivan. 2022. "Student Exhibit at Berkeley Hearst Museum Aims to Decolonize Philippine History." *Berkeley News*, 31 October 2022. https://news.berkeley.edu/2022/10/31/student-exhibit-at-berkeley-hearst-museum-aims-to-decolonize-philippine-history.

Nelson, N. C. 1909. "Shellmounds of the San Francisco Bay Region." *University of California Publications in American Archaeology and Ethnology* 7:310–348.

Nelson, N. C. 1910. "The Ellis Landing Shellmound." *University of California Publications in American Archaeology and Ethnology* 7:357–426.

Nelson, Peter. 2021. "Where Have All the Anthros Gone? The Shift in California Indian Studies from Research 'On' to Research 'With, For, and By' Indigenous Peoples." *American Anthropologist* 123:469–473.

Nettl, Bruno. 1965. "The Songs of Ishi: Musical Styles of the Yahi Indians." *Musical Quarterly* 51:460–477.

Nevins, M. Eleanor. 2017. " 'You Shall Not Become This Kind of People': Indigenous Political Argument in Maidu Linguistic Text Collections." In *Engaging Native American Publics: Linguistic Anthropology in a Collaborative Key,* edited by Paul V. Kroskrity and Barbra A. Meek, 61–81. London: Routledge.

Newman, Stanley S. 1944. *Yokuts Language of California*. New York: Viking Fund.

Newman, Stanley S. 1946. "The Yawelmani Dialect of Yokuts." In *Linguistic Structures of Native America,* edited by C. Osgood, 222–248. New York: Viking Fund.

Newman, Stanley S. 1958. *Zuni Dictionary.* Indiana University Research Center in Anthropology, Folklore, and Linguistics Publications 6. Bloomington: Indiana University Press.

Newman, Stanley S. 1965. *Zuni Grammar.* Albuquerque: University of New Mexico Press.

Newman, Stanley S. 1996. "Sketch of the Zuni Language." In *Languages,* edited by Ives Goddard, 483–506. Handbook of North American Indians 17. Washington, DC: Smithsonian Institution.

Newmeyer, Frederick J. 2020. "Outside of the Palace Walls: Generative Linguists in the 1970s and 1980s." *Language* 96:e173–e199.

Newsom, Gavin. 2019. Executive Order N-15-19. Executive Department, State of California. https://www.gov.ca.gov/wp-content/uploads/2019/06/6.18.19-Executive-Order.pdf.

Ngũgĩ wa Thiong'o. 1986. *Decolonising the Mind: The Politics of Language in African Literature.* Woodbridge, UK: James Currey.

Nickliss, Alexandra M. 2018. *Phoebe Apperson Hearst: A Life of Power and Politics.* Lincoln: University of Nebraska Press.

Nijmeh, Charlene. 2020. Letter (for the Muwekma Ohlone Tribe of the San Francisco Bay Area) to Paul Fine, Chair, Building Name Review Committee, University of California, Berkeley, 14 August 2020. https://chancellor.berkeley.edu/sites/default/files/kroeber_muwekma_ohlone_tribe_public.pdf.

NoiseCat, Julian Brave, Ruth Orta, Jonathan Cordero, and Corrina Gould. 2019. "Landless in the Bay Area." SFMOMA's *Open Space* 13. https://openspace.sfmoma.org/2019/11/landless-in-the-bay-area/.

Nomland, Gladys Ayer, and A. L. Kroeber. 1936. "Wiyot Towns." *University of California Publications in American Archaeology and Ethnology* 35:39–48.

North, Griswold. 1900. "A Summer Home in California." *The Puritan* 7: 593–599.

Norton, Jack. 1979. *Genocide in Northwestern California: When Our Worlds Cried.* San Francisco: Indian Historian Press.

Ocasio, Rafael. 2020. *Race and Nation in Puerto Rican Folklore: Franz Boas and John Alden Mason in Porto Rico.* New Brunswick, NJ: Rutgers University Press.

"Old Ellis Mound to Disappear Soon." 1913. *San Francisco Call,* 21 June 1913, 10.

Older, Cora Baggerly. 1936. *William Randolph Hearst, American.* New York: D. Appleton-Century.

O'Meara, Carolyn, and Gabriela Pérez Báez. 2011. "Spatial Frames of Reference in Mesoamerican Languages." *Language Sciences* 33:837–852.

O'Neale, Lila M. 1932. "Yurok-Karok Basket Weavers." *University of California Publications in American Archaeology and Ethnology* 32:1–184.

O'Neale, Lila M., and Juan Dolores. 1943. "Notes on Papago Color Designations." *American Anthropologist* 45:387–397.

O'Neale, Lila M., and A. L. Kroeber. 1930. "Textile Periods in Ancient Peru." *University of California Publications in American Archaeology and Ethnology* 28: 23–56.

O'Neill, Sean. 2008. *Cultural Contact and Linguistic Relativity among the Indians of Northwestern California*. Norman: University of Oklahoma Press.

Osborn, Henry Fairfield. 1921. "The Second International Congress of Eugenics Address of Welcome." *Science* 54:311–313.

"Our Founder: Phoebe Apperson Hearst." n.d. Phoebe A. Hearst Museum of Anthropology, UC Berkeley. https://hearstmuseum.berkeley.edu/phoebe-heast/.

"Our History." n.d. Berkeley Haas, UC Berkeley. https://haas.berkeley.edu/about/at-a-glance/history/.

Owsley, Douglas W., and Richard L. Jantz, eds. 2014. *Kennewick Man: The Scientific Investigation of an Ancient American Skeleton*. College Station: Texas A&M University Press.

Paddock, Richard C. 2008. "Native Americans Say Berkeley Is No Place for Their Ancestors." *Los Angeles Times,* 13 January 2008.

Padilla, Sedna Villavicencio. 2019. "The UCLA Fowler Museum & Collaborative Repatriation: An Analysis of NAGPRA Compliance Working with California Indian Tribes." Master's thesis, University of California, Los Angeles. https://escholarship.org/uc/item/6jj7q7rd.

Padilla Deza, Fernando. 2018. El concepto y la representación de lo indio en la propuesta política de Julio César Tello Rojas (1917–1929). Magíster en historia, Universidad Nacional Mayor de San Marcos. https://core.ac.uk/download/pdf/323349895.pdf.

Palmer, Bill, Jonathon Lu, Jonathan Schlossberg, and Alice Gaby. 2017. "How Does the Environment Shape Spatial Language? Evidence for Sociotopography." *Linguistic Typology* 21:457–491.

Pandey, Triloki Nath. 1967. "Factionalism in a Southwestern Pueblo." Unpublished PhD dissertation, University of Chicago.

Pandey, Triloki Nath. 1972. "Anthropologists at Zuni." *Proceedings of the American Philosophical Society* 116:321–337.

Pandian, Anand. 2019. *A Possible Anthropology: Methods for Uneasy Times*. Durham, NC: Duke University Press.

Panich, Lee M. 2020. *Narratives of Persistence: Indigenous Negotiations of Colonialism in Alta and Baja California*. Tucson: University of Arizona Press.

Panich, Lee M., GeorgeAnn DeAntoni, and Tsim D. Schneider. 2021. " 'By the Aid of His Indians': Native Negotiations of Settler Colonialism in Marin County, California, 1840–70." *International Journal of Historical Archaeology* 25:92–115.

Panich, Lee M., and Tsim D. Schneider, eds. 2014. *Indigenous Landscapes and Spanish Missions: New Perspectives from Archaeology and Ethnohistory.* Tucson: University of Arizona Press.

Papac, Luca, Michal Ernée, Miroslav Dobeš, Michaela Langová, Adam B. Rohrlach, Franziska Aron, Gunnar U. Neumann, et al. 2021. "Dynamic Changes in Genomic and Social Structures in Third Millennium BCE Central Europe." *Science Advances* 7:eabi6941.

"Papal Bulls Used to Aid Indian Cause at Hearing." 1954. *Oakland Tribune,* 2 July 1954, 5.

Parry, Milman. 1923. "A Comparative Study of Diction as One of the Elements of Style in Early Greek Epic Poetry." Master's thesis, University of California. Reprinted in *The Making of Homeric Verse: The Collected Papers of Milman Parry*, edited by Adam Parry, 421–436. Oxford: Clarendon Press, 1971.

Parry, Milman. 1928. *L'épithète traditionelle dans Homère: Essai sur un problème de style homérique.* Paris: Société d'éditions "Les Belles Lettres." Thèse pour le doctorat ès lettres presentée à la Faculté des Lettres de l'Université de Paris. Translated and reprinted in *The Making of Homeric Verse: The Collected Papers of Milman Parry,* edited by Adam Parry, 1–190. Oxford: Clarendon Press, 1971.

Parry, Milman. 1971. Edited by Adam Parry. *The Making of Homeric Verse: The Collected Papers of Milman Parry.* Oxford: Clarendon Press.

Parsons, Elsie Clews. 1880–1980. Elsie Clews Parsons papers. Mss.Ms.Coll.29, American Philosophical Society.

Parsons, Elsie Clews. 1917. *Notes on Zuñi: Part II.* Memoirs of the American Anthropological Association. Lancaster, PA: American Anthropological Association.

Pederson, Eric, Eve Danziger, David Wilkins, Stephen C. Levinson, Sotaro Kita, and Gunter Senft. 1998. "Semantic Typology and Spatial Conceptualization." *Language* 74:557–589.

Pellegatti, Paolo. 2020. "Sunk." *From Many Basements.* Phoebe A. Hearst Museum of Anthropology blog. 17 July. http://pellegatti.blogspot.com/.

Penfield, Susan D. 2005. "Mohave Remembered." *Journal of the Southwest* 47: 81–105.

Penfield, Susan D., Angelina Serratos, Benjamin V. Tucker, Amelia Flores, Gilford Harper, Johnny Hill, Jr., and Nora Vasquez. 2008. "Small Languages and Small Language Communities." *International Journal of the Sociology of Language* 191:187–202.

Penfield, Susan D., and Benjamin V. Tucker. 2011. "From Documenting to Revitalizing an Endangered Language: Where Do Applied Linguists Fit?" *Language and Education* 25:291–305.

Perley, Bernard C. 2011. *Defying Maliseet Language Death: Emergent Vitalities of Language, Culture, and Identity in Eastern Canada*. Lincoln: University of Nebraska Press.

Perley, Bernard C. 2012. "Zombie Linguistics: Experts, Endangered Languages and the Curse of Undead Voices." *Anthropological Forum* 22:133–149.

Perley, Bernard C. 2013. "*Remembering* Ancestral Voices: Emergent Vitalities and the Future of Indigenous Languages." In *Responses to Language Endangerment in Honor of Mickey Noonan: New Directions in Language Documentation and Language Revitalization,* edited by Elena Mihas, Bernard C. Perley, Gabriel Rei Doval, and Kathleen Wheatley, 243–270. Amsterdam: John Benjamins.

Perry, Jean. 2003. "When the World Was New: Ishi's Stories." In *Ishi in Three Centuries,* edited by Karl Kroeber and Clifton Kroeber, 275–292. Lincoln: University of Nebraska Press.

Peterson, Brent. 2014. "Passage through Mohave Territory, Part 1." Video presented by Colorado River Historical Society. https://www.youtube.com/watch?v=SqgBY0jE-7w.

Phillips, Julie. 2019. "Ursula Le Guin Was a Creator of Worlds." *Humanities* 40 (1). https://www.neh.gov/article/ursula-k-le-guin-was-creator-worlds.

Phillips, Julie. 2022. *The Baby on the Fire Escape: Creativity, Motherhood, and the Mind-Baby Problem*. New York: W. W. Norton.

Pike, Kenneth L. 1947. *Phonemics: A Technique for Reducing Languages to Writing.* Ann Arbor: University of Michigan Press.

Pike, Kenneth L. 1999. *Mary R. Haas, January 12, 1910–May 17, 1996: A Biographical Memoir.* Washington, DC: National Academies Press.

Pinker, Steven. 2002. *The Blank Slate.* New York: Viking Penguin.

Pinker, Steven. 2011. *The Better Angels of Our Nature: Why Violence Has Declined.* New York: Viking.

Pinker, Steven. 2018. *Enlightenment Now: The Case for Reason, Science, Humanism, and Progress.* New York: Penguin.

Pitkin, Harvey. 1884–1980. Harvey Pitkin papers. Mss.Ms.Coll.78, American Philosophical Society.

Platt, Tony. 2009. "Grave Matters: A Brief History of the Desecration of Native American Cemeteries in Humboldt County." *North Coast Journal,* 18 June 2009. https://www.northcoastjournal.com/humboldt/grave-matters/Content?oid=2129764.

Platt, Tony. 2011. *Grave Matters: Excavating California's Buried Past*. Berkeley, CA: Heyday.

Platt, Tony. 2012–2013. "The Yokayo vs. the University of California." *News from Native California* 26 (2):9–14.

Platt, Tony. 2020a. Kroeber Hall: What's in an In-naming [sic]: Addendum. Public comment on the Proposal to Un-Name Kroeber Hall. https://chancellor.berkeley.edu/sites/default/files/kroeber_platt_addendum_august_31_public.pdf.

Platt, Tony. 2020b. "What's in an Un-naming? Berkeley's Kroeber Hall." *History News Network,* 2 August 2020. https://historynewsnetwork.org/article/176677.

Pope, Saxton, Jr. 1972. Interview with Saxton Pope concerning his reminiscences of Ishi. #24-448, Phoebe A. Hearst Museum of Anthropology, University of California, Berkeley. http://cla.berkeley.edu/item/11890.

Pope, Saxton T. 1920. "The Medical History of Ishi." *University of California Publications in American Archaeology and Ethnology* 13:175–213.

"President and Senate to Make Treaty with Aborigine." 1911. *Oroville Daily Register,* 4 September 1911, 1.

Protzen, Jean-Pierre, and David Harris, eds. 2005. *Explorations in the Pisco Valley: Max Uhle's Reports to Phoebe Apperson Hearst, August 1901 to January 1902.* Berkeley: University of California Archaeological Research Facility. https://escholarship.org/uc/item/3xp8j2b3.

Proulx, Paul. 1985. "The Semantics of Yurok Terms Referring to Water." *Anthropological Linguistics* 27:353–362.

Putnam, Edna Hildebrand. 1917. "Ah-Pura-Way: The Dance of the White Deer Skin and Other Klamath Indian Worship Dances. *Overland Monthly* 69:277–283.

Putnam, F. W., ed. 1905. *The Department of Anthropology of the University of California*. Berkeley, CA: University Press.

Putnam, F. W., ed. 1906. *Guide to the Collections of the Department of Anthropology at the Affiliated Colleges, San Francisco.* Berkeley: University of California Press.

Quinby, Alysoun. 2003. "Dialectology of River Yurok: A Preliminary Exploration." Senior honors thesis, Department of Linguistics, University of California, Berkeley.

Radin, Paul. 1948. *Winnebago Hero Cycles: A Study in Aboriginal Literature.* Indiana University Publications in Anthropology and Linguistics, Memoir 1. Baltimore, MD: Waverly Press.

Raff, Jennifer. 2022. *Origin: A Genetic History of the Americas.* New York: Twelve.

Ram, Tala. 2014. "Ever Notice How Often 'Hearst' Appears on Our Campus?" *Daily Cal,* 26 February 2014.

Ramirez, Louise J. Miranda. 2008–2009. "Breathing Language." *News from Native California* 22:8–12.

Ramón Joffré, Gabriel. 2014. *El neoperuano: Estilo nacional y paisaje urbano en Lima, 1910–1940.* Lima: Municipalidad Metropolitana de Lima, Sequilao.

Rasmussen, Morten, Martin Sikora, Anders Albrechtsen, Thorfinn Sand Korneliussen, J. Victor Moreno-Mayar, G. David Poznik, Christoph P. E. Zollikofer, et al. 2015. "The Ancestry and Affiliations of Kennewick Man." *Nature* 523:455–464.

Ratzel, Friedrich. 1904. Geschichte, Völkerkunde und historische Perspektive. *Historische Zeitschrift* 93: 1–46. Reprinted in Friedrich Ratzel, *Kleine Schriften,* vol. 2, edited by Hans Helmolt, 488–525. Munich: Oldenbourg, 1906.

Ray, Arthur J. 2006. "Kroeber and the California Claims: Historical Particularism and Cultural Ecology in Court." In *Central Sites, Peripheral Visions: Cultural and Institutional Crossings in the History of Anthropology,* edited by Richard Handler, 248–274. Madison: University of Wisconsin Press.

Redman, Samuel J. 2016. *Bone Rooms: From Scientific Racism to Human Prehistory in Museums.* Cambridge, MA: Harvard University Press.

Redman, Samuel J. 2021. *Prophets and Ghosts: The Story of Salvage Anthropology.* Cambridge, MA: Harvard University Press.

Register of Pupils. 1892–1899. Records of the Stewart Indian School, Record Group 75, Records of the Bureau of Indian Affairs, National Archives and Records Administration, San Bruno, California.

Reichmann, Charles P. 2018. "Anti-Chinese Racism at Berkeley: The Case for Renaming Boalt Hall." *Asian American Law Journal* 25:5–20.

Reid, Donald Malcolm. 1985. "Indigenous Egyptology: The Decolonization of a Profession?" *Journal of the American Oriental Society* 105:233–246.

Reid, Donald Malcolm. 2015. *Contesting Antiquity in Egypt: Archaeologies, Museums, and the Struggle for Identities from World War I to Nasser.* Cairo: American University in Cairo Press.

Reid, Donald Malcolm. 2020. "Pharaonic Heritage in Modern Egypt." In *A Companion to the Ancient Near East,* 2nd ed., edited by Daniel C. Snell, 471–486. Hoboken, NJ: Wiley-Blackwell.

Reisner, George A. 1905. *The Hearst Medical Papyrus: Hieratic Text in 17 Facsimile Plates in Collotype with Introduction and Vocabulary.* Leipzig: J. C. Hinrichs.

"Relics Found in Humboldt Guano Cave." 1911. *Elko Weekly Independent,* 29 September 1911, 1.

Rice, Julian. 1992. *Deer Women and Elk Men: The Lakota Narratives of Ella Deloria.* Albuquerque: University of New Mexico Press.

Richardson, Jane, and A. L. Kroeber. 1940. "Three Centuries of Women's Dress Fashions: A Quantitative Analysis." *Anthropological Records* 5 (2):111–153.

Riley, Tom. 1959. "Indians Owe Land Victory to Famed Anthropologist." *Oakland Tribune,* 16 August 1959, 14.

Rizzo, Martin Adam. 2016. "*No Somos Animales*: Indigenous Survival and Perseverance in 19th Century Santa Cruz, California." PhD dissertation, University of California, Santa Cruz. https://escholarship.org/uc/item/72n1q0vz.

Roberts, Harry K. 2011. *Walking in Beauty: Growing Up with the Yurok Indians.* Trinidad, CA: The Press at Trinidad Art.

Roberts, Meranda Diane. 2018. "Resiliency of Native American Women Basket Weavers from California, Great Basin, and the Southwest." PhD dissertation, University of California, Riverside. https://escholarship.org/uc/item/422088q0.

Robins, R. H. 1958. *The Yurok Language: Grammar, Texts, Lexicon,* vol. 15 of *University of California Publications in Linguistics.* Berkeley: University of California Press.

Robinson, Judith. 1991. *The Hearsts: An American Dynasty.* San Francisco: Telegraph Hill.

Roche, Gerald. 2020. "Abandoning Endangered Languages: Ethical Loneliness, Language Oppression, and Social Justice." *American Anthropologist* 122:164–169.

Rollings, Willard Hughes. 2004. "Citizenship and Suffrage: The Native American Struggle for Civil Rights in the American West, 1830–1965." *Nevada Law Journal* 5:126–140.

Rolston, Scott L. 2011. *The Big Picture Man: Reflections on the Life and Thought of Alfred Louis Kroeber.* New York: iUniverse.

Rose, Steve. 2021. " 'I Work with the Dead. But This Can Help the Living': The Anthropologist Investigating the Tulsa Race Massacre." *The Guardian,* 8 July 2021. https://www.theguardian.com/society/2021/jul/08/.

Rosen, Lawrence. 1980. "The Excavation of American Indian Burial Sites: A Problem in Law and Professional Responsibility." *American Anthropologist* 82: 5–27.

Rowe, John Howland. 1954. "Max Uhle, 1856–1944: A Memoir of the Father of Peruvian Archaeology." *University of California Publications in American Archaeology and Ethnology* 46:1–134.

Rowe, John Howland. 1962. "Alfred Louis Kroeber, 1876–1960." *American Antiquity* 27:395–415.

Royster, Hayden. 2022. "This Land Is Their Land." *California Magazine,* Summer 2022. https://alumni.berkeley.edu/california-magazine/2022-summer/this-land-is-their-land/.

Rugg, Linda. 2021. "Berkeley Talks: Linda Rugg on Native American Repatriation at UC Berkeley." https://news.berkeley.edu/2021/07/02/berkeley-talks-native-american-repatriation/.

Rumsey, Alan. 1999. "The White Man as Cannibal in the New Guinea Highlands." In *The Anthropology of Cannibalism,* edited by Laurence R. Goldman. Westport, CT: Bergin & Garvey.

Rutherford, Adam. 2021. "Race, Eugenics, and the Canceling of Great Scientists." *American Journal of Physical Anthropology* 2021:1–5. https://doi.org/10.1002/ajpa.24192.

Sackman, Douglas Cazaux. 2010. *Wild Men: Ishi and Kroeber in the Wilderness of Modern America.* Oxford: Oxford University Press.

Salah, Margo. 2019. "4 Things You Probably Didn't Know about the Hearst Family." *Daily Cal,* 29 July 2019.

Sallabank, Julia. 2017. "Purism, Variation, Change and 'Authenticity': Ideological Challenges to Language Revitalisation." *European Review* 26:164–178.

Sandos, James. 2004. *Converting California: Indians and Franciscans in the Missions.* New Haven, CT: Yale University Press.

Sapir, Edward. 1910. "Yana Texts." *University of California Publications in American Archaeology and Ethnology* 9:1–235.

Sapir, Edward. 1923. "Text Analyses of Three Yana Dialects." *University of California Publications in American Archaeology and Ethnology* 20:263–294.

Sapir, Edward. 1929. "The Status of Linguistics as a Science." *Language* 5:207–214.

Sapir, Edward. 1933. "La réalité psychologique des phonèmes." *Journal de Psychologie Normale et Pathologique* 30:247–265. Translated as "The Psychological Reality of Phonemes," *Selected Writings of Edward Sapir in Language, Culture and Personality*, edited by David G. Mandelbaum, 46–60. Berkeley: University of California Press, 1949.

Sapir, Edward, and Morris Swadesh. 1960. *Yana Dictionary.* Berkeley: University of California Press.

Sarris, Greg. 2022. *Becoming Story: A Journey among Seasons, Places, Trees, and Ancestors.* Berkeley, CA: Heyday.

Sawchuk, Elizabeth A., Susan Pfeiffer, Carla E. Klehm, Michelle E. Cameron, Austin C. Hill, Anneke Janzen, Katherine M. Grillo, and Elisabeth A. Hildebrand. 2019. "The Bioarchaeology of Mid-Holocene Pastoralist Cemeteries West of Lake Turkana, Kenya." *Archaeological and Anthropological Sciences* 11:6221–6241.

Saxton, Dean. 1963. "Papago Phonemes." *International Journal of American Linguistics* 29:29–35.

Saxton, Dean, and Lucille Saxton. 1973. *O'othham hoho'ok a'agitha: Legends and Lore of the Papago and Pima Indians.* Tucson: University of Arizona Press.

Saxton, Dean, Lucille Saxton, and Susie Enos. 1983. Edited by R. L. Cherry. *Dictionary, Papago/Pima–English, O'othham–Mil-gahn, English–Papago/Pima, Mil-gahn–O'othham.* 2nd ed. Tucson: University of Arizona Press.

Scheer, Robert. 2021. "Tony Platt: California's Grim Genocidal Past Implicates the University of California." Scheerpost, 19 November 2021. https://scheerpost.com/2021/11/19/tony-platt-californias-grim-genocidal-past-implicates-the-university-of-california/.

Scheib, C. L., Hongjie Li, Tariq Desai, Vivian Link, Christopher Kendall, Genevieve Dewar, Peter William Griffith, et al. 2018. "Ancient Human Parallel Lineages within North America Contributed to a Coastal Expansion." *Science* 360:1024–1027.

Schenck, W. Egbert. 1926. "The Emeryville Shellmound: Final Report." *University of California Publications in American Archaeology and Ethnology* 23:147–282.

Scheper-Hughes, Nancy. 2002. "Coming to Our Senses: Anthropology and Genocide." In *Annihilating Difference: The Anthropology of Genocide,* edited by Alexander Laban Hinton, 348–381. Berkeley: University of California Press.

Scheper-Hughes, Nancy. 2003. "Ishi's Brain, Ishi's Ashes." In *Ishi in Three Centuries,* edited by Karl Kroeber and Clifton Kroeber, 99–131. Lincoln: University of Nebraska Press.

Scheper-Hughes, Nancy. 2020. "Alfred Kroeber and His Relations with California Indians." *Berkeley Blog,* 24 July 2020. https://blogs.berkeley.edu/2020/07/24/alfred-kroeber-and-his-relations-with-california-indians/.

Scheper-Hughes, Nancy. 2022. "Goodbye Kroeber, Kroeber Hall, and the Man We Know as Ishi." *BEROSE International Encyclopaedia of the Histories of Anthropology.* https://www.berose.fr/article2565.html.

Schevill, Margot Blum. 1986. "Lila Morris O'Neale." *Kroeber Anthropological Society Papers* 65–66:129–137.

Schevill, Margot Blum. 1988. "Lila Morris O'Neale (1886–1948)." In *Women Anthropologists: A Biographical Dictionary,* edited by Ute Gacs, Aisha Khan, Jerrie McIntyre, and Ruth Weinberg, 275–281. New York: Greenwood Press.

Schevill, Margot Blum. 1992. "Lila Morris O'Neale: Ethnoaesthetics and the Yurok-Karok Basket Weavers of Northwestern California." In *The Early Years of Native American Art History,* edited by Janet Catherine Berlo, 162–190. Seattle: University of Washington Press.

Schneider, David M., and John M. Roberts. 1965. *Zuni Kin Terms.* Human Relations Area Files Press. Originally appeared in 1956 as Note Book no. 3, Laboratory of Anthropology, University of Nebraska.

Schneider, Tsim D. 2009. "Shell Mounds of China Camp and Tomales Bay State Parks, Marin County." *Proceedings of the Society for California Archaeology* 21:63–68.

Schneider, Tsim D. 2021. *The Archaeology of Refuge and Recourse: Coast Miwok Resilience and Indigenous Hinterlands in Colonial California*. Tucson: University of Arizona Press.

Schneider, Tsim D., John Holson, Lori D. Hager, Samantha S. Schell, and Lucian N. Schrader III. 2014. "Obsidian Production and Mortuary Practices at CA-NAP-399, Napa Valley: Inferences from AMS Radiocarbon Assays." *California Archaeology* 6:191–218.

Schneider, Tsim D., and Lee M. Panich. 2019. "Landscapes of Refuge and Resiliency: Native Californian Persistence at Tomales Bay, California, 1770s–1870s." *Ethnohistory* 66:21–47.

Schnell, Stefan. 2018. "Reflections on the Role of Language Documentations in Linguistic Research." In *Reflections on Language Documentation 20 Years after Himmelmann 1998,* edited by Bradley McDonnell, Andrea L. Berez-Kroeker, and Gary Holton, 173–182. Honolulu: University of Hawai'i Press.

Schoeninger, Margaret J., Jeffrey L. Bada, Patricia M. Masters, Robert L. Bettinger, and Tim D. White. 2011. "Unexamined Bodies of Evidence." *Science* 332:916.

Schoep, Ilse. 2018. "Building the Labyrinth: Arthur Evans and the Construction of Minoan Civilization." *American Journal of Archaeology* 122:5–32.

Schultze, Leonhard. 1908. "Einleitung." In *Zoologische und anthropologische Ergebnisse einer Forschungsreise im westlichen und zentralen Südafrika, 1, Systematik und Tiergeographie,* edited by Leonhard Schultze, v–viii. Denkschriften der medicinisch-naturwissenschafltlichen Gesellschaft zu Jena. Jena: Gustav Fischer.

Schultze, Leonhard. 1910. "Südwestafrika." In *Das deutsche Kolonialreich: Eine Länderkunde der deutschen Schutzgebiete, Zweiter Band: Togo, Südwestafrika, Schutzgebiete in der Südsee und Kiautschougebiet,* edited by Hans Meyer, 131–295. Leipzig: Bibliographisches Institut.

"Scion of Indian Aristocracy Paints for University Professors." 1914. *San Francisco Chronicle,* 25 October 1914.

Seifart, Frank, Nicholas Evans, Harald Hammarström, and Stephen C. Levinson. 2018. "Language Documentation Twenty-five Years On." *Language* 94:e324–e345.

Seiler, Hansjakob. 1977. *Cahuilla Grammar.* Morongo Indian Reservation. Banning, CA: Malki Museum Press.

Selinker, Larry. 1972. "Interlanguage." *International Review of Applied Linguistics in Language Teaching* 10:209–232.

Selvin, Paul. 1991. "The Raging Bull of Berkeley." *Science* 251:368–371.

Senior, W. A. 1996. "Cultural Anthropology and Rituals of Exchange in Ursula K. Le Guin's 'Earthsea.'" *Mosaic: An Interdisciplinary Critical Journal* 29:101–113.

Sewell, William H., Jr. 1999. "The Concept(s) of Culture." In *Beyond the Cultural Turn: New Directions in the Study of Society and Culture,* edited by Victoria E. Bonnell and Lynn Hunt, 35–61. Berkeley: University of California Press.

Seymour, Susan. 1988. "Cora Du Bois (1903–)." In *Women Anthropologists: A Biographical Dictionary,* edited by Ute Gacs, Aisha Khan, Jerrie McIntyre, and Ruth Weinberg, 72–79. New York: Greenwood Press.

Seymour, Susan C. 2015. *Cora Du Bois: Anthropologist, Diplomat, Agent.* Lincoln: University of Nebraska Press.

"Shell Mounds in 'Faculty Glade.'" 1914. *Oakland Tribune,* 5 October 1914, 5.

Shelmerdine, Cynthia W., ed. 2008. *The Cambridge Companion to the Aegean Bronze Age.* Cambridge, UK: Cambridge University Press.

Sherer, Lorraine M. 1965. "The Clan System of the Fort Mojave Indians: A Contemporary Survey." *Southern California Quarterly* 47:1–72.

Sherer, Lorraine M. 1966. "Great Chieftains of the Mojave Indians." *Southern California Quarterly* 48:1–35.

Shok, Katherine. 2020. "Building Unnaming, Heritage Month Cannot Be All CA Does to Respect Indigenous Communities." *Daily Cal,* 1 December 2020.

Shook, David. 2020. "Poetry as Wonder, Desire, Rage, and Memory: A Conversation with Natalie Diaz." *World Literature Today* 94:12–15.

"Sideshows Want Indian: Vaudeville Agents Storm Aborigine." 1911. *Chico Enterprise,* 6 September 1911, 3.

Silverstein, Michael. 1978. "Yokuts: Introduction." In *Handbook of North American Indians, Volume 8: California,* edited by Robert F. Heizer, 446–447. Washington, DC: Smithsonian Institution.

Silverstein, Michael. 2015. "From Baffin Island to Boasian Induction: How Anthropology and Linguistics Got into Their Interlinear Groove." In *The Franz Boas Papers, Vol. 1, Franz Boas as Public Intellectual: Theory, Ethnography, Activism,* edited by Regna Darnell, Michelle Hamilton, Robert L. A. Hancock, and Joshua Smith, 83–127. Lincoln: University of Nebraska Press.

Simpson, Audra. 2018. "Why White People Love Franz Boas, or, the Grammar of Indigenous Dispossession." In *Indigenous Visions: Rediscovering the World of Franz Boas,* edited by Ned Blackhawk and Isaiah Wilner, 166–181. New Haven, CT: Yale University Press.

Sims, Hank. 2006. "'Speak It Good and Strong': Yurok Youth Vow to Bring Back the Language of Their Ancestors." *North Coast Journal,* 12 January 2006. https://www.northcoastjournal.com/011206/cover0112.html.

Sinclair, Upton. 1923. *The Goose-Step: A Study of American Education*. Pasadena, CA: Upton Sinclair.

Smith, Anna V. 2020. "An Indigenous Effort to Return Condors to the Pacific Northwest Nears Its Goal." *Audubon News,* 5 November 2020. https://www.audubon.org/news/an-indigenous-effort-return-condors-pacific-northwest-nears-its-goal.

Smith, Anthony D. 2009. *Ethno-symbolism and Nationalism: A Cultural Approach*. London: Routledge.

Smith, Carolyn. 2016. "Weaving *pikyav* (to-fix-it): Karuk Basket Weaving in-Relation-with the Everyday World." Unpublished PhD dissertation, University of California, Berkeley. https://escholarship.org/uc/item/8hx01626.

Smith, Duane A. 2003. "'Here's to Low-Grade Ore and Plenty of It': The Hearsts and the Homestake Mine." *Mining Engineering* 55 (9):23–27.

Smith, Laura. 2022. "Into the Ishi Wilderness." *California Magazine,* Summer 2022. https://alumni.berkeley.edu/california-magazine/2022-summer/into-the-ishi-wilderness/.

Smith, Martyn. 2007. "Pyramids in the Medieval Islamic Landscape: Perceptions and Narratives." *Journal of the American Research Center in Egypt* 43:1–14.

Smith, Wayland H. 1909. "In re California Indians to Date." *Out West* 30:130–147.

Smith, William Stevenson. 1963. "The Stela of Prince Wepemnofret." *Archaeology* 16:2–13.

Smith-Ferri, Sherrie. 1998. "The Development of the Commercial Market for Pomo Indian Baskets." *Expedition: Magazine of the University of Pennsylvania Museum of Archaeology and Anthropology* 40:15–22.

Sowry, Nathan. 2020. "Museums, Native American Representation, and the Public: The Role of Museum Anthropology in Public History, 1875–1925." Unpublished PhD dissertation, American University. https://dra.american.edu/islandora/object/auislandora:85282.

Soza War Soldier, Rose Delia. 2013. "'To Take Positive and Effective Action': Rupert Costo and the California Based American Indian Historical Society." Unpublished PhD dissertation, Arizona State University.

Sparkman, Philip Stedman. 1908. "The Culture of the Luiseño Indians." *University of California Publications in American Archaeology and Ethnology* 8:187–234.

Sparks, Corey S., and Richard L. Jantz. 2002. "A Reassessment of Human Cranial Plasticity: Boas Revisited." *Proceedings of the National Academy of Sciences* 99:14636–14639.

Sparks, Corey S., and Richard L. Jantz. 2003. "Changing Times, Changing Faces: Franz Boas's Immigrant Study in Modern Perspective." *American Anthropologist* 105:333–337.

Spiro, Jonathan Peter. 2009. *Defending the Master Race: Conservation, Eugenics, and the Legacy of Madison Grant.* Burlington: University of Vermont Press.

Spivak, Gayatri Chakravorty. 1988. "Can the Subaltern Speak?" In *Marxism and the Interpretation of Culture,* edited by Cary Nelson and Lawrence Grossberg, 271–313. Basingstoke, UK: Macmillan Education.

Spott, Robert. 1926. "Address." *Transactions of the Commonwealth Club of California* 21:133–135.

Spott, Robert, and A. L. Kroeber. 1942. "Yurok Narratives." *University of California Publications in American Archaeology and Ethnology* 35:143–256.

Spriggs, Matthew, and David Reich. 2020. "An Ancient DNA Pacific Journey: A Case Study of Collaboration between Archaeologists and Geneticists." *World Archaeology* 51:620–639.

Stanlaw, James. 2022. "Alfred Kroeber and the Development of Linguistic Anthropology: A Brief Reassessment." *BEROSE International Encyclopaedia of the Histories of Anthropology.* https://www.berose.fr/article2564.html.

Starn, Orin. 2004. *Ishi's Brain: In Search of America's Last "Wild" Indian."* New York: Norton.

Stauder, Jack. 1974. "The 'Relevance' of Anthropology to Colonialism and Imperialism." *Race* 16:29–51.

Steenland, Patricia. 2015. "Lost Stories and Cultural Patrimony." *Public: A Journal of Imagining America* 3 (1). http://public.imaginingamerica.org/blog/article/105-2/.

Stein, Barbara R. 2001. *On Her Own Terms: Annie Montague Alexander and the Rise of Science in the American West.* Berkeley: University of California Press.

Stephan, Tara. 2017. "Writing the Past: Ancient Egypt through the Lens of Medieval Islamic Thought." In *Arabic Humanities, Islamic Thought: Essays in Honor of Everett K. Rowson,* edited by Joseph E. Lowry and Shawkat M. Toorawa, 256–270. Leiden: Brill.

Stern, Alexandra Minna. 2015. *Eugenic Nation: Faults and Frontiers of Better Breeding in Modern America.* 2nd ed. Berkeley: University of California Press.

Steward, Julian H. 1933. "Ethnography of the Owens Valley Paiute." *University of California Publications in American Archaeology and Ethnology* 33:233–250.

Steward, Julian H. 1934. "Two Paiute Autobiographies." *University of California Publications in American Archaeology and Ethnology* 33:423–438.

Steward, Julian H. 1938. *Basin-Plateau Aboriginal Sociopolitical Groups,* vol. 120 of *Bulletin of the Smithsonian Institution Bureau of American Ethnology.* Washington, DC: US Government Printing Office.

Steward, Julian H. 1962. *Alfred Kroeber, 1876–1960: A Biographical Memoir.* Washington, DC: National Academy of Sciences.

Steward, Julian H. 1973. *Alfred Kroeber.* New York: Columbia University Press.

Stewart, Kenneth M. 1983. "Mohave." In *Southwest,* edited by Alfonso Ortiz, 55–70. Handbook of North American Indians 10. Washington, DC: Smithsonian Institution.

Stewart, Omer C. 1961. "Kroeber and the Indian Claims Commission Cases." *Kroeber Anthropological Society Papers* 25:181–191.

Stewart, Omer C. 1978. "Litigation and Its Effects." In *Handbook of North American Indians, Vol. 8, California,* edited by Robert F. Heizer, 705–712. Washington, DC: Smithsonian Institution.

Stock, Chester. 1918. "The Pleistocene Fauna of Hawver Cave." *Bulletin of the Department of Geology* 10:461–515.

Stocking, George W., Jr., ed. 1974. *A Franz Boas Reader: The Shaping of American Anthropology, 1883–1911.* Chicago: University of Chicago Press.

Strange, Adelaide Weihe. 1976. "I Remember Ishi." Recording of a talk given to the Antioch Soroptimist Club, 17 March 1976. Robert L. Day collection, University of California, San Francisco, Archives and Special Collections, MSS.2011.23, Box 26, item 13.

Stringfellow, Kim. 2020. "Bringing Creation Back Together Again: The Salt Songs of the Nuwuvi." The Mojave Project, June 2020. https://mojaveproject.org/dispatches-item/bringing-creation-back-together-again-the-salt-songs-of-the-nuwuvi/.

Strong, Herbert A., Willem S. Logeman, and Benjamin Ide Wheeler. 1891. *Introduction to the Study of the History of Language.* New York: Longmans, Green.

Stubblefield, Phoebe R. 2011. "The Anatomical Diaspora: Evidence of Early American Anatomical Traditions in North Dakota." *Journal of Forensic Sciences* 56:1324–1327.

"Students Discover First Skeletons of Pomos." 1906. *San Francisco Examiner,* 16 June 1906, 8.

Sussman, Robert Wald. 2014. *The Myth of Race: The Troubling Persistence of an Unscientific Idea.* Cambridge, MA: Harvard University Press.

Sveen, Karin. 2014. *The Immigrant and the University: Peder Sather and Gold Rush California.* Berkeley: University of California Press.

Swartzlow, Ruby. 1971. Ad Kessler interview. Tape recording in Butte County Library, call number 2016-050-0007. https://archive.org/details/corob_000234a.

TallBear, Kim. 2013. *Native American DNA: Tribal Belonging and the False Promise of Genetic Science.* Minneapolis: University of Minnesota Press.

Tantaleán, Henry. 2014. *Peruvian Archaeology: A Critical History.* Translated by Charles Stanish. London: Routledge.

Taylor, Alexander S. 1860–1863. *The Indianology of California, or, Fragmentary notes, selected and original, on the Indian tribes of the countries formerly called Alta and Baja California, in four series of 150 separate numbers, published in the California Farmer from 1860 to 1863.* San Francisco.

Tedlock, Barbara. 1992. *The Beautiful and the Dangerous: Encounters with the Zuni Indians.* New York: Viking.

Tedlock, Dennis. 1971. "On the Translation of Style in Oral Narrative." *Journal of American Folklore* 84:114–133.

Tedlock, Dennis. 1983. *The Spoken Word and the Work of Interpretation.* Philadelphia: University of Pennsylvania Press.

Teeter, Wendy Giddens, Desiree Martinez, and Dorothy Lippert. 2021. "Creating a New Future: Redeveloping the Tribal-Museum Relationship in the Time of NAGPRA." *International Journal of Cultural Property* 28:201–209.

Tello, Julio C. 1909. *La antigüedad de la sífilis en el Perú.* Lima: Sanmartí.

Tello, Julio C. 1912. "Prehistoric Trephining among the Yauyos of Peru." In *Actas del XVII Congreso internacional de americanistas, sesión de Buenos Aires, 17–23 de mayo de 1910,* edited by Robert Lehmann-Nitsche, 75–83. Buenos Aires: Coni hermanos. Reprinted in Richard L. Burger, ed., *The Life and Writings of Julio C. Tello: America's First Indigenous Archaeologist*, 112–124. Iowa City: University of Iowa Press, 2009.

Tello, Julio C. 1913. *Arawak (fragmento de linguística indígena sudamericana).* Lima: Imp. Del centro editorial.

Tello, Julio C. 1917. "Los antiguos cementerios del Valle de Nasca." In *Proceedings of the Second Pan American Scientific Congress: Section I, Anthropology,* 283–291. Washington, DC: US Government Printing Office.

Tello, Julio C. 1918. *El uso de las cabezas humanas artificialmente momificadas y su representación en le antiquo arte peruano.* Lima: Ernesto R. Villaran.

Tello, Julio C. 1921. *Introducción a la historia antigua del Perú.* Ciudad de los Reyes del Perú: Editorial Euforion.

Tello, Julio C. 1923a. "Ortografia fonética de las lenguas indígenas: Sistema de sonidos de la Keshwa." *Inca* 1:375–382.

Tello, Julio C. 1923b. *Wira-Kocha.* Lima. Reimpresso de la Revista "Inca," vol. I, nos. 1 y 3, Lima, 1923.

Tello, Julio C. 1943. "Discovery of the Chavín Culture in Peru." *American Antiquity* 9:135–160.

Tello, Julio C. 1960. *Chavín, cultura matriz de la civilización andina.* Con revision de Torribio Mejía Xesspe. Lima: Impr. De la Universidad de San Marcos.

Tello, Julio C. 2009a. "Collision of Two Civilizations." Translated by Freda Wolf de Romero. In *The Life and Writings of Julio C. Tello: America's First Indigenous Archaeologist,* edited by Richard L. Burger, 110–111. Iowa City: University of Iowa Press. Originally published in *Introducción a la historia antigua del Perú,* 1921.

Tello, Julio C. 2009b. "The Museum of Peruvian Anthropology." Translated by Freda Wolf de Romero. In *The Life and Writings of Julio C. Tello: America's First Indigenous Archaeologist,* edited by Richard L. Burger, 103–109. Iowa City: University of Iowa Press. Originally published in *El Comercio,* 14 December 1924.

Tello, Julio C., and Toribio Mejía Xesspe. 1959–1979. *Paracas.* 2 vols. (vol. 1, New York: Institute of Andean Research; vol. 2, Lima: Universidad Nacional Mayor de San Marcos).

Thieberger, Nicholas. 2013. "Extinction in Whose Terms? Which Parts of a Language Constitute a Target for Language Maintenance Programmes?" In *Language Endangerment and Language Maintenance: An Active Approach,* edited by David Bradley and Maya Bradley, 310–328. London: Curzon.

Thomas, David Hurst. 2000. *Skull Wars: Kennewick Man, Archaeology, and the Battle for Native American Identity.* New York: Basic Books.

Thomason, Sarah Grey. 2002. "Creoles and Genetic Relationship." *Journal of Pidgin and Creole Languages* 17:101271.

Thomason, Sarah Grey. 2003. "A Response to Mufwene's Response." *Journal of Pidgin and Creole Languages* 18:289–298.

Thompson, Bonnie. 2013. "The Student Body: A History of the Stewart Indian School, 1890–1940." Unpublished PhD dissertation, Arizona State University. https://hdl.handle.net/2286/R.I.20910.

Thompson, Laura. 1991. *Beyond the Dream: A Search for Meaning.* Mangilao, Guam: University of Guam, Micronesian Area Research Center.

Thoresen, Timothy H. H. 1973. "Folkloristics in A. L. Kroeber's Early Theory of Culture." *Journal of the Folklore Institute* 10:41–55.

Thoresen, Timothy H. H. 1975. "Paying the Piper and Calling the Tune: The Beginnings of Academic Anthropology in California." *Journal of the History of the Behavioral Sciences* 11:257–275.

Thornes, Tim. 2020. "Kuiyuidɨkadɨ (Pyramid Lake Reservation, Nevada)." *International Journal of American Linguistics* 86 (Suppl. 1):S147–S150.

Tobin, Kate. 2017. "Rare Audio of Indigenous Languages Saved by Invention 100 Years Later." NSF *Science Nation,* 7 August 2017. https://www.youtube.com/watch?v=H6AqEppqUDA.

Tolkien, J. R. R. 1954–1955. *The Lord of the Rings.* 3 vols. London: Allen and Unwin.

Trafzer, Clifford E. 2015. *A Chemehuevi Song: The Resilience of a Southern Paiute Tribe.* Seattle: University of Washington Press.

Trafzer, Clifford E., and Joel R. Hyer, eds. 1999. *Exterminate Them: Written Accounts of the Murder, Rape, and Slavery of Native Americans during the California Gold Rush, 1848–1868.* Lansing: Michigan State University Press.

Treuer, David. 2019. *The Heartbeat of Wounded Knee: Native America from 1890 to the Present.* New York: Riverhead.

Trombley, Trent, Sabrina C. Agarwal, Patrick Beauchesne, and Caroline Goodson. 2018. Evidence for Teeth-as-Tools and Palliative Oral Hygiene at Late Medieval Villamagna. Stahl Research Report no. 26. Berkeley: University of California Archaeological Research Facility. https://escholarship.org/uc/item/34t3t8bq.

Tuohy, Donald R., and L. Kyle Napton. 1986. "Duck Decoys from Lovelock Cave, Nevada, Dated by ^{14}C Accelerator Mass Spectrometry." *American Antiquity* 51:813–816.

"Twenty-Two Skeletons." 1908. *Sacramento Bee,* 7 April 1908, 6.

"UC Berkeley Needs to Be Efficient about Confronting Problematic Building Names. 2018. *Daily Cal,* 14 September 2018.

"UC Co-ed and Indian Marry." 1935. *Oakland Tribune,* 20 November 1935, 1.

UC News. 2018. The University of California Is Born: How a World-Class University Got Its Start 150 Years Ago. University of California, 22 March 2018. https://www.universityofcalifornia.edu/news/university-california-born.

Uhle, Max. 1907. "The Emeryville Shellmound." *University of California Publications in American Archaeology and Ethnology* 7:1–106.

"Unearthed Indian Skeletons." 1908. *Petaluma Daily Morning Courier,* 31 December 1908, 1.

United States of America. 1990. Congressional Record: Proceedings and Debates of the 101*st* Congress, Second Session. Friday, 26 October 1990.

"University Folk Crowd to View 'Wild Man.'" 1911. *San Francisco Examiner,* 16 October 1911, 12.

University of California. 1904. *Register, 1903–1904.* Berkeley: University Press.

"University Professor Inspects Guano Cave." 1911. *Reno Gazette-Journal,* 5 December 1911, 2.

"Untainted Life Revealed by Aborigine." 1911. *San Francisco Examiner,* 6 September 1911, 1.

Valtin, Tom. 2003. "Zuni Salt Lake Saved." *Planet Newsletter.* Sierra Club. https://vault.sierraclub.org/planet/200307/zuni.asp.

Velleman, Barry L. 2008. "The 'Scientific Linguist' Goes to War: The United States A.S.T. Program in Foreign Languages." *Historiographia Linguistica* 35: 385–416.

Villalba-Mouco, Vanessa, Camila Oliart, Cristina Rihuete-Herrada, Ainash Childebayeva, Adam B. Rohrlach, María Inés Fregerio, Eva Celdrán Beltrán, et al. 2021. "Genomic Transformation and Social Organization during the Copper Age-Bronze Age Transition in Southern Iberia. *Science Advances* 7:eabi7038.

Vizenor, Gerald. 1994. *Manifest Manners: Narratives on Postindian Survivance.* Lincoln: University of Nebraska Press.

Vizenor, Gerald. 1995. "Ishi and the Wood Ducks: Postindian Trickster Comedies." In *Native American Literature: A Brief Introduction and Anthology,* 299–336. New York: HarperCollins.

Vizenor, Gerald. 2003. "Mister Ishi." In *Ishi in Three Centuries,* edited by Karl Kroeber and Clifton Kroeber, 363–372. Lincoln: University of Nebraska Press.

Vizenor, Gerald. 2008. "Aesthetics of Survivance: Literary Theory and Practice." In *Survivance: Narratives of Native Presence,* edited by Gerald Vizenor, 1–23. Lincoln: University of Nebraska Press.

Vizenor, Gerald. 2009. *Native Liberty: Natural Reason and Cultural Survivance.* Lincoln: University of Nebraska Press.

Wade-Gery, H. T. 1952. *The Poet of the Iliad.* Cambridge, UK: Cambridge University Press.

Waggoner, Ben M., and Dave Smith. 2006. John C. Merriam (1869–1945). UC Museum of Paleontology. https://ucmp.berkeley.edu/history/merriam.html.

Walker, Rob. 2016. "The Shifting Symbolism of the Gadsden Flag." *New Yorker,* 2 October 2016. https://www.newyorker.com/news/news-desk/the-shifting-symbolism-of-the-gadsden-flag.

Wallace, Anthony F. C. 1999. *Jefferson and the Indians: The Tragic Fate of the First Americans.* Cambridge, MA: Harvard University Press.

Wallace, Grant. 1911. "'The Heaven of the White People' Ishi Calls the Orpheum." *San Francisco Call,* 8 October 1911, 4–5.

Wallace, William J., and Donald W. Lathrap. 1952. "An Early Implement Assemblage from a Limestone Cavern in California." *American Antiquity* 18: 133–138.

Wallace, William J., and Donald W. Lathrap. 1975. *West Berkeley (CA-Ala-307): A Culturally Stratified Shellmound on the East Shore of San Francisco Bay,* vol. 29 of *Contributions of the UC Archaeological Research Facility.* Berkeley: University of California, Archaeological Research Facility. https://escholarship.org/uc/item/4616g044.

Walton, John. 1993. *Western Times and Water Wars: State, Culture and Rebellion in California.* Berkeley: University of California Press.

Wares, Alan Campbell. 1968. *A Comparative Study of Yuman Consonantism.* The Hague: Mouton.

Warma, Zachary. 2018. "The Golden State's Scientific White Supremacist." *Boom California,* 5 November 2018. https://boomcalifornia.org/2018/11/05/the-golden-states-scientific-white-supremacist/.

Warren, Stephen, and Ben Barnes. 2018. "Salvaging the Salvage Anthropologists: Erminie Wheeler-Voegelin, Carl Voegelin, and the Future of Ethnohistory." *Ethnohistory* 65:189–214.

Washington, Daisy. 1908. "Stenography—Its Use and Value." *Indian Leader,* 31 July 1908, 1, 4.

Waterman, T. T. 1917. "Ishi, the Last Yahi Indian." *Southern Workman* 46: 528–537.

Waterman, T. T. 1918. "The Yana Indians." *University of California Publications in American Archaeology and Ethnology* 13:35–102.

Waterman, T. T. 1920. "Yurok Geography." *University of California Publications in American Archaeology and Ethnology* 16:177–314.

Waterman, T. T., and A. L. Kroeber. 1938. "The Kepel Fish Dam." *University of California Publications in American Archaeology and Ethnology* 35:49–80.

Watkins, Mark Hanna. 1937. "A Grammar of Chichewa: A Bantu Language of British Central Africa." *Language* 13 (2), Language Dissertation No. 24:5–158.

Wear, Kimberly. 2021. "Restoring the Name of Sue-meg State Park." *North Coast Journal,* 1 October 2021. https://www.northcoastjournal.com/NewsBlog/archives/2021/10/01/restoring-the-name-of-sue-meg-state-park.

Weigel, William. 2005. "Yowlumne in the Twentieth Century." Unpublished PhD dissertation, University of California, Berkeley.

Weinberg, Jessica P., and Susan D. Penfield. 2000. "Mohave Language Planning: Where Has It been and Where Should It Go from Here?" *Coyote Papers* 11:85–91. https://repository.arizona.edu/handle/10150/226605.

Weiss, Marc A. 1986. "Urban Land Developers and the Origins of Zoning Laws: The Case of Berkeley." *Berkeley Planning Journal* 3:7–25. https://escholarship.org/uc/item/26b8d8zh.

Wheeler, Benjamin Ide. 1885. *Der griechische Nominalaccent.* Strassburg: Karl J. Trübner.

Wheeler, Benjamin Ide. 1887. *Analogy and the Scope of Its Application in Language,* vol. 2 of *Cornell University Studies in Classical Philology.* Ithaca, NY: Cornell University Press.

Wheeler, Benjamin Ide. 1912. "Dr. Wheeler Voices Gratitude: Gifts to U.C. Invaluable." *San Francisco Examiner,* 4 December 1912, 15.

Wheeler, Benjamin Ide. 1926. *The Abundant Life.* Berkeley: University of California Press.

Wheeler, Benjamin Ide, and F. W. Putnam. 1902. "Ethnological and Archeological Survey of California." *Science* 18:570–571.

White, Leslie A. 1946. "Kroeber's 'Configurations of Culture Growth.'" *American Anthropologist* 48:78–93.

Wilder, Craig Steven. 2013. *Ebony and Ivy: Race, Slavery, and the Troubled History of America's Universities.* New York: Bloomsbury.

Wilkinson, Toby. 2020. *A World beneath the Sands: The Golden Age of Egyptology.* New York: W. W. Norton.

"Will Investigate the Desert Plants." 1906. *Santa Barbara Independent,* 25 August 1906, 2.

Williams, Samantha M. 2022. *Assimilation, Resilience, and Survival: A History of the Stewart Indian School, 1890–2020.* Lincoln: University of Nebraska Press.

Williams, Sloan R., Kathleen Forgey, and Elizabeth Klarich. 2001. *An Osteological Study of Nasca Trophy Heads Collected by A. L. Kroeber during the Marshall Field Expeditions to Peru.* Fieldiana, Anthropology, New Series, 33. Chicago: Field Museum of Natural History.

Williams, Tara, and Susan M. Tracz. 2016. "Taking Back the Fire: Schooling Experiences of Central California Indian People across Generations." *Journal of American Indian Education* 55:75–98.

Willis, William S., Jr. 1972. "Skeletons in the Anthropological Closet." In *Reinventing Anthropology,* edited by Dell H. Hymes, 121–152. New York: Pantheon.

Wilner, Isaiah Lorado. 2015. "Friends in This World: The Relationship of George Hunt and Franz Boas." In *The Franz Boas Papers, vol. 1, Franz Boas as Public Intellectual: Theory, Ethnography, Activism,* edited by Regna Darnell, 163–189. Lincoln: University of Nebraska Press.

Witt, John Fabian, G. Leonard Baker, Tom A. Bernstein, David Blight, Beverly Gage, Jonathan Holloway, Lalani Perry, et al. 2016. Report of the Committee to Establish Principles on Renaming. Yale University. https://president.yale.edu/advisory-groups/presidents-committees/committee-establish-principles-renaming-0.

Wolf, Eric R. 2001 [1981]. "Kroeber Revisited." In *Pathways of Power: Building an Anthropology of the Modern World,* 23–37. Berkeley: University of California Press.

Wolfe, Patrick. 1999. *Settler Colonialism and the Transformation of Anthropology: The Politics and Poetics of an Ethnographic Event.* London: Cassel.

Wong, Laiana. 1999. "Authenticity and the Revitalization of Hawaiian." *Anthropology and Education Quarterly* 30:94–115.

Wood, Michael. 1998. "The Use of the Pharaonic Past in Modern Egyptian Nationalism." *Journal of the American Research Center in Egypt* 35:179–196.

Woodbury, Anthony C. 1998. "Documenting Rhetorical, Aesthetic, and Expressive Loss in Language Shift." In *Endangered Languages: Language Loss and Community Response,* edited by Lenore A. Grenoble and Lindsay J. Whaley, 234–258. Cambridge, UK: Cambridge University Press.

Woodbury, Anthony C. 2003. "Defining Documentary Linguistics." *Language Documentation and Description* 1:35–51.

Woodbury, Anthony C. 2011. "Language Documentation." In *The Cambridge Handbook of Endangered Languages,* edited by Peter K. Austin and Julia Sallabank, 159–186. Cambridge, UK: Cambridge University Press.

Woodbury, Anthony C., and Nora England. 2006. "Training Speakers of Indigenous Languages of Latin America at a US University." *Linguistic Discovery* 4 (1). http://dx.doi.org/10.1349/PS1.1537-0852.A.301.

Woolford, Andrew John. 2015. *This Benevolent Experiment: Indigenous Boarding Schools, Genocide, and Redress in Canada and the United States.* Lincoln: University of Nebraska Press.

"Workmen Uncover Indian Skeletons." 1910. *San Francisco Call,* 24 May 1910, 2.

"Workmen Unearth Many Indian Skeletons." 1904. *Sacramento Bee,* August 31, 1904, 6.

Yamane, Linda. 2001. "New Life for a Lost Language." In *The Green Book of Language Revitalization in Practice,* edited by Leanne Hinton and Ken Hale, 429–430. San Diego: Academic Press.

Yates, Edith. 1988. Remembering Ishi: Ms., 5 December 1988. BANC MSS 99/229 c, Bancroft Library, UC Berkeley.

Younger, John G., and Paul Rehak. 2008. "Minoan Culture: Religion, Burial Customs, and Administration." In *The Cambridge Companion to the Aegean Bronze*

Age, edited by Cynthia W. Shelmerdine, 165–185. Cambridge, UK: Cambridge University Press.

"Yurok Tribe Celebrates Reclaiming Sacred Artifacts." 2010. *All Things Considered,* NPR, 13 August 2010. https://www.npr.org/templates/story/story.php?storyId=129182536.

"Y.W.C.A. Host Gathered in Tent City." 1912. *San Francisco Call,* 19 May 1912, 55.

Zanjani, Sally. 2001. *Sarah Winnemucca.* Lincoln: University of Nebraska Press.

Zepeda, Ofelia. 1983. *A Papago Grammar.* Tucson: University of Arizona Press.

Zumwalt, Fred H., Jr. 2003. "A Personal Remembrance of Ishi." In *Ishi in Three Centuries,* edited by Karl Kroeber and Clifton Kroeber, 11–17. Lincoln: University of Nebraska Press.

Zumwalt, Rosemary Lévy. 2019. *Franz Boas: The Emergence of the Anthropologist.* Lincoln: University of Nebraska Press.

Zumwalt, Rosemary Lévy. 2022. *Franz Boas: Shaping Anthropology and Fostering Social Justice.* Lincoln: University of Nebraska Press.

"Zuni Life Studied by Berkeley Man." 1916. *San Francisco Chronicle*, 21 August 1916, 6.

Zuni People, The. 1972. *The Zunis: Self-Portrayals.* Albuquerque: University of New Mexico Press.

INDEX

The letter *f* following a page number denotes a figure; the letter *t* denotes a table. Lower case *n* followed by a number indicates an endnote.